THE HISTORY OF
THE HOLY WAR

Ambroise's *Estoire de la Guerre Sainte*

To Wolfgang van Emden

THE HISTORY OF
THE HOLY WAR

Ambroise's *Estoire de la Guerre Sainte*

Translated by
MARIANNE AILES

with notes by MARIANNE AILES
and MALCOLM BARBER

THE BOYDELL PRESS

First published 2003
as volume II of
The History of the Holy War: Ambroise's Estoire de la Guerre Sainte
The Boydell Press, Woodbridge
Reprinted in paperback 2011

ISBN 978 1 84383 662 9

Transferred to digital printing

The Boydell Press is an imprint of Boydell & Brewer Ltd
PO Box 9, Woodbridge, Suffolk IP12 3DF, UK
and of Boydell & Brewer Inc,
668 Mt Hope Avenue, Rochester, NY 14620, USA
website: www.boydellandbrewer.com

A CIP catalogue record for this book is available
from the British Library

The publisher has no responsibility for the continued existence or accuracy of
URLs for external or third-party internet websites referred to in this book, and
does not guarantee that any content on such websites is, or will remain,
accurate or appropriate.

Papers used by Boydell & Brewer Ltd are natural, recyclable products
made from wood grown in sustainable forests

Contents

Preface

Although the editing of the text and the translation are by Marianne Ailes and the bulk of the historical notes by Malcolm Barber, we have nevertheless tried to make this a fully collaborative venture between a specialist in French medieval literature and a historian of the crusades. To that end we have consulted closely at every stage and hope that, as a consequence, the result is an integrated whole.

We have called upon the varied skills of many friends, colleagues and family members; their generous help has made a substantial contribution to the work and we are very grateful. We would like particularly to thank Adrian Ailes, Colin Ailes, Katherine Ailes, Elizabeth Barber, Keith Bate, Matthew Bennett, Jim Brundage, Ted Evergates, John Gillingham, Bernard Hamilton, Tony Hunt, Zsolt Hunyadi, Alex Kerr, Mike Lacey, Piers Mitchell, Vincent Moss, Helen Nicholson, Peter Noble, Al and Janet Rabil, Helen Roberts, Sara Scanlon, Françoise Vielliard, Nicholas Vincent, the Whichard family and, most of all, Wolfgang van Emden, to whom this book is dedicated.

Acknowledgements

The authors are grateful to Professor Peter Edbury and to Cambridge University Press for permission to reproduce the map of Cyprus in P.W. Edbury, *The Kingdom of Cyprus and the Crusades, 1191–1374* (Cambridge, 1991), p.xvi, and to Editions du Centre National de la Recherche Scientifique for permission to use Carte 1 in Joshua Prawer, *Histoire Royaume de Jérusalem*, vol.2 (Paris, 1970), p.47, as the basis for Map 2, The Siege of Acre.

Abbreviations

A-ND	*Anglo-Norman Dictionary*, ed. W. Rothwell, Publications of the Modern Humanities Research Association 8, 7 vols (London, 1977–92)
DNB	*Dictionary of National Biography*
Godefroy	F. Godefroy, *Dictionnaire de l'Ancienne Langue Française*, 10 vols (Paris, 1881–1902)
HC	*A History of the Crusades*, gen. ed. K. Setton, vol.1 ed. M.W. Baldwin, vol.2 ed. R.L. Wolff and H.W. Hazard (2nd ed., Madison, 1969)
HL	*The Crusade of Richard Lion-Heart by Ambroise*, trans. and annotated M.L. Hubert and J.L. La Monte (New York, 1941; reprint 1976)
Itinerarium	*Itinerarium Peregrinorum et Gesta Regis Ricardi*, in *Chronicles and Memorials of the Reign of Richard I*, vol.1, ed. W. Stubbs, Rolls Series 38 (London, 1864)
Landon	L. Landon, *The Itinerary of Richard I*, Pipe Roll Society n.s. 13 (London, 1935)
MGH SS	*Monumenta Germaniae Historica, Scriptores*
Nicholson	*Chronicle of the Third Crusade: A Translation of the Itinerarium Peregrinorum et Gesta Regis Ricardi*, trans. H.J. Nicholson, Crusade Texts in Translation 3 (Aldershot, 1997)
Paris	*L'Estoire de la Guerre Sainte par Ambroise*, ed. and trans. G. Paris, Documents inédits sur l'Histoire de France (Paris, 1897)
RHCr	*Recueil des Historiens des Croisades*
RRH	*Regesta Regni Hierosolymitani*, ed. R. Röhricht, 2 vols (Innsbruck, 1893–1904)
Stone	*The History of the Holy War*, trans. E.N. Stone, in *Three Old French Chronicles of the Crusades*, University of Washington Publications in the Social Sciences (Seattle, 1939), pp.1–160
T-L	*Tobler-Lommatzsch Altfranzösisches Wörterbuch*, 11 vols (Stuttgart, 1989–)
WT	Guillaume de Tyr, *Chronique*, ed. R.B.C. Huygens, Corpus Christianorum Continuatio Mediaevalis 63, 63A (Turnhout, 1986)

Chronology

1187

1 May	Defeat of the Templars and Hospitallers at the Springs of Cresson
4 July	Battle of Hattin
10 July	Saladin captures Acre
Between 14 July and mid-August	Arrival of Conrad of Montferrat at Tyre
4 September	Saladin captures Ascalon
2 October	Saladin captures Jerusalem
29 October	Issue of the encyclical *Audita tremendi*
November	Richard, Count of Poitou, takes the Cross

1188

27 March	Frederick Barbarossa takes the Cross
Summer	Arrival of the Sicilian fleet under Margaritone on the Palestinian and Syrian coast

1189

9 April	*EASTER*
11 May	Departure of Frederick Barbarossa's army from Ratisbon
6 July	Death of Henry II at Chinon
20 July	Richard I and Philip II agree to go on crusade together
28 August	Beginning of the siege of Acre
1 September	Arrival of James of Avesnes at the siege of Acre
3 September	Coronation of Richard I at Westminster
10 September	Arrival of the Danish and Frisian fleets at Acre
14–22 September	Saladin's first counter-attack at Acre
4 October	Defeat of the Christian forces at Acre and death of Gerard of Ridefort, Master of the Temple
12 December	Richard sails from Dover to Calais
30 December	Meeting between Richard I and Philip II at Nonancourt, at which regulations for the crusade are laid down

1190

16 March	Further meeting between the two kings at Dreux
25 March	*EASTER*
10 June	Drowning of Frederick Barbarossa in the River Saleph
June	Richard issues ordinances for the regulation of his crusading fleet
21 June	Arrival of the German crusaders at Antioch under Frederick, Duke of Swabia
24–27 June	Richard at Tours
Late June	Philip II departs from the Abbey of Saint Denis for the crusade
2–4 July	The two kings assemble their armies at Vézelay
4 July	Departure from Vézelay
10–13 July	Richard stays at Lyons
c.28 July	Arrival of Henry, Count of Champagne, and Thibaut, Count of Blois, at Acre
31 July	Richard arrives in Marseilles
7 August	Richard sails for Genoa
14 August	Richard leaves Genoa
20 August	Richard reaches Pisa
22–30 August	Richard's fleet at Marseilles
14 September	Richard's fleet reaches Messina
16 September	Philip arrives at Messina
23 September	Richard arrives at Messina
24 September	Unsuccessful attack on the Tower of Flies at Acre by the Pisans
29 September	Arrival of Baldwin, Archbishop of Canterbury, and a large party of English crusaders, at Acre
4 October	Seizure of Messina by Richard
6 October	Peace made between Richard and Tancred of Lecce
7 October	Arrival of Frederick, Duke of Swabia, at Acre
Before 21 October	Death of Queen Sibylla of Jerusalem
24 November	Marriage of Conrad of Montferrat and Isabella of Jerusalem

1191

20 January	Death of Frederick, Duke of Swabia
30 March	Philip sails for Acre
Spring	Arrival of Leopold V, Duke of Austria, at Acre
2 April	Richard sends Walter of Coutances back to England in order to resolve governmental problems
10 April	Richard's fleet leaves Messina
14 April	*EASTER*
17 April	Richard arrives in Crete
20 April	Philip arrives at Acre

1191 cont.

22 April	Richard arrives in Rhodes
1 May	Joanna and Berengaria anchor off Limassol
6 May	Richard arrives at Limassol and captures it
11 May	Guy of Lusignan arrives in Cyprus
12 May	Marriage of Richard and Berengaria at Limassol
31 May	Isaac Comnenus surrenders to Richard
1 June	Arrival of Queens Joanna and Berengaria at Acre
1 June	Death of Philip, Count of Flanders, at the siege of Acre
5 June	Richard departs from Cyprus
8 June	Richard lands at Acre
2 or 3 July	Unsuccessful attack on Acre by Philip II and the French
12 July	Fall of Acre to the crusaders
12 July	Richard orders the removal of the banner of Leopold of Austria from Acre
28 July	The two kings confirm Guy of Lusignan as king for his lifetime, but determine that Conrad of Montferrat and Isabella or their issue shall succeed him
31 July	Departure of Philip II for Tyre, leaving Hugh III, Duke of Burgundy, in command of the French
2 August	Philip II departs for France from Tyre
c.16 August	Massacre of the Muslim prisoners by Richard
22 August	Departure of the Christian army from Acre
26–27 August	The army encamps below Haifa
28–29 August	The army stays at Destroit
29 August	Richard goes ahead to La Merle, where he is joined by the army
30 August	The army encamps at the Crocodile River (Nahr al-Zarqa)
31 August	The army reaches Caesarea
1–3 September	The army camps at the Dead River (Nahr al-Mafijr)
3–4 September	The army camps at the Salt River (Nahr al-Qasab)
5–6 September	The army camps at the River Rochetaille (Nahr al-Falik)
7 September	Battle of Arsuf
7 September	Death of James of Avesnes
9 September	The army camps at 'the river of Arsur' (Nahr al-'Auja)
10 September	The army arrives at Jaffa
29 September	Richard is almost captured near Jaffa
29 September–3 October	Conrad of Montferrat enters negotiations with Saladin
3 October	Richard begins peace negotiations with Saladin through envoys
c.7–13 October	Richard returns to Acre to rally the rest of the army
17 October–14 November	Further negotiations between Richard and Saladin's representatives, during which Richard proposes to Saphadin (al-Adil) that he marry his sister, Joanna

1191 cont.

31 October	The army leaves Jaffa and camps between Casel des Plains (Yazur) and Casel Maen (Bait Dajan)
3 November	Further negotiations between Saladin and Conrad of Montferrat
6 November	Christian victory over the Turks near Bombrac
7–8 November	Saphadin returns to Richard's camp for negotiations
9 November	Saladin considers a possible alliance with Conrad against Richard
Between c.15 and 22 November	The army departs from the Casels towards Ramla
17 November	Saladin moves to Latrun
8–23 December	The army stays at Ramla
12 December	Saladin moves to Jerusalem
23–c.27 December	The army stays at Latrun
27 December	Philip II returns to Paris
c.27 December	The army moves to Bait Nuba
28 December	Successful foraging expedition by the Hospitallers and Templars

1192

After 6 January	On the advice of the military orders and the local barons Richard decides to return to Ascalon and not to proceed to Jerusalem
13 January	The army returns to Ramla
19 January	The army reaches Ibelin
20 January	The army reaches Ascalon
Late January–Easter	Rebuilding of Ascalon by the crusaders
February	The French return to Acre after a quarrel between Richard and Hugh of Burgundy
20 February	Richard makes peace between the Pisans and the Genoese in Acre
27 March	Richard goes to Jaffa
31 March	Richard returns to Ascalon
5 April	*EASTER*
15 April	Arrival of Robert, Prior of Hertford, with news of problems in England
16 April	Richard announces he must leave for England, and the army elects Conrad of Montferrat as King of Jerusalem
28 April	Murder of Conrad of Montferrat by the Assassins in Tyre
c.2 May	Election of Henry of Champagne as King of Jerusalem
5 May	Henry of Champagne marries Isabella of Jerusalem
After 5 May	Guy of Lusignan takes over the government of Cyprus
17 May	Beginning of the siege of Darum

1192 cont.

22 May	Capture of Darum by the crusaders
23 May	Arrival of Hugh of Burgundy and Henry of Champagne at Darum
25 May	The army leaves Darum and arrives at La Forbie (Harbiyah)
26 May	The army arrives at Tell al-Hasi
27 May	Attack on the Castle of the Figs (Khirbat al-Burj), but it has been abandoned
1 June	The army moves to Bait Jibrin (Bethgibelin)
4 June	Richard announces that he will remain in Palestine until Easter 1193, and that he will besiege Jerusalem if it is possible
7 June	The army leaves Ascalon
11 June	The army reaches Bait Nuba
21 June	Expedition by Richard to find a fragment of the True Cross. Later that day he goes to Galatia (Qaratiya) in anticipation of an attack on a Muslim caravan
23 June	Capture of the Muslim caravan at the Round Cistern, near Bir Khuwailifa
24 June	Richard returns to Ramla, where he meets Henry of Champagne, who has come from Acre with additional forces
29 June	Richard returns to the main army at Bait Nuba, but decides that an attack on Jerusalem is not possible
4 July	The army returns to Ramla
4–20 July	Peace negotiations between Richard and Saladin
11 July	The army returns to Ascalon
26 July	The army returns to Acre
28 July	Saladin attacks Jaffa
29 July	Richard sails to relieve Jaffa
30 July	The garrison at Jaffa is besieged in the citadel
1 August	Richard and his forces retake Jaffa after a landing from the seaward side
4 August	Saladin retreats to Casel des Plains (Yasur)
5 August	Unsuccessful attempt by a party of Mamluks to capture Richard
7 August	Richard decides to stay in Palestine
27 August	Saladin moves to Ramla
28–29 August	New peace negotiations
2 September	Treaty of Jaffa, establishing a three-year truce from the previous Easter
7 September	The Muslims begin the demolition of Ascalon
9 September	Richard goes to Haifa
September	Parties of Christian pilgrims visit Jerusalem
29 September	Queens Joanna and Berengaria sail from Acre
9 October	Richard sails from Acre

1192 cont.

11 November	Richard arrives in Corfu
20 December	Richard is captured at Vienna by the men of Leopold, Duke of Austria

1193

4 March	Death of Saladin

1194

4 February	Release of Richard by Emperor Henry VI

1199

6 April	Death of Richard I

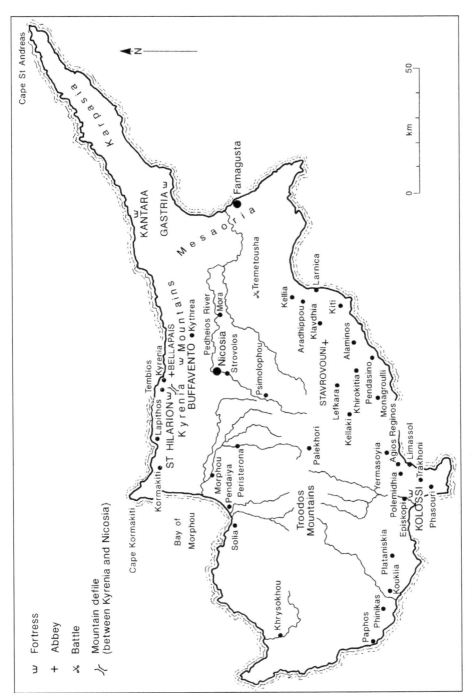

Map 1. Cyprus

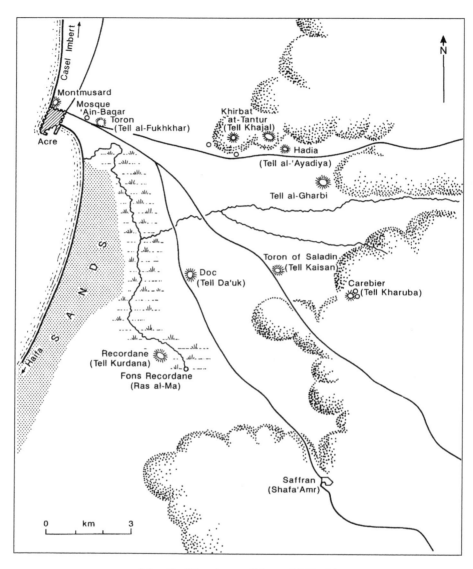

Map 2. The siege of Acre, 1189–91

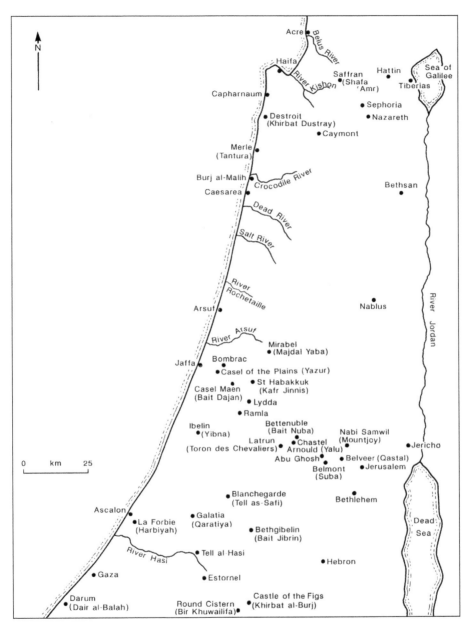

Acre
Belus River
Haifa
River Kishon
Saffran
(Shafa
'Amr)
Hattin
Sea of
Galilee
Capharnaum
Tiberias
Sephoria
Destroit
(Khirbat Dustray)
Nazareth
Merle
(Tantura)
Caymont
Burj al-Malih
Crocodile River
Caesarea
Bethsan
Dead River
Salt River
River
Rochetaille
Arsuf
Nablus
River Arsuf
Mirabel
(Majdal Yaba)
Jaffa
Bombrac
Casel of the Plains (Yazur)
Casel Maen
(Bait Dajan)
St Habakkuk
(Kafr Jinnis)
Lydda
Ramla
Ibelin
(Yibna)
Bettenuble
(Bait Nuba)
Nabi Samwil
(Mountjoy)
Latrun
(Toron des Chevaliers)
Chastel
Arnould (Yalu)
Jericho
Abu Ghosh
Belveer (Qastal)
Belmont
(Suba)
Jerusalem
Blanchegarde
(Tell as-Safi)
Bethlehem
Ascalon
Galatia
(Qaratiya)
La Forbie
(Harbiyah)
Bethgibelin
(Bait Jibrin)
Dead
Sea
River Hasi
Tell al-Hasi
Hebron
Gaza
Estornel
Darum
(Dair al-Balah)
Round Cistern
(Bir Khuwailifa)
Castle of the Figs
(Khirbat al-Burj)
River Jordan

0   km   25

Map 3. The campaigns of the Third Crusade

Introduction

The Author and the Date

Nothing is known about the author of the *Estoire de la Guerre Sainte* apart from what he tells us himself. He names himself as Ambroise at several points in the text (lines 171, 728, 2397, 3221, 3728, 4554, 4822, 5913, 6005). This reference to himself in the third person does not mean that the poem has been adapted from another work, but is simply one of the conventions of the emerging vernacular genre of chronicle.[1] Most of the text is, in fact, recounted in the first person, in both singular and plural forms, and from the perspective of an eyewitness. He confirms his authority to tell and argue the case for the crusade on the grounds that 'we saw it who were there' (line 12195). Where he sees the need to give background information, notably at the siege of Acre, he makes it clear when he has not seen something, but that it is necessary to know it in order to understand what is going on (ll.2383–404); in such instances he assures his audience that some of these details have been supplied by authorities 'which should be believed' (l.704). Indeed, he readily acknowledges the limitations of his knowledge (for example, ll.928ff), a technique common in early chronicles in order to add extra force to those matters he does claim to have seen.[2]

Gaston Paris, the first editor of the text, thought that he was a jongleur, an entertainer, on the basis that he shows some knowledge of well-known, vernacular narrative poems. He dismisses any suggestion that Ambroise might have been a cleric on the grounds that he does not have a particularly high level of learning, since all the texts mentioned are popular tales. His undoubted piety, Paris argues, is only what might be expected from any pilgrim on crusade.[3] On the other hand, a number of unacknowledged biblical echoes suggest something more than popular learning, while the rhetoric used by Ambroise is not only more extensive than in the majority of other early vernacular chronicles, but is also more sophisticated than most. Thus the lack of much overt display of

---

[1] See P. Damian-Grint, *The New Historians of the Twelfth-Century Renaissance. Authorising History in the Vernacular Revolution* (Woodbridge, 1999), pp.98–100. The same third-person techniques are found on occasion in other genres too: for example, Béroul in his version of the story of Tristan and Yseut, see *Tristan et Yseut: Les poèmes français, la saga norroise*, ed. D. Lacroix and P. Walter (Paris, 1989), ll.1268, 1790. On the poet in the text, see C. Croizy-Naquet, 'Les Figures du jongleur dans l'Estoire de la Guerre Sainte', *Le Moyen Age* 104 (1988), 229–56.

[2] See Damian-Grint, pp.166–8.

[3] See Paris, pp.vi–xii.

learning in the intertextual references may have more to do with the reception of the text and the attitudes of those for whom it was intended than with the culture of the author. Both the strong moral purpose which runs through the poem and the level of language employed suggest that Ambroise was a cleric, at least in minor orders, and a man of some education. Some possible confirmation may be found in an entry in the Liberate Rolls for 10 October 1200 in which King John authorises a payment of 25 shillings to Eustace the chaplain and Ambroise 'our clerks, who sang the *Christus vincit* at our second coronation and at our anointing and crowning of Queen Isabella, our wife',[4] an event which had taken place at Westminster two days before. Both the duties performed and the fact that Ambroise was also present at the coronation of Richard I in September 1189 (ll.190–205) suggest that it could be the same person.

He was probably from the Evrecin region of Normandy. His language is Norman, with some overlay from an Anglo-Norman scribe.[5] Although he provides no direct information about himself, his reference to the Norman conquerors of Sicily as 'our ancestors' (l.618), his evident admiration for Richard I,[6] and his detailed knowledge of the Norman crusaders, especially those associated with Robert, Earl of Leicester, who held extensive lands around Breteuil and Pacy, all point to Norman origin.[7] Moreover, his greatest praise is for the Normans, in contrast to his frequent (although not invariably) contemptuous remarks about the French, which makes it difficult to believe he can be identified with any of the crusaders from the Ile-de-France. On this basis he has the authority of a member of the army or train of Richard I of England, who can

---

4   *Rotuli de Liberate ac de Misis et Praestitis, Regnante Johanne*, ed. T.D. Hardy (London, 1844), p.1; *Rotuli Normanniae*, ed. T.D. Hardy (London, 1835), p.34. He may perhaps have either been given or adopted the name of Ambroise for professional purposes, given the use of Ambrosian chant in the twelfth century.

5   Paris, pp.x–xiii. See also ed. M. Ailes and M. Barber, vol.1, pp.2–3.

6   See B. Levy, 'Pèlerins rivaux de la 3e croisade: les personnages des rois d'Angleterre et de France d'après les chroniques d'Ambroise et d'"Ernoul" et le récit Anglo-Normand de la *Croisade et Mort Richard Coeur de Lion*', in *La Croisade – réalités et fictions: Actes du colloque d'Amiens, 1987* (Göppingen, 1989), pp.143–55; C. Hanley, 'Reading the Past through the Present: Ambroise, the Minstrel of Reims and Jordan Fantosme', *Mediaevalia* 20 (2001), 265–71; M.J. Ailes, 'Heroes of War: Ambroise's Heroes of the Third Crusade', in *Writing War: Medieval Literary Responses to Warfare*, ed. C. Saunders, F. Le Saux and N. Thomas (Cambridge, 2004), pp. 29–48.

7   See J.H. Round, 'Some English Crusaders of Richard I', *English Historical Review* 18 (1903), 475–81, and J.G. Edwards, 'The *Itinerarium regis Ricardi* and the *Estoire de la Guerre Sainte*', in *Historical Essays in honour of James Tait*, ed. J.G. Edwards, V.H. Galbraith and E.F. Jacob (Manchester, 1930), pp.68–9. A passing reference to *Duens* may be a clue to his place of origin, in that, although it is a rhyme for *bons*, it might be thought that Ambroise could have found a better-known place if he had wanted, but it is not identifiable on modern maps. In addition, at one point he has Richard vow to act 'by St Lambert of Liège', while he describes Richard's horse, Fauvel, as the best 'from here to Ypres', but both were well-known towns which could be conveniently used to rhyme with *siege* and *Cypre*, so it seems unlikely that the references are significant. For a different view of the identity of the author see F. Vielliard, 'Richard Coeur de Lion et son entourage normand: le témoignage l'*Estoire de la guerre sainte*', *Bibliothèque de l'Ecole des Chartes* 160 (2002), 5–52.

draw both upon what he witnessed himself and on information acquired from fellow Normans and others in the Angevin army.[8]

The text appears to have been written towards the end of the twelfth century. It must have been completed after the release of Richard from captivity in 1194, as this is mentioned in the poem, but before the king's death in 1199.[9] The linguistic evidence would support this dating.[10] Indeed, Ambroise's poem has the immediacy and impact of an account written within a few years of the events it describes.

Historical Context

In the autumn of 1187, Joscius, Archbishop of Tyre, set sail for the West, the sails of his galley painted black so that, says one of the French continuators of the great chronicle of William, Joscius's predecessor, 'whenever the galley came near to land the people who saw it would know that it brought bad tidings'.[11] For the true Christian believer the news was indeed shattering: on 4 July 1187, on the Horns of Hattin, a parched hillside overlooking the Sea of Galilee, Saladin, ruler of Egypt and Syria, and the dominant political leader in the Muslim Middle East, had defeated and destroyed the greatest army ever put into the field by the Latin settlers. The fragments of the True Cross, always carried into battle by the Christians, had fallen into Muslim hands. Less than a week later, the city of Acre, the most important Frankish port, tamely capitulated, followed in July and August by Sidon, Beirut and Ascalon. Then, on 2 October, after a devastating campaign throughout the kingdom, Saladin captured the city of Jerusalem itself where, according to the contemporary Muslim historian, Ibn al-Athir, he ordered that the Dome of the Rock be 'cleansed of filth and impurities' so that on the following Friday, Muslims could once again enter for communal prayers.[12] Nor was this the end of the Christian trauma. Even as the archbishop was crossing the Mediterranean, cities and castles continued to fall: in the course of the year after Hattin, Muslim forces captured the great castles of Belvoir, Montréal, Kerak and Safad. In the Kingdom of Jerusalem only the port of Tyre remained in Christian hands, saved not by the Latins of the East, who had been on the verge of giving it up, but by the arrival from Constantinople of Conrad, eldest son of William III, Marquis of Montferrat, who had himself been

---

8 On the concept of eyewitness and truth, see J. Beer, *Narrative Conventions of Truth in the Middle Ages* (Geneva, 1981), pp.23–4, and Damian-Grint, pp.68–74.

9 Levy, p.144.

10 Paris, pp.xiii–l. See also ed. M. Ailes and M. Barber, vol.1, pp.2–3.

11 *La Continuation de Guillaume de Tyr (1184–1197)*, ed. M.R. Morgan, Documents relatifs à l'histoire des Croisades publiés par l'Académie des Inscriptions et Belles-Lettres 14 (Paris, 1982), p.82; trans. P.W. Edbury, *The Conquest of Jerusalem and the Third Crusade: Sources in Translation* (Aldershot, 1996), p.73.

12 *The Chronicle of Ibn al-Athīr for the Crusading Period from al-Kāmil fī 'l-ta 'rīkh. Part 2*, trans. D.S. Richards. Crusade Texts in Translation 15 (Aldershot, 2007), p.334.

captured at Hattin. Further north the only important cities left to the Christians were Tripoli and Antioch.

Archbishop Joscius already had a reputation as a mediator and a diplomat. He first visited William II, King of Sicily, whose prompt reaction in sending a fleet in the summer of 1188 was crucial in saving Tripoli, and then went on to Pope Urban III in Rome. Urban did not survive long enough to take any effective action, but his successor, Gregory VIII, issued the encyclical *Audita tremendi* on 29 October 1187, calling on 'those with contrite hearts and humbled spirits' to activate themselves in the cause of the holy places. For those who 'undertake the labour of this journey and die in penitence for their sins and with right faith we promise full indulgence of their faults and eternal life'.[13] On 21 January 1188, Joscius met the kings of England and France, Henry II and Philip II, together with Philip of Alsace, Count of Flanders, near Gisors in Normandy, where he persuaded them to make common cause for the sake of the Holy Land. In November 1187, quite independently, Richard, Count of Poitou, Henry's eldest surviving son, had already taken the Cross, the first of the great western rulers to make such a commitment. Although Henry at once began a vigorous campaign to raise money for the forthcoming expedition, he died on 6 July 1189, leaving Richard to succeed to both his extensive English and continental lands and to his crusading plans. On 20 July, Richard and Philip agreed to crusade together, a promise consolidated by further meetings at Nonancourt on 30 December (where regulations for the conduct of the crusade were promulgated) and at Dreux on 16 March 1190.

In the end it was the forces of these men and their vassals that formed the backbone of the Third Crusade, but there is no doubt that the defeat at Hattin was profoundly significant for all of Latin Christendom. According to the anonymous author of the first book of the *Itinerarium*, incorporated into the chronicle of the Augustinian canon, Richard de Templo, sometime between 1217 and 1222, 'a great many men sent each other wool and distaff, hinting that if anyone failed to join the military undertaking they were only fit for women's work'.[14] Events offered the opportunity for the heroic qualities of Richard I to take centre-stage, a theme moulded by Ambroise into his powerful story of the lion-hearted king. However, initially by far the most formidable army assembled was that of the German Emperor, Frederick Barbarossa. Frederick took the Cross on 27 March 1188, and set out from Ratisbon on 11 May 1189, taking the overland route through Gallipoli and Asia Minor. It seems probable that the sheer size of his forces determined Frederick's decision to take this route rather than obtain sea transport in the way that Philip and Richard were to do, but it was a decision that entailed severe risks.[15] No crusader army had crossed Asia Minor

---

[13] *Historia de expeditione Friderici imperatoris*, in *Quellen zur Geschichte des Kreuzzuges Kaiser Friedrichs I.*, ed. A. Chroust, *MGH SS*, n.s., vol.5 (Berlin, 1928), pp.6–10; trans. L. and J. Riley-Smith, *The Crusades: Idea and Reality 1095–1274* (London, 1981), p.67.

[14] *Itinerarium Peregrinorum et Gesta Regis Ricardi*, in *Chronicles and Memorials of the Reign of Richard I*, vol.1, ed. W. Stubbs, Rolls Series 38 (London, 1864), 1.17, p.33; trans. H. Nicholson, *Chronicle of the Third Crusade* (Aldershot, 1997), p.48.

[15] See J. Prawer, *Histoire du Royaume Latin de Jérusalem*, vol.2 (Paris, 1970), p.34.

without terrible suffering; he himself must have remembered this from his own experiences as a young man during the Second Crusade in 1147, and even as they marched he seems to have been having second thoughts. In fact he himself paid the price, drowning while crossing the River Saleph in Cilicia on 10 June 1190. When they heard the news, the Muslim garrison at Acre, pinned in by Latin forces since the previous August, was jubilant, while Saladin, who had been attempting to lift the siege by counterattacking the Latins, was profoundly relieved. Although important German forces took part in the eastern campaigns of the crusade, most notably under the emperor's son, Frederick of Swabia, and Leopold, Duke of Austria, the death of the emperor so undermined their role that they were never in a position to challenge Richard's dominance. The bitterness this caused culminated in Richard's capture and imprisonment in Germany between December 1192 and February 1194.

The preparations made by the kings of France and England were extensive and necessarily lengthy: Philip did not reach Acre until 20 April 1191, while Richard only appeared on 8 June. Meanwhile, others had taken matters into their own hands, most notably Guy of Lusignan, King of Jerusalem at the time of Hattin, and the man whose decision to leave a good defensive position on the springs of Sepphoria in order to march to relieve Tiberias had been primarily responsible for the Christian defeat. Guy had been captured in the battle, but had been released in May or June 1188 in exchange for the surrender of Ascalon the previous September and a promise not to fight the Muslims in the East again. In fact, his options were quite limited, for he had been king by virtue of his marriage to Sibylla, sister of Baldwin IV, who had died in 1185, a position established by the coup the couple had staged in the late summer of 1186. Yet there was little left of his kingdom except for the great port of Tyre, held by Conrad of Montferrat, who clearly saw himself as the future ruler. Most of the surviving baronage had agreed that Conrad should hold the city until the arrival of the western kings. Conrad therefore refused first Geoffrey of Lusignan, Guy's brother, and then Guy and Sibylla, entry into the city, where he had been consolidating his position by grants of privileges to the Italian and French maritime cities.[16] By the summer of 1189 Guy was a king without a kingdom, with his military reputation at a low ebb, and with few prospects back in Poitou. In these circumstances his desperate and apparently reckless march to besiege Acre makes some sense, although his chances of success must have seemed small to any knowledgeable observer. He may have been encouraged in this course by Gerard of Ridefort, the Master of the Temple, who had been released by Saladin at the same time, and who had been the main influence upon the king on the eve of Hattin.

Guy was greatly helped by Saladin's apparent reluctance to take the move seriously, for he allowed the Christians to march unopposed to Acre and to set

---

[16] See H.E. Mayer, 'On the Beginnings of the Communal Movement in the Holy Land: The Commune of Tyre', *Traditio* 24 (1968), 448–52, and D. Jacoby, 'Conrad, Marquis of Montferrat, and the Kingdom of Jerusalem (1187–92)', in *Atti del Congresso internazionale 'Dai feudi monferrine e dal Piemonte ai nuovi mondi oltre gli Oceani', Alessandria 2–6 aprile 1990* (Alessandria, 1993), pp.187–238.

themselves up on Tell-Fukhkhar, a low hill to the south-east of the city. Saladin may not have wished to be diverted from the siege of Beaufort, whose lord, Reynald of Sidon, had exploited his previous acquaintance with Saladin and his ability to speak Arabic to delay its fall. However, Saladin's failure even to block the coast north of Acre (where it was possible to land supplies) enabled the Christian forces not only to survive, but to act as a focal point for contingents from the West, which began to arrive within days of the establishment of Guy's camp on 28 August 1189.[17] The most important of the newcomers was James of Avesnes, vassal both of the count of Flanders and of the count of Hainaut, who landed on 1 September, two days before Richard had even been crowned. Thereafter, the besiegers were steadily reinforced: fleets from Denmark and Frisia, soldiers from northern Italy, major regional leaders like Ludwig of Thuringia, Frederick of Swabia, Leopold of Austria, Robert of Dreux and Henry of Champagne, and great ecclesiastical lords like Philip of Beauvais, Baldwin of Canterbury and Hubert Walter of Salisbury.

By the time Philip II arrived, the Christians had therefore been fighting on two fronts for nearly twenty months. During that time Saladin's perspective had entirely changed, for he now saw this as a major confrontation important enough to justify calling in troops from as far away as Armenia, Iraq and Egypt. A measure of the intensification of the conflict can be seen by the toll this took upon the European nobility, unequalled by any previous crusade. Before either Philip or Richard had even set foot on the Syrian mainland, the crusaders had already lost Everard, Count of Brienne, and his brother Andrew, Henry, Count of Bar-le-Duc, William Ferrers, Earl of Derby, Theobald, Count of Blois, Stephen, Count of Sancerre, Ranulf Glanville, the former justiciar of England, Baldwin, Archbishop of Canterbury, and Guy of Senlis, Butler of France, among others. Philip of Alsace, Count of Flanders, died shortly after King Philip's arrival. Among the eastern Franks, Gerard of Ridefort, Master of the Temple, was killed in the major Christian defeat on 4 October 1189, while Queen Sibylla and her two daughters appear to have succumbed to disease sometime before 21 October the following year. If it is true, as the English chronicler Roger of Howden reported, that one of the reasons for Philip's departure so soon after the fall of Acre in July 1191 was his fear of death, then he certainly had some justification.[18]

However, while the new crusaders undoubtedly helped to change Saladin's attitude towards the attack on Acre, they were unable to take the city. Indeed, if the gloomy letter to the convent at Canterbury by Archbishop Baldwin's chaplain, dated 21 October 1190, is any indication, the Muslims were beginning to gain the upper hand against an army ridden by faction and undermined by

---

[17] See, however, H.A.R. Gibb, *The Life of Saladin from the Works of 'Imad ad-Din and Baha' ad-Din* (Oxford, 1973), pp.59–61, who argues that most of the blame falls on Saladin's generals, who were disinclined 'to cut across country and intercept the Crusaders on their march'.

[18] See J. Richard, 'Philippe Auguste, la croisade et le royaume', in *La France de Philippe Auguste: Le Temps des Mutations*, ed. R.-H. Bautier (Paris, 1982), p.422.

immoral behaviour.[19] It was the arrival of the royal forces which made the decisive difference, even though Imad al-Din, Saladin's secretary, claims to have been unimpressed by Philip II's relatively modest fleet. 'His mediocrity gave us pleasure', he wrote.[20] In fact, even Ambroise, who had scant sympathy for the French king, concedes that Philip was generous in his subsidies and energetic in his desire to mount an immediate attack. The king himself took a prominent part in the fighting, as well as financing the building of some formidable siege engines. Nevertheless, Richard could deploy much greater resources, at least partly because, as the Winchester chronicler Richard of Devizes drily put it, 'the king most obligingly unburdened all those whose money was a burden to them'.[21] He had equipped large fleets which, according to Roger of Howden, sailed 'from the different harbours of England, Normandy, Brittany and Poitou, immediately after Easter [25 March 1190]'.[22] By the time he set out from Messina, where he had overwintered between mid-September 1190 and April 1191, there may have been as many as 180 transports and 39 galleys.[23]

The kings had been a long time coming. Richard, in particular, had a direct financial interest in the Sicilian kingdom, for William II had died in November 1189 without direct heirs, and the consequent seizure of the throne by his cousin, Tancred of Lecce, had left Joanna, William's widow and Richard's sister, isolated in the kingdom. Richard intended to collect her dower as well as sums bequeathed to his father by the late king. On 4 October Richard's seizure of Messina obliged Tancred to make terms which, among other things, enabled him to increase his war chest. Even so it had meant further delay because by this time the 'inclemency of the winds and the waves and weather' made it impossible to sail before the spring. Richard had gained further resources from the conquest of the island of Cyprus, which he seized from its ruler, Isaac Comnenus, in the course of May 1191. Therefore, by June 1191 the Christian position had been transformed from Guy's rather forlorn foray of late August 1189. At that time his small force was perched on top of an isolated hill some three-quarters of a mile (1,200 metres) from the nearest city wall; now Acre was completely invested and really continuous pressure could be brought to bear which Saladin was unable to do much to mitigate. A series of assaults in early July brought capitulation on the 12th, and the kings moved in to occupy the city, Richard in the citadel, Philip in the fortress of the Templars on the northern promontory.

19 *Epistolae Cantuarienses*, in *Chronicles and Memorials of the Reign of Richard I*, vol.2, ed. W. Stubbs, Rolls Series 38 (London, 1865), pp.328–9; trans. Edbury, *Conquest of Jerusalem*, p.171.

20 Imad al-Din al-Isfahani, *Conquête de la Syrie et de la Palestine par Saladin*, trans. H. Massé (Paris, 1972), pp.289–90.

21 Richard of Devizes, *The Chronicle of Richard of Devizes of the Time of King Richard the First*, ed. and trans. J.T. Appleby (London, 1963), p.9.

22 Roger of Howden, *Chronica*, vol.3, ed. W. Stubbs, Rolls Series 51 (London, 1870), p.42.

23 See C. Tyerman, *England and the Crusades, 1095–1588* (Chicago and London, 1988), p.66, and S. Painter, 'The Third Crusade: Richard the Lionhearted and Philip Augustus', in *A History of the Crusades*, vol.2, ed. R.E. Wolff and H.W. Hazard (Madison, 1969), p.61.

According to Roger of Howden, little account was taken of the efforts and suffering of the besiegers, some of whom had been there for nearly two years. The kings, he says, divided everything between themselves; but when they eventually agreed to share the spoils, 'since they delayed in doing so, many were forced by poverty to leave them'.[24] They did, however, settle the outstanding question of the future kingship of Jerusalem, which had been a festering sore in the army ever since Guy's release from captivity and Conrad's refusal to receive him in Tyre. Since then, with the death of Sibylla, the balance of power had shifted further towards Conrad and, on 24 November, he had seized the opportunity to marry Isabella, Sibylla's half-sister, despite the fact that she was apparently happily married to a local baron, Humphrey of Toron. The agreement, made on 28 July 1191, reflected this: Guy was to retain the kingship during his lifetime, but it was to be Conrad and Isabella or, if they predeceased Guy, their heirs, who would succeed. Resources were supposed to be divided between them, but Conrad's effective control of key cities, strengthened further by Philip II's grant of his half of the city of Acre, left him in much the stronger position.

This was Philip II's last significant act in the East, for nothing could now deflect him from his determination to return to France. The English chroniclers are uncompromising in their view. 'How shameful, how outrageous', says the *Itinerarium*, 'wanting to leave when there was so much pressing business to be done! . . . What an extraordinary way of discharging a vow, when he had hardly entered the country and had such brief triumphs against the Turks!'[25] Roger of Howden claimed that when he arrived in Rome, the king's main objective was to vilify Richard, a policy continued thereafter when he 'defamed the king of England among his neighbours, accusing him of many crimes'. According to Roger, the real reason he had left was because the death of Philip of Flanders had opened up the possibility 'that he might subjugate the county of Flanders'.[26] The French chronicler, Rigord, is the only voice in his defence, claiming that the king 'was then oppressed by a most serious illness',[27] an explanation clearly not believed in the crusading army, nor by other contemporaries unconnected with Richard.[28]

Underlying the English chroniclers' attitudes, of course, were the rivalries stemming from the continuing conflict over the continental lands of the Angevins, and it appears that Richard did extract an oath from Philip that he would not attack his lands while he remained in the East, although he cannot have had much confidence in its efficacy. However, Richard cannot have been entirely displeased to see him leave; with Frederick Barbarossa dead and Philip departed, he was undoubtedly the greatest leader in the crusader host. For

---

[24] Roger of Howden, *Chronica*, vol.3, p.123.

[25] *Itinerarium*, 3.21, p.236; trans. Nicholson, p.223.

[26] Roger of Howden, *Chronica*, vol.3, pp.166–7, 111. See, too, *La Continuation de Guillaume de Tyr*, pp.130–1.

[27] Rigord, *Histoire de Philippe Auguste*, ed. and trans. E. Carpentier, G. Pon and Y. Chauvin. Sources d'Histoire Médiévale publiées par l'Institut de Recherche et d'Histoire des Textes 33 (Paris, 2006), pp.304–7.

[28] See Richard, 'Philippe Auguste, la croisade et le royaume', p.421, who says that the king was healthy by the time he reached Apulia, and J. Gillingham, *Richard I*, 2nd ed. (New Haven and London, 1999), p.163, n.43, p.164, n.48.

Ambroise it was the ideal opportunity to fashion the story of the Third Crusade around him, and it would indeed have been an appropriate dramatic climax if the expedition had culminated in the recapture of the city of Jerusalem. Controversially, then and since, it did not happen. Although Acre had been retaken, Saladin's army remained intact and most of the rest of the former Kingdom of Jerusalem was still in Muslim hands. Success therefore depended upon Richard's future strategy and the extent to which Saladin could prevent him executing it. As there were limits to the determination and resources of even a man like Richard, the degree to which the Muslims could hinder and delay him was the crucial element. As the famous incident of the massacre of the 3,000 Muslim prisoners, taken when Acre fell, shows, it is clear that the king thought that this was his opponent's main goal, for the prisoners could not be taken south with the crusader army, and Richard appears to have believed that Saladin was deliberately prevaricating in fulfilling the terms of their repatriation. Even so, some historians have argued that Richard contributed decisively to his own failure by his own over-cautious policy and by his willingness to be diverted into other minor forays which, although sometimes profitable, did little to further the major objective of the crusade.[29] By the time Richard was eventually forced to leave on 9 October 1192 – finally succumbing to the urgent messages suggesting that his presence was vitally needed in England and on the continent – it is arguable that the crusade had completely lost focus.

When Richard led the crusaders south from Acre on 22 August he chose to take the coastal route, his right flank protected by the sea. Saladin could not prevent this, although he did as much as he could to make the march slow, uncomfortable and costly. Even so, on 7 September, the Muslims were brought to battle near Arsuf and suffered a heavy but not totally crushing defeat. Richard de Templo saw this as regrettable, claiming that with more persistence, 'the Turks would have been swept off the face of the earth, leaving it free for the Christians to inhabit'.[30] Three days later Richard arrived at Jaffa, the port from which the original besiegers of Jerusalem had been supplied during the First Crusade in 1099. Control of Jaffa was obviously vital and during the next two months Richard refortified the city with the evident intention of using it as a base for a march inland to Jerusalem. Joshua Prawer sees this as a second chance to launch a successful attack, having already missed the opportunity to march directly inland after the departure from Acre. For Prawer the king failed to capitalise upon the high morale of the army after Arsuf.[31] Certainly Richard did become entangled in a series of fruitless negotiations with Saladin and his brother, al-Adil, which lasted throughout October and most of November. Separate contact between Saladin and Conrad of Montferrat suggests that the intention was not only to exploit the evident divisions among the Christians, but also to sow enough confusion to bring the impetus generated by the victory at Arsuf to a halt.

---

[29] See, for example, M. Markowski, 'Richard Lionheart: Bad King, Bad Crusader?' *Journal of Medieval History* 23 (1997), 351–65.

[30] *Itinerarium*, 4.21, p.278; trans. Nicholson, p.259.

[31] Prawer, *Histoire du Royaume Latin*, vol.2, pp.77–83.

Richard himself, while presenting the situation in a very positive light, never-theless in a letter to Garnier of Rochefort, Abbot of Clairvaux, on 1 October 1191, showed that he was well aware of the problem. 'Since his defeat that day [at Arsuf]', he says, 'Saladin has not dared to do battle with the Christians. Instead he lies in wait at a distance out of sight like a lion in his den, and he is intent on killing the friends of the cross like sheep led to the slaughter.'[32] Between mid-November and early December the army ventured no further inland than Ramla and Lydda; indeed, by this time the wet weather had made the movement of large forces extremely difficult as well as causing equipment to rust or rot. At the end of October Richard had had to return to Acre to bring back some elements in the army who preferred the comforts to be found there to the privations of the crusader camp. In early January 1192, the king was obliged to accept the advice of the heads of the military orders and the local Frankish leaders that an attack on Jerusalem was not feasible at that time. More weeks passed while the crusaders concentrated upon refortifying cities further south, most notably Ascalon, the walls of which were expensively rebuilt between January and Easter, 1192. Here, Richard may have had in mind a wider strategy contemplated the previous year, to bring pressure on Saladin by threatening Egypt. Saladin had certainly lost much of what he had gained in the aftermath of Hattin, for the coast from Tripoli to Ascalon was once more in Christian hands, and it no longer seemed that the Latins would be driven out altogether; more-over, Richard had shown that he could defeat his great army of allies drawn from across the Muslim world. Even so, by April 1192 it seemed as if Saladin's dogged attritional strategy had paid off, for Richard's doubts about the practi-cality of besieging Jerusalem were reinforced by news of political problems in England which demanded his personal attention. On 16 April, just when improvements in the weather seemed to offer an opportunity to resume campaigning, the king announced that he would have to return to England.

In some ways this was the most logical step. Richard had been away from his complex and sprawling lands for nearly two years. Neither his brother John nor Philip II could be trusted not to exploit this absence, while in the East Saladin had effectively created a stalemate from which it was difficult to see any other outcome than compromise. In February Richard had quarrelled with Hugh of Burgundy, effectively the leader of the French and Philip's representative since the previous July, since Hugh disapproved of the attention paid to Ascalon, yet was prevented from much independent action by a lack of funds, a situation which Richard would do nothing more to alleviate. Although Henry, Count of Champagne, and his vassals remained with Richard, Hugh of Burgundy and the majority of the French withdrew to Acre. Even if Richard decided to stay on, there was a clear danger that the crusade would disintegrate around him. Not surprisingly, in these circumstances the crusaders were now willing to accept Conrad as king, a decision to which Richard had no alternative but to accede.

Less than two weeks after his election as king, however, Conrad was murdered in Tyre by two members of the messianic Muslim sect known as the

---

[32] Roger of Howden, *Chronica*, vol.3, p.132; trans. Edbury, *Conquest of Jerusalem*, p.180.

Assassins. As presented by the chroniclers, the crusaders spontaneously chose Henry of Champagne to replace him and, on 5 May, Henry married Isabella. In fact, Richard must have been one of the prime movers in the affair for he could not have afforded to leave a power vacuum in the kingdom for very long. These events seem to have suspended Richard's plan to depart, despite new information about an alleged conspiracy against him by Philip and John. Even Ambroise presents his hero as tortured by indecision: 'it was not to be wondered that he did not know what to do'.[33] In the end he continued campaigning, capturing Darum on 22 May, and once more drawing the bulk of the army behind him when Hugh of Burgundy and Henry of Champagne arrived in support. By 4 June he had changed his mind, perhaps as a result of the strength of opinion in the crusader army, and had decided he would try once more for Jerusalem. On 23 June the capture of a rich Muslim caravan at the Round Cistern, south of Bait Jibrin, gave the army both a psychological boost and a welcome renewal of resources.

The fundamental situation, however, had not changed. A march on Jerusalem remained a formidable undertaking which Richard was reluctant to undertake except under the most favourable circumstances possible, circumstances which would include the assembly of the strongest available force. Although by 11 June Richard had advanced to Bait Nuba, only about twelve and a half miles (or about twenty kilometres) from Jerusalem, he nevertheless kept the main army waiting there until 3 July while Henry of Champagne gathered together those crusaders still in Acre. Saladin could not be expected to remain passive during this new delay, and his continual attacks upon the lines of communication back to the coast offered a preview of what would happen if they settled in to besiege Jerusalem. On 29 June the king decided for a second time to withdraw. 'You never saw such a chosen people so depressed and dismayed', says Ambroise, a line which quite evidently reflects his own deep disappointment as well.[34] In these circumstances Richard's proposal that they should attack Egypt instead could hardly be expected to set light to the fires of enthusiasm. Although Richard did not leave until October the decision to abandon the attack on Jerusalem for a second time effectively ended the crusade, for no other policy could have held the various elements in the army together long enough to pose any really coherent threat to Saladin.

Saladin now knew that there would have to be a negotiated settlement and he once more moved onto the offensive in an effort to secure the most favourable terms possible. Moreover, as Prawer has very clearly demonstrated, the Ayubid empire depended upon effective communication between Egypt and Syria, a position which could not be maintained while the Franks controlled Ascalon and Darum.[35] Saladin's sudden attack on Jaffa on 28 July 1192 can thus be explained in this context and, although its garrison was saved three days later by a typical piece of bravado by Richard, it was evident that there would have to be peace negotiations. The key for Saladin was Ascalon, the fortifications of which he

---

33 Lines 9121–2.
34 Lines 10667–8.
35 Prawer, *Histoire du Royaume Latin*, vol.2, p.98.

wanted dismantled; not surprisingly, previous negotiations had broken down on this point, since the Christians had only rebuilt the walls and towers the previous spring at great cost and effort. The extent to which Richard was forced to lower his sights can be seen by the eventual outcome, embodied in the truce known as the treaty of Jaffa, agreed on 2 September. It was to last for three years and the Christians would retain the coastal lands between Tyre and Jaffa. The walls of Ascalon were to be demolished. Access to Jerusalem was permitted to certain pilgrims approved by Richard, among whom the French were not included. Richard did not avail himself of this opportunity, perhaps partly because of his state of health, but perhaps partly, too, because he genuinely intended to return. Richard de Templo, writing with a longer perspective than Ambroise and in the knowledge that Richard had not been able to go back, wanted nothing to detract from the achievements of these crusaders. 'Afterwards some people used to taunt them and go foolishly on and on saying how little the pilgrims had achieved in the country of Jerusalem since they had not yet recovered Jerusalem. They did not know what they were saying, because they were criticising things which they had not experienced and knew nothing about.'[36]

Historical Value

'You never saw any one like him; he will always be at the front; he will always be found at the place of need, as a good and tested knight. It is he who cuts so many of us down. They call him Melec Richard.' In Ambroise's epic poem of the Third Crusade the Saracen emirs assemble before Saladin, their heads bowed with the shame of their defeat by the crusaders at the battle of Arsuf on 7 September 1191. When Saladin berates them, only one man, called Sanguin of Aleppo by Ambroise, can bring himself to speak. We fought courageously, he tells the sultan, but no one could prevail against the Franks led as they are by such a man as Melec Richard, who 'should hold land, conquer and dispense wealth' (ll.6790–825). Sanguin's speech is, of course, pure fiction, and Ambroise's audience, familiar with the genre of the *chansons de geste*, would have known this very well, but, equally importantly, they would have known too that Ambroise had woven this story into a vivid, first-hand narrative of events which really had taken place and at which the story-teller had either actually been present or knew those who had. On the one hand, therefore, Ambroise writes in epic style with heroes and villains, dramatic confrontations and individual deeds of daring, and colourful speeches and imaginary dialogue. Yet, at the same time, his listeners would have understood that this was serious history, authenticated by the teller's evident status as an eyewitness and participant. Ambroise had been present at the meeting between Henry II and Philip II on 21 January 1188, he had observed the great court which had followed Richard's coronation on 3 September 1189, he had sailed to Sicily and Cyprus in 1190 and

36 *Itinerarium*, 6.35, p.439; trans. Nicholson, p.379.

1191, he had seen the fall of Acre on 12 July 1191 and the battle of Arsuf in the following September, and he was still there when, three years after Richard's coronation, select groups of English and Norman crusaders were allowed to visit and pray at the holy sites in Jerusalem, sites which they had failed to recapture despite the greatest expenditure of blood and resources since the First Crusade.

The only Christian source with comparable chronological coverage is that of another possible participant, Richard de Templo, Prior of the Augustinian house of the Holy Trinity in London, the probable author of the Latin chronicle known as the *Itinerarium*, which was most likely put together between 1217 and 1222.[37] There are many similarities between Ambroise and the *Itinerarium*; indeed, it used to be thought that they derived from a common source, now lost.[38] It now seems that both can be regarded as independent authors, but that Richard de Templo drew upon various sources, of which Ambroise's poem was by far the most important, to produce his own version of events. This he attached to an account of the beginning of the crusade and the siege of Acre by another writer, possibly English like himself. However, Ambroise and Richard de Templo were aiming at different audiences, each of whom would have admired their manner of presentation. Although Ambroise's listeners would have included many clerks, his primary target would have been knights and their followers, perhaps even including men who had fought in the East, who understood the vernacular better than Latin, and were carried along by the rhythm; Richard was writing in Latin prose for his fellow monks and scholars, who would have appreciated his skill in compiling such a narrative from a number of sources. Nevertheless, different as their techniques were, both men drew credibility from the fact that they had been there, and neither had any time for armchair critics safely ensconced in England or Normandy. After his account of the taking of the Cross and the Mediterranean journeys of the two kings, Ambroise pauses to tell his listeners 'how it came about that the city of Acre was besieged', making it clear that this came not from his own experience but from what he had read, for 'he did not see any of this' (ll.2383–404). At the appropriate dramatic moment, he returns to his own witness: 'so Ambroise wishes to complete his tale here, carry on to his goal, tie the knot and join the tale of the two kings who came to the siege of Acre and what they did there and recall what he can remember of the story of how Acre was taken, as he saw it with his own eyes' (ll.4545–62). For Richard de Templo, his account could be believed because 'we saw and experienced the trials and difficulties which they [the crusaders] bore'.[39] Similarly, the English crusader who appears to have been the original author of book one of the *Itinerarium*, while making the obligatory disclaimer about his lack of a cultured style, at once turns it into a virtue by telling any critics that 'they should

---

37 On the authorship and dating of the *Itinerarium*, see H.E. Mayer, *Das Itinerarium: Eine zeitgenössische englische Chronik zum dritten Kreuzzug in ursprünglicher Gestalt* (Stuttgart, 1962), pp.1–44; H. Möhring, 'Eine Chronik aus der Zeit des dritten Kreuzzugs: das sogennante *Itinerarium peregrinorum 1*', *Innsbrucker historische Studien* 5 (1982), 149–62; Nicholson, pp.6–15.
38 For example, see Edwards, p.68.
39 *Itinerarium*, 6.35, p.439; trans. Nicholson, p.379.

realise that we wrote this while we were in the military camp, where the battle's roar does not allow leisure for peaceful thought'.[40] In fact, he need not have worried, for the anonymous Latin continuation of William of Tyre, probably written in England in the 1190s, offers a more ordered version of events, largely based on this writer's account.[41]

A fourth eyewitness was Roger, Parson of Howden in Yorkshire. In many ways Roger of Howden, whose temperament and technique were quite different, complements Ambroise and Richard de Templo. Unlike them, he wrote within the wider context of the reigns of Henry II and Richard, which he recorded from the viewpoint of one who had been a royal clerk and judge in Henry's courts in the 1170s and 1180s, as well as a much travelled royal and episcopal representative.[42] Although he was not present when the kings set out from Vézelay in July 1190, he had joined the king's party by the time it left from Marseilles on 7 August, apparently sent to convey the complaints of Hugh du Puiset, Bishop of Durham, against William of Longchamp, whom Richard had left in charge of the government of England. He remained with the crusade until after the fall of Acre in July the next year, probably because of the value of his experience as an administrator. He returned to the West, joining the small fleet of Philip II soon after it had left Tyre on 2 August 1191, apparently as part of a group sent by Richard to warn about Philip's supposed plans to attack the Angevin lands. Roger was deeply interested in administration, incorporating a range of documents in his chronicle, and taking care to make precise notes of his itineraries. Between 1170 and 1192 he made an independent record of events, including his notes on the crusade; soon after his return he revised his account of the crusade for his *Chronica*, taking cognisance of information which was not to hand for his first draft.[43]

Other chroniclers, while not on the crusade itself, gathered information from those who had been. Ralph, Abbot of the small Cistercian monastery of Coggeshall in Essex, was a neighbour of Hugh of Neville, one of a group of Anglo-Norman knights closely linked to the king. Hugh held lands at Wethersfield, about twelve miles (or about nineteen kilometres) to the northwest of Coggeshall.[44] Richard of Devizes, while not naming his sources, clearly spoke to several participants, who left the crusade at different times. His account

---

[40] *Itinerarium*, Prologue, p.4; trans. Nicholson, p.22.

[41] *Die lateinische Fortsetzung Wilhelms von Tyrus*, ed. M. Salloch (Leipzig, 1934). See also Nicholson, pp.3–4. William of Tyre's own narrative is the most important history of the crusader states up to the early 1180s.

[42] Roger of Howden, *Gesta Regis Henrici II et Ricardi I*, vol.2, ed. W. Stubbs, Rolls Series 49 (London, 1867), pp.110–99, and *Chronica*, vol.3, pp.36–133, 155–61, 165–7, 179–86.

[43] See J. Gillingham, 'Roger of Howden on Crusade', in *Richard Coeur de Lion: Kingship, Chivalry and War in the Twelfth Century* (London and Rio Grande, 1994), pp.141–53; A. Gransden, *Historical Writing in England c.550–c.1307* (London, 1974), pp.222–6; D. Corner, 'The *Gesta Regis Henrici Secundi* and *Chronica* of Roger, Parson of Howden', *Bulletin of the Institute of Historical Research* 56 (1983), 126–44.

[44] Ralph of Coggeshall, *Chronicon Anglicanum*, ed. J. Stevenson, Rolls Series 66 (London, 1875), p.45. See Gransden, pp.238–9, on Ralph's sources of information.

of the journey of the crusaders to Sicily, for example, suggests that it is based on the recollection of somebody who did not know the outcome of the crusade and so might have returned to England with Walter of Coutances in April 1191. Later on, his graphic description of the wretched condition of Christian captives in Jerusalem may well have derived from Hubert Walter, Bishop of Salisbury, who had led one of the pilgrim parties to Jerusalem in September 1192.[45] Ralph of Diceto (perhaps Diss in Norfolk), who was Dean of St Paul's from about 1180, knew a great deal about the early stages of the siege of Acre, before the arrival of the kings, because William, his chaplain, was there.[46] Indeed, among the English chroniclers, only William, a canon in the Augustinian priory of Newburgh in Yorkshire, seems to lack the specific or anecdotal detail of eye-witnesses, although, in compensation, his crisp and succinct summary of events is much more chronologically balanced than Richard of Devizes or Ralph of Diceto.[47] Others wrote letters during the course of the crusade, describing what was happening and expressing their feelings about the situation, among them the king himself, Hubert Walter, Archbishop Baldwin of Canterbury, and the archbishop's chaplain.[48]

Given the importance of these sources, it is not surprising that a crusade which included Danes, Frisians, Germans, Hungarians, Pisans, Genoese, Sicilians, Flemings, Picards and French, among others, as well as the local baronage of the Kingdom of Jerusalem and the Principality of Tripoli, should appear to be largely the work of the Anglo-Normans under the inspired leadership of the English king, Richard I. As William of Newburgh described it, the siege of Acre was transformed by the arrival of the king, and the city fell because of his fervour and power.[49] Although the legend grew during the next generation, nevertheless other contemporaries, unconnected with the Anglo-Normans, expressed similar sentiments. An anonymous Nestorian Christian, observing

45 *The Chronicle of Richard of Devizes of the Time of King Richard the First*, ed. and trans. J.T. Appleby (London, 1963), pp.2, 84.

46 Ralph of Diceto, *Ymagines Historiarum*, in *The Historical Works of Master Ralph of Diceto*, vol.2, ed. W. Stubbs, Rolls Series 68 (London, 1876), pp.80–1.

47 William of Newburgh, *Historia rerum Anglicarum*, in *Chronicles of the Reigns of Stephen, Henry II and Richard I*, vol.1, ed. R. Howlett, Rolls Series 82 (London, 1884), pp.249–75, 284–6, 303–7, 324–30, 346–67, 372–83. William cuts between events in England and France and the course of the crusade. This may, however, be a matter of style, for there is good reason to believe that he obtained information from both Roger of Howden and Philip of Poitiers, Richard's chief clerk on the crusade from the time of the capture of Cyprus in May, 1191. See J. Gillingham, 'Royal Newsletters, Forgeries and English Historians: Some Links between Court and History in the Reign of Richard I', in *La cour Plantagenêt (1154–1204). Actes du Colloque tenu à Thouars du 30 avril au mai 1999*, ed. M. Aurell (Poitiers, 2000), pp.179–85.

48 Examples in *Epistolae Cantuarienses*, in *Chronicles and Memorials of the Reign of Richard I*, vol.2, ed. W. Stubbs, Rolls Series 38 (London, 1865), pp.328–30; Ralph of Diceto, vol.2, pp.88–91. Indeed, Richard's three letters written from the East in 1191 seem to be conscious attempts at 'news management', intended not only to present the king's version of events, but also to influence contemporary English chroniclers, see Gillingham, 'Royal Newsletters', pp.172–3.

49 William of Newburgh, p.355.

events from the region of Mosul about 1192, saw Raymond of Tripoli as a 'second Judas', who had fled from the battle of Hattin, whereas there came to Acre, 'the young lion, the king of England, the shining light. He fought without pause, both day and night.'[50] Neither of the other great kings could provide the raw material for such an epic narrative: Philip II's crusade was recorded by Rigord, a monk of St Denis, but in much less detail and without the verisimilitude which comes from actually being present,[51] while the account of the anonymous cleric who did travel with Frederick Barbarossa's army, could nevertheless only offer the limited perspective of a chronicler whose chief focus had died before he could take any effective action, leaving his army demoralised and diminished.[52]

Ambroise's major historical value therefore is as a narrative of Richard's crusade; the events of the years between 1187 and 1190 are better understood through sources originating in the East, Old French, Latin and, especially Arabic. In the western accounts the eastern Franks are generally members of the supporting cast, their attitudes largely determined by their relationship to the major figures of Richard, Philip and Conrad. However, the death of William of Tyre in 1186 removed the one man capable of real insight into the motivations of the eastern Franks and of explaining the pressures upon them. A younger contemporary of William of Tyre was Ernoul, who wrote an account in Old French of the history of the kingdom of Jerusalem from the capture of the city in 1099 to 1227. Almost nothing is known about him, except that he appears to have been, at some point, a squire of Balian of Ibelin, Lord of Ramla, and to have lived through the dramatic events which preceded the Third Crusade. Although he wrote in prose, his approach can be compared to that of Ambroise in that he often makes his point through anecdote or invented dialogue which, while clearly based upon contemporary events, brings his account close to the borderline between 'history' and 'romance'. However, while Ambroise saw Guy of Lusignan as a man 'who had endured so much suffering and trouble in order to uphold the land of God' (ll.1704–6), Ernoul's perspective was governed by his close connection to the Ibelin family, from whom he must have gathered much of his information. William of Tyre's chronicle was also continued in Old French in a number of different versions which, while quite extensive, nevertheless present considerable difficulties for the historian. The status and value of these continuations remain a matter of controversy, both because of the problem of their relationship to each other and because of the piecemeal nature of narratives added to and modified in later years by anonymous compilers whose own intentions and motives are themselves impossible to discover. These compilers

[50] J. Richard, *L'Esprit de la Croisade* (Paris, 1969), pp.116–19.
[51] Rigord, pp.272–309.
[52] *Historia de expeditione Friderici imperatoris*, in *Quellen zur Geschichte des Kreuzzuges Kaiser Friedrichs I.*, ed. A. Chroust, *MGH SS*, n.s., vol.5 (Berlin, 1928). Events between November, 1190 and 1197 were added to this account by an Austrian cleric, whose name may have been Ansbert.

cut and pasted to suit themselves, leaving a series of narratives now known as *L'Estoire d'Eracles* (after the French translation of the opening words of William of Tyre's chronicle), some of which incorporated material drawn from Ernoul's narrative. Although they were all composed in the East, the extant versions of the Old French continuations are more distant from the Third Crusade than Ambroise, since they all postdate 1204, and, in their present form, some were compiled as late as the 1240s.[53] Nevertheless, they do, ultimately, derive their information from contemporaries who lived there.

This may also be true for three further Latin sources for the period. The anonymous *Libellus de Expugnatione Terrae Sanctae per Saladinum* appears to have been written by an Englishman, possibly with connections in Essex, although it is not clear whether he was a crusader or a settler in the East.[54] It has been pointed out that he shows a reluctance to blame the Temple for any of the disasters,[55] which may suggest membership of the Order. Whatever is the case, he had valuable and detailed information from participants, both in the battle of Hattin (possibly from a member of the entourage of Raymond of Tripoli who escaped with his party) and in the siege of Jerusalem, where he may be describing his own direct experience. He only continues to 1190, but evidently knew of the existence of Ambroise's poem and, seemingly, read the *Itinerarium*, for he concludes that 'if anyone desires to learn more, he should read the book which the lord prior of the Holy Trinity of London translated from the French language into Latin in a style both elegant and truthful'.[56] In addition there are two Latin poems. One, which extends slightly further than the *Libellus* to incorporate the actual fall of Acre in July 1191, is by Aimery, Archbishop of Caesarea between 1180 and 1197, a Florentine who was Patriarch of Jerusalem from 1197 until his death in 1202. He survived the siege of Tyre and was present in the East throughout all the events of these years, the only senior eastern cleric

---

53 For discussion of these problems, see especially P.W. Edbury, 'The Lyon *Eracles* and the Old French Continuations of William of Tyre', in *Montjoie: Studies in Crusade History in Honour of Hans Eberhard Mayer*, ed. B.Z. Kedar, J. Riley-Smith and R. Hiestand (Aldershot, 1997), pp.139–53, and B. Hamilton, *The Leper King and his Heirs: Baldwin IV and the Crusader Kingdom of Jerusalem* (Cambridge, 2000), pp.6–13. Attempts have been made to establish the text closest to Ernoul's original. Ruth Morgan believed that this was the so-called Lyon *Eracles*, *La Continuation de Guillaume de Tyr (1184–1197)*, ed. Morgan; trans. Edbury, *Conquest of Jerusalem*, pp.11–145. Edbury disagrees, arguing that the nearest text is that found in *La Chronique d'Ernoul et de Bernard le Trésorier*, ed. L. de Mas Latrie, Société de l'Histoire de France (Paris, 1871). In addition, Gillingham, 'Roger of Howden', 147, n. 33, believes that Ernoul's contribution only encompasses the years up 1187 and that material after that was put together in the 1220s. If this is true, none of the Old French sources on the Third Crusade itself are as close to the events as Ambroise.

54 *Libellus de Expugnatione Terrae Sanctae per Saladinum*, in *Radulphi de Coggeshall Chronicon Anglicanum*, ed. J. Stevenson, Rolls Series 66 (London, 1875), pp.209–62.

55 See S. Runciman, *A History of the Crusades*, vol.2 (London, 1952), pp.478, 487.

56 *Libellus*, p.257.

to be so.[57] The other is an anonymous, but contemporary account of the siege of Acre.[58]

There are three detailed contemporary narratives of the Third Crusade which provide a Muslim perspective, as well as a selection of important letters written by those involved. Two of the narrators – Imad al-Din, Saladin's secretary and chancellor, and Baha'al-Din Ibn Shaddad, Saladin's Qadi of the army – were at the centre of affairs; the third, the Mesopotamian chronicler, Ibn al-Athir, while making extensive use of these two writers, as well as witnessing some of the events himself, was also able to place the crusade in a wider context of the Muslim world as a whole.[59] A later anthologist, Abu Shama, although writing in the mid-thirteenth century, gathered and reproduced other contemporary documents, including letters written by the Qadi, al-Fadil, a man who had Saladin's confidence (and who recommended Imad al-Din to him), and additional material by Imad al-Din, lost in its original form, but which he edited and abridged. Abu Shama also includes material from a fourth chronicler, Ibn Abi Tayy, whose work is known only through later references such as this.[60] If, as some historians of Islam argue, there are two historiographical traditions for the Muslim history of Syria during this period, then they are represented here by, on the one hand, those close to Saladin – Imad al-Din and Baha'al-Din – and, on the other, by Ibn al-Athir, strongly pro-Zangid in his presentation of events. Indeed, the rifts which were never far from the surface in the Muslim world – as seen by, among others, Turks, Mamluks and Kurds – reappear under the pressures brought about by the invasion of the crusaders. More surprisingly, Ibn Abi Tayy, a Shi'ite from Aleppo, is usually favourable to Saladin.[61]

Like Ambroise and Richard de Templo, Imad al-Din claims to write only about what he has witnessed or obtained from sources whom he trusted. Equally, like them, he was committed to the idea of the holy war, the *jihad*, promoted so effectively by his two chief employers, Nur al-Din and Saladin. Unlike the western chroniclers, however, he had the advantage of the insider, who generally accompanied Saladin on his travels, drafted a great range of different types of documents for him, and acted as confidant and adviser on all kinds of matters. Imbued with the literary culture of what D.S. Richards calls the Islamic secretary class, he writes in an elaborate style characteristic of

---

57 Roger of Howden, *Chronica*, vol.3, pp.cv–cxxxvi (appendix to the preface). For Aimery, see B. Hamilton, *The Latin Church in the Crusader States: The Secular Church* (London, 1980), pp.122, 135, 243.

58 'Ein zeitgenössisches Gedicht auf die Belagerung Accons', ed. H. Prutz, *Forschungen zur deutschen Geschichte* 21 (1881), 449–94.

59 'Imad al-Din al-Isfahani, *Conquête de la Syrie et de la Palestine par Saladin*, trans. H. Massé (Paris, 1972); Baha' al-Din Ibn Shaddad, *The Rare and Excellent History of Saladin*, trans. D.S. Richards, Crusade Texts in Translation 7 (Aldershot, 2001); Ibn al-Athir, *The Chronicle of Ibn al-Athîr for the Crusading Period from al-Kâmil fi'l-ta'rîkh*. Part 2, trans. D.S. Richards. Crusade Texts in Translation 15 (Aldershot, 2007).

60 Abu Shama, *Le Livre des Deux Jardins*, in *RHCr, Historiens Orientaux*, vol.4 (Paris, 1870).

61 See H.A.R. Gibb, 'The Arabic Sources of the Life of Saladin', *Speculum* 25 (1960), 58–72. However, see also the comments of M.C. Lyons and D.E.P. Jackson, *Saladin: The Politics of the Holy War* (Cambridge, 1982), pp.1, 385, on Ibn al-Athir and Imad al-Din.

contemporary conventions in the administrative circles of his time, but this should not obscure for the modern reader his prime importance as a source for the Third Crusade. Imad al-Din came from Isfahan and had gained his early education and training in Baghdad before moving to Syria in 1167; here he worked for Nur al-Din until his death in 1174 and for Saladin from 1175 until his death in 1193. He was therefore an older contemporary of Baha' al-Din, Ibn al-Athir and Ibn Abi Tayy, all of whom made use of his work. Moreover, his admiration for Saladin does not prevent him for seeing the virtues of Nur al-Din.[62] Baha' al-Din, who was born in Mosul, was twenty years younger than Imad al-Din, and did not enter Saladin's service until 1188 but, like Imad al-Din, he too was a genuine insider, present at most of the key moments of the Third Crusade. He is especially valuable for his perception of the vicissitudes of the military engagements, as seen by the Muslim leaders.

The Third Crusade, like the First, attracted massive interest in western Christendom; consequently the actual course of the expedition is well known. Narratives by participants of different kinds, as well as Muslim accounts closely associated with Saladin, can be supplemented by the versions told by western chroniclers who were not there, but who talked to some of those who were, and by compilations drawn from the experiences of some of the eastern Franks involved. Many others wrote letters, ranging from the chaplain of Baldwin of Canterbury on one side to Saladin's Qadi, al-Fadil, on the other; these survive either independently and/or as part of larger narratives and compilations. By any standards Ambroise's poem is a narrative of central importance, both in itself and as a source for others, most importantly, Richard de Templo. Unsurprisingly, Ambroise concentrates upon the deeds of Richard I; indeed, following the death of Frederick Barbarossa and the departure of Philip Augustus, it could hardly be otherwise, even had the author not been born in Normandy. He has, nevertheless, other heroes, such as James of Avesnes and Andrew of Chauvigny and, in that sense, the poem is also a celebration of the values and mores of western European chivalry embodied in those who rallied to the holy war and who died in unprecedented numbers in its cause. At the same time, however, Ambroise did have some feeling for the low-born, for the common people who took the brunt of the famines and of the terrible living conditions, and it is possible that they too could be numbered among the listeners to his poem. It was not a 'people's crusade', but it rested upon a huge popular base, which the leaders could not ignore when taking decisions which affected the whole. Ambroise knew how to tell a story and he was not reluctant to write his own script, but he was too close to events and there were too many surviving participants and their relatives for him to produce a fantasy. Moreover, he was not simply trying to entertain, for he had a serious moral purpose; he starts and ends with the fundamental social point that men are responsible for the consequences of their actions, and that, ultimately, God would ensure that whatever these

---

[62] See D.S. Richards, 'Imad al-Din al-Isfahani: Administrator, Littérateur and Historian', in *Crusaders and Muslims in Twelfth-Century Syria*, ed. M. Shatzmiller (Leiden, 1993), 133–46.

actions were, the end would be just. What happened in 1187 'was through God, who wished to bring to Himself his people whom He had redeemed and who at that time served Him not at all' (ll.32–4).

The Estoire *as Literature*

The *Estoire* has a significant place in the history of Old French literature. Most of Ambroise's predecessors, twelfth-century writers of verse chronicles in French, such as Wace, Gaimar and Benoît de Sainte-Maure, were, to some extent, translators and adaptors of Latin, or in the case of Gaimar, Anglo-Saxon, texts.[63] Moreover, they generally deal with the fairly distant past. One important exception to this generalisation is the *Chronique* of Jordan Fantosme, a contemporary eyewitness account of the events of 1173–4 (the struggles between Henry II and his rebellious sons and the king of Scotland). Fantosme wrote in French verse in a fluent and relatively unadorned style, very different from that of Ambroise.[64] Writing with openly didactic intent about recent events, in French, Ambroise had no vernacular model to follow. If he knew the work of Wace, Benoît and Gaimar he could have used them as models only in a very general way, as inspirations to write vernacular verse chronicle. His style is distinctive.

The *Estoire* is not without literary merit and Ambroise also shows some knowledge of literary texts. There are direct references to the heroes of the *chansons de geste*, the epic of medieval France. Stylistically, formulaic descriptions of splitting an enemy 'to his teeth' or images such as the arrows sticking out like prickles of a hedgehog, are reminiscent of the hyperbolic style of the epic. The form, however, is that of other narrative genres; the text is written in rhyming couplets, not the *laisses*, rhymed or assonanced strophes of variable length, of the *chansons de geste*. He also uses extensive, witty rhetoric; the rhetoric of the *chanson de geste* is of a different, more colloquial kind, although some writers of romances do use the more scholastic type of rhetoric.[65] Ambroise uses a number of devices extensively and effectively. Accumulatio, the listing of verbs, nouns or adjectives, is generally used for emphasis and binary structures and binomials (the use of two terms, strictly speaking nouns, of similar meaning) are used in a similar way. Annominatio, a punning device

63 Benoît de Sainte-Maure, *Chronique des ducs de Normandie*, ed. C. Fahlin, Bibliotheca Ekmaniania 56 and 60 (Uppsala, 1951–4); Geffrai Gaimar, *Estoire de Engleis*, ed. A. Bell, Anglo-Norman Text Society 14–16 (Oxford, 1960); Wace, *Roman de Brut*, ed. I. Arnold, 2 vols, Société d'anciens textes français (Paris, 1938–40); Wace, *Roman de Rou*, ed. A.J. Holden, 3 vols, Société d'anciens textes français (Paris 1970–3). See Damian-Grint, p.49.

64 *Jordan Fantosme's Chronicle*, ed. R.C. Johnston (Oxford, 1987).

65 S. Kay, 'The Nature of Rhetoric in the Chansons de Geste', *Zeitschrift für romanische Philologie* 94 (1978), 304–20, examines the link between genre and rhetoric and distinguishes between the rhetoric of the schools and 'rhetoric as a feature of literary texts' (p.305); on the links between chronicles and other narrative genres see J. Beer, *Villehardouin, Epic Historian* (Geneva, 1968).

which can involve using two words from the same root, or two words which sound the same but have different meanings, can provide humour as well as ornamentation. For example, at one point Ambroise creates a word to form a punning link between emperor, *empereor*, and the verb to make worse, *empirer*, to both comic and didactic effect (ll.1392–3). His enjoyment of language is seen in the wit with which he uses this device, often drawing attention to it by using it as a rhyme. Stone, an earlier translator of the text, refers to this as 'the poet's weakness for "homonymous rhymes" '.[66] Other devices affect the rhythm of the text, with many forms of parallels. The use of the proverb, *sententia*, is part of Ambroise's expression of his didactic intentions.

While chronicles, unlike epics or romances, were probably not intended for extensive public reading or recitation, they retain many of the stylistic devices of this oral delivery.[67] Most obvious of these is the use of the apostrophe, addressing the reader, drawing him (or, today, her) into an involvement with the text. This is a feature common to the vernacular chronicles.

Another dramatic feature the chronicle shares with other narrative genres is extensive use of direct speech,[68] although Ambroise uses less than many texts, with only about 5% of the text in this form. In eyewitness chronicles, such as that of Ambroise or, for example, Villehardouin's *Conquête de Constantinople*, the direct speech may seem to carry some authority. However, one need only look at the priest's address to Richard (ll.9562–655) to realise that these speeches are a literary construct, a dramatisation of the reality. Richard was agonising between returning to deal with his errant brother and staying to finish the job in the Holy Land; his dilemma would not have been articulated in highly rhetorical rhyming couplets. Not only does this dramatise the text but in this particular case it also presents a touchingly human side to a man otherwise presented as a hero. Ambroise is partial in his depictions of character, but draws his characters effectively, using the dramatic epic devices of showing his deeds of prowess and the reaction of others to him, but also using the monologue, the internal debating, more common in the romance. This dramatisation may offer difficulties of interpretation. Saladin's address to his emirs (ll.6766–89) may have some truth in it or may be pure fabrication, but whatever an enraged Saladin may have said to his defeated men it would not have been in the carefully constructed rhetorical speech reported by Ambroise, making sarcastic use of the well-worn *ubi sunt* theme. The purpose of his monologue is to dramatise and entertain, while reconstructing the sort of thing he may have said.

---

66 Stone, note to ll.4755–6.

67 Paris, p.x, considered that the poem was intended for public recitation, citing the numerous appeals to the audience and the mixture of use of the first and third person and references to 'what the book says'. These do appear to be mere conventions of the genre and cannot be considered evidence of oral delivery.

68 S. Marnette, 'Narrateur et point de vue dans les chroniques médiévales: une approche linguistique', in *The Medieval Chronicle: Proceedings of the First International Conference on the Medieval Chronicle, Utrecht, 13–16 July 1996*, ed. E. Kooper (Amsterdam, 1999), pp.176–90. Marnette uses only prose chronicles here. Her work on direct and indirect discourse on chronicle is part of a larger study on genre and discourse. See *Narrateur et points de vue dans la littérature française médiévale: une approche linguistique* (Berne, 1998).

Brevity may not be considered one of Ambroise's literary virtues. However, he can use economy of style. Thus, when relating a number of incidents during the siege of Acre he gives only a few dozen lines to each incident, beginning and ending each with the same formula. Ambroise makes his intentions clear. He is writing to show the consequences of folly and sin (ll.10–19), but also to justify the crusade (ll.12188–220) and to depict the sufferings of the crusaders. He illustrates the virtues of the crusaders, while not hesitating to condemn their sloth or sin, and he extols Richard's qualities, while showing him to be caught in a very human dilemma: to stay or not to stay.[69] That he also sets out to entertain is seen in his choice of anecdote: the dedication of the dying woman who wishes her body to be used to help fill the trench (ll.3620–55), the tale of the crusader caught 'with his trousers down' (ll.3578–619), or the Saracen emir killed by the spilling of Greek fire on the more tender parts of his anatomy (ll.3656–94). All such incidents are clearly included for purposes other than edification.

Ambroise's merits are not easily discernible in a translation as they generally concern his use of language. There he stands at least on an equal level with the other few examples extant of early vernacular chronicle. If he does not tell his narrative with the economy of Villehardouin, he is more witty. If he has not Robert of Clari's eye for visual detail, he shows more interest in the main characters. If his 'hero', Richard, is not given the expansive treatment accorded to William Marshal in the *Histoire de Guillaume le Maréchal*, then that may be because the *Estoire* is after all the story of the war, not just the account of one man.[70]

Ambroise also shows considerable technical skill. His rhymes are nearly always accurate, with only very few inadequate rhymes (e.g. ll.6593–4, *gaire* rhymes with *Angletere*; ll.6992–3, *Haste* rhymes with *chase*; ll.8976–7, *toli* rhymes with *lui*) in over 12,000 lines of poetry. He is not averse to the use of homophones at the rhyme; indeed rhyme-words that are identical in sound but different in meaning are part of his rhetorical style (e.g. ll.2147–50, *ataindre/ateindre, atainte/ateinte*; ll.5710–11, *a traire/atraire*). His ability to scan is less clear, given the corrupt nature of the only manuscript of the text. With only the minor correction made in our edition the text has still a very high proportion of octosyllabic lines (96.5%) which suggests that the original was accurate. The use of 'continental' scansion, regular syllable count, rather than the less clear-cut scansion of Anglo-Norman, which seems to be dependent on syllabic stress, reinforces the linguistic evidence that this is a Norman, not Anglo-Norman, text.[71]

---

69 Levy, pp.143–55; Ailes, 'Heroes of War'.
70 Villehardouin, *La Conquête de Constantinople*, ed. J. Dufournet (Paris, 1969); Robert de Clari, *La Conquête de Constantinople*, ed. P. Lauer (Paris, 1924); *History of William Marshal*, ed. A.J. Holden, with English translation by S. Gregory and historical notes by D. Crouch, Anglo-Norman Text Society, 3 vols (2002–6).
71 There has been considerable discussion about the nature of Anglo-Norman scansion for a number of years. J. Vising, *Anglo-Norman Language and Literature* (London 1925), pp.79–88. Vising writes of the 'decline of versification' (p.79). Compare R.C. Johnston, 'Jordan Fantosme's Experiments in Prosody and Design', in *Mélanges offerts à P. Jonin* (Aix-en-Provence, 1971), pp.355–67, and P.E. Bennett, 'La Chanson de Guillaume, poème

Ambroise's *Estoire de la Guerre Sainte* deserves an important place in the emerging lists of vernacular chronicle texts of the twelfth century. It is clearly a well crafted, sometimes witty, example of the emerging genre. It is entertaining and yet at the same time didactic. Above all it informs the reader that here are events recounted by someone who was actually present, events of great magnitude and deeds of arms by men such as Richard whom future generations could emulate.

The Translation

Previous translations
There have been three previous translations of the *Estoire*:

Paris's edition is followed by a translation into French (Ambroise, *L'Estoire de la Guerre Sainte: histoire en vers de la troisième croisade (1190–92)*, ed. and trans. into modern French by Gaston Paris (Paris, 1897)). This is generally accurate, although with some simplification of Ambroise's rhetorical style.

The History of the Holy War, trans. E.N. Stone, in *Three Old French Chronicles of the Crusades*, University of Washington Publications in the Social Sciences (Seattle, 1939), pp.1–160. This was written in what was, even at the time of writing, a difficult and old-fashioned style, the normal register for translations of medieval texts at that period. Some sentences would be nearly incomprehensible to today's undergraduates. Though generally quite accurate some lines are omitted in the translation. Stone's practice of translating silently where Gaston Paris has filled lacunae either from the context or from the *Itinerarium* is also not satisfactory for the modern scholar. It is, moreover, no longer very accessible.

Ambroise, *The Crusade of Richard the Lion-Heart*, trans. M.J. Hubert, with notes by J.L. La Monte (New York, 1941, reprinted 1976). This verse translation is the most widely used translation of the text. The translator claims that 'our purpose throughout has been to render as faithfully as possible the words, rhymes and meanings of the author'.[72] This is probably an impossible task and the exigencies of the verse greatly reduce the accuracy of the translation; what is gained in charm is lost in accuracy. The use of verse does, however, remind the reader of the literary nature of the text. Hubert and La Monte indicate where

---

anglo-normand?' in *Au carrefour des routes d'Europe: la chanson de geste. Xe congrès international de la Société Rencesvals pour l'étude des épopées romanes, Strasbourg, 1985*, Senefiance 21 (Aix-en-Provence, 1986), pp.259–81. M.L. Colker, 'A Newly-Discovered Manuscript Leaf of Ambroise's *L'Estoire de la Guerre Sainte*', *Revue d'Histoire des Textes* 22 (1992), 159–67, declines to correct the fragment on the basis that 'in Anglo-Norman efforts at octosyllabic versification, the poet himself, rather than the scribe, was frequently responsible for deviation from eight-syllable lines' (p.166), ignoring the evidence that the poet was Norman rather than Anglo-Norman.

[72] HL, p.ix.

they have translated Paris's reconstructions of lacunae by using the conventional square brackets.

The present translation

The translator always faces an impossible task. The desire to be faithful to the text pulls against the desire to render it into good English. The primary purpose of this translation is to provide an accessible and accurate translation to benefit historians and undergraduate students of history as much as those interested in French literature. Accuracy has therefore been our primary aim. It is impossible, particularly within the constraint of accuracy, to reproduce all the forms of rhetoric used by Ambroise. We have, however, endeavoured to keep all cases of accumulatio (listing) and binomials. The more interesting forms of rhetoric, his punning and word-play, including the coining of words not attested elsewhere, cannot always be translated into English. It is clear that in some instances terms are used for their word-play potential rather than their meaning. While we have given the meaning in the translation the importance of the word form itself is indicated in a note. The effect of keeping even some of the rhetorical devices in English is rather heavy and laboured, but this does show the contrived nature of the text. This is a style which is not natural in modern English, indeed not even part of our recent literary tradition. The use of repetitions and accumulations often results in rather unnatural use of English. Ambroise's fondness for using different parts of the same verb or different words with a close etymological link can sometimes be reflected in English; although the effect may be stilted this does reflect the contrived nature of Ambroise's language while, of course, not being able to do justice to Ambroise's French. The dramatic effect created by the expression 'Eth vos', the Old French equivalent of modern French 'Voici' and 'Voilà', English 'Behold', has been expressed by the use of structures involving inversion. Addresses to the reader, a technique common in early chronicle, are kept. Names are translated to the normal English form. In Old French verb tense can shift between the past and the present, although this is a less common practice in chronicle than in fictional genres; tense usage has been standardised, using the past for the narrative tense and with the present being kept only when it refers to the present or where a statement has a more universal reference.

Some terms pose particular challenges to the translator: grifon was an insulting term to designate the Greeks; words such as preux, translated as 'valiant' or 'noble' depending on the context, refer to qualities important in a militaristic, feudal society, but have no direct translation in modern English; the general term gens may be translated as 'men' or 'people' depending on the context. Conjunctions such as et are frequently used to create anaphora (succeeding lines beginning with the same word) and do not always need to be translated.

Old French assumes that the reader will work within the context of the text. The use of pronouns, which can be omitted in Old French, can be confusing. The referent is not always clear. In the translation this is sometimes clarified by the use of nouns.

Line-filling interpolations protesting the veracity of the account sound rather clumsy in English, and in the French their main purpose is often clearly to provide syllables or a rhyme, but they are retained as they also serve as a constant reminder of the presence of the author in his text and are, moreover, characteristic of early chronicle discourse.[73]

The present translation is based on our own edition. We had available not only the work of our predecessors, but also major reference works not available to them, the *Tobler-Lommatzsch* dictionary (*T-L*) and the *Anglo-Norman Dictionary* (*A-ND*). These, along with Godefroy's dictionary (Godefroy), the less comprehensive Larousse, *Dictionnaire de l'ancien français*, and new *Old French–English Dictionary*, were our essential tools. While we have not consciously copied the work of our predecessors we may have inadvertently echoed them and in places we have coincidentally chosen similar formulations. Major differences of interpretation are indicated in the notes. We acknowledge our debt to their work.

---

[73] Damian-Grint, pp.143–71.

TRANSLATION

The Crusade Begins

[1–34]   He who would deal with a long story must take great care that he does not burden himself by beginning a work he cannot finish. Rather, if he undertakes such a task, he should do it in such a way that he is able to complete what he has undertaken. For this reason I have begun briefly, so that the subject will not be too burdensome. I want to get right to my subject for it is a story that should be told, a story which tells of the misadventure that happened to us, and justly so, a few years ago in the land of Syria, because of our excessive folly.[1] For God did not wish us to continue without feeling the consequences. And He certainly did cause us to feel them, in Normandy and in France, and throughout Christendom. Whether the folly was great or whether it was little, the consequences were felt directly; all this because of the Cross which the world worships and which at that time was taken away and moved by the pagans from the land where it was to be found, the land where God deigned to be born and to die [. . .][2] [the land] of the Hospital and of the Holy Temple,[3] causing much pulling of the temple,[4] [the land] of the Sepulchre, where God was placed, lost to us through sin. This is not how it should be said – it was through God, who wished to bring to Himself his people whom He had redeemed and who at that time served Him not at all.

[35–86]   Through this great disaster all people, throughout the world, of high or low estate, were afflicted and could scarcely be comforted. The dances, the sounds, the songs, the words and all earthly joys of Christian people were abandoned, until the pope in Rome, Gregory the Eighth,[5] as is written in the accounts, through whom God saved many men, issued a pardon that brought relief; for God's sake and in contempt of the devil he declared that any man who went against the infidels who had disinherited the worthy King of Truth, will be

---

1   On 4 July 1187, at the battle of Hattin in Galilee, Saladin, ruler of Egypt, Damascus, and Aleppo, inflicted a crushing defeat upon the Latin forces of the Kingdom of Jerusalem. Most of the Christians were killed or captured, leaving the crusader states virtually defenceless, and the True Cross, carried in the army, was lost. Saladin followed up this victory by capturing most of the important cities, towns and castles, most importantly taking Jerusalem on 2 October. The assembly of armies known as the Third Crusade was a direct response to this crisis.

2   It is difficult to account for the disjointed syntax here other than by positing a lacuna of two lines after l.26.

3   The two military orders of the Hospital and the Temple. The Hospitallers had developed from the hospices attached to the Benedictine monastery of St Mary of the Latins established in Jerusalem before 1071. The Templars were founded in c.1119 to defend pilgrims travelling to the Holy Sepulchre. The orders received papal recognition in 1113 and 1129 respectively. During the 1130s the Hospitallers added military functions to their medical and charitable roles. By the time of the Third Crusade, the two orders formed the backbone of the permanent military forces in the East. See J. Riley-Smith, *The Knights of St. John in Jerusalem and Cyprus c.1050–1310* (London, 1967) and M. Barber, *The New Knighthood: A History of the Order of the Temple* (Cambridge, 1994).

4   ll.27–8. This kind of punning rhetorical device, annominatio, is used frequently by Ambroise, but cannot always be reproduced in translation.

5   Elected 21 October 1187, consecrated 25 October, died on 17 December.

acquitted of all his sins.[6] Because of this many kings and counts and other men beyond number took the Cross to seek God in the distant land of Syria. All the most esteemed men took the Cross together.

Richard, the valiant count of Poitiers,[7] did not wish to fail God at the time of His need and His call. So he took the Cross for love of Him. He was the first of the great men of the lands from which we came [to do so]. Then the king entered His service, expending great effort and expense.[8] No-one put off the taking up of the Cross, even if it meant selling his inheritance.[9] No knight, whether old or young, sought to hide what was in his heart; all wanted to show how heavy upon them was the need to take vengeance for the shame committed against God, who had not deserved it, because of His land that had been devastated, where His people were so pressed that they did not know what to do. But no-one should be surprised that they were then defeated. They were a good people, a chosen race, but it was the will of God that they should die and that others should come to their aid. They died in body but live on in heaven. This is what happens to those who die there but who abide in the service of God.[10]

[87–154]   There was a long-standing war between France and Normandy,[11] a war at once cruel, terrible and mighty, full of wickedness and danger. The war was between King Philip[12] and King Henry of England, Henry, head of a fine

---

6   Gregory VIII issued a plenary indulgence in the encyclical *Audita tremendi* (29 October 1187), *Historia de expeditione Friderici imperatoris*, in *Quellen zur Geschichte des Kreuzzuges Kaiser Friedrichs I.*, ed. A. Chroust, *MGH SS*, n.s., vol.5 (Berlin, 1928), pp.6–10. To this pope and his predecessor, Urban III, this meant a full remission of the penance imposed by the Church, as had been offered at the Council of Clermont in November 1095. However, since the beginning of the crusading movement, most participants had interpreted this to mean that death on crusade would make them holy martyrs, received in Heaven. For discussion of the indulgence, see H.E. Mayer, *The Crusades*, 2nd ed. (Oxford, 1988), pp.23–36. For *Audita tremendi*, see J. Riley-Smith, *The Crusades. A History*, 2nd ed. (London 2005), pp. 134, 137.

7   Richard was the third son of Henry II and Eleanor of Aquitaine, born on 8 September 1157. When, on 6 January 1169, Henry II divided his continental lands among his sons, Richard received Aquitaine. He was enthroned as Count of Poitou on 10 June 1172. He took the Cross at Tours in November 1187. The most recent biographies of Richard are J. Gillingham, *Richard I*, 2nd ed. (New Haven and London, 1999) and J. Flori, *Richard the Lionheart. King and Knight*, trans J. Birrell (Edinburgh, 2006). K. Norgate, *Richard the Lion Heart* (London, 1924) remains valuable, see pp.91–263 for the crusade.

8   Henry II, King of England, 1154–89. Henry took the Cross on 21 January, 1188.

9   Reminiscent of Matthew 8, Luke 9 and Luke 14, which tell of those who thought up excuses to put off following Christ. 'No man, having put his hand to the plough, and looking back, is fit for the kingdom of God' (Luke 9:62).

10   This echoes the feelings expressed by Paul in Philippians 1:21, 'For to me to live is Christ, and to die is gain.'

11   The origins of the war can be found in the conquest of England by William, Duke of Normandy, in 1066, an achievement which made William more powerful than his ostensible overlord for the duchy, the Capetian king, Philip I. In 1154, William's great-grandson, Henry, Count of Anjou, became King of England, continuing the long-standing rivalry with the French kings, represented by Louis VII (1137–80). See W.L. Warren, *Henry II* (London, 1973), pp.51–3.

12   Philip II, King of France, 1180–1223. The most detailed study of his reign is A. Cartellieri, *Philipp II. August, König von Frankreich*, 4 vols (Leipzig, 1899–1922; reprint 1969). Vol.2 describes his role in the crusade. See also J. Bradbury, *Philip Augustus: King of France*

family, noble, wise and prudent, the good father of the Young King,[13] who jousted with such vigour, the father of Richard [who is] shrewd, wise and full of talent, the father of Geoffrey of Brittany,[14] who also did great deeds, and the father of John Lackland[15] because of whom he suffered such trouble and war.

The king who had such a family and who knew himself to be rich could easily sustain a war if anyone wished to wage war on him and had he done what they wanted, to people such as they were.[16] The two kings were in disagreement, so that no-one could make them agree until God brought them together, at a meeting that was of such great importance; it was held between Gisors and Trie[17] in the great and lovely meadow. Much was said there, words of wisdom and of foolishness. One was concerned for peace; the other had no such concern. There were many people there, of all sorts, who could not see how peace was to be sought, but, it seems to me, God willed that they should take the Cross together. At that meeting many quarrels were raised, old and new, many quarrels which were troublesome, arousing pride and haughtiness; these were followed up without rest. That was on a very fine day.

There was there an archbishop, come from Tyre as a messenger,[18] a wise man and a noble one, sent by the Syrians on account of his good sense, which they knew and had seen. We saw him go to great trouble to put the kings on the right way. God took such pains over this, as did the wise men and the noble, that both kings took the Cross and there they kissed one another. They kissed with tears and praised God, worshipping Him because of their great joy and because they knew of God's great need of their help. There you might have seen knights running up eagerly to take the Cross. They did not seem a downhearted people. I saw there such a large press around the bishops, the archbishops and the abbots (may God help me and protect me) and so many people rushing forward that,

1180–1223 (London, 1998), pp.72–105, and Richard, 'Philippe Auguste, la croisade et le royaume', pp.411–24.

13 Henry, Henry II's second son, born 28 February 1155. He became heir to the throne with the death of his brother, William, in 1156, but predeceased his father, dying on 11 June 1183.

14 Henry II's fourth son, born 23 September 1158. He became Duke of Brittany in 1171, having been betrothed to Constance, the heiress, two years before. He died on 19 August 1186.

15 Henry II's fifth son, born (probably) on 24 December 1167. He was crowned King of England on 27 May 1199, following the death of Richard on 6 April.

16 Paris assumes a lacuna of at least two lines, but the syntax is not interrupted. Nevertheless, it is difficult to make sense of the text as it stands.

17 This seems to have been the traditional meeting-place, on the borders between Normandy and France. This conference was held on 21 January 1188. Roger of Howden, *Gesta*, vol.2, pp.29–30; William of Newburgh, p.272; Ralph of Diceto, p.51. The *Itinerarium*, 1.17, pp.33–4, describes the meeting at Gisors, and returns to the subject in 2.3, pp.140–1, where the details correspond more closely to those given by Ambroise.

18 Joscius, Archbishop of Tyre, 1186–c.1201, and Chancellor of Jerusalem, 1192–c.1201, had come to the West in order to reinforce the appeals for help which had been sent by Conrad, Marquis of Montferrat (who was holding Tyre against Saladin), the leaders of the military orders, and the prelates of the Church. He had first visited William II, King of Sicily, who sent immediate help in the form of a fleet in the spring and summer of 1188. For the archbishop's career, see Hamilton, *The Latin Church in the Crusader States*, pp.81, 120–1, 243–5, 248.

with the great heat (may no-one ever demand a greater) they were nearly suffocated.

[155–204]   Because of the joy that resulted from this meeting, the peace and the taking up of the Cross, all men were coming to take up the Cross, for no-one could prevent himself, nor could any man refuse the great pardon. However, the delay to the expedition is much to be regretted, for the devil made great efforts to restore the discord between the two kings, for the accord could not be established before one of them died and death overcame him. This was the old king of England, Henry, who wished to search out the Holy Sepulchre and follow God, but death was able to overtake him.[19] Ambroise, the writer of this book, says that he is wise who at once fulfils the vow that he has vowed to God, his avowed Lord.[20]

After the death of the king, their father, there remained only the two brothers: the elder was called Richard, the renowned count of Poitiers; John Lackland was the name of the younger, a young man, as yet unformed. Richard, the elder, had the crown given to him by right, and the treasure and riches and the land, and to him was homage given. Because he was the first of all to take the Cross, as we related to you, he was willing to suffer hardship for God. Therefore he prepared his journey and travelled to England. Little time passed before he had himself crowned in London.[21] There I saw great gifts given and I saw such gifts of food that no-one could tell how much nor keep account of it. Never in all my life did I see a court served in more courtly a manner; I saw such rich vessels in that most lovely hall. I saw the tables so laden that they could not be counted. But why should I give you long account of this? Each of you knows what it means, what a great court can be held by him who holds England.

[205–76]   The feast was great, rich and stately. It lasted three full days. The king gave great gifts and gave to his barons their fiefs and their inheritances and invested them in their lordships. When the members of the court had departed, each one went to his own place. Everyone took himself off to his own dwelling place, but they could not long remain there, for the king had sent for each by name and commanded that they make ready for their journey by borrowing or acquiring [what was needed]. For he wanted to get his ships and his equipment on the move so that he could in good time make the crossing to go on his pilgrimage. Night and day his heart yearned for his noble men who awaited him in Normandy and Anjou, Gascony and Poitou, Berry and Burgundy,[22] for there were many of them in this undertaking. Before his departure, he placed in his churches in England and throughout his lands, bishops and archbishops where

---

19   Henry II died at Chinon on 6 July 1189, Landon, p.1.
20   The reference to the author in the third person is the normal convention. The *Itinerarium*, 2.4, p.141 (Nicholson, p.144) gives the sententia in a more impersonal way: 'A person who is bound by a voluntary vow should be absolutely condemned if it remains unfulfilled through negligence, because there was no obligation to vow.'
21   Richard was crowned in Westminster on 3 September, Landon, p.3.
22   1.227. HL, p.39, n.39, assume that this is a mistake for Brittany, since all the other regions were part of Richard's lands. However, Ambroise does make a deliberate rhyme with *besoigne*.

there were none. He did not wish to wait for winter. He busied himself preparing for his voyage and loaded on board his rich treasure, a task he could well accomplish. He spent little time by the sea for God prepared the weather conditions and sent a good wind that took him over to Normandy.

As soon as he was seen there he was received with much joy, as you may very well believe;[23] at once he hurried on his way and sent men forward straight to Lions to celebrate [the Nativity].[24] The king held his feast at Lions for the celebration of the Nativity, when God willingly took human form. But there was little singing of epic songs, rather he quickly had a letter written and sent for a swift messenger; the letter was sent to the king of France and Richard commanded the messenger that as well as the letter he should say at once that he was completely ready to go. From this a meeting was arranged between them,[25] if I am not mistaken, and they met before Dreux, seven leagues from Evreux.[26]

While the kings were speaking, planning the journey, there came a messenger, in great haste. With his head bowed he came before the king of France and said that the Queen had died.[27] On account of this sorrow, and another which was both strong and heartfelt, the death of the king of Apulia,[28] there was, and still is, much mourning. The people were very distressed and the journey to Syria was nearly put off, but thanks to God this was not so; it was only postponed until the Feast of St John, which is celebrated by all.[29]

[277–346]   When the rose was sweet of scent the time came when God willed that the pilgrims should set out and that others should choose [to join them] and that all should be ready with that which God had given them, ready to endure suffering for God, to move on the Feast of St John, so that on the eighth day, without delay, the army assembled at Vézelay.[30] The king [of France] left Paris and took his leave at St Denis.[31] There were there many chosen knights who had not yet set out, while most of the noble French men had already gone. The duke

---

[23] Cf. *Itinerarium*, 2.6.

[24] Richard sailed from Dover to Calais on 12 December, and from there he travelled to Normandy. He spent Christmas at Lion-la-Forêt (Eure), Landon, p.23.

[25] Richard and Philip met first at Nonancourt on 30 December, where they laid down regulations for the crusade. A further meeting at Dreux on 16 March confirmed this agreement, although they were obliged to postpone their departure, originally set for 1 April, until 1 July, Landon, pp.24, 27.

[26] A league varied from 2.4 to 4.6 miles, although an English unit was usually approximately 3 miles.

[27] Isabelle of Vermandois or Hainaut died in childbirth on 15 March 1190. Rigord, pp.272–3.

[28] William II died on 17 November 1189, leaving no direct heirs. He was married to Joanna, Richard's sister, 1165–99.

[29] Feast of St John the Baptist, 24 June.

[30] The octave of the Feast of St John, 2 July 1190, Landon, p.36.

[31] At the abbey of St Denis on 24 June, Philip II received the staff and scrip of the pilgrim, together with the *oriflamme*, the banner of the abbey, from William, Archbishop of Reims, before setting out to meet Richard at Vézelay. Rigord, pp.272–5. See Cartellieri, vol.2, pp.106–7.

of Burgundy[32] then moved with the king in his task. The count of Flanders[33] immediately set out; he did not delay long. There you could see so great a movement of people, so many people pouring in from all parts, such a company to send them off and such sadness at their departure that those who were accompanying them nearly broke their hearts with sorrow.

King Richard was at Tours, with all his armour and all the accoutrements of war.[34] The city was so full of people that they could scarcely all be accommodated. He sent straightaway to the sea, to summon at once his fleet. He had his fleet put out to sea and entreated that they should go without delay.[35] One hundred and seven ships were counted when they were out at sea, not counting those that followed, all of which followed closely after. They all passed the straits and the narrows, the dangerous waters, the perilous straits of Africa, where the waves beat and storm all day, but not a single boat was lost, nor battered or broken. It is thanks to God that they sailed until they arrived at Messina.

King Richard and his nobles left Tours in high spirits. There were there many good knights and renowned crossbowmen. You should have seen the army as it set out. The whole land trembled. All the people knew sadness over their valiant lord. The ladies and girls, young and old, beautiful and ugly, were all in tears.

---

[32] Hugh III, Duke of Burgundy, 1162–92. He died in July 1192, probably at Acre. Richard of Devizes, pp.79–80; Roger of Howden, *Chronica*, vol.3, p.184. In 1178, he had been offered marriage to Sibylla, heiress to the Kingdom of Jerusalem, but negotiations had broken down and he did not appear in the East in 1180, WT, 21.25(26), pp.996–7. For the background to this, see Hamilton, *Leper King*, pp.139–41, 144–5, 150–4. The reason for his reluctance to leave Burgundy appears to have been the critical political situation following the accession of Philip II in September, 1180.

[33] Philip of Alsace, Count of Flanders, 1168–91. He died of disease on 1 June 1191 at the siege of Acre, Roger of Howden, *Chronica*, vol.3, p.111. The counts of Flanders had been involved in the crusades from the outset. Robert II was one of the leaders of the First Crusade, while Thierry, Philip's father, went on four separate expeditions between 1139 and 1164. Philip himself campaigned controversially in the East between August 1177 and Easter 1178, during which time he declined the offer of overall authority in the Kingdom of Jerusalem, J. Phillips, *Defenders of the Holy Land: Relations between the Latin East and the West, 1119–1187* (Oxford, 1996), pp.231–7. For a jaundiced view of his intervention at that time, see WT, 21.13(14)–18(19), pp.979–87, analysed by J. Dunbabin, 'William of Tyre and Philip of Alsace, Count of Flanders', *Mededelingen var de Koninklijke Academie voor Wetenschappen, Letteren en Schone Kunsten van België. Klasse der Letteren* 48 (1986), 110–17. See Hamilton, *Leper King*, pp.119–31, for a full account of the pressures which induced Philip to act as he did.

[34] Cf. *Itinerarium*, 2.7. Richard was at Tours between 24 and 27 June, Landon, p.35.

[35] The main fleet sailed from a number of different ports in England, Normandy, Brittany and Poitou from early April onwards. Some reached Silvia in Portugal, recently reconquered from the Moors, although the larger part assembled in Lisbon. They were able to provide some help against the Moors, but some of them pillaged Lisbon and about 700 men were imprisoned. They finally departed on 26 July and joined the rest of the fleet at the mouth of the River Tagus. It reached Marseilles on 22 August, having failed to meet Richard there as planned, since it was three weeks late. Richard had arrived in Marseilles on 31 July, Roger of Howden, *Gesta*, vol.2, pp.115–23; Roger of Howden, *Chronica*, vol.3, pp.42–51; Landon, pp.33–4. For the routes of the Third Crusade, see *The Atlas of the Crusades*, ed. J. Riley-Smith (London, 1991), pp.62–5.

Pity and sorrow weighed on their hearts for their loved ones who were leaving. You never saw a more pitiful company nor a more sorrowful group of people returning. There many tears were shed and many good vows made. Those accompanying them returned and the pilgrims went on their way. So it was that at the time which the kings had set, neither earlier nor later than they had said, the army gathered at Vézelay, an army stolen by God from the devil. Stolen? No! He took them openly and it is for Him that they have stirred themselves.

[347–64] God lodged his people at Vézelay, in the mountain. In the valley there were many people who had set out for love of God. Many mothers' sons filled the slopes and the vineyards. The day was warm; the night was calm. God had drawn there the finest young men who had ever been gathered together in this world. For God had they left their lands and their households and mortgaged their inheritance, or lost it for the remainder of their days. They had allowed themselves to be dispossessed that they might buy the love of God, for there can be no better bargain than [to gain] the love of the Heavenly King.[36]

[365–412] At Vézelay, where the kings were, they swore an oath to one another that whatever fortune befell [them] they would be sure of each other and whatever they gained together they would share loyally.[37] They also undertook, in their pledge, that whoever came first to Messina, at whatever time and by whatever means, that he would wait for the other. This is how they made their alliance. They left Vézelay.[38] The two kings rode ahead, talking of the expedition. They honoured each other greatly in every place they came to. So the army moved forward in such harmony that you would not hear any disturbance from it. I saw there such acts of courtesy towards these people that should not be passed over in silence. May God help me, as the army went on its way you would have seen young men and women and girls with fine pitchers and jugs, with buckets and bowls, bringing water to the pilgrims. They came straight to the road, to the army, holding their bowls in their hands, and would say: "God, King of Heaven, from where do all these people come? What can this mean? Where were all such young men born? Look at their glowing cheeks! How sad their mothers must be, their families, their sons, their brothers, their friends, all those belonging to them – these men whom we see coming in such numbers." They commended the whole army to God and wept for them when they had passed. They prayed to God for them both tenderly and fervently, that He would lead them in His service and, if it be His will, bring them back again. Then, by the grace of God, who blessed them and will bless them again, they came straight to Lyons on the Rhône, with great joy and happiness, without anger or sadness, without insult or scorn, without mockery.

[413–48] The army stopped at Lyons on the fast-flowing Rhône.[39] The two

---

36 Cf. Luke 12:33–4.
37 This is similar to the sometimes limited oaths taken by companions at arms, see M. Keen, 'Brotherhood in Arms', *History* 47 (1962), 1–17, and for further literary examples, M.J. Ailes, 'The Medieval Male Couple and the Language of Homosociality', in *Masculinity in Medieval Europe*, ed. D.M. Hadley (London, 1999), pp.214–37, 221; cf. *Itinerarium*, 2.9.
38 The kings left Vézelay on 4 July 1190, Landon, p.37.
39 Richard stayed at Lyons between 10 and 13 July. He and Philip then proceeded by different routes to Messina. Richard reached Marseilles on 31 July and remained there until 7 August,

kings waited there for those who were still to come. Such a marvellous sight was never seen, nor was there ever such a great movement of people. They were estimated at a good one hundred thousand, most of whom were billeted in the town. The kings were lodged neither in the town nor among the trees. They had their pavilions erected beyond the Rhône, to await the army – and wait they must – for many men were still coming and they waited there until they saw them arrive and gather together. When they had waited long enough to be certain that they knew for sure and in truth that the whole army had come, they rejoiced in their coming. They struck camp, taking down the tents which were so fine and so costly, from all along the strand, because of the army which came some distance behind. The two kings travelled together as long as their routes were the same; then each one went to his port with great joy and happiness. King Philip of France had already arranged his passage with the Genoese for they are both skilful and wise in such things. Richard, king of England, followed the coast, from region to region straight to Marseilles by [the grace of] God, who guides us in all good things.

[449–80]   When the army knew that the kings were setting out, there were those who got up before daybreak, others who rose as early in the morning as they could because of the Rhône which they had to cross. Those who had got up before dawn had no trouble at all; they crossed the bridge first, with no delay; but those who crossed during the morning and who crowded upon the bridge, they were ill-fated, for one arch of the bridge over the water gave way, for it was excessively high over the water, which was not safe. There were more than a hundred men on that arch, which was made of pinewood; there was too much weight. The arch fell; the men fell; the people shouted and yelled. Each one, not knowing, thought he had lost whatever [companion] he had, son or brother, or anyone else belonging to him. But God then worked so that of all those who fell there, there were only two who perished, as far as can be ascertained, I mean, but no-one could dare make certain of this for the water is so strong and fast-flowing that no creature who falls into it could ever be rescued. If they perished in this world they are [now] before God pure and purified. They were going about His business and He will have mercy on them, as is right.[40]

[481–510]   The arch of the bridge was broken down and the people completely turned from their way: they did not know which way to go, whether upstream or downstream. The bridge could not provide any help, nor was there any workman there. There was on the Rhône neither boat nor barge that was big enough or wide enough to allow them to follow or reach those who had already crossed. When they could find no other solution, they did the best they could. They passed over with great difficulties in very narrow little skiffs in which the people suffered great discomfort. This is how it is for those who suffer for God.

The crossing took three days and there was a great crowding together of people. Then both wise and foolish sought their place of embarkation. A great

when he sailed to Genoa. Philip II had gone directly to Genoa, where he met Richard again on 13 August, Landon, pp.37–9.

40 For different accounts of this episode, see the *Itinerarium*, 2.10, and Roger of Howden, *Gesta*, vol.1, p.112. Nicholson, p.153, n.36, discusses their relative credibility.

multitude to be wondered at went to Marseilles, the nearest port; very noble Christians went to the port of the Venetians; at that time so many went to the Genoese that they could not now be numbered; so many went to Barletta and to Brindisi that they were much talked of; many went to Messina and waited until the two kings arrived.

Messina

[511–34]   Messina is a city about which writers have written much.[41] It is a fine town, well-situated, for it sits at the extreme point of Sicily, above the Pharos across the straits from Reggio, which Agoland took in his expedition.[42] Messina was full of comforts, but we found them an evil people. The king, who was called Tancred,[43] had much pure gold, amassed by his ancestors who had reigned there since the time of Robert Guiscard.[44] There was there a lady of Palermo who had lived there for a long time; she had been queen of their kingdom, the espoused wife of King William, but, and this was a great misfortune, the noble and gifted king died without an heir. The queen was the sister of the king of England who undertook to have her dower restored to her, so that Tancred, who held both the dower and the queen herself, did not dare make any objection.[45]

---

[41] Cf. *Itinerarium*, 2.11.

[42] This is one of several references by Ambroise to characters from the *chansons de geste*. Agoland is a Saracen king who invades Calabria, *Chanson d'Aspremont*, ed. L. Brandin, Les Classiques Français du Moyen Age, 2 vols (Paris, 1923–4, reprint 1970) (trans. M.A. Newth, New York, 1989). The *Itinerarium* has an error, stating that 'it was once conferred on the famous Agoland for his service', *Itinerarium*, 2.11 (Nicholson, p.154). Nicholson, n.40, notes that, 'Gaston Paris believed that the author of the *Itinerarium* had mistranslated Ambroise's French. In Bk. 5, ch. 21, . . . he translated the same incident correctly. Yet it is odd that an educated clerk did not know this story about Charlemagne.' The tale contained in the *Chanson d'Aspremont* seems to have been quite well known in the Middle Ages. HL, p.48, n.31, note that the 'Pharos of Messina derived its name from the famous lighthouse which stood there in antiquity. The name passed from the lighthouse to the strait.' The lighthouse was destroyed in the fourteenth century.

[43] Tancred of Lecce, King of Sicily, 17 November 1189 to 20 February 1194. Tancred was an illegitimate son of William I's elder brother, Roger, Duke of Apulia. When William II died without heirs, he had seized the throne, perhaps contradicting William's grant of the kingdom to his aunt, Constance, wife of the Emperor, Henry VI. For the circumstances, see D.J.A. Matthew, *The Norman Kingdom of Sicily* (Cambridge, 1992), pp.286–91.

[44] Robert Guiscard, ruler of Apulia and Sicily, 1061–85. Guiscard was the leading member of the Hauteville family, the most successful of the Normans who had invaded southern Italy in a piecemeal fashion in the first half of the eleventh century. In 1059 he was granted Apulia and Calabria by Pope Nicholas II, as well as the island of Sicily if he should be able to conquer it. Together with his brother, Roger, he had largely achieved this by 1085. For the context, see Matthew, pp.9–32.

[45] Joanna was the third daughter of Henry II and Eleanor of Aquitaine. She married William II in Palermo in 1177. Tancred had not given Joanna the dower to which she was entitled, a circumstance which led to conflict with Richard. Agreement was reached between the two kings in November 1190. See *DNB*, vol.30, pp.143–4, and below p.45.

[535–58]   You who have mind and memory, you have indeed heard how the
navy and the marvellous fleet of snacks, had passed by Spain.[46] The fleet
arrived at Messina, where it awaited Richard, to whom England belonged.[47]
Never in all my life did I see such a fleet. There were people of all sorts, with
tents and pavilions and banners set up all along the shore, for the city was
forbidden to them. They stayed near the shore until the kings arrived, because
the burgesses, the Grifon rabble of the town and the louts, descendants of
Saracens, insulted our pilgrims, putting their fingers to their eyes and calling us
stinking dogs.[48] Each day they ill-treated us, murdering our pilgrims and
throwing them into the latrines. Their activities were well attested.

[559–80][49]   My lords, it is the custom and tradition that when princes of high
degree, as high as the king of France, who is of such repute throughout the
world, and as high as the king of England, who has such honour throughout the
lands, should enter a city or a town or a land, such as Sicily, then he should come
as a great lord, on account of some people and their talk, for it is a good saying, I
believe, which says, 'As I see you so I regard you.'[50] I say this, for when the
kings came there, there came many people. The king of the French was the first
to arrive at Messina,[51] where many people gathered to see him. But they did not
see his face for he had only one ship and there was such a great press and crowd
of people on the shore that to avoid such a crowd he disembarked at the palace
itself.

[581–604]   When King Richard arrived,[52] then were there just as many on the
shore who sought to see him, both wise men and frivolous, who had never seen

---

46 The kind of ships referred to here are *eneques* or snekkars, which were oared transport ships of
a Scandinavian type, longer and narrower than the bulkier and slower dromonds. See N.A.M.
Rodger, *The Safeguard of the Sea: A Naval History of Great Britain*, vol.1: 660–1649 (London,
1997), pp.46–7; R.H.F. Lindemann, 'The English *Esnecca* in Northern European Sources', *The
Mariner's Mirror* 74 (1988), 75–82, compares the accuracy of terms in Ambroise and in the
Itinerarium, noting that Ambroise is relatively precise. For this reason we have decided to
distinguish in the translation between *dromond* and *snack*, the two main types of transport
ship.

47 Paris translates ll.541–2 as 'où elle attendait le roi Richard d'Angleterre', that is 'where it [the
fleet] awaited Richard'. Paris makes this correction partly on the basis of the *Itinerarium*, which
refers to the fleet 'waiting at Messina for the king to arrive' (Nicholson, p.155). In French *li reis
Richarz* is definitely in the subject case, and the preceding *que*, referring to the fleet, is the
object form, but what follows suggests that it is the boats that wait for the king. According to
Roger of Howden, *Gesta*, vol.2, p.124, the fleet left Marseilles on 30 August, arriving in
Messina on 14 September. Richard arrived on 23 September, Landon, pp.40–1. It seems that,
here, the grammar contradicts both the actual chronology of events and the sense of the passage.

48 The 'Grifon rabble' translates *grifonaille*. Ambroise generally uses the mocking term *grifon*,
here adding a deprecating suffix for good measure.

49 Cf. *Itinerarium*, 2.13.

50 1.570. The quoting of this Old French proverb in the *Itinerarium*, 2.13, could suggest that
Ambroise is indeed the original. See J. Morawski, *Proverbes français antérieurs au XVe siècle*
(Paris, 1925), no. 2324. The form *tel le veez, tel le prenez* is also included in E. Schulze-
Busaker, *Proverbes et expressions proverbiales dans la littérature narrative du moyen âge
français* (Geneva, 1985), p.310.

51 Philip II arrived at Messina on 16 September 1190, Landon, p.40.

52 Richard arrived on 23 September 1190, Landon, p.41.

him and who wished to see him on account of his valour. He came with such pomp that the whole sea was covered by galleys full of competent people, fighters, bold of countenance, with little pennoncels and with banners.[53] Thus came the king to the shore, and his barons came to meet him. They brought to him his fine war-horses, which had already arrived on the dromonds.[54] He and all his people mounted. Those who saw the procession said that this was how a king should enter, a king to hold his land well. But the Grifons were angry and the Lombards grumbled because he came into their city with such a fleet and such pomp and circumstance.[55]

[605–14][56] When the two kings had arrived the Grifons then kept the peace, but the Lombards would quarrel and threaten our pilgrims with the destruction of their tents and the taking of their goods, for they feared for their wives, to whom the pilgrims spoke, but they did this to annoy those who would not have thought of doing anything.

[615–86] The Lombards and the townsfolk always had bitterness against us, for their fathers said to them that our ancestors conquered them.[57] So they could not love us but rather they tried to starve us.[58] They did not do this to build us up, for they built up their towers and deepened their ditches. All this made the matter much worse, with the disputes and threats that rose all around.

So it happened one day that a woman who was called, it is said, Ame, brought her bread for sale among the army.[59] A pilgrim saw the bread, that it was soft

---

53 *A New Dictionary of Heraldry*, ed. S. Friar (London, 1987), p.267, defines a pennoncel as 'a small pennon, usually no more than 18 inches (45cm) in length, triangular or swallow-tailed and carried at the head of a lance'. See also R. Gayre, *Heraldic Standards and Ensigns* (Edinburgh and London, 1959), pp.1–11.

54 Dromonds were galleys with either a single or double bank of oars, and one or more masts with lateen (triangular) sails. They are first mentioned in Byzantium in the sixth century. From the tenth century they had a beak, intended to facilitate the boarding of an enemy vessel and to cause sufficient damage to immobilise it. See J.H. Pryor, *Geography, Technology and War: Studies in the Maritime History of the Mediterranean, 649–1571* (Cambridge, 1988), especially pp.57–60. According to WT, 20.13, p.927, the Byzantine fleet sent to help the Latins attack Damietta in 1169 included ten or twelve *dromones*, carrying food, arms, and siege machines. See J.H. Pryor, 'Transportation of Horses by Sea during the Era of the Crusades: Eighth Century to 1285 A.D., Part I: To c.1225', *The Mariner's Mirror* 68 (1982), 17–18. Evidently they could be used both as warships and as transports.

55 The Norman penetration of southern Italy in the first half of the eleventh century had been greatly facilitated by the political disunity of the region, in particular the continuing divisions between the Lombards, whose ancestors had been established there since the late sixth century, and the Greeks, who considered Italy to be an integral part of the Byzantine empire. To an outsider like Ambroise, Grifons and Lombards remained quite distinct. For the situation during the period of the Normans' arrival, see Matthew, pp.11–19.

56 Cf. *Itinerarium*, 2.14.

57 See above, note 43.

58 Paris, followed by Stone, assumes a lacuna here, but it is not clear why.

59 1.628, Ame is translated by Paris as Emme and by Stone as Emma. Ambroise is using the established technique of enhancing his authority by apparently candidly admitting when he knows something only by hearsay. See Damian-Grint, pp.166–8. Cf. *Itinerarium*, 2.15, p.158 (Nicholson, p.159), where the woman is depicted more negatively: 'Then the woman suddenly flew into a great temper because he had offered less for the loaf than she wanted, and attacked

and warm and he haggled with her over it. The woman was indignant at the price
he offered for it, so that she nearly struck him, so angry and so beside herself
was she. Such a commotion arose that the townspeople joined in. They then took
the pilgrim, beat him, tore his hair and badly ill-treated him. The noise reached
the ears of King Richard; he asked them to keep peace and friendship between
them; he sought and achieved peace among them and sent the people away. But
the devil, who by his nature hates peace more than anything in all creation,
revived the fight the next day.[60] It was not to be resolved without difficulty. The
two kings were together at a meeting, so I believe, with the justices of Sicily and
the great men of the town; there they spoke of making peace.[61] At the very time
when this was going on, even while the two kings were speaking of peace and
thought they could achieve it, the news came that our people were attacked.
Twice there came messengers with the news that much harm was being done;
the third messenger, who came after, said to the king, "It is an evil way of peace,
when the men of this land kill the men of England, both within and without the
city." This then is the truth: the Lombards went out, saying to the kings that it
was to appease the trouble, but they lied. It was for nothing but to cause trouble.
Jordan del Pin and Margaritone[62] – may ill-fortune attend them – these two
stirred up bad trouble and they were the cause of it. The king of France was
there and the king of England with him. With them was he who recounted this
tale. The king of England mounted and went there to break up the disturbance,
but as he went the people of the town hurled insults after him and reviled him
and the king hastened to arm himself and had them attacked from all sides, by
sea and by land, for there was not another such warrior anywhere in the world.
[687–829]   Great was the noise and the confusion and the tumult was tremendous.[63] The French came to seek their lord at the lodging of the king of England,
for the town was in such uproar that they thought they would never find him. He
returned [with them] to the palace where he was staying. Then the Lombards
came to him and held him by the left stirrup; they gave him gifts and promises
and granted that his was the day; they beseeched him to maintain them in the

---

the man with a stream of abuse, barely restraining herself from hitting him with her fist or
   pulling out his hair.'
[60] Cf. *Itinerarium*, 2. 16.
[61] The meeting with the justices took place on 4 October 1190, Landon, p.42.
[62] Margaritone of Brindisi had been William II's admiral, sent by the king to assist the Christians
   in the summer of 1188. He had appeared first at Tyre, but had not been welcomed by Conrad of
   Montferrat, already entrenched in the city and not prepared to countenance any competition
   from William II. See below, p.50. Thus Margaritone's main contribution to the defence of the
   crusader states was in Tripoli and Antioch. Jordan del Pin was governor of Messina:
   F. Chalandon, *Histoire de la domination normande en Italie et en Sicile*, vol.2 (Paris, 1907),
   pp.415–17, 438–9; Mayer, 'On the Beginnings of the Communal Movement', 446–7. The
   Byzantine historian and imperial official, Niketas Choniates, describes Margaritone as 'the
   most formidable pirate on the high seas', *O City of Byzantium, Annals of Niketas Choniates*,
   trans. H.J. Magoulias (Detroit, 1984), p.204.
[63] In his translation, but not his edition, Paris corrects 'noise', translated here as 'tumult', to
   'ville'; l.687 would then be translated as 'the city was in a sorry pass', the translation given by
   Stone, p.20.

town and retain them in his service and under his authority, expending both money and effort, until the king hastily armed himself and, according to one who should be believed, he helped the people of that land more than he helped the people of the king of England.

Then did the uproar increase and the disturbance grow throughout the army. The French were in the town, relaxing at their leisure, for the Lombards trusted them, but those in our army did not care about this. The gates were closed and the people of the town armed and up on the walls [of the city] in defence, but later they had to come down and those who had sallied forth and attacked the lodgings of lord Hugh le Brun[64] were all fighting together when the king of England arrived. I do not think that he had twenty men with him at the beginning. The Lombards left off their threats as soon as they saw him and turned and fled and the noble king pursued them. Ambroise witnessed this when it happened, for when they saw the king come they would have reminded you of sheep fleeing the wolf; as the oxen strain against the yoke so did they strain to reach the postern on the Palermo side.[65] He forced them forward, cutting down I do not know how many of them. The army gave the alarm and mounted, even as they were attacked by the Lombards in their arrogance, and by the enraged false Grifons. But those who undertook the task were men who had taken many towns; they were Normans and men of Poitou, Gascons and men of Maine, and Angevins, and there were more than one could number of Englishmen. They attacked them boldly; when they saw them on the top [of the wall] they ran all round the city and did not stop until they were within. Then their enemies using bows and crossbows which they had at hand were shooting and firing at them from the top, doing much harm; they hurled rocks and stones and struck our men hard. Bolts and arrows flew, doing much harm to our pilgrims. They murdered three of our knights who went in at a gate; one was Peter Tireproie whom they threw down among the spoils,[66] and with him they threw down dead Maheu of Sauçoi and Ralph of Rouvray was also found dead.[67] This is the proven truth; they were much mourned and lamented. May God grant them

---

64 Hugh IX, lord of Lusignan, became Count of La Marche in 1199. He was the grandson of Hugh VIII, who had been captured by Nur al-Din at the battle of Artah, in July 1164, and died in prison, WT, 19.9, p.875. Hugh IX was therefore the nephew of Geoffrey, Guy, and Aimery of Lusignan, see below, pp.55, 70. He died at Damietta on 11 August 1219 during the Fifth Crusade. See S. Painter, 'The Houses of Lusignan and Chatellerault', *Speculum* 30 (1955), 375–6, and 'The Lords of Lusignan in the Eleventh and Twelfth Centuries', *Speculum* 32 (1957), 27–47.

65 ll.731–3. The second image is less apt and is partly an excuse for word play with *traire*, translated here as 'strain'.

66 l.762. Paris rejects the manuscript reading *enmi la proie*, 'in the middle of the booty', replacing it with *en la voie*, 'in the way' or 'on the road'. However, using the name of the victim Tireproie as the basis for the rhyming word is very typical of Ambroise.

67 Ralph was one of three brothers of Osbert II of Rouvray-Catillon (Seine-Maritime), twenty miles north-east of Rouen. See D.J. Power, 'Between the Angevin and Capetian Courts: John de Rouvray and the Knights of the Pays de Bray, 1180–1225', in *Family Trees and the Roots of Politics: The Prosopography of Britain and France from the Tenth to the Twelfth Century*, ed. K.S.B. Keats-Rohan (Woodbridge, 1997), pp.361–84. The other two knights are not known, although Maheu can possibly be identified with Saussey (Manche). Cf. *Itinerarium*, 2.16, p.162, for a slightly different rendering of their names.

salvation! If the Lombards had been steadfast the king's men would have paid
dearly for it. It was inevitable that their folly would harm them; it kindled in us a
fire to burn them. Those who defended the town numbered more than fifty
thousand on the walls and the towers, equipped with long shields and with round
shields.[68]

There you might have seen an assault of strength and power. The galleys went
to the attack near the palace buildings. But the king of France took his stand on
the shore and defended the port against the galleys so that they could not take it;
they fired upon them until they killed two rowers – a misdeed. But from the
other side, from the land, the king of England attacked, coming upon the
Lombards so that many of them fell. There you might have seen his men
mounting and climbing the embankments, and cutting the bars of the gates;
many were taken or killed. Some fought together in the streets but regretted it
for those who were in the upper rooms were throwing [missiles down] and
taking aim at them. Despite all their efforts they were taken in that assault and
whoever may have been among the last the king was one of the first who dared
enter the town. Then there entered a good ten thousand men.

There you might have heard our men shouting, beating and storming,
injuring, harming, hitting of heads. They took Messina in less time than it takes
a priest to say matins; many would have been killed there if the king had not had
pity on them. You may believe in truth that great wealth was lost when the crowd
entered, for the town was soon pillaged and the galleys, which were neither poor
nor mean, were burned. They acquired women, fair, noble and wise women. I do
not know the whole story, but whether it was folly or wisdom, before it was well
known through the army, the French could see our pennoncels and our banners
of many kinds on the walls.[69] The king of France was jealous of this, a jealousy
that was to last all his life and there was the war conceived which led to the
devastation of Normandy.[70]

---

[68] l.776, *targes* and *roeles*; *targe* is glossed in the *A-ND* as 'light shield', and *roele* as 'round
shield'. D. Nicolle, *Arms and Armour of the Crusading Era, 1050–1350*, 2 vols (New York,
1988), vol.2, p.618, defines *targe* as a 'large shield, probably kite-shaped' and *roiele* as 'possibly a small round shield used by a horse archer, of three layers of leather'. Both types of shield
were used in the eleventh and twelfth centuries. Round shields, often large enough to protect
the body from neck to thigh, had been extensively used in the Carolingian era, while long,
narrow, kite-shaped shields (similar to those seen in the Bayeux Tapestry), with both flat and
curved surfaces, were equally useful for both mounted warriors and foot soldiers. They were
generally made of wood covered with leather with a metal boss and sometimes a metal rim. The
very ubiquity of these two types of shield is suggested by their inclusion in Ambroise's list of
synonyms, see below, p.52. See K.R. DeVries, *Medieval Military Technology* (Peterborough,
Ontario, 1992), pp.59, 63–4, 66–7. There were many variants on these two basic types. See the
illustrations in Nicolle, pp.286, 778; 290–1, 781; 302–4, 788–92; 322, 804; 513–14, 916–18.

[69] Richard took Messina on 4 October 1190, the same day as the conference with the justices. See
above, p.40.

[70] Philip II left Tyre to return to France on 2 August 1191, following the fall of Acre on 12 July.
See below, p.105. Richard remained in the East until October 1192 and was captured during the
journey home. He did not gain his release until February 1194. Philip took advantage of this
long absence to renew the war in Normandy, thus continuing the conflict which had begun with
the agglomeration of Henry II's lands in the 1150s. See above, p.30. For a concise overview of
the issues involved, see J. Gillingham, *The Angevin Empire*, 2nd ed. (London, 2001).

[830–47]⁷¹   When the king had taken Messina and placed his banners on the towers, then the king of France, jealous and annoyed, as were his people, that Richard had raised his banners there, sent word to him that his men would lower the banners and they would raise his own on the walls of the city.⁷² He did indeed send word to him that in doing this Richard had offended Philip's dignity and that this displeased him greatly. My lords, I ask you to judge which of them had the better right to raise their banners – he who did not wish to undertake the attack on the city, or he who dared such an undertaking.

[848–89]   King Richard heard of this business. He did not deign to make a long dispute over such a request, against the other king, who was raising such a storm over the matter; however, many words were said which were full of hatred and folly; but one should not write about all such follies nor put them into a book. However, all the high clerics and the great men spoke about peace a great deal and in divers ways until at the end both kings had their banners on the towers and turrets.⁷³ Then they turned their attention to send news to the king of Sicily [to tell] of the people of the town, of the villainy and excesses that they had suffered against them and their people. King Richard's messengers asked him on the king's behalf that he demanded with insistence the dower of his sister and her part of the great treasure that it be given to her as was right, for this would be right and reasonable, along with whatever belonged to the lady.⁷⁴ The messengers were named; they were great noblemen, men of renown, men of high lineage and great nobility, men of great importance, the men who would deal with this business. One of those who set about the task was the duke of Burgundy, another [was] Robert of Sablé, a noble man of high birth and great affability,⁷⁵ and there could have been others whose names I do not know. They set off and rode away and went so far on their way that they soon told their message to the king of Palermo.

---

71 Cf. *Itinerarium*, 2.17.

72 The translation here partly depends on the context. The Old French has an error, with *le roi de France* in the object, while the rest of the sentence structure suggests it is the subject; as this also makes more sense in the context I have followed Paris and Stone and corrected according to sense.

73 The *Itinerarium*, 2.17, p.165 (Nicholson, p.164), is less uncritical of Richard here, writing that 'at last King Richard's indignation cooled, and the abusive words ceased. He put up little resistance to the coaxings of his companions, although he had appeared invincible in the face of his enemies' attacks . . . So he who remained strong and unbending in the face of threats and bragging words bent before flattery and entreaties.'

74 Cf. *Itinerarium*, 2.18, which gives more details of the quarrel between Richard and Philip.

75 Robert of Sablé was a leading vassal of Richard I, holding extensive lands in the Sarthe valley. He was one of the five fleet commanders named by Richard in June 1190. He was later one of Richard's representatives on a committee established by the two kings which laid down regulations for the conduct of the armies while they were in the Kingdom of Sicily, Landon, p.44. In 1191 he became Master of the Temple, a post vacant since the death of the last Master, Gerard of Ridefort, in October 1189. His appointment clearly reflects Richard's influence. He died in 1192 or 1193. For his biography, see M.-L. Bulst-Thiele, *Sacrae Domus Militiae Templi Hierosolymitani Magistri: Untersuchungen zur Geschichte des Templeordens 1118/9–1314* (Göttingen, 1974), pp.123–34.

[890–931][76] King Tancred, who was very cunning,[77] listened to the words of the messengers. He had had many adventures and he was a good clerk, skilled at writing. He knew the matter well, so he did not linger long before giving his reply and responding. He replied without more thought to the men of the king of England that he would deal with this quarrel according to the established way of his land, the barons of his land and the customs of King William[78] and he would do what seemed good to all; if the townspeople of Messina had offered foolish provocation and given the kings cause for anger redress would be certainly made. When the messengers who had come from King Richard heard this, there were some who said that the king would not bargain over this. Many words were exchanged; good goblets were given to the messengers of France; the others suffered this with patience. Now hear about the great discord, which has been recorded then and since, which the king of France caused. He must have sent privately to Tancred over this affair (I do not know what he hoped to gain from it) asking that Tancred would do what he, Philip, wanted and that he would defend his right, that he would not move to war for the king of England and that he would be bound to him by oath. If this is how it was then it was ill-done; the history cannot be certain that the king thought of such villainy but the people assert it as truth that he sent such a message, whatever be the truth of it.

[932–949][79] Those who did not receive any cups returned as soon as they could; they retained their message well and returned to Messina. At that time King Richard was having a work carried out that pleased him greatly; it was a castle, Mategrifon, which caused much grief to the Grifon.[80] The messengers came to the king and said to him all that they had asked of King Tancred and the message he in turn was sending to Richard and what he asked of him, according to the established ways of the land and in the eyes of his barons. King Richard replied without hesitation that he would not plead with him and that he would pursue the matter.

[950–1049] When the news was known that no peace or truce would hold, war was then expected because of the support of the king of France [for our enemies], for the cunning Lombards had allied with him. Then was our food supply cut off, so that throughout the army not a penny's worth came and had it not been for God and the navy many would have had a poor time of it. However, the boats had their provision: cereal and wine, meat and other supplies. The town was watched over by night and the army was similarly guarded. The kings were at odds with one another, because of jealousy, which always causes discord. This was neither good nor honourable. The important men took great pains to bring agreement and peace between them; they rode to the palace, to

---

76 Cf. *Itinerarium*, 2.19.
77 1.890. The word used is *sage* which has a wide range of meaning from 'wise' to 'cunning'. Stone translates it as 'prudent'.
78 It is not clear whether William I, 1154–66, or William II, is meant here. On the king's role in the administration of justice, see Matthew, pp.184–8.
79 Cf. *Itinerarium*, 2.20.
80 Ambroise explains the meaning in 1.939, the following line; *mater* means to 'put into check, to bruise or batter', i.e. 'it caused the Grifon much trouble'.

Mategrifon and back by the same route, but they could bring no end to it and did not know how to deal with it – so the writings testify – until the king of Sicily, who knew the wrongs [committed by] the town, took the son of his chancellor,[81] and with him a knight, to the best of my knowledge his constable,[82] whom he held to be noble and trustworthy, and sent him to the king of England and told him that he did not want war with him but that if he was willing to accept compensation for the quarrel he was seeking that he would willingly make peace: he would give him twenty thousand ounces of gold that he would take from his treasury and if he wished to speak of a marriage, in a way which would have the approval of his barons, then he would give one of his unmarried daughters, a fair girl and noble damsel, to Arthur of Brittany[83] and for this business to be carried out [. . .][84] twenty thousand ounces of gold, on condition that he would return the gold if Arthur did not take the child. He would, moreover, send him back his sister. When the king had heard this he did not wait for long before sending back other men to seek a firm and durable peace: the archbishop of Monreale,[85] the loyal archbishop of Reggio,[86] John, the bishop of Evreux[87] who endured much effort and cost, to these men he entrusted the message. They well understood the matter and the business; other men went with them. Peace was what they sought and peace they brought back; they brought back the money of which I told you. When they came back everyone rejoiced over the peace. Then were the charters read and examined and copied and the peace established and sworn; the safety of the people was guaranteed by this.[88] They weighed and examined the money, which was no burden to the king for he desired it greatly, to spend it in the service of God. His sister, who was worth a great ransom, was restored to him. Then it was the king's will that everything that his people had taken that belonged to the people of the town should be restored without delay; for this he received great praise. It was restored on confession, under pain of excommunication, on the good and noble advice of the archbishop of Rouen.[89]

---

81 Richard, son of the chancellor, Matthew of Ajello (Salerno). Matthew and his sons, Richard and Nicholas, were closely associated with the dynasty, and Matthew played a key role in securing the election of Tancred. Chalandon, *Domination normande*, vol.2, pp.422–3, 440, 476.

82 Perhaps William of San Severino, royal justiciar and constable between 1178 and 1187. E. Jamison, *The Norman Administration of Apulia and Capua*, ed. D. Clementi and T. Közler (Darmstadt, 1987), pp.366–8.

83 Arthur was born on 29 March 1187, the posthumous son of Geoffrey of Brittany, Ralph of Diceto, vol.2, p.48. He died in April 1203. See *DNB*, vol.2, pp.543–5.

84 After l.994, there is a lacuna.

85 William, Prior of the monastery of Monreale, succeeded Abbot Theobald as bishop in 1178. Pope Lucius III agreed to elevate him to archbishop in 1183. See Matthew, pp.203–4. According to Roger of Howden, *Gesta*, vol.2, p.147, he died at the siege of Acre in 1190. However, as can be seen, he was in Messina in October 1190, and Richard I's letters of January 1191 show that the king thought he was still alive at the time. See below, p.87, n.273.

86 William, Archbishop of Reggio, Roger of Howden, *Chronica*, p.62.

87 John, Bishop of Evreux, 1180–92. He arrived at Acre from Cyprus in late June 1191 and died at Jaffa in June the next year.

88 The agreement with Tancred was made on 6 October 1190, Landon, p.43. The text is given by Roger of Howden, *Gesta*, vol.2, pp.133–5, and *Chronica*, vol.3, pp.61–4.

89 Walter of Coutances, Archbishop of Rouen, 1184–1207, formerly Bishop of Lincoln, 1183–4. Richard sent him back to England on 2 April 1191 in order to subdue the growing conflict

So was the town in a good state, free from dispute and confusion, and if anyone dared arouse such he was hanged or killed. Among the army there was great justice: blessed be the soul who brought this about. Then, once again, the roads were trodden; we obtained good provisions, horses and food; thus did the business end, without fail. The townspeople made peace with us again and lodged the pilgrims, and the two kings were in agreement with each other, though after that they would disagree again many times. And they shared the goods between them; each one had his due.

[1050–1105][90] The knights who had been there during the summer moaned and complained and grumbled at the expense they incurred. The complaints spread among high and low and reached King Richard who said that he would give each one enough money that he would be able to congratulate himself. Richard – who is not mean nor miserly – gave them such great gifts of silver chalices and gilded cups, brought to the knights according to their station, that all men praised him for his fine gifts, those of high, middle and low degree, and he did them such honour that even he who went on foot had one hundred sous from him; to the disinherited ladies who had been ejected from Syria, to the ladies and to the girls, he gave great gifts at Messina. Similarly the king of France also gave generously to his people. So all the army rejoiced because of this honour and generosity and because of the peace that had come.

So a great celebratory feast was held on the day of the Nativity.[91] Truly King Richard had it announced that all should come and celebrate the feast with him. He made such great efforts that the king of France was brought to eat with him. The feast was at Mategrifon, in the Hall, which the king of England had built by his authority, against the wishes of the people of that land. I was present at the feasting in the hall and I saw no dirty table-linen, nor wooden chalice or bowl. Rather I saw there rich vessels, embossed, with images cast on them, and richly set with precious stones, not in any way paltry. I saw there such good service that everyone had what he wanted. It was a good and honourable feast as is appropriate for such a festival; I have not, it seems to me, seen so many rich gifts given at once as King Richard gave then, handing over to the king of France and to his people vessels of gold and silver.

[1106–93] The time came for our departure; he who was wise and prudent was prepared. By my estimation the army stayed in Messina from the Feast of the Nativity of Our Lady in September to the end of Lent,[92] all the while looking forward to the day when they would be at the taking of Acre, with those who dared such an undertaking, for they had much discomfort, much more than they knew; they suffered much pain and trouble and labour in that half-year. When

---

between William of Longchamp, the chancellor, and Count John and some of the barons. He became chief justiciar in October 1191. See J.T. Appleby, *England without Richard, 1189–1199* (Ithaca, 1965), pp.59–68, 78–80, 82–3, and *DNB*, vol.13, pp.712–14, for his important role in English affairs thereafter.

90 Cf. *Itinerarium*, 2.23; *Itinerarium*, 2.22, contains an account of a meeting between Richard and Tancred not given by Ambroise.

91 Cf. *Itinerarium*, 2.24.

92 In 1191 Easter fell on 14 April, so Lent began on 3 March and Palm Sunday was 7 April. The Nativity of Mary is celebrated on 8 September.

they had stayed there for that time and God had prepared the way for them, then, truly, did the king of France set out on the sea with his company, a little before Palm Sunday.[93] King Richard could not move for he did not have ready all that was needful to go against that pack of curs – his galleys and his transport ships[94] for the carrying of his fast war-horses, his armour and his provisions. Because of this he had to stay, the better to prepare his journey. He went with the king of France on his galleys, then made his way beyond the straits, straight to Reggio whence news had been sent to him that his mother had arrived there bringing to the king his beloved. She was a wise maiden, a fine lady, both noble and beautiful, with no falseness or treachery in her. Her name was Berengaria; the king of Navarre was her father.[95] He had given her to the mother of King Richard who had made great efforts to bring her that far. Then was she called queen and the king loved her greatly. Since the time when he was count of Poitiers she had been his heart's desire. He had brought her straight to Messina with her female attendants and his mother.[96] He spoke to his mother of his pleasure and she to him, without keeping anything from him. He kept the girl, whom he held dear, and sent back his mother to look after his land that he had left, so that his honour would not decrease. Walter, the archbishop of Rouen, a most wise man, had the care of England with her. They had much war. Gilbert of Vascueil (who allowed Gisors to be taken) went back with them.[97]

From then on the king did not stop. Then were his ships prepared and loaded, all fitted out, and his galleys similarly. There was no more delay. He has the barons set out to sea and with them his beloved, the noble and wise lady, and with his beloved went his sister, that they might encourage one another, and with

[93] Philip II sailed from Messina for Acre on 30 March 1191. He arrived at Acre on 20 April, Landon, pp.47,48.

[94] 1.1126. Fr. *uissiers*. On uissiers as horse transports, see Pryor, 'Transportation of Horses by Sea during the Crusades', 21–2.

[95] Berengaria (d. c.1230) was the daughter of Sancho VI, King of Navarre. She arrived at Messina on 30 March 1191 and married Richard at Limassol on 12 May, Landon, pp.47, 49. The marriage seems to have been aimed at strengthening Richard's ties with Navarre and Aragon, which could provide valuable support in his prolonged conflict with Raymond V, Count of Toulouse. It did, however, necessitate the breaking of Richard's long-standing engagement to Alice of France, Philip II's sister (arranged in 1169), an action which further jeopardised relations between the two kings. On the political implications of the marriage, see J. Gillingham, 'Richard I and Berengaria of Navarre', *Bulletin of the Institute of Historical Research* 53 (1980), 157–73. For her life, see *DNB*, vol.5, pp.321–2.

[96] Eleanor of Aquitaine (c.1122–1204) was the daughter of William X, Duke of Aquitaine and Count of Poitou. She married Louis VII of France in July 1137, was divorced from him in March 1152, and in May married Henry of Anjou. For concise biographies, see E.A.R. Brown, 'Eleanor of Aquitaine: Parent, Queen, and Duchess', in *Eleanor of Aquitaine: Patron and Politician*, ed. W.W. Kibler (Austin and London, 1976), pp.9–34, and *DNB*, vol.18, pp.12–22. See also J. Martindale, 'Eleanor of Aquitaine', in *Richard Coeur de Lion in History and Myth*, ed. J.L. Nelson (London, 1992), pp.17–50, for a reassessment of historians' views on the queen.

[97] Gilbert of Vascueil was a Norman knight, sent back from Messina by Richard on 2 April 1191, to accompany Queen Eleanor and, thereafter, to take over as castellan of the key fortress of Gisors. His surrender of Gisors in April 1193 to the French, was seen as treachery by some chroniclers. For the context, see F.M. Powicke, *The Loss of Normandy 1189–1204*, revised ed. (Manchester, 1961), p.96.

them a great body of knights, all on one great dromond. He had his heavy dromonds put at the head and set sail towards the rising sun. But the rapid and mobile snacks did not move until the king had eaten; then the whole of this wonderful fleet moved off in good order.

It was in Holy Week that the fleet drew out of Messina to go the aid of God and to his glory.[98] On the Wednesday of that week during which God endured pain and suffering we too were to suffer in fear and watchfulness. And so Messina, where so many ships were seen to gather has reason to boast that never has the sun risen over such a rich fleet.

Cyprus

[1194–1229][99] The fleet went in good order towards the abused land of God, across the straits, straight to the high seas, on the way to Acre. We went to overtake the dromonds. Then we saw the wind drop, so that the king wished to return. Whether it pleased us or troubled us, we had to spend the night between Calabria and Mount Gibel.[100] On Maundy Thursday He who had taken away the wind, Who takes [all] and gives [all], gave it back to us and left it with us for the whole day.[101] But the wind was feeble and the rich and honoured fleet came to a halt. On Good Friday we met a contrary wind, near Viaires, to our left.[102] The sea was stirred in its depths; the wind was strong, whipping up the waves in great billows. A great wound opened in each fold. We could only be blown off-course. We were afraid and uneasy, sick at heart, mouth and head. But we endured all our sufferings, as we ought, most willingly, for Him who deigned to come on that day to suffer His passion for our redemption. The wind was strong, urging us on until evening, when it was growing dark. Then we had a softer wind, favourable and pleasant.

[1230–83]   King Richard, whose heart was always quick to respond, did a worthy deed. He had the custom of having on his ship a great candle in a lantern, lit at night. It threw a clear light and burned all through the night to show others the way. He had with him able seamen, worthy men, who knew their work well. All the other ships followed the king's flame, keeping it in near view, and if the fleet ever moved away he would willingly wait for them. In this way he led the proud fleet, as the mother hen leads her chicks to food. This was both worthy and natural. Through the night we sailed on, untroubled and without hindrance. On the next day, Saturday of Holy Week, God led us again, without error, for the whole of the night and through Easter Day.[103] For three days the fleet went on at

---

98   The fleet left Messina on 10 April 1191, Landon, p.48.
99   Cf. *Itinerarium*, 2.27.
100   Mount Etna.
101   Maundy Thursday, 11 April 1191.
102   The context suggests Cape Spartivento on the south-eastern tip of Calabria. Paris, p.569.
103   Easter Day was 14 April, and therefore they reached Crete on 17 April and sailed on towards Rhodes on 18 April.

full speed and without lowering its sails, the king himself sailing at its head. On the Wednesday we saw Crete; there the king of England turned to hug the coast of the island. There he lay and the whole fleet with him. However, that night twenty-five of our swift snacks lost us. The king was very angry, indeed enraged, by this. In the morning of Thursday, with sails raised, we moved on to Rhodes, another island nearby. The wind was strong and the waves high. The ship sailed as swift as a swallow in flight, mast bending [before the wind]. As we went along the coast of Rhodes God gave us great speed and wonderful sailing, so that it seemed that He was pleased with the way His people took. I tell you truly, we sailed on very quickly until darkness fell. In the morning we came into the straits and lowered our sails. There we were untroubled and rested there until Sunday. The next day we were in Rhodes, the city where Herod was born.[104]

[1284–1351] Rhodes was a great city, of ancient antiquity, almost as great as Rome. One could scarcely appreciate the whole of it, for there were so many houses that had been destroyed, ruined walls and towers, and so many great churches that still stand (because of the number of people who have been there through the years and across the ages and under so many different lordships) that no man could count them without difficulty. Nor could anyone estimate its greatness and nobility, now fallen through age. However, there lived there people who sold us food. As the king was ill and unwell we had to wait a while at Rhodes. The king searched out and made enquiries about where his ships had gone and waited for his galleys that followed him from land to land. He also asked about and made enquiries about the tyrant who held Cyprus[105] and detained his pilgrims. We stayed at Rhodes for ten days.[106] It was, I believe, the first of May when we moved on, when the fleet raised its sails and left Rhodes in good order straight to the Gulf of Sattalia, a most dangerous passage.[107] No more dangerous passage is found on any course, for there four seas battle against one another, each striving against the others. As we were entering the Gulf a wind came against us and brought us in the evening back to where the fleet had entered it. The wind, which changes frequently, came round again and

---

104 Richard landed at Rhodes on 22 April. In the manuscript *li eredes*. Stone notes that there is no other reference to Rhodes as the birthplace of Herod and that 'it looks as if Ambroise has invented this circumstance for the sake of the rhyme'. Given his fondness of word-play the anagrammatic nature of the connection may also have contributed.

105 Isaac Ducas Comnenus (c.1155–c.1195), the former Byzantine governor of Cilicia, was the brother-in-law of the Norman admiral, Margaritone. Late in 1183, or early in 1184, he had gained control of Cyprus, perhaps on the basis of forged letters of authority or perhaps as a legitimate appointee. However, during the troubled reign of Andronicus I Comnenus (1183–5), he was among those who revolted against a man widely seen by the Byzantine aristocracy as a usurper. In 1184 he took the title of 'Basileus', apparently considering himself to be the only legitimate Byzantine emperor, rather than merely ruler of a province that had seceded. With the help of the Sicilian fleet under Margaritone, he survived an attempt to overthrow him by Emperor Isaac II Angelus in 1186, but the death of his ally, King William II of Sicily, in 1189 left him vulnerable to outside attack, R.H. Rudt de Collenberg, 'L'empereur Isaac de Chypre et sa fille (1155–1207)', *Byzantion* 38 (1968), 123–53.

106 Cf. *Itinerarium*, 2.28.

107 Adalia or Sattalia (medieval), Antalya (modern).

gave us a more courteous exchange, coming behind us as it pushed us so quickly that we all feared, on account of the Gulf where we were and of which we were much afraid. The king's ship was first, as was always customary. The king looked out over the high sea and saw a transport ship, a buss,[108] coming from Syria. He hailed it to enquire news of the Holy Land, for this was a matter dear to his heart. They said that it was certain that the king of France was already there, waiting for him before Acre and that every day he was busy making machines to take the town. However, King Richard already had another plan in mind. So the vessel passed on and the king struggled against the wind until God brought him to shore before Cyprus near the land that God gave him in conquest. There he found his sister, his people and his beloved.[109]

[1352–1435][110]   Listen, my lords, this land of Syria had endured such wrongs and such great misadventures, such opposition and such attacks, so many delays and so much waiting, so much suffering and so many needs, such assaults and such burdens before help could come! Great harm was done to the needs of the work because of the emperor of Germany who had such magnificence and yet died so suddenly.[111] The Holy Land suffered much through the death of the king of England, good King Henry, who knew so much and had so much. By him would the land have been maintained and the town of Tyre supported. It was a great loss to the Holy Land that good King William died, for he had saved it many times. His death was a great loss. The land had suffered much from these sad mishaps. But nothing had done it so much damage and set back [its cause] as that caused by the well-endowed island of Cyprus, an island near to Syria, which used to bring it much aid but now did nothing on its behalf, for there ruled there a tyrant who leaned only towards evil. He was more treacherous and more evil than Judas or Ganelon.[112] He turned away from Christians and was the intimate friend of Saladin.[113] It was said with some certainty that they had drunk each

---

[108] Old French *boce* (l.1333). On the 'buss', see Pryor, 'Transportation of Horses', 20.

[109] The ship carrying Joanna and Berengaria had anchored off Limassol on 1 May 1191, Landon, p.48.

[110] Cf. *Itinerarium*, 2.29.

[111] Frederick I, Barbarossa, the Staufen emperor, drowned in the River Saleph in Cilicia on 10 June 1190. He had taken the Cross on 27 March 1188, and set out from Ratisbon (modern Regensburg) on 11 May 1189 at the head of a huge army. However, the overland journey had already devastated its ranks; even before Frederick's death, it had lost about three-fifths of its initial manpower. See F. Opll, *Das Itinerar Kaiser Friedrich Barbarossas (1152–1190)* (Vienna, Cologne and Graz, 1978), pp.97–109, and R. Hiestand, ' "precipua tocius christianismi columpna": Barbarossa und der Kreuzzug', in *Friedrich Barbarossa Handlungs- spielraume und Wirkungsweisen des staufischen Kaisers*, ed. A. Haverkamp, Vorträge und Forschungen 40 (Sigmaringen, 1992), pp.51–108.

[112] The betrayal of Roland and his companions by Ganelon in the *Chanson de Roland* implicitly parallels the betrayal of Christ by Judas.

[113] Al-Nasir Salah al-Din Abu'l-Muzaffar Yusuf ibn Ayyub, 'sultan' of Egypt, was born c.1138, the son of Ayyub, a Kurd from Dvin, near Tiflis. He spent his early years in Damascus. He gained power in Egypt following the death of his uncle, Shirkuh, vizier to the Caliph, in March 1169. Shirkuh and Saladin had been acting on behalf of Nur al-Din, ruler of Aleppo and Damascus. When Nur al-Din died on 15 May 1174, Saladin was able to use Egypt as a base from which to expand his power. See Lyons and Jackson, pp.1–69.

other's blood as a sign of their alliance, and this was later known to be true. So he had made himself emperor, not truly imperial but imperilor, for he did much harm.[114] He never ceased to commit evil and pursue evil ends, as far as he was able, and to pursue the Christians of God. There were there three wrecked ships belonging to Richard, with men of his entourage.[115] They had escaped the wreck but were now in dire straits. The emperor had forced them to give up their arms, then he had them taken, through treachery; having guaranteed them safety, a guarantee that did not last long, he – whose word should never be trusted – promptly attacked them. However, their foes paid dearly for their rage; they defended themselves well with only three bows that they had and of which the Grifon knew nothing. There was there Roger of Harcourt,[116] a companion of the king and one of his court, who, mounted on a pathetic pack-horse reduced their numbers greatly. There was also the good archer William of Bois- Normand,[117] who fired arrows, striking them in front and behind and was more feared than a catapult [. . .][118] In their sight they drew back to the dromonds, which were in the port, having brought the queen. There was a great battle with the prisoners fighting well. When the king, who had arrived in the port, learned of the perfidy, of the trials of his men, when he saw the dromond in which his sister was awaiting him in terror,[119] when he saw the shore covered with the perfidious Greeks, he had no desire to hunt out Saracens worse than these. He had himself taken towards the land that the tyrant thought to defend, but where he dare not await the noble king.

[1436–81]   God had ordained that it would be on a Monday morning[120] that the king would do his will, that he would seek out the shipwrecked men, that he would set his sister free, that he would take his beloved elsewhere. The two ladies cursed the day that had brought them there for the emperor would have taken them both prisoner had he been able. There were many willing to defend the port that the king wished to take, for the emperor himself was standing there on the shore, with as many men as he could muster, either for money or by his

---

114 The play on words (annominatio) is difficult to render into English. The annominatio stresses the harm he did by punning on *empereor*, 'emperor', and *empirer*, 'to make worse'. The word he uses is not attested elsewhere and is apparently coined for the purpose.

115 Cf. *Itinerarium*, 2.30.

116 Roger or Roges was a member of a prominent Anglo-Norman family from Harcourt, near Brionne (Eure). The family held lands from the honour of Beaumont and in several English counties, in particular from the earls of Leicester and Warwick. Roger was with the king in Westminster and Dover in 1189 and was one of a major group of Normans which arrived in Acre on 8 June 1191, the day after the king, so he must have travelled with the royal fleet. This confirms Ambroise's description of him as a companion of the king: C.L. Loyd, *The Origins of some Anglo-Norman Families*, Publications of the Harleian Society 103 (Leeds, 1951), p.51; Powicke, pp.342–3; Landon, pp.15, 22, 50.

117 William of Bois-Normand was a Norman knight from the region of Evreux, who held lands from the earl of Leicester. Loyd, p.29.

118 After l.1419, there is a lacuna. According to the *Itinerarium*, 2.30, the crusaders were rescued by their companions who drew them back to the boats. There is much more detail given in the *Itinerarium*.

119 Cf. *Itinerarium*, 2.32.

120 6 May 1191, Landon, p.48.

commands. The king took a messenger and had him rowed to the shore; he was sent to the emperor to ask him courteously to return their goods to the prisoners and to redress the wrongs he had done to the pilgrims, causing many orphans to mourn. The emperor mocked the messenger to such an extent that he was enraged and could not temper his anger. He said to the messenger "Pah sir!", nor would he ever give a more courteous reply, but rather began to growl mockingly.[121] The messenger retired promptly and took the reply back to the king faithfully. The king heard the dishonourable reply and said to his men, "Arm yourselves." They did so at once. They had to embark, fully armed, in the rowing boats attached to the snacks. There embarked many good knights and bold crossbowmen. Their enemies also had crossbows and men ready on the shore, as well as five galleys, fully armed. But when they saw our arms their men felt little confidence.

[1482–1697]   In the town of Limassol, where the battle and fighting began, they had left intact nothing that could be used as a weapon: neither door nor window, barrel nor cask, round shields nor long shields, old galley nor old boats, plank nor beam, nor step.[122] All were eagerly taken down to the shore to inflict damage on the pilgrims. They stood at the shore, fully armed, more arrogant than any people alive, with pennoncels and with banners of rich fabrics and rich colours, on great horses, strong and fleet, and on mules, both strong and fine. They bayed at us, like dogs, but soon their pride left them. We had the worse hand, for we were coming from the sea, in tiny little boats, exhausted by the storms, crippled by the waves, weighed down with our arms and all on foot.[123] They were on their land. We, however, better understood the business of war.

Our crossbowmen attacked, and there were among them those who would not miss! First they fired upon the boatmen, who were not learned in warfare. They hurt and injured so many of those in the galleys that they jumped into the sea, four by four. Then you could see one fighting another. Then were their galleys taken and put with our snacks. The archers and the bowmen fired thick and fast, forcing the Greeks to move their position. Then you might have heard our men baying as they had bayed at us before we had moved. From both sides came firing and hurling [of missiles] and the oarsmen moved forward while it rained bolts and arrows wherever they went. The strand and the shore were covered with these wild people. There you might have seen a bold undertaking and men learned in war. When the king saw his companions struggling to reach land he leapt into the sea from his skiff[124] and, reaching the Greeks, attacked them. All

---

121 1.1463. The text has *Trop* (literally 'too much'), which Paris changes to 'Tprout!', an invented exclamation of contempt. It is clear from the context that an insult is intended.

122 ll.1486–8. Pairs of near synonyms are put together accumulatively for rhetorical effect. The last term *degré*, translated here as step, is probably used to provide word-play with *de gré*, 'willingly/eagerly' in l.1489.

123 ll.1505–8. The disadvantages of the crusaders' position are stressed through the rhetorical technique of anaphora (each line beginning with the same word, in this case *et*, 'and') building up to the single line 'and they were on their land'.

124 Ambroise appears to be referring to a ship's boat, carried for emergencies, and used for victualling, embarking and landing. See J.H. Pryor, 'The Naval Architecture of Crusader Transport Ships', *The Mariner's Mirror* 70 (1984), 372–3.

the others leapt in after him and the Grifons defended themselves, but our men went along the shore striking and overcoming them. There you might have seen arrows flying and Greeks dying and being killed. They forced them into the town, striking them down, striking blows. They went after them like lions, striking at them and at their horses. Both Greeks and Armenians fled before the brave Latins; they were chased as far as the fields so fiercely that they pressed the emperor, who fled. The king gave pursuit after him until he soon acquired a pack-horse or beast of burden, I do not know which, with a bag strapped to the saddle and stirrups of thin cord.[125] He leapt from the ground into the saddle and said to the false and perfidious emperor, "Emperor, come, joust!" But the emperor did not fancy jousting. That night, without any delay, the king had many horses disembarked from the snacks.[126] The emperor had no idea that he had brought horses with him. The horses were walked about, because they were all stiff and lame and dazed after being at sea for a month, standing the whole time, unable to lie down. The next day, without giving them any more rest than they had had (although they deserved more), the king, having taken the matter in hand, mounted. There in an olive grove, next to the road, were the Greeks, with their banners and their pennoncels of all sorts. The king had them hunted out. He put on his steel helmet and followed them swiftly. There you might have seen bold and noble men! The front runners pursued them; they fled and our men followed until they saw the body of their army. Our men followed and they fled. Then they stopped. Our men followed and they yelled; such noise and such shouting there was (so said those who heard it) that the emperor in his tent, more than half a league away, heard them, or so I understand. He had retreated there because of the fighting; there he had dined and slept, but he and his men were greatly disturbed [by this]. Then he mounted and his men mounted and they crossed the mountains to see what their people were doing, for they knew nothing beyond the shooting of bows. They continued to circle around, baying at us, and our people stood their ground. Then an armed clerk, Hugh de la Mare[127] was his name, came to the king, advising him thus, "Sir, get away, for they have hordes of people, beyond counting." The king said, "Sir clerk, concern yourself with your writing and come out of the fighting; leave chivalry to us, by God and Saint Mary." He and others said this to the king on account of the great numbers of people that they saw there; there were not with the king at that time more than forty, or at the most fifty, knights. The noble king, who would wait no longer, rushed upon his enemies, faster than a bolt of lightening, as alert as a hobby going after a lark. (Anyone who saw the attack admired it greatly.) He struck into the press of hostile Greeks, so that they became perforce in disarray, and he so disordered them that they could not remain together, until his people came.

---

125 *roncin ou jument* can both be translated 'pack-horse', but Ambroise distinguishes between them. Translating *jument* as 'mare', does not, however, adequately reflect the status of the animal, which was not a war-horse but a beast of burden.

126 Cf. *Itinerarium*, 2.33.

127 Hugh seems to have been a member of the Marra family, two of whom (both called William) served in the Exchequer under Henry II and Richard. The first William died in c.1190 and the second helped run the Exchequer while Richard was on crusade.

When they arrived they grew in numbers and came upon them, they killed and took so many that no-one could count the dead (not counting those who fled shamefully). For those who had horses fled across mountains and valleys, and the foot-soldiers, the lesser people, were all dead or taken. The battle was hard-fought and fierce. You would have seen so many horses lying there, hauberks[128] and swords and lances and pennoncels and cognisances.[129] Horses, with their burdens, stumbled. The emperor saw that his men could not endure against our men and that our strength increased continuously. He fled into the mountain with his Greeks and his Armenians,[130] leaving the plain to our people.

When Richard, the king of England, realised that they were fleeing thus and leaving their people he struck the man carrying the emperor's banner in such a way that he gained the banner and he gave commands that it should be well guarded. Then the king saw their people retreating in disarray, fleeing like a strong wind, with many a bleeding body and head; he did not have them pursued for they could not be overtaken and the pursuit by the bold Franks had already lasted for two leagues. So he came back, slowly. But the men-at-arms did not leave it at that; they took rich and fine vessels of gold and silver, which the emperor had left behind where his tent was pitched; they took his arms and his very bed, cloths of silk and of scarlet dye, horses and mules burdened as if for market, hauberks and helmets and swords, thrown down by the Grifons, oxen and cattle and pigs and goats, which were agile and not docile, sheep and ewes and lambs, mares with their fine, fat foals, capons and pullets and cocks, fat mules bearing embroidered cloth, good doublets and elegant, beautiful clothes, and good horses, of more worth than ours which were exhausted. They also took

---

128 The hauberk was a coat of mail made of iron rings, interlinked in a variety of patterns. There is some controversy over whether this coat covered the entire body or was simply some kind of hood. Padding might have been attached to the garment or worn underneath it as a separate item. P. Contamine, *War in the Middle Ages*, trans. M. Jones (Oxford, 1984), pp.184–8, summarises this discussion. For illustrations, see Nicolle, *Arms and Armour*, pp.291, 782; 300, 786; 302, 788; 320, 803.

129 *Cognisances* are defined in *A New Dictionary of Heraldry*, p.97, as 'any device used for the purpose of identification. In heraldry generally taken to mean a badge'.

130 Armenia is the mainly mountainous area south of the Black Sea, which lies between eastern Asia Minor and the Mesopotamian lowlands. Although it had been Christianised by the early fourth century, the Armenian Church had rejected the doctrine on the Trinity, promulgated at the Council of Chalcedon (451), in favour of monophysite belief, that the divine and human natures of Christ were hypostatically united. Given its geographical position, it is not surprising to find that it was an area of perennial conflict between the Byzantine and Persian empires, a situation further complicated by the Arab invasions from the 640s. In any case the mountains made it difficult to achieve political unity even in favourable circumstances, so Armenia seldom enjoyed much autonomy and its people were often to be found scattered throughout Asia Minor and the Middle East. The only coherent Armenian political structure at this time was to be found in Cilicia in south-eastern Asia Minor, where the Katholikos, the head of the Armenian Church, had established himself by the late eleventh century, and it may be that the Armenians in the service of Isaac Comnenus came from this region, since he had once been governor there. For the geography and history of medieval Armenia and the Armenian Church see the articles by N.G. Garsoïan and K.H. Maksoudian respectively in *Dictionary of the Middle Ages*, vol.1, ed. J.R. Strayer (New York, 1982), pp.470–87 and pp.498–505.

the dragoman of the emperor, whom I heard called John,[131] and so many Grifons and Armenians that they blocked the road, and so many good wines and so much good food that no-one could keep a count or tally of it. The king had an announcement made that all those of the land who did not want war could come and go in safety and those who did not want peace would have neither peace nor truce from him.

[1698–761][132] On the Saturday of that same week[133] in which the Greek rabble suffered in this way, there came to Limassol three galleys, from Cyprus, carrying the much respected king of Jerusalem.[134] This was Guy of Lusignan,[135] who had endured so much suffering and trouble in order to uphold the land of God, that he had had to come [to Cyprus]. For the king of France wished to do him so much harm that he wanted to make the marquis [of Montferrat] king,[136] which caused him much pain in his heart. For this reason he had left the land to come to the king of England [to ask] that he would give him his support in protecting the land. The king was pleased about his arrival and hurried to greet him. You may know and understand that he received him with great eagerness, for he was of a very great lineage and good family, and [those of] his family who were there did not give the appearance of being people who had come from nothing. The king showed great joy towards him, honouring him in many ways, and giving him goods – which was both courteous and wise – giving him two thousand marks and twenty drinking vessels out of his treasury, two of them of fine gold – no mean gift.

The next morning the young woman [the princess of Navarre] was married

---

131 This man probably acted as Isaac's interpreter and intermediary with foreign powers.

132 Cf. *Itinerarium*, 2.34.

133 11 May 1191, Landon, p.49.

134 'From Cyprus' does not make sense and these words are not in the *Itinerarium*. HL, p.93, n.28, suggest that it should read 'from Syria'.

135 Guy of Lusignan was King of Jerusalem, 1186–92. During Lent (5 March – 30 April) 1180 he married Sibylla, sister of the reigning king, Baldwin IV (1174–85), and mother of his successor, the infant Baldwin V. When the seven-year-old Baldwin died in August 1186, Guy and Sibylla seized the throne with the support of Heraclius of Caesarea, Patriarch of Jerusalem, and Gerard of Ridefort, Master of the Temple. Guy was a younger son of Hugh VIII, lord of Lusignan in Poitou, and vassal of Richard I. The most detailed account of these events is M.W. Baldwin, *Raymond III of Tripolis and the Fall of Jerusalem (1140–1187)* (Princeton 1936; reprint Amsterdam, 1969), pp.35–40, 76–8. However, Baldwin's distinctive interpretation – in particular his presentation of two parties consisting of the 'court' and the 'native baronage' – has been strongly challenged. See P.W. Edbury, 'Propaganda and Faction in the Kingdom of Jerusalem: The Background to Hattin', in *Crusaders and Muslims in Twelfth-Century Syria*, ed. M. Shatzmiller (Leiden, 1993), pp.173–89, and Hamilton, *Leper King*, pp.150–8. Hamilton concludes that there was a division in the kingdom, but that it was 'between the king's maternal and paternal kin'.

136 Conrad, Marquis of Montferrat (1188–92), was the son of William III. His defence of Tyre in 1187–8 saved the Kingdom of Jerusalem from complete collapse in the face of Saladin's attacks, following the latter's victory at Hattin in July 1187. See above, p.29 and below, pp.69–70. Since King Guy was at that time a captive of Saladin, Conrad emerged as a viable challenger for the throne, a claim strengthened by the death of Sibylla in 1190. See Jacoby, 'Conrad, Marquis of Montferrat', pp.187–238.

and crowned at Limassol.[137] [She was] beautiful, with a bright countenance, the wisest woman, indeed, that one could hope to find anywhere. There was the king in great glory, rejoicing in his victory and in his marriage to the woman to whom he had pledged his troth.

There came the galleys that he had awaited so long, so well-armed and equipped that we had never seen such in our lives, and with them were the five that we had seized there [at Limassol]. With the others in the different ports of which he had the full use, that made a good forty armed [vessels] that were worth fifty others. Later he took the marvellous ship where there were counted eight hundred warriors, Turks and Persians, unbelievers. So the king was emboldened to go against the accursed Greeks and Armenians. Then he got his army ready, setting his watchmen for the night, to go after the emperor and take him in his own land.[138]

[1762–1797]   After this defeat which so shamed the Greeks, the emperor was at Nicosia with his company, angry, upset and despairing over the men he had lost and over the pursuit after him. He would not be comforted. He was greatly hated in his land and he feared the king of England, so he sent to him to ask for a meeting for the emperor to make amends to the king. He said that he would come and pledge loyalty, bringing in his company five hundred mounted men, as far as Syria, for the service of God, and that he would do all that the king wanted. It was all in the agreement, so that the king could be sure of it, that he would give as a surety his castles and all his rich inheritance, and as reparation for his people three thousand five hundred marks of silver; if he served faithfully he would regain his lands in recompense. The king agreed to a meeting, as did the emperor. A time was decided upon by both parties with no delay. The meeting was held in a fig grove between the shore and the way to Limassol, as I believe, with his people gathered there.[139] That which was stipulated there was better than what was done.[140]

[1798–1829]   The king called his entourage, the wisest of his men, and said to those who were with him, those most desirous of peace, "My lords, you are my right hand: see if this peace can hold; take care, for your honour lies in it and take care that there should be no compromising. For if it pleases you the peace will be made, or set aside if it pleases you not." "My lord" they said, "it pleases us, and such a peace is honourable to us." They went straight back and agreed to the peace. The emperor straight away swore the oath to the king, and gave him the kiss of fealty. The king returned to his army, which was nearby. He soon

---

137 The marriage took place on the Feast of St Pancras, 12 May 1191, Landon, p.49. Cf. *Itinerarium*, 2.35.

138 Cf. *Itinerarium*, 2.36.

139 l.1795. *E les sues iloc ensemble* translated by Paris as 'c'est là qu'il se rencontrèrent' with the note that this is a conjectural translation, l.1795 being corrupt and incomprehensible. I have translated *les sues* as 'his people' reading *sues* as a form of *soes*, the stressed feminine possessive plural, here representing 'ses gens'.

140 ll.1796–7. Paris translates as 'on y dit des choses meilleurs que celles qui furent faites' (better things were said there than were done), interpreting 'retraite' as meaning to recount. The *A-ND*, vol.6, p.649, includes the gloss 'draw up (of document), to stipulate, lay down', which would imply here a formal agreement, not just discussion.

reached them. Without delay he commanded to be packed rich vessels in plenty and three rich tents that he had taken at the defeat of the evil Grifons – these belonged to the king and were of fustian. He most courteously sent them to the emperor, who took the vessels and erected the tents at that very place where the meeting that we recounted took place.

[1830–75]   That same evening when the peace had been concluded there was with the emperor a slanderous knight. His name was Pagan of Caiphas.[141] He was false and more evil than a cur.[142] He gave the emperor to understand that the king wanted him taken, but he was making him believe a lie. The emperor at once mounted a fleet horse named Fauvel.[143] On Fauvel he fled, but as if he were going out for pleasure, leaving equipment and tents, as well as two fast and fleet horses, like a man going out of his mind, riding away as quickly as he could. The king heard that he had taken flight but he did not wish him pursued because he did not mean to break the treaty and no horse would have been able to catch up with him. But when he saw his flight he did not wish him to go scot-free so he searched for him by land and sea and made great efforts to look for him. His galleys left by night and in time arrived at Famagusta. He himself went there, for he wished greatly to undertake this. He said to the king of Jerusalem that he should accompany him, going by land, following the emperor, perjurer and traitor that he was, to know if he had been seen. King Guy set off arriving – and this is the truth – in three days at Famagusta, which the people had deserted. The king arrived there with his galleys; with his galleys he had the ports watched and guarded so that the emperor could not go by sea without coming across them. They were there for three days after parting from the snacks.

---

141 Pagan, lord of Haifa (Caiphas) was one of the leading barons of the Kingdom of Jerusalem since, apart from Haifa, he held lands in the Principality of Galilee and money fiefs on the royal domain at Acre, S. Tibble, *Monarchy and Lordships in the Latin Kingdom of Jerusalem, 1099–1291* (Oxford, 1989), pp.68–9, 75–6. He last appears on a charter of the kingdom in 1191, *RRH*, no.703, p.188. He was one of a group allied to Conrad of Montferrat which included Balian of Ibelin, his wife, Maria Comnena, and Reynald of Sidon. These were instrumental in effecting the marriage of Conrad to Isabella, Maria Comnena's daughter by King Amalric, despite the fact that she was already married to Humphrey of Toron. See below, pp.88–9. According to Roger of Howden, *Gesta*, vol.2, p.168, Pagan was responsible for upsetting the peace between Isaac and Richard, since Conrad of Montferrat wished to undermine any advantage gained by Guy of Lusignan, his rival for power in the Kingdom of Jerusalem. However, it is also a name heavy with resonance. *Chaiphas*, as well as being a place, was the name of the High Priest who found Jesus guilty of blasphemy and sent him to Pilate. Cf. *Itinerarium*, 2.38.

142 l.1835. *gaignon*, 'mastiff', translated here as 'cur' because of the implication of meanness. Stone translates as 'surly dog'.

143 Paris notes that Fauvel is 'à la fois nom propre et désignation par la couleur . . . on retrouve le nom du cheval Fauvel de Chypre dans le poème anglais de *Richard, Coeur de Lion*'. Nicholson, p.191, n.134, notes that this was 'a French name for a dun-coloured horse'. Fauvel was one of the most common names for horses in *chansons de geste*. A. Moisan, *Repertoire des noms propres de personnes et de lieux cités dans les chansons de geste* (Droz, 1986), vol.1, p.401, lists a dozen texts featuring a horse called Fauvel.

[1876–1983]   During this time of waiting there came two messengers from France, Dreux of Mello,[144] I believe, and with him the bishop of Beauvais,[145] to ask the king to make haste; they put great pressure on him to move at once against Acre, for the king of France would not on any account make an assault at any point before his arrival. They greatly pestered and pressed him, and in pressing him they insulted him, so much so that the king became angry, raising his eyebrows. Such things were said as should not be written down. Yet they pressed him in vain, wasting words for nothing, for the king had made haste himself, and he had so tested the Greeks that he would not concern himself with Syria, not for half the wealth of Russia, until Cyprus was subjected to him – Cyprus, that island that produces so much food – nor would he consent to leave it without recompense before he had taken it.[146] For this reason they came to press him, holding him to be in a good position.[147]

So he left at once with his assembled army to head directly for Nicosia. Each one took with him his provisions and all his accoutrements for battle; the emperor, hiding nearby, kept watch. The king took the rearguard that they might suffer less from the rear. The emperor suddenly jumped out of his place of ambush with at least seven hundred of his personal entourage who had been as if spellbound by cowardice. They went to shoot upon the vanguard and the vanguard allowed them to approach. The emperor came on the flanks, harrying them like a Turcopole,[148] until he came to the rearguard of which King Richard

144 Dreux of Mello was Constable of France from 1193. He came from a family of castellans near Senlis, and was an active member of Philip II's administration until his death in 1218. See J.W. Baldwin, *The Government of Philip Augustus: Foundations of French Royal Power in the Middle Ages* (Berkeley and London, 1986), pp.104–5.

145 Philip of Dreux, Bishop of Beauvais between 1175 and his death in 1217, was a cousin of Philip II, and a leading member of his government. He was captured by Richard I in 1197 and not released until 1200. At the battle of Bouvines in 1214 he commanded the left wing of the French army together with his brother, Robert II, Count of Dreux. See Baldwin, *Government of Philip Augustus*, pp.105–6, 216.

146 l.1903, *N'il ne la deignast pas sanz prise*. Paris offers the correction *s'emprise* and the translation 'il n'aurait jamais voulut la laisser'. Stone translates 'nor would he deign to give over his emprise'. I suspect that Ambroise's choice of words was based on the possibility of creating *annominatio/paronomasia*, with *prise* = 'prize', 'reward', and *prise* = taken. This would require no correction and, while being clumsy and contrived, is perfectly in keeping with Ambroise's style.

147 l.1900, *en grant estal l'en teneient*. This line is obscure. Paris offers 'croyaitaient qu'il se reposait', but glosses under *estal*, 'qui l'en pressaient beaucoup (la traduction est inexacte)'. Stone translates 'who pressed him so greatly in this matter', noting that the manuscript's reading is uncertain.

148 Turcopoles were lightly armed and mobile mounted troops, characteristic of crusader armies in the East, where they had been developed in imitation of similar forces in Muslim and Byzantine armies. They were recruited both from baptised Turks and from the local Christian population. See J. Richard, 'Les Turcopoles au service des royaumes de Jérusalem et de Chypre: Musulmans convertis ou Chrétiens orientaux?' *Revue des études islamiques* 54 (1986), 259–70. The French Rule of the Temple, in a section probably put together in the mid-1160s, designates an office of Turcopolier, the holder of which was responsible for the use of such troops by the Order, *La Règle du Temple*, ed. H. de Curzon, Société de l'Histoire de France (Paris, 1886), cl.169–72, pp.127–9.

had the charge. He shot at once against him two poisoned arrows.[149] Then the king spurred on, coming out of the ranks, and almost succeeded in wreaking vengeance on this emperor, who was totally lacking in goodness, but the emperor was mounted on Fauvel who, fleet as a fleeing deer, carried him on, full of sorrow, straight to his castle at Kantara. When the king saw that he could not take the emperor he turned towards Nicosia, but our men had taken good horses and injured and taken many of the Greek rabble who had come too close to us. They made their way, following the king, having nothing more to fear or doubt. They came to Nicosia in the morning; the townspeople did not hold back. They came to the king from all directions, taking him as their rightful lord; they came to him as to a father. The king had their beards shaved. When the emperor heard tell of it he nearly went out of his mind with rage – he ill-treated both his men and ours; his own men who had surrendered and those of ours whom he could take, when he could get hold of them. He had their feet or hands chopped off, their eyes put out, or their nose cut off, since he could not [in any other way] take vengeance.[150] The king meanwhile accepted the homage of the most valiant and the most wise, who willingly turned from the emperor, whom they hated. The king split and divided the army into three divisions and caused siege to be laid to three castles, two of which were taken easily. One division went to Kyrenia which was taken in time. The king of Outremer gave it to Richard, conducting matters well and bringing back [his men].[151] Near the castle he had the army armed, and besieged it by land and sea, attacking in strength. The inhabitants had no support so could not hold out but had to make terms. They had to give up to the warrior King Guy the castle and with it the emperor's daughter.[152] This was such a shock to him that he ever after was out of his mind and his senses and he would not be comforted. King Guy had the banners of the king raised on the tower, put his guards to the castle and then led the army to Didemus.[153]

---

[149] l.1923, *entuchiees en desheites*. Paris notes the obscurity of the term which he glosses as 'sans doute "en un moment, aussitôt" '.

[150] From the late sixth century onwards, beards came to symbolise both political power and masculinity in Byzantium. As contacts with clean-shaven westerners began to increase from the mid-eleventh century, beards became even more important as a means of marking the distinction between the Byzantines and the Latins, *The Oxford Dictionary of Byzantium*, ed. A.P. Kazhdan, vol.1 (Oxford, 1991), p.274. According to WT, 11.11, p.511, it was customary for both Greeks and other easterners to take great care over their beards, so that they regarded it as the greatest insult if even one hair were plucked from them.

[151] Outremer is a common name for the Holy Land in medieval texts.

[152] She was born c.1177/8, and was his daughter by his Armenian wife. Her name is unknown, although Rudt de Collenberg speculates that it may have been Beatrice, 174–5.

[153] The Kyrenian Mountains extended across the north coast of Cyprus into the Karpasian peninsula to the north-east. Kyrenia itself is the nearest port to Nicosia, reached through a pass to the north-west, dominated by the castle of St Hilarion (Didemus). By this route the distance is approximately 16 miles (about 26 kilometres). Buffavento about 6 miles (10 kilometres) to the south-east of Kyrenia, and Kantara (Candaire) about 2 miles (3 kilometres) inland on the north-east coast at the entrance to the Karpasian peninsula, occupied similarly strategic peaks in this range. All these places were fortified by 1191. See P.W. Edbury, *The Kingdom of Cyprus and the Crusades 1191–1374* (Cambridge, 1991), p.13 and map one.

[1984–2005]   Didemus is a strong castle that could never be taken by force, but those who had been sent there [by the emperor] were so stupefied by the news that they heard that they could scarcely hold it; yet they did on several occasions cast down large stones [on our men]. The castle would have had nothing to fear, but the cowardly lot were afraid. Nonetheless, King Guy sat there for so many days after he began to besiege it, before the emperor ordered that it should surrender, bringing down from their vantage point those [who held it]. When they had surrendered to the king, as I have heard, King Guy took possession of it. He commanded that the young girl should be kept well-guarded in the tower, so that she could not be taken away secretly. Then he brought his army back, but he found great shortages in the land.[154]

[2006–61]   King Richard at Nicosia had been struck down by illness. As soon as he felt better he laid siege to Buffavento, a most strong castle. Listen now to a strange adventure that happened to the recreant emperor on account of his sins.[155] He had shut himself away in Kantara, given himself up to his sorrow and shame. When he heard about the siege of Buffavento, then he was as in a trap. He knew that his daughter, whom he loved more than any living thing, was taken and put in a castle tower; this led him to seek peace with eagerness at whatever cost it would be to himself. It was a cursed cost – costing him those castles that he had and his riches, which he lost through his cowardice, but what had mortally injured and ruined him was that all his people had abandoned him. He had to do it; he did not tarry. He went down from Kantara, and went to give himself up to Richard, not intending to protect himself from him.[156] Before he came he sent word to the king, asking that he would have pity on him, saying that he would surrender everything to his mercy, so that nothing would remain to him, of land, castles, houses but, for his honour and as was right, he asked that the king would spare him on one count: that he would not be put in iron chains or fetters. Nor was he, but, on account of the protests of the people, he was put in bonds of silver. He came on his knees humbly before the king, asking for mercy. The king saw that this was sincere and saw his hurts and his losses and saw that this was God's will and that the emperor could do no more [harm]. Then he wanted to complete this task and had the emperor raised and sat him next to himself and let him see his daughter. When he saw her he was more joyful than if he were holding the feet of God. He kissed her one hundred times, weeping. What more can I say? In two weeks, as I do not lie, since God willed it so, the king held Cyprus securely, so that it was inhabited by Franks.[157]

[2062–294][158]   When the king had Cyprus under his dominion,[159] taken in the

---

154   1.2005, *mult trova la terre chiere*; *chiere* and the noun *chierté*, translated as 'shortages' and later as 'scarce', can also mean 'expensive'. The meanings are clearly related and I have translated as seems appropriate in the context.

155   Cf. *Itinerarium*, 2.40.

156   Isaac surrendered on 31 May, Landon, p.49.

157   1.2061. Paris interprets: 'au pouvoir des Francs'; Stone has 'in the possession of the Franks'. I have kept to a more literal translation because Ambroise goes on to tell us of the expulsion of Greeks.

158   Cf. *Itinerarium*, 2.41.

159   For a succinct account of Richard's conquest of Cyprus, see Edbury, *Kingdom*, pp.1–12.

service of God, a good omen, and the castles and the fortresses from which he had expelled the Greeks, he found that the towers were stocked with treasures and riches, with pots and pans of silver, great vats, cups and bowls of gold, spurs, bridles and saddles, rich and precious stones, which were powerful against infirmity, cloths of scarlet and of silk (I have not seen any like them anywhere else I have been) and all other riches appropriate to the high and mighty; the king of England conquered all this in the service of God and to take His land. He sent the army to Limassol and beseeched his companions to make haste themselves and with his ship, to waste no time at all. He gave the emperor into the guard of King Guy, the warlike.[160] His daughter, who was most beautiful and a very young girl, he had sent to the queen to be taught and instructed.[161] So the army turned straight back to the fleet and made their preparations, loaded up and moved on as soon as they could.[162] They gathered on board the snacks and set sail when they saw their opportunity, taking with them the queens and the dromonds that were there. The king left in the land men who well knew the art of war; they sent food – barley, wheat, sheep and cattle – with which the land was well provided, and which would be of great value in Syria.[163]

Then came the news by sea, brought and told to the king, that the taking of the city of Acre had been undertaken and that the city would be taken before he could get there.[164] "This should not be", he said, "that anyone could take it without me." Then he did not want to wait but for the coming of his companions

---

[160] l.2085, *Guion le poigneür*. This kind of formula, applying a single epithet to a hero, as if summing him up in one word, is common in the Old French epic. In fact, Richard sent Isaac to Tripoli in the custody of his chamberlain, Ralph FitzGodfrey. When Ralph died on 8 June, Isaac was handed over to Garnier of Nablus, Master of the Hospital, who imprisoned him in the castle of Margat: Roger of Howden, *Gesta*, vol.2, pp.167, 172, 173; Landon, p.50. He was released in 1193 or 1194, and died c.1195 in the course of a revolt against the reigning Byzantine emperor, Alexius III, Rudt de Collenberg, 154–5.

[161] Isaac's daughter remained with the two queens, who arrived at Acre on 1 June 1191, Landon, p.50. She also travelled to Italy and France with them in 1192–3. For a short time in 1194 she was promised in marriage to Leopold, son of Leopold V, Duke of Austria. Between c.1200 and c.1202/3 she was the fourth wife of Raymond VI, Count of Toulouse. When he repudiated her, she married Thierry, an illegitimate son of Philip of Alsace, Count of Flanders (see above, p.34). In 1203 he unsuccessfully claimed the island of Cyprus by right of his wife. She may have spent the later part of her life in Constantinople, where, in 1207, her husband joined his cousin, the Latin emperor, Henry, Rudt de Collenberg, 155–75.

[162] Cf. *Itinerarium*, 2.42.

[163] Richard left Richard of Camville (one of his fleet commanders) and Robert of Turnham as governors of Cyprus, Roger of Howden, *Gesta*, vol.2, p.167.

[164] Saladin had captured Acre on 10 July 1187. In what appears to have been a desperate bid to reassert his authority as king, Guy of Lusignan had laid siege to it in August 1189, thirteen months after his release by Saladin. Guy had promised to withdraw from the conflict but, according to western sources, once free he was absolved from his oath. According to Ambroise, see below, p.69, Saladin had released him from his promise on the basis that he would rather fight the unwarlike Guy than some other, possibly more formidable opponent. However, Baha' al-Din (1145–1234), who was Saladin's Qadi of the Army, says that Guy broke his word, having been released from imprisonment at Tortosa in return for the cession of Ascalon and a promise that 'he should not draw sword against him ever again', *Baha' al-Din*, p.91.

to accompany him [. . .][165] beyond this I do not know how many came together. At Famagusta he put to sea[166] and had his galleys armed, going himself onto one of them which was marvellously large, strong and speedy. There is not under the heavens any port or harbour that would not be dismayed by such marvellous galleys with such bellicose men. Then did the galleys move forward, each one a chosen craft, the king in front, as was his custom, hale and hearty and light as a feather. As quickly as a running stag he travelled across the sea. Then he saw Margat,[167] on the coast of the land rightfully belonging to God. After Margat he saw Tortosa, which was also sited on the tumultuous sea. He quickly passed Tripoli, Infré[168] and Botron and then saw Gibelet, with the tower of its castle.

Before Sidon, near Beirut, the king noticed a ship full of Saladin's men.[169] It had been sent by Saphadin,[170] who had manned it with the best Turks he could find in pagandom. They could not land at Acre and had only turned back until they could more readily come about. But their intention was thwarted. The king had his galley push forward and advance to take them.[171] When he reached it he saw the ship, great, wide and tall, masted with three masts; it did not seem like a hastily-built vessel. The curs had covered it on the one side with a green felt and on the other side with a yellow felt. They saw the boat so decorated, as if it were the work of the fairy, and with such provisions that they could not be counted nor numbered. One who knew it, who was there at Beirut when the boat was loaded, which was to lose its load so ignominiously, recounts that he saw one hundred camels charged with good armaments, well-sharpened – bows, spears, bolts, cruel frame-mounted crossbows and hand-operated crossbows[172] – eight

---

[165] After 1.2113 there is a lacuna of at least one line; the rhyme is deficient and the syntax interrupted.

[166] Richard left Cyprus on 5 June, Landon, p.50.

[167] Margat was a Hospitaller castle, situated on the coast in a key area on the borders of Antioch and Tripoli. The Order had acquired it in 1186 from its lord, Bertrand le Mazoir, as part of an active expansion of its military role in the region. It fell to the Mamluks in May 1285, Riley-Smith, *Knights*, pp.68–9, 131, 137, 195, 464–5, and H. Kennedy, *Crusader Castles* (Cambridge, 1994), pp.163–79.

[168] Infré is the castle of Nephin, situated on the coast between Gibelet and Tripoli, Kennedy, pp.66–7.

[169] Richard's fleet met the Saracen ship on 7 June, Roger of Howden, *Gesta*, vol.2, pp.168–9.

[170] Saphadin was al-'Adil Saif al-Din. He joined Saladin in Egypt in about 1170 and soon became a vital member of his brother's forces. While Saladin campaigned further north, he was effectively ruler of Egypt. He was then transferred to Aleppo in 1183 at his own request. He was governor of the Jazira (Upper Mesopotamia) between 1186 and 1193. On Saladin's death he quickly asserted himself and remained the dominant figure in the complex and often riven political structure left by his brother until his own death on 31 August 1218. In August 1200, he made himself sultan of Egypt and Syria, maintaining his position by exploiting the rivalries among Saladin's sons and negotiating a series of truces with the Franks: Lyons and Jackson, pp.39, 77, 129, 165, 186–7, 208–9, 211, 295, 307, 323, 337–8; H.A.R. Gibb, 'The Aiyubids', in *HC*, vol.2, pp.693–9.

[171] 1.2148 added by a later hand.

[172] Contamine, p.186, refers to the *arbalète à tour* as 'the more powerful cross-bow on a stand'; Nicolle, *Arms and Armour*, p.584, refers to it as 'probably a frame-mounted cross-bow'. See also D. Nicolle, *Medieval Warfare Source Book*, vol.1, *Warfare in Western Christendom* (London, 1995), pp.130–1.

hundred chosen Turks, prompted by devils, large amounts of equipment and provisions beyond count or tally, flasks of Greek fire,[173] of which much has been said; there were also put into the ship two hundred dark and ugly snakes[174] (according to the written tale and the word of him who helped in putting them there) that they intended to let loose among the army to imperil the people of God.

The galley approached so near that it almost touched them. The oarsmen, who did not know who they were, greeted them and asked whence they were coming and from which lord they held their dominions. They had a French interpreter and replied that they were English and were going to Tyre.[175] Then a wind rose up from Arsuf[176] that took them away from the galley. A sailor had taken good note of the galley and of those aboard it for they willingly parted from them. He said to the king, "My lord, listen. May I be killed or hanged if this is not a Turkish vessel." The king said, "Are you sure of this?" "Yes, sir, certain. Send at once another galley after them, which will not greet their people; see what they do and to what faith they belong." The king gave his commands; another boat went towards them, but they did not greet them. The enemy having no business with them, began to shoot upon them with Damascus bows[177] and with crossbows. The king was nearby and the people were ready. They attacked

---

173 Greek fire was first used by the Byzantines against the Arabs during the siege of Constantinople in c.673. It may have been invented by a Syrian, Kallinikos of Heliopolis (Baalbek), who had fled to Constantinople, but it is just as likely that it was developed by the Byzantines in Constantinople and that Kallinikos was responsible for finding a way of firing it through siphons. Initially, such siphons were usually on the prow of ships, but Greek fire was soon used on land, projected by various means in earthenware pots. It seems to have consisted of petroleum mixed with solid materials such as pine resin and sulphur, and pitch. The petroleum could not be extinguished with water and the sulphur caused the mixture to stick to surfaces; the only way to deal with it was by soaking wood and leather with vinegar or urine, or with sand. Moreover, the solid materials increased the range and stability of the flame. Although the Byzantines attempted to keep its ingredients secret, it was clearly well known to the Arabs in the twelfth century who, after all, controlled the lands where petroleum was found. See J.R. Partington, *A History of Greek Fire and Gunpowder* (Cambridge, 1960), pp.1–41.

174 According to an eighth- or ninth-century Byzantine text on tactics, scorpions and snakes might be thrown at the enemy, Partington, p.18.

175 Paris, in his translation, p.358, corrects l.2188, following the *Itinerarium*, 2.42, which says that they first claimed to be French and then that they were Genoese. He thus interprets the passage as 'our sailors greeted them, not knowing who they were'. Given what follows, it does seem likely that it is the English ships which greet the foreign ship. It is not unusual in Old French, where the use of the subject pronoun is optional, for the subject to be ambiguous, the context being used to clarify.

176 I.e. an offshore wind.

177 This presumably means a shortbow, commonly used by mounted archers in the East, but rare in the West. This was a composite bow made up of three parts, a centre and two wings. Horn was glued to the inside and sinew to the outside. The characteristic wave-like shape marks them as quite different in manufacture from ordinary wooden bows. For their size they were extremely powerful, although it took great skill to use them effectively, particularly from the back of a horse or the deck of a ship. See J. Bradbury, *The Medieval Archer* (Woodbridge, 1985), pp.12–14, and G. Rausing, *The Bow: Some Notes on its Origin and Development*, Acta Archaeologica Lundensia 6 (Lund, 1967), especially pp.145–51. Illustrations in Nicolle, *Arms and Armour*, pp.xix; 289–90, 781; 322, 804; 324, 805; 513, 916.

them forcefully when they saw them shoot upon our people. The enemy defended themselves very well, shooting and drawing bow against us, arrows raining down like hailstones. On both sides there was general fighting. The ship sailed with but little wind and they often reached it, but did not dare to board, nor could they overcome them. The king swore at that time that he would hang the oarsmen if they relaxed their efforts or if the Turks escaped them. They launched themselves forward, like a storm, dived in [to the water], heads and bodies, passing under the ship, going to and fro [under the ship]. They fastened ropes to the rudder of the ship belonging to the vile and filthy race, in order to dominate and destroy them and to bring the ship low. They clambered up and moved forward enough to throw themselves on to the ship. The Turks, who were not slow off the mark, ran across to slaughter them. Those who were skilled in such matters boarded the boat in force. They cut off hands and feet, harming them in every way.[178] The oarsmen gave chase until they chased them into the harbour.[179] Fearing death greatly the Turks on their part rallied with force and new men, well-equipped with decorated armour, climbed up in companies according to a pre-arranged plan. They fought from both sides, struggling even on the boat itself. The Saracens made such efforts that they forced the oarsmen to retire to the galleys to begin the assault again. The king told them that they should ram the boat until it sank. They launched themselves forward, colliding with it so that it gave way in several places; because of these holes the vessel foundered. Then was the battle finished; the Saracens, defeated, leapt into the sea in their dozens. Everyone tried to kill them. There you would have seen great blows flying as the king struck fierce blows, killing and bringing death, and, I believe, taking thirty-five whom he kept alive, emirs and engineers, who were knowledgeable about many machines. The others, Turks, Persians and renegades, were drowned. If the ship had arrived at Acre then the city would never have been taken, such means of defence would have been brought.[180] This was the work of God, who cares for his people, and of the good and strong king of England, a keen fighter of battles.

The Saracens on the mountain had seen these deeds. They sent word to Saladin, for they were angered and saddened by it. When Saladin heard tell of it he pulled his beard three times, out of sorrow. Then he spoke as a man overcome: "God! Now have I lost Acre, and my people of whom I was sure. You have brought too much misfortune upon me."[181] The army of pagans lamented

---

178 There is the potential for some confusion as to who is doing what here. Stone has the Turks doing the cutting up, but I see no reason to assume a change of subject. See n.175 above.
179 The text is slightly confused in that the scribe originally wrote the lines in the wrong order (correction to edition, ll.2239, 2242, 2240, 2241) then added marginal marks to indicate his error; his correction is, however, still wrong. There may also be dittography in the manuscript here as ll.2245 and 2246 end in the same word, but this would not be the only case of *rime identique* in the text and it makes sense as it stands so we have not changed it.
180 Baha' al-Din, p.151, agrees that the ship was indeed intended to resupply Acre, although he says that the captain deliberately sank it when he realised that the position was hopeless.
181 Cf. *Itinerarium*, 2.1. The expression of Saladin's sorrow and his railing against his god here could well be a motif derived from the epic, where defeated Saracens often do this, sometimes defacing their idols. Cf. *Itinerarium*, 3.1.

so much, so we are told by those who saw it, that the Turks cut off their hair and ripped their clothes, because in the ship perished their friends and their lords.

Acre

[2295–2350] When the king had taken this strong ship and conquered the people by force, his desire turned to Acre and so he set off there most willingly, his galleys in order, having taken their revenge on the ship. As he and his fleet went on their voyage God sent them the Boreal wind.[182] Heartened, and with his men heartened, he spent the night before Tyre. In the morning the noble king, the Lion-Heart,[183] saw Scandelion and passed Casel Imbert. Then he saw Acre, clearly exposed, with the flower of the world encamped around it. He saw the slopes and the mountains, the valleys and the plains, covered with Turks and tents and men who had it in their hearts to harm Christianity, all there in very great numbers. He saw the tents of Saladin and those of his brother Saphadin, so near to our Christian army that the pagans pressed upon them. Elsewhere Quahadin,[184] the seneschal of all pagandom, guarded the sea and the land, making war on the Christians, making violent attacks on them and all too readily pursuing them. The king looked and studied, continually drawing up and re-drawing his plans. When he came near to the shore there you would have seen all the nobility of the army, behind the king of France, coming eagerly to meet him; many were they who came to greet him. He disembarked from the galley on to land; you would have heard the trumpets trumpeting to welcome Richard the peerless.[185] All the people together were joyful at his arrival. The Turks in Acre, however, knew great fear because of his arrival and because of the number of galleys he had brought with him, for they knew that this would be the end of their comings and going that had caused the loss of so many [of our] men. The two kings went together, always side by side. King Richard came to his tents and put much thought and consideration into how Acre could be conquered and how it could most easily be taken.

---

182 l.2302, *vent de boire*, translated by Paris as *vent du nord* and glossed as such in *T-L*, but the only examples given in the dictionary are this case and one case in Villehardouin, *La Conquête de Constantinople*, ed. J. Dufoumet (Paris, 1969), § 242, p.97 (see *T-L*, vol.1, 1030–1), where it could be interpreted as the name of a particular wind, the Boreal. Stone translates as 'wind out of the North'.

183 The first reference to Richard as 'lion-hearted' seems to have been by Gerald of Wales in his *Topographia Hibernica* in or before 1187, B.B. Broughton, *The Legends of King Richard I Coeur de Lion: A Study of Sources and Variations to the Year 1600* (The Hague, 1966), pp.116–17.

184 Al-Muzaffar Taqi al-Din 'Umar Shahanshah ibn Ayyub, lord of Hamah, and nephew of Saladin. His victory over Qilij Arslan, Sultan of Rum, in 1179, secured Saladin's lands in northern Syria from Seljuq expansion. He governed Egypt, 1183–6, and commanded the right wing of the Muslim army at the battle of Hattin. He died on 11 October 1191: Baha' al-Din, p.190; Lyons and Jackson, pp.138, 208, 246, 256.

185 Cf. *Itinerarium*, 3.2.

[2351–82]   Great was the joy, the night was clear. I do not believe that any mother's son ever saw or told of such joy as the army expressed over the king's presence. Bells and trumpets, horns, pipes and cornet all sounded. There you would have seen such joy unconfined, expressed among people of all degree. Fine songs and ballads were sung. Cup-bearers bore wine in beautiful vessels through the streets to serve the great men and the lowly, for it had brought great joy to the army that the king had taken Cyprus, whence came so much food, which sustained the whole army. All were full of hope. It was on a Saturday evening.[186] I think you would never have seen, anywhere you might go, such lights and candles so that it seemed to the Turks in the opposing army that the whole valley was ablaze. When they heard of the arrival of the king on whose account the celebrations were held they gave the impression of great excitement. In the morning the whole valley was filled with the cruel and evil people firing on us, crossing the ditch, harassing and pressing in on the army.[187]

[2383–2404]   Now let us leave this for the moment (for he who bears with me a while will hear me return to it when the material lends itself to this); let us move on from the two kings and their arrival, about which I have said enough to bring them to Acre. Listen and pay attention, for I am going to break off my thread and interrupt the matter, but it will be picked up again and re-attached later. For the kings came last to the siege, not first. So Ambroise would tell and instruct those who wish to learn how it came about that the city of Acre was besieged. He did not see any of this; I know only what I have read. Now you will hear what men took part and how bold was the undertaking.

[2405–14]   You have heard me recount and relate – and it is worthy of the re-telling – at the beginning of this account, if you remember, the great loss and damage that happened in Syria. This was in the time of King Guy, who suffered much persecution. But not everyone knows yet how he was betrayed, because of jealousy.

[2415–42]   There was in Outremer a king called Amalric,[188] brought up there. A son had been born to him, King Baldwin the leper,[189] who lived his time out until he was given to the worms. He had two sisters, young ladies, worthy, wise and beautiful. One was wife to a baron, Humphrey of Toron; the other had been taken to wife by William Longsword, lord of Jaffa on the sea, brother to the marquis of Montferrat. The lady bore to him a male heir, also called Baldwin, in truth. The child lived; the count died; this is how fortune turns. Guy of Lusignan greatly desired the countess and he married her. The child was king, but not for long. Thus does God govern these matters. When the child died the kingdom reverted to the lady, as was right and just, and Guy was crowned king, a deed which later caused many blows to fall.[190]

---

186   Richard landed at Acre on 8 June 1191, Landon, p.50.
187   Cf. *Itinerarium*, 3.3. The *Itinerarium* does not have the explanatory digression which follows.
188   Amalric, King of Jerusalem, 1163–74.
189   Baldwin IV, King of Jerusalem, 1174–85. He was Amalric's son by his first wife, Agnes of Courtenay.
190   The two sisters were Sibylla and Isabella. Sibylla was Baldwin IV's sister who, in 1176, married William Longsword, lord of Jaffa, and the eldest son of William III, Marquis of

[2443–83] There had long been an alliance between the disloyal Count Raymond and Saladin, of whom I tell, an alliance that was much talked of in Syria. This Raymond thought to have the kingdom, because of his wealth and because he was count of Tripoli.[191] But, thank God, it was not his. When King Guy, to whom God gave this honour, had himself crowned [he summoned to his coronation][192] all the barons. The count of Tripoli was sent for – but it is needless to ask if he mocked this summons, replying with rudeness. The messenger came back and the count went on his way, to moan to Saladin that he could no longer remain on his land because of Count Guy, who had succeeded to the kingdom and who hated him. He said to him, lying through his teeth, that Christendom suffered and that as he held him dear he should help him take revenge. My lords, the treason was planned at that meeting which led to the loss of the Holy Cross and the suffering of Christianity. The count was called again to the court with much pleading, but he did not want to come nor to hold anything from King Guy. The king sent for him a third time, saying he would give him all his rights and he came, bringing ill-fortune, for he had already decided to bring distress to the land. Through him came misfortune but later he was to die shamefully because of it, as the account tells us.

[2484–525] You have heard repeatedly and heard tell again, how when this Guy was newly made king he did not rest for two months before summoning his people throughout the land of Syria, calling on them to come to his help, for Saladin had already sent men to ride through the country; his army had entered the land, disturbing his people – there were one hundred chosen knights who had killed James of Mailly, to the great sorrow of the Templars.[193] From this

---

Montferrat, and thus the brother of Conrad, the saviour of Tyre. He died in June 1177, leaving a posthumous son, the future Baldwin V. Isabella was half-sister to Baldwin IV and Sibylla, since she was Amalric's daughter by his second wife, Maria Comnena. She married Humphrey IV of Toron in 1183. See below, pp.86, 88–9.

191 Raymond III, Count of Tripoli, c.1140–87. His alliance with Saladin was effected in late 1186. As Raymond saw it, the purpose was self-defence, for he felt threatened by King Guy and his supporters. Raymond had been accepted as *bailli* or procurator in the autumn of 1174, following the death of King Amalric the previous July. The new king, Baldwin IV, was only thirteen years old and had not reached his majority. Raymond was Baldwin's closest adult relative, since his mother, Hodierna, was a younger sister of Queen Melisende (d.1161), heiress to the throne on the death of her father, King Baldwin II, in 1131, and wife of King Fulk (1131–43). Raymond was again *bailli* in 1184/5 during the king's illness. He was certainly among the wealthiest of the barons since, apart from the county of Tripoli, he had also acquired the lordship of Galilee in c.1174, when he had married Eschiva of Bures, widow of Walter of Falconberg, Prince of Galilee. See Baldwin, *Raymond III*, pp.17–18, 25–6, 57–8, 79–94; R.C. Smail, 'The Predicaments of Guy of Lusignan', in *Outremer: Studies in the History of the Crusading Kingdom of Jerusalem presented to Joshua Prawer*, ed. B.Z. Kedar, H.E. Mayer and R.C. Smail (Jerusalem, 1982), pp.159–76; Edbury, 'Propaganda and Faction', 173–89; Hamilton, *Leper King*, pp.1–2, 40–1, 88–90, 93–106, 130–3, 136–7, 146–7, 151–8, 165–9, 194–6, 205–9, 211, 214–24, 227–31, 239, 241, 243.

192 After l.2453 the line is left blank in the manuscript; Paris's conjectural reading does help make sense of the passage.

193 On 1 May 1187, a combined force of Templars and Hospitallers was destroyed at the Springs of Cresson, north-east of Nazareth, by a large Muslim troop sent by al-Afdal, Saladin's son. Saladin had asked permission for this force to enter the kingdom through Raymond's lands,

defeat came the misfortunes that orphaned Christendom for ever. The count of
Tripoli, who was always in a sulk,[194] then sent word to King Guy, that he would
come to his aid. He came and made peace with him. However, the people later
bore witness that this was a false agreement and that the count betrayed him
suddenly in a great battle where they both were and where so many good men
died.[195] It is indeed possible that he did so and it is possible that he did not – but
most people testify with certainty that he betrayed him in the battle and if he did
this he should be struck down. Saladin had summoned his people from all of
his nine realms,[196] armed with bows, hauberks, helmets. They came in great
force; neither weak nor strong remained behind. There were many renowned
emirs, many noble men of renown, prepared to leave their lands to bring down
Christianity.

[2526–73]   King Guy and the Christians, accompanied by the Venetians, the
men of high rank and of lesser rank, had come together, one army at Sepphoria
and the other at the port of Tiberias. Our army advanced to a blessed end, going
down to Tiberias, for those who lost their lives there gave their souls to God. The
count of Tripoli led them, with treason in his heart. Our men were not suspicious
of him; what he said they did. He said and did and laboured so to the point that
their army pushed ours as far as the Sea of Galilee, until they were short of
water. The waters of the sea being sweet and good to drink, the traitor caused
them to drink.[197] But, when it came to the lowering of the lances, when he
should have pushed the hardest, then he fled, leaving them behind to lay down
their lives. I do not know who struck whom, who escaped and who perished. I
was not present at the battle. But this I tell you in truth, that God had planned all
this for He had seen such sin in the world and people so turned towards evil, that
few would come to Him without this. It was at Marescallia, near Tiberias, that

---

a request the count was in no position to refuse because of his previous alliance. Only
three Templars escaped from a Christian contingent of 140. Among the dead was a leading
Templar, James of Mailly.

194 l.2503, *ce qui toz jorz pendeit la lipe*, translated by HL as 'his lip hung always in a pout', interpreting this as a physical characteristic. They note that 'this peculiarity of Raymond's is not
mentioned by any other writer, and we incline to the opinion that it was inserted in the *Estoire*
merely for the rhyme', p.125, n.13. It may well be the case that the description is largely a
rhyme-maker but it seems to be concerned with his temperament rather than his appearance.

195 Raymond of Tripoli was one of the few to escape from the battle of Hattin, a circumstance
which led some contemporaries to accuse him of treachery. Baha' al-Din, p.74, saw it somewhat differently: 'The Count was a clever and shrewd leader of theirs. He saw that the signs of
defeat were already upon his co-religionists and no notion of aiding his fellows stopped him
thinking of himself, so he fled at the beginning of the engagement before it grew fierce and
made his way towards Tyre, pursued by a group of Muslims.'

196 Saladin's empire was divided among his large family, upon which he relied throughout his
lifetime. The four most important 'realms' were based at Damascus, Aleppo, Cairo, and in the
Jazira and upper Mesopotamia. They were held by his three sons, al-Afdal, az-Zahir and
al-Aziz, and by his brother, al-Adil. In addition, al-Adil's son, al-Mu'azzam, ruled Kerak and
the Transjordan on his father's behalf. Three smaller provinces at Hamah, Homs, and Baalbek
were held by the other family members. The ninth province was Yemen, generally subordinate
to Egypt, Gibb, 'The Aiyubids', p.693.

197 Calling him a traitor here is not implying that this act is treacherous but rather that this is the
nature of the man. In fact, the army never reached the water.

King Guy fought, killing so many Saracens. But all our men were killed, cut down and beheaded, and there was no deliverance. They came quickly down upon the king, so that he was brought to the ground, ill-treated and beaten. He had embraced the Holy Cross; without this it would have suffered much damage when taken. But God showed that He was taking care of it.

[2574–713]   When the battle was over as God had ordained, the king was taken and the Cross was taken and nearly all the people killed (for this reason many took the Cross, leaving behind their worldly goods to do so). Then Saladin took the whole land as it pleased him, except for only Tyre and Ascalon – and Jerusalem, which he took soon after[198] – thus does God give and take away His land. He laid siege to Ascalon, which he thought to take easily. However, they held out firmly and loyally against him. Many Saracens died there before it was taken. In the end they[199] were shown their king, bringing him before the walls, in the hope that they might have the town in exchange for him. The king made known to those within that they should hold firm and do nothing for him. But they could not hold out and had to make terms. They surrendered Ascalon in exchange for him and left with all their goods and chattels.[200] King Guy was then delivered under the following terms, as it is written, that he would go overseas and give up the kingdom. To fulfil his covenant he immediately took to the sea and arrived at the island of Tortosa. So then were his people very troubled. There, word came to him from Saladin, who was a cunning Saracen.[201] He knew that Guy was an unfortunate man and neither fierce nor ardent [in war]; he did not wish to exchange him for another who might be a threat to him, so he released him from his oath. The king then returned to Tripoli beside the sea. He found there the queen and the count who had hated him (so that it was said he had betrayed him) and who now feted the king, whatever he thought behind his back. It is not worth wasting words on this traitor, this evil count who brought sorrow to Christianity and orphaned many children. He would pay dearly for his treachery and evil deeds for he made a bad death (thanks be to God) and that suddenly. Nor is it worth telling of the siege of Tyre, which was bitter for Saladin, where William of the Chapel[202] did such fine and valiant deeds and where the brothers of Tiberias,[203] who defended the city, showed such loyalty to God and to His kingdom. Nor should I make a long tale about the marquis [of Montferrat] who,

---

198 Jerusalem was taken on 2 October 1187.

199 I.e. the Saracens showed the king to the Christian army that the Saracens might receive the town in exchange for him.

200 Ascalon surrendered on 4 September 1187.

201 1.2611, *saives* has the same meaning as *sage* and can be translated as either 'wise' or 'cunning'.

202 He may be the same person who served Philip II as a *bailli* in the royal domain between 1201 and 1217, first in Orléans and later at Caux. See Baldwin, *Government of Philip Augustus*, pp.130–4, 172, 222, 430, 432.

203 Hugh, William, Osto, and Ralph were the sons of Walter of Falconberg, Prince of Galilee, and Eschiva of Bures (and thus the stepsons of Raymond of Tripoli). The most famous of these was Ralph, who had become lord of Tiberias by March 1198 (d. c.1220). He became one of the great jurists of the early thirteenth century. See J. Riley-Smith, *The Feudal Nobility and the Kingdom of Jerusalem, 1174–1277* (London, 1973), pp.22–3, 114, 122–4, 152, 156–9.

having come after the land was taken, there began with good deeds, and was for a while in the service of God – but from this good beginning came a sad and sorry ending. This is rather about King Guy who came out of captivity, and I do not want to fail or go astray from my subject. We will stick to this matter. For he had come back to Tripoli to the delight of all, of high and low degree, but King Guy of Jerusalem was as poor and defenceless a creature as any man released from prison. He did not do any wrong in taking; he could do nothing but take, yet he had to give.[204] He knew that Acre was taken and the people sent out and expelled and this was the key to his land, and he did not know to whom to turn. He spoke of his troubles to God and God wrought good from it.[205] One morning as the bell was ringing there came to Guy the prince of Antioch[206] to ask him to grant that he should return to Antioch [with him] and stay there and remain there until he could find, gather together and assemble his people and until he knew where he could go to gain something back from the Turks. The king went with the prince to his province of Antioch, remaining there a short while. He shed many tears for the land he had held, lost during his reign. He returned to Tripoli, and prepared and equipped himself. With what he could borrow he prepared and summoned such men as he could muster, for he did not want to wait any longer. While he was waiting there, concerned with the assembling of his men, there came his brother, Geoffrey of Lusignan,[207] held to be the most valiant vassal in the land, well-trained for war. First he had arrived at Tyre but he did not find his intimates there, for at that time the marquis and those who were with him closed the port to him. Geoffrey then turned to Tripoli, where he found his brother, King Guy, who rejoiced with his mother's son.

When the king had gathered together his people, when they were prepared, he came along the shore to Tyre, with but few men and barons. He found the gate closed and everything barred against him. The marquis, from jealousy and in a mad undertaking, closed it against him. Some malevolent inspiration caused him to shut the king out of his own domain. The king saw that he could not enter and said that he would not put up with this. He set up his tent on the sand and sat there with a firm resolve.[208]

---

204 ll.2654–7 are difficult lines with much annominatio. Paris translates, 'Il ne prenait plus que son dû, car il n'avait rien au monde à prendre et il était obligé de depenser', and is followed by Stone, 'He took nothing that was not his due, nor had he aught in the world to take, but spend he must, perforce.'

205 Romans 8:28, 'all things work together for good . . .' The implication is not that everything that happens to those who trust God is good, but rather that God can bring good out of all things, which is the point Ambroise is making here.

206 Bohemond III of Antioch, 1163–1201, son of Raymond of Poitiers and Constance of Antioch.

207 Geoffrey of Lusignan was Guy's elder brother. By 1169 both his father, Hugh VIII, and his elder brother, Hugh, had died, and Geoffrey was the leading adult member of the family. In 1173–4 he was involved in the revolt of Henry II's sons against their father and in 1183 and 1188 he rebelled against Richard. It was not until the crusade that this family was reconciled with the king. He was granted the lordships of Jaffa and Ascalon in 1191.

208 Conrad refused entry to Geoffrey in the summer of 1188, and to Guy and Sibylla at the end of April 1189. He clearly saw Tyre as his own conquest and believed that Guy had forfeited his right to be king, Mayer, 'On the Beginnings of the Communal Movement', 443–57. Mayer describes Conrad's own ambition to be king as 'transparent', 453.

[2714–37]   The army assembled near Tyre; you must know how troubled the king was to see the city closed to him; this had been determined by the false marquis of Montferrat, son of the worthy, valiant Conrad who was taken in the great battle.[209] Conrad would certainly not have closed it, for he was a noble man and loyal, but his son was disloyal. The people of Tyre, who loved God and called upon Him, soon left the city and came to the king with his army. These were the noble Germans who held an important place at that time, and the brothers of Tiberias, the most loyal people in Syria. There were also the valiant men of Pisa,[210] who were in the service of God and left their homes and much of their property, bringing their wives and children before Acre, where the Saracens were.

[2738–81]   The king celebrated his brother's arrival, so goes the tale that does not falter, staying for four months before he turned to the strand before Tyre, a city rightly his. When he had brought his people, assembled from across his land, including the men who came with his brother who were an important element, he had only four hundred knights and only seven thousand infantrymen to bring to besiege Acre. For sure no [other] man would have dared do it. Without the protection of God what he considered would have needed a miracle, to go against men who were one hundred and four men to any four of his. But God willed that which came to pass, that the great army would come to Acre, which Saladin was making great efforts to fortify, for well he knew that the people came with the intention of taking it back. The king undertook this adventure for the Lord God in whom he put his trust. He led such forces as he had by a route that he knew between Acre and Tyre, along a difficult pass, the army passing along quickly. This is the Scandelion Pass.[211] That route did King Guy take. Saladin, however, did not know this, for all the gold in Russia would not have prevented them from being cut down had he known it. But God willed it otherwise, and this was the beginning of the deliverance of Christendom, a deliverance that developed greatly thereafter. So there was the army before Acre, in the name of the Holy Body, which we honour, which is worshipped by us, the Christians. There he was, on the Toron.[212]

209   Ambroise means William III of Montferrat, captured at Hattin and freed in May 1188.

210   The initial settlement of the Latin states would not have been possible without the help given by the maritime cities of Italy, especially Venice, Genoa and Pisa. In return they had received extensive juridical and commercial privileges within the cities thus captured. Conrad of Montferrat confirmed and extended the Pisan privileges in Tyre in 1187–8, as well as in Acre and Jaffa, even though both the latter were still in Muslim hands, *RRH*, nos.665, 667–8, 674–5, pp.177–8, 180. The Pisan fleet made a vital contribution to the siege of Acre both by blockading the city and facilitating the supply of crusaders on the Toron by means of the River Belus. For the relationship of the Pisans to the other powers in the East, see Jacoby, 'Conrad, Marquis of Montferrat', pp.191–203.

211   A castle had been built here, Iskandaruna, in c.1117, about 9 miles (15 kilometres) south of Tyre, D. Pringle, *Secular Buildings in the Crusader Kingdom of Jerusalem: An Archaeological Gazetteer* (Cambridge, 1997), no.106, p.51 (map 3).

212   The siege of Acre began on 28 August 1189. Guy's army took up position on Tell al-Musallabin or Tell al-Fukhkhar, a hill (toron) about 118 feet (36 metres) high, and about ¾ mile (1,200 metres) to the east of the city. See Prawer, *Histoire du Royaume Latin*, vol.2, pp.43–4 and map, p.47. According to the *Itinerarium*, 1.26, p.62, 'That mountain rises loftily

[2782–809]   On the Toron, before Acre, were the Christians who had come from Tyre and it is without doubt true that they climbed there in the dark of night. They did not dare remain in the woods so they positioned themselves on the heights. In the morning when the Turks came out of the city and saw them then was Acre in total uproar, the knights disturbed. They sent word to Saladin that a handful of Christians had come upon them in madness and that he should come at once to cut off their heads, for they themselves did not dare mount a defence. When Saladin heard of this, at the siege of Beaufort,[213] which he was attacking with strength, he was filled with joy. He made a general summons to his vassals, and had the order issued throughout his land that everyone who was under his lordship should come to Syria, where great gains were to be had. Many, many people came – may they be cursed by God, who made the skies and the earth and the whole world. Had they made mincemeat of our people there would not have been a pinch for each of them.

[2810–79]   On the third day after our people arrived,[214] positioned on the heights of Toron, keeping armed all night because of the Saracens who were attacking them, there came Saladin's people – Turks, Bedouins and Persians – come to take and occupy the whole land. On the third day of the week came Saladin himself, truly expecting to have the heads of our people. So it is not to be wondered at if those who thought to lose their heads were frantic with watching and labouring, for the Turks attacked the Toron, where they were, both night and day, attacking them so often that they could scarcely eat. Geoffrey of Lusignan endured great labour in the defence of the army; he was already [held to be] noble and daring; from then on he was highly praised.[215] There they were in peril from the Monday until the Friday.[216]

Now you will hear how God looks upon those whom He takes into His care. Nothing can harm him who wishes to devote himself to His service. Just as they were in such fear, pleading with God to send them some sort of help, the king and all his company looked far out to sea. There coming straight towards them was a whole fleet of snacks, full of men coming to them. It was James of Avesnes in Flanders.[217] I think that Alexander, Hector and Achilles were not

---

on the eastern side of the city, and from it a clear view spreads out all around before the roving eye, far and wide across the plains' (Nicholson, p.71).

213   The castle of Beaufort (Qal'at ash-Shaqif Arnun) is approximately 20 miles (32 kilometres) north-east of Tyre, above the Litani River. According to Baha' al-Din, pp.90–1, 95–6, 108, Saladin had intended to attack it in late April, 1189, but was deceived by the delaying tactics of its lord, Reynald of Sidon, who offered to surrender it. By the time that Saladin realised that he had no intention of doing this, 'he and his army had lost three months in which nothing had been achieved'. Saladin eventually gained the castle on 22 April 1190, in return for Reynald's release: Kennedy, pp.41–5; Pringle, *Secular Buildings*, no.44, p.31 (map 4).

214   Baha' al-Din, p.97, says that Saladin first heard of the Frankish move on 27 August, and that he blockaded them on the Toron two days later.

215   According to the *Itinerarium*, 1.25, Geoffrey was driven not only by the common cause, but also 'by a personal desire to avenge his brother's injuries' (Nicholson, p.69).

216   Saladin's main attack started on Friday 14 September, and was renewed on Monday 18 September, lasting until Friday 22 September, Baha' al-Din, pp.98–9.

217   The family came from Avesnes-sur-Helpe in Hainaut, and held lands from both Baldwin V, Count of Hainaut, and Philip of Alsace, Count of Flanders. James of Avesnes was a far from

more worthy than he, nor better knights.[218] This James had sold, mortgaged and spent all his land and his inheritance and in a most wise deed, had given every-thing, heart, body and soul, to the service of the King who rose from death to life. He had with him a good fourteen thousand men of renown. There came too the Danish fleet and many a noble castellan from the Marches and from Cornwall, so says one who knows well.[219] They had with them good horses, brown and piebald, strong and fleet. When they were about to land, then you might have seen the Turks going out of their minds with rage; they ran down to the water and even hurled themselves into the sea, drawing thick and fast against them, as did those inside Acre. But those on the Toron came down, so they were holding their own on two sides, pressing them hard, but the Turks, who drew upon them all the time, repulsed them; yet the Christians advanced. At the sight of the army Saladin said, "Now is our prey the greater."

[2880–907]   When the High King, whom men adore, had increased the army in such little time, so that they were reassured who would have lasted but little time [. . .][220] But all together they rejoiced and came down from the heights of Toron, put up their tents and made an encampment and besieged the city of Acre,[221] so that they were oppressed and besieged on both sides. The Pisans did good service, camping out on the strand and defending the shore from the cruel Saracens so that when ships came to the shore they could neither take them nor damage them. One Friday, in the morning, there was a fierce battle near Montmusard,[222] with dead on both sides. Those from the town sallied out and took back, by force, a large caravan of camels, loaded with food, and took to

docile vassal; among other incidents, in 1175/6 he was involved in a serious revolt against Philip of Alsace, seemingly having a particular resentment against what he saw as the count's 'low-born' administrators. See E. Warlop, *The Flemish Nobility before 1300*, trans. J.B. Ross and H. Vandermoere, vol.1 (Kortrijk, 1975), pp.275, 325–6, and J. Falmagne, *Baudouin V, Comte de Hainaut 1150–1195* (Montreal, 1966), pp.119–22. He took the Cross in November 1187, and in company with Hellin Wavrin, Seneschal of Flanders, travelled overland to Messina, from where they sailed to Acre, arriving on 1 September 1189, H. van Werweke, 'La contribution de la Flandre et du Hainaut à la troisième croisade', *Le Moyen Age* 78 (1972), 58, 67–8, 85.

218 The *Itinerarium*, 2.5, makes a similar comparison between these epic heroes and Richard earlier in the text.

219 A combined Danish-Frisian fleet of at least fifty vessels left in the spring of 1189, reaching Sandwich in Kent on 15 May. From there they sailed first to Portugal and then to Messina, where they met an army of Flemings, including James of Avesnes, which had travelled over-land. They left Messina together at about the beginning of August and arrived at Acre on 10 September. P. Riant, *Expéditions et pèlerinages des Scandinaves en Terre Sainte au temps des croisades* (Paris, 1865), pp.275–86.

220 After l.2883 there is a lacuna of at least two lines.

221 l.2886. Paris interprets *logierent* as 'erect *feuillées*' or 'bowers', which Stone translates as 'lodges'. Whatever form this encampment took it is evident later in the siege that it consisted not only of tents but also of some sort of temporary structures.

222 Montmusard was to the north of the city. In the thirteenth century it developed as an important suburb. See D. Jacoby, 'Montmusard, Suburb of Crusader Acre: The First Stage of its Devel-opment', in *Outremer: Studies in the History of the Crusading Kingdom of Jerusalem presented to Joshua Prawer*, ed. B.Z. Kedar, H.E. Mayer and R.C. Smail (Jerusalem, 1982), pp.205–17.

Saladin the booty that they had taken. They came and went from Acre because they had the power to do so.

[2908–41]   Know that the people who were within Acre were neither ploughmen nor carters. It became known that among those who did not believe in God there were none better than these at guarding and defending a town or taking a castle by force. Less than two weeks passed before the count of Brienne came and with him Andrew his brother;[223] they were from a good mother and a good father. The seneschal of Flanders[224] came and with him more than twenty barons, and the landgrave of Germany,[225] with good Spanish horses. There came also the bishop of Beauvais, who was neither old nor infirm, and his brother Count Robert, an agile and skilled knight.[226] There came also the count of Bar;[227] there was no more courtly a man than he from here to the Far. Many another noble and wise man came to the army at that time. But the strange thing was that the more who came the less the Saracens feared them, attacking them and coming right up to their tents. Those of the town sallied out and the others continually increased in number so that the land was overrun by them and our army felt hemmed in. Yet they always held firm to the High King for whom they came.

[2942–51]   No priest nor cleric nor deacon could tell or relate the great hardships and martyrdom that the Christians suffered when the war took place before Acre, until the arrival of the kings of England and of France, to bring down the walls of Acre, with the good people who moved in the love and faith of God.

[2952–3071]   I recall one particular day, a Friday in the month of September, when a dreadful, fearful thing happened to our people.[228] The Saracens attacked them; they did not fail to do so on any day. The Christians armed and in good order, divided into pre-planned companies. The Hospitallers were on the strand, where there were many Saracens; the Templars were in the front rank; this was always how it began. The count of Brienne and his household, who were in the middle of the army, the landgrave and those of Germany, who were a large company, positioned themselves close to the place of idolatry, as is just.[229] King Guy and the Pisans and the other men of great undertakings, were to the right,

---

223 Everard II, Count of Brienne, 1161–92, and Andrew of Brienne, lord of Ramerupt, died 4 October 1189.

224 Hellin of Wavrin, Seneschal of Flanders, 1176–89/90. His family were hereditary seneschals, responsible for provisioning the court, the administration of justice, and some military operations. He may perhaps be seen as a representative of Philip of Alsace, Count of Flanders, who did not arrive until April 1191. See below, p.94. Hellin died sometime during the siege of Acre. Two brothers, Robert and Roger, also participated; the latter was Bishop of Cambrai, who also died during the crusade. Van Werweke, 69–70, 72, 84.

225 Ludwig III, Landgrave of Thuringia, 1172–90. He died on 16 October during his return from the crusade.

226 Robert II, Count of Dreux, 1184–1218, was the cousin of King Philip II and brother of Philip of Dreux, Bishop of Beauvais. On him, see Baldwin, *Government of Philip Augustus*, pp.198, 216.

227 Henry I, Count of Bar-le-Duc, 1170–91, who was killed during the siege of Acre.

228 4 October 1189, Baha al-Din, pp.101–5. Ambroise, in his care to be very precise, to the naming of the day, is reminding us that he is an eyewitness, even if the facts are wrong.

229 l.2970. The word used in French is *mahomerie* which normally refers to a mosque. This is the mosque of 'Ain-Baqar (today 'Ain-Sitt) situated about quarter of a mile (about 400 metres)

on the hill of Toron, to keep watch on the Turks and their activities. The Saracens came forward with great tumult. There you might have seen many men in good order. The Templars and the Hospitallers charged and came to grips with the first ranks, defeating them and putting them to flight. They fled and were pursued. Our men followed and the Saracens fell back, but there were so many of them that none of the Christians knew which way to turn. The Turks could not turn back. They were already near to the mountain when the devil accomplished a deed through which many of our people died and perished and suffered. This was because of a horse that escaped from a German who went after it and asked his companions to follow, but they could not catch it. The horse fled towards the town and more than one hundred thousand Saracens thought that our people fled and that they gave way. They turned upon them and attacked and that day those whose duty was to attend to the army had enough to do to defend themselves, for they were twenty-four to every one of ours, making every effort to kill us and those who had club and bludgeon left some of our men dead in the field. There Andrew of Brienne was killed, may his soul never suffer, for never did another such knight die, nor any who came to the rescue of so many. There was the marquis of Montferrat so surrounded by the infidel that had not King Guy rescued him he would have perished that day. At that time was also killed the Grand Master of the Templars,[230] who spoke well, having been well-schooled. When, at the time of the attack, the bold and the cowardly had said to him, "Come away my lord, come away" – and he might have gone had he wished – he said this, "May it not please God that I should ever be in another place, nor the Templars ever be reproached because I have been caught in flight." He did not go, so he died, for so many Turks came against him. There were a good five thousand lesser men whose bodies were left there naked. When those of the town knew that our men had been defeated they mounted on Arab horses and came out; they met with our men so furiously that it would have gone ill with them had they not defended themselves. But they made their stand; there were acts of knighthood seen and blows against the men of the hated race. There the king himself, King Guy, of whom we have told you, did well, as did Geoffrey of Lusignan, who suffered much trouble, and the noble James of Avesnes, who did such heroic deeds in the land, and others who succeeded in holing their enemies up in Acre.

   This is how the day went, how Fortune arranged matters.[231] Then the Saracens rejoiced (may God curse them as I curse them!) for now they harassed

---

east of the city between the Accursed Tower and the Franks' position on the Toron. See Prawer, *Histoire du Royaume Latin*, vol.2, pp.43, 49, 56, and map, p.47. The belief that Muslims worshipped idols is reflected in much of the literature of the period, see N. Daniel, *Heroes and Saracens: An Interpretation of the Chansons de geste* (Edinburgh, 1983).

230 Gerard of Ridefort, Master of the Temple, 1185–9. He died on 4 October. For his career, see Bulst-Thiele, pp.106–22.

231 The image of Fortune, rising and falling like a wheel, was a commonplace in the twelfth and thirteenth centuries, most often applied to political or military affairs. It derives from *The Consolation of Philosophy* by the Roman consul, Boethius (480–524), who presented Fortune as an arbitrary goddess, Boethius, *Consolation of Philosophy*, trans. V.E. Watts (Harmondsworth, 1969), p.55.

and pressed upon the Christians more than ever before. When the valiant warriors saw this then the barons said, "My lords, we achieve nothing here. Let us think of some means of succour against the Devil's mob who come upon us every day and at night steal our horses." This is how they decided to tackle the matter: they would dig a great ditch, deep and wide, into which they would put many shields, light shields and long shields and sharp, broken pieces of timber.[232] In this way there was a barrier between the two areas. The Saracens [still] attacked, allowing them no respite.

[3072–93] Listen and hear about the great trouble that came because of the slaughter about which I have told you, that brought sorrow to the French. The day after these deeds and this defeat of the best, the elite, of our army, there were lesser men dead, who had come there for God, and Saladin had all the bodies of the dead taken and returned to us by throwing them into the river of Acre.[233] You could see the dreadful butchery, for the bodies came down river until they reached the army. Such was the stench coming from there as the pile of dead bodies mounted, that the whole host retired from there, until they were buried. Even after their burial for a long time men continued to flee from the stink.

[3094–3137] The Christians dug the trench in which they were entrenched; they held firm in the ditch when the Saracens came, harassing them as they did by day and night, in cold and in heat. Over the trench was the battle between the people of God and the scum of the earth. Our men sought to dig it; they sought to destroy it. There you might have seen in a short space of time[234] more than five hundred thousand arrows handed from the diggers to those who were defending them. There you might have seen bold and courageous men on both sides. There you might have seen men keel over, fall and be disembowelled, great blows exchanged until night parted them.

For the whole of the time that the army besieged Acre, until All Saints' Day[235] – I know this and have often heard it said – people did not cease to come who could hold their place well. The count of Ferrers[236] came, who put more than a hundred Turks on their biers, for he was such a good archer that there was no better from here to Duens;[237] also Guy of Dampierre,[238] who held many fine

---

[232] l.3068, *de pons parties*, is obscure. Paris translates as 'morceaux de ponts (?)'. As these items are clearly intended for defence I have interpreted *pons* as a form of *poinz* meaning 'something sharp'. Stone has 'pieces of timber', and HL have 'timber-ends'.

[233] River Belus (Nahr Na 'aman).

[234] l.3104. See also note to l.1923. Paris writes in his glossary, 'on a évidemment dans ces deux passages le même mot qui doit être *en dessaietes* – mais le sens n'est pas clair: sans doute "en un moment, aussitôt" ' (obviously in these two passages we have the same word, the meaning of which is unclear, no doubt 'at once'). Paris also includes a row of dots in his edition, suggesting a lacuna; Stone assumes a lacuna. I see no need to assume such a lacuna; Ambroise is clearly again enjoying annominatio, punning *dessaietes* and *saietes*, 'arrows'.

[235] 1 November 1189.

[236] William Ferrers, Earl of Derby, died during the siege in the autumn of 1190.

[237] There is no evident equivalent in modern France, although some guesses could be made based upon the rhyme with *bons*. Given its obscurity it could be a clue to the author's place of origin, but there is no other evidence by which it could be identified. See the introduction, above, pp.1–3, for a discussion of the author's background.

[238] Guy of Dampierre, vassal of Henry II, Count of Champagne.

stone castles, and the bishop of Verona,[239] considered to be a most worthy man. They all came at this time and became martyrs and confessors of the faith, for the most comfortable [now] lived a life of sacrifice, in fear and watching, labouring night and day, for they had no respite and could take none until they had completed the trench over which there was such loss.

[3138–69] The day before All Hallows Eve[240] something happened to the army that was so astonishing – at once astonishing and dreadful – something really serious, both evil and harsh. While the Christians were enduring the hardships that lasted too long, those on the hill of Toron looked out over the headland of Caiphas. There they saw a great fleet of armed galleys, coming from Babylon, which had long been giving support to Acre.[241] The fleet came in good order and the news rapidly spread through the army that it was advancing. No-one in the army knew anything about it, but some believed that it was the fleet of Pisans, or Genoese, or Venetians, that it came from Marseilles or Sicily, coming to attack the town. While they were speculating the galleys approached, coming nearer and nearer until they had moored in Acre. During this approach they took one of our snacks which carried both food and men and took it by force into the town where the men were killed and the provisions taken.

[3170–85] Now listen to what the Turks did to God and how they worked evil against Him. On the day of that celebrated feast, when many a tear was shed, on the day of the feast of all the saints gathered in heaven, on that very day the hated people in defiance hanged from the walls of Acre the bodies of the Christians whom they had taken from the snack, whom they had killed. They were indeed participants, as the preachers tell us, in the great and everlasting joy that is for ever and is without end, the joy of those whose feast was celebrated that very day.

[3186–227] The fleet of which I told you guarded so well the port and the way by which God's people would come, that everyone avoided the port and that no help came to those who were committed to God [there]. Winter was approaching without them being able to make any provision. The ditch was finished, but later filled in again by force. That winter they made siege towers, giant catapults and mangonels, cats, sows and cercleia, labouring ceaselessly.[242]

---

239 Adelardo Cattaneo, Bishop of Verona, 1188–1214, cardinal, 1214–28.

240 30 October 1189.

241 Looking south beyond Haifa at the approaching Egyptian fleet.

242 The catapults and mangonels were trebuchets, that is a rotating beam set upon a wooden frame. They were worked either by traction, that is ropes pulled by a team of men, or by counterweights. The latter form was more efficient and accurate, and was much more widely used from the later twelfth century, although it is not clear if its principles were known at the time of the Third Crusade. The siege engines were tall wooden castles with armoured roofs, which could be rolled forward on wheels, and were known by a variety of names, including cat, sow and weasel. See Contamine, pp.102–5; DeVries, pp.127–42; J. France, *Western Warfare in the Age of Crusades 1000–1300* (London, 1999), pp.117–27; and R. Rogers, *Latin Siege Warfare in the Twelfth Century* (Oxford, 1992), pp.251–73. *Cercleies* were protective wooden covers used by besiegers, which varied in size and solidity. The presence of crossbowmen inside such a constructions suggests that they could be quite substantial, while Kings Philip and Richard each had their own more elaborate versions. See below, pp.99, 100. According to the *Itinerarium*, 3.8, p.220, they were made from a rigid wooden framework covered with hide.

The enemy fortified the town with more than thirty thousand workers, building gates and towers, new, strong barbicans, reinforcing the town on all sides in so many ways that they challenged the whole world. Saladin, who had no intention of renouncing [his claim], had put in place so many mangonels and catapults, machines of all sorts, so many skilled engineers, from his lands and elsewhere, such stores of vessels of Greek fire, such instruments of war of all sorts, that it was known from then on as a truth that never was there castle nor city that had so many arms, such defence, such provision of food, at such expense. Thus passed that winter, until the coming of the soft season of spring. Then in the season of Lent, as Ambroise says and understands, the Germans built the very first windmill ever constructed in Syria,[243] before the eyes of the race accursed by God; they looked on in astonishment and were most terrified by it.

[3228–3361]   There came some news to the army, at first good and encouraging news, though later the tidings were heavy and worrying, distressing and bitter. This was news of the good emperor of the Germans who came in strength to the Holy Sepulchre to seek the grace of God, but, and herein lay the sorrow, in the crossing of a river, at a ford, which he had not first tested, he died, in accordance with the will of God. Inside Acre there was such rejoicing when they heard the news that there was dancing and playing of drums, and they worked at nothing else. They climbed into the turrets to tell the news to our people for Saladin knew of it and had told them of it.[244] They shouted in a loud voice, many times, from the turrets, and had it shouted by the renegades: "Your emperor has drowned." Then there was in the army such sadness, such despair and such distress, that they were not concerned for their well-being, except for the approaching arrivals, the hope and the promise, spread throughout the army, of the coming of the great men, the kings whose subjects we are, those of France and of England, who after this arrived in the land. The army took heart from this.

So the news came a little after Easter[245] that the fleet was coming from Tyre. There it was, come into the harbour. Then you might have been reminded of the scrabbling of ants coming out of an anthill in all directions – in that same way did the Turks come out of the town, more than ten thousand armed men, both they and their galleys covered with drapes of silk and of baize, of buckram and of samite. So they came against the fleet that the north wind brought along the shore,[246] breaking through the waters. The other fleet awaited them, having come out to fight them in strength. They responded in the same way, coming up

---

243 The windmill was developed in England in the course of the twelfth century. Ambroise is probably correct in asserting that it was unknown in Syria at this time. See E.J. Kealey, *Harvesting the Air: Windmill Pioneers in Twelfth-Century England* (Berkeley and Los Angeles, 1987), pp.38–43, and R. Holt, *The Mills of Medieval England* (Oxford, 1988), pp.20–1, 171–5.

244 According to Baha' al-Din, p.106, Saladin heard about Barbarossa's march in October 1189, information which 'greatly troubled him'. He received news of the emperor's death quite soon after the event in a letter from Basil, Bishop of Ani, the Armenian Katholikos (head of the Armenian Church), pp.114–16.

245 Easter 1190 was 25 March.

246 *vent de boire*. See above, n.182.

boldly. There was the marquis who held Tyre, who came against the Turkish fleet with fifty armed vessels, well-appointed and equipped. There you might have seen so many banners, so many valiant and skilled men, bold, quick and alert! Then the Turks sent a volley from their crossbows. This was the beginning of the battle of the fleets.[247] There was no cowardice there. The men of Genoa and those of Pisa were attacked in their little boats with crossbows and long shields; they came down upon our people but our people drew and shot back until the Turkish fleet retired, and by sheer brute force they led one galley into the harbour. Then you would have heard great celebration. Then you would have seen women coming, knives in their hands, taking the Turks by the hair, pulling them to their great pain, then cutting off their heads, bearing them to the ground. In both fleets a racket ensued, each in turn pushed back, often coming together, throwing Greek fire against each other, beginning fires, extinguishing them; they fought each where they met, striking each other, making great efforts and drawing towards the harbour. Never was such a battle seen. No man ever witnessed such a fight – but our people had the worst of it, those of the army of God who were at the siege, for through sorrow over the galley that our people had taken, the Turks were so moved that each day their numbers increased and there was such a great press at the trench while the battle was waged at sea, for there was no Christian in the army, high or low, young or old, however bold or renowned, however confident or daring, who did not suffer from onslaught of the Turks.[248] For they came down like flies, competing to be the first to do their share to fill and destroy the trench. There you might have seen them covering the plains from here to the foot of the mountain, the land as covered and overrun with the Turks coming down upon it, as stubble covering a field, for they did not cease to come. They hurled themselves into the trench so densely that they knocked each other down. There was there in great number and full of evil intent a hideous black people, against God and against nature, with red head-dresses on their heads – never did God make more ugly creatures.[249] There were great numbers of them, all turned towards evil. The waves of people in red caps were like cherry trees covered with ripe fruit. There were so many other Turks that they were estimated at five hundred thousand. Yet more Turks from within the town came out with their banners, thus attacking on two fronts. That

---

247 This battle cannot be dated precisely, but it probably took place at about the end of March 1190. The *Itinerarium*, 1.34, p.82, explains more clearly that the captured Muslim galley was drawn up on the beach, where its occupants were killed by the women in the crusader host.

248 *Raosche*, 1.3332, is not attested elsewhere. It is glossed by Paris as 'presse? attaque? importunité?'. There may be a semantic or etymological link to *r(o)uche* meaning 'to swarm', or the Middle English *russche* used to mean attack. The Middle English comes from *reûsser*.

249 Black Africans had formed a large proportion of the army of the Fatimid Caliphate. In August 1169, Saladin put down a revolt of these soldiers in Cairo shortly after he had become vizier on 29 March. The Qadi, al-Fadil, Saladin's administrator, whose letters are a valuable source for Saladin's life, confirms Ambroise's observation, for al-Adil, Saladin's brother, brought troops to Acre in November 1189, and they included Negroes. Lyons and Jackson, pp.22, 32, 34–6, 307. Cf. *Itinerarium*, 1.38. 'There were also peoples deformed through adapting to the southern sun: they are called Mauros or Mauritanians from the Greek word *Mauron*, which means black' (Nicholson, p.92).

day and on many days the Christians feared their assaults that went on for so
long.

[3362–427]   Those with the red caps had a standard to which they all rallied;
this was the standard of Mohammed, whose image was there in chief and in
whose name they came to fight, to defeat Christianity.[250] These scum protected
themselves with great projectiles that they carried. This was the great land battle
the army fought. At sea the battle lasted all day. However, thanks to God our
fleet had the victory, for day by day there were established divisions of barons
within the army, on the galleys, good men and well-armed, who fought a hard
battle. By sheer force they drove the galleys beyond the chain [which closed the
harbour], so that the Christian fleet did so much damage to the Turks of the
town, who then numbered forty thousand, for they had no help from the sea.
Then they had so little food that they suffered greatly from the shortage.

On a Thursday, Ascension Day,[251] the day of holy procession, when God went
up to the highest Heaven, as is recounted in the gospel, our people wanted to go
up into Acre in the name of the True Body which is venerated. We had
siege-towers, well covered to protect against the Greek fire of the infidels.[252]
There were three large towers that three great men of the army had had made –
the Landgrave and King Guy and the marquis with his Genoese. These three
were in their towers on the day of the attack. The people of God attacked and
those within leapt to the walls. Vigorous was the attack and the defence. Men
with few provisions defended themselves vigorously and made us pay dearly for
their suffering. Never was there a people as good in defence as these devil's
minions! Some were beating drums, others rushing to the point of need. The
Turks from the mountains for their part rushed up in great number to the ditches
and leapt into them, as soon as our people attacked, so that the army had to
attack and defend itself at the same time. The assault lasted a long time, until the
night began to fall, but in the evening they had to stop for they would never be
able to repel the defenders. The Turks threw Greek fire on the three towers
which caught fire so that they had to get out of them and watch them burn into
cinders.

[3428–51]   The curs inside Acre had long been short of food. As time passed
and their food went down, they were in such a state of misery and disarray that
they ate all their beasts, hooves and innards, necks and heads. They expelled the

---

[250] Such depiction would be impossible, being against the tenets of Islam, but is very like the
imputed heraldry given to literary characters; thus in the *chanson de geste*, *Fierabras*, the
eponymous hero, a Saracen who will be converted, carries a shield bearing the image of
Apollo, ed. Kreober and Servois (Paris, 1860), 1.667. L.A. Mayer, *Saracenic Heraldry*
(Oxford, 1933), considers eastern devices to be truly heraldic since they were both hereditary
and concerned with armoury and the shield; for a succinct summary of the influence of the
crusades on heraldry, see A. Ailes, *The Origins of the Royal Arms of England* (Reading,
1982), pp.35–7. On the heraldic standard, see Gayre, *Heraldic Standards*, pp.51–85.

[251] Ascension Day 1190 was 3 May.

[252] Baha' al-Din, pp.110–11, says these towers were covered with hides soaked in vinegar to
prevent them catching fire. However, a young metal-worker from Damascus devised a
naptha-based mixture which, when hurled in pots against the towers, caused them to burst into
flames immediately. See also above, p.63.

Christians, the old prisoners, the decrepit, keeping the young, those who appeared lively, to load the catapults. They experienced such suffering, misfortune, pain and fatigue that it cannot be told. [They suffered these things] until after the Feast of Saint John, when the devils sent to them three ships which were wrecked and broken up there, some of the Turks perishing, but the besieged gathered up the food. When they had the food that rabble of curs took heart. They would often sally out, hemming in our men.

[3452–89] A terrible day came to the army, to those who were devoted to God. It was on the Feast of St James.[253] But the devil, who takes no rest, overtly carried out a deed, by which the army was [much] decreased. But I lie – it was not the devil who did it, but God who permitted it, wishing to gather more martyrs to himself and welcome them on high, in heaven. The finest soldiery that was then or ever will be, who were poor and needy, went out from the camp of God, with no defence. They were in dire straits, for there was little comfort in the army. There were ten thousand of them, all armed. They left the camp all together in their companies and ranks and headed straight for the tents of the Turks, which was their aim. When the Turks saw them they did not dare wait for them. They arrived and pillaged all the best that they could find; when the Turks saw them burdened it was a gift for them. They launched themselves on them so that they left there more than seven thousand [dead], for they received no help apart from some knights who hurried over, but there was not a large number of them, so the foot-soldiers died quickly. There Thorel of Mesnil[254] was killed, but only after making great efforts. He was that day greatly mourned. This was one of many evil things that happened to the army.

[3490–3515] That hated race made many attacks and assaults against the army of God. God permitted his people to endure many hard and terrible deeds. God tested His people in the same way that He tested the saints, as we know, putting them through many trials, like gold tested in the furnace.[255] Those who had offered themselves to God had suffered much there.

As they were suffering, so there came the barons of France, around August, at the best time for the journey before winter. The lord of Champagne, Count Henry came, with a great company, and also Count Theobald of Blois, though he did not survive more than three months. Count Stephen also came and died without protection;[256] the noble count of Clermont,[257] who was useful to God

---

253 Feast of St James, 25 July.

254 Evidently a Norman knight, but difficult to identify beyond that. The name Thorel or Thoril does not appear in the Pipe Rolls, while Mesnil is a common place name in Normandy.

255 Isaiah 48:10; Zechariah 13:9; 1 Corinthians 3:13.

256 These were all members of the powerful house of Champagne, which included William aux Blanches Mains, Archbishop of Reims, who had crowned Philip II on 1 November 1179. Henry II, of Champagne, Count of Troyes, 1181–97, married Isabella, the widow of Conrad of Montferrat in 1192 and thereafter ruled the Kingdom of Jerusalem until his death in 1197. See below, pp.152–4. Theobald V, Count of Blois, 1152–91, and Stephen, Count of Sancerre, 1152–91, were his uncles, younger brothers of Henry's father, Henry the Liberal. This family, once rivals of the Capetians, was closely associated with the monarchy by this time. On its importance, see Baldwin, *Government of Philip Augustus*, pp.8–9.

257 Ralph, Count of Clermont, c.1162–91.

and the world, also came and the count of Châlons,[258] a great man, tall and mighty, with many other valiant men, so many that they could not be counted or numbered.

[3516–55]   Before Acre, while the noble and honoured people stayed there for their salvation and for the pure love of God, many things happened that are written down to be remembered and many miracles performed, coming from the power of God. There were in the army many catapults, with many men coming and going in front of them and behind them and many things happened there that were held to be miracles at the time of their happening. There were within the city, as the history tells us in truth, many catapults that hurled [missiles] so well that you never saw the like. There was one which was so powerful that it did us much harm, continually breaking into pieces our catapults and cerceleia, for it hurled the stones so that they flew as if they had wings; it took two men to load the sling, according to the written word, and when the sling let fly, when the stone fell, it had to be looked for a full foot into the ground. This very catapult struck a man in the back and if the man had been a tree, or a column of marble, he would have been cut in half, but the good man did not feel it, for God did not permit it. One should have faith in such a Lord, for such a miracle inspires faith.

[3556–77]   Time passed and many an incident happened. Around April and May, at the turn of the month a very strange thing happened to a man-at-arms who was in the army. He was in the trench surrounding the walls, equipped with a coif and a hauberk and a very finely decorated pourpoint.[259] One of the enemies of the Creator was holding a windlass-spanned crossbow;[260] through a loop-hole he fired a bolt at the man-at-arms which struck him on the chest, below his head, piercing the pourpoint and the coif, passing through the hauberk; by the grace of God the man-at-arms had at his neck a letter that protected him for the names of God were written on it. Those who were there saw that when the bolt touched it it bounced back out. This is how God acts; those whom He protects have nothing to fear.

[3578–619]   Time passed and many an incident happened. It happened that one day a knight, his back to the ditch, was doing what everyone has to do. While he was bent over to relieve himself at his need a Turk came at great speed from the vanguard while the knight was not paying much attention. It was a base and villainous deed to seek to harm a knight when he was about such business. The attacker was some distance from the vanguard, his lance couched ready to kill the knight, when the men of the army shouted to him, "Run, sir, run, run!" He got up with difficulty, but he did manage to get to his feet, his business finished, when his enemy came as fast as his horse could bring him, expecting to lay him out on the ground. But, by the grace of God, he did not succeed, for the knight

258   William II, Count of Châlons-sur-Marne, 1168–1203.

259   According to C. Blair, *European Armour, circa 1066 to circa 1700* (London, 1958), 'it seems likely that the *pourpoint* was a general term covering any type of quilted defence', p.33.

260   l.3565, *arbalast a tur*, clearly not here a heavy frame-mounted device, see above, n.172. Nicolle, *Medieval Warfare*, p.130, assumes that sometimes this would be a heavy bow which could be rested on a wall or parapet. Illustrations in Nicolle, *Arms and Armour*, pp.211–12, 742; 286, 778.

leapt aside. [As he did so] he grabbed two stones in his hands (listen what a just avenger God is) and as the Turk turned to have another go, the knight aimed and as he planned, as the other was coming towards him, threw one of the stones he was holding, striking the temple below the headgear; at once he fell dead. The knight took the horse, leading him away by the reins. He who told me about this saw the knight mount and ride to his tent, where he had the horse well-kept.

[3620–55]   Time passed and many an incident happened. One thing that happened is worth the telling. Many people were attacking the walls, and many time they wearied. There were some who did not cease gathering stones that they carried,[261] the lords bearing them on their war-horses and their packhorses. There were many women who carried them there; it pleased them to do so. Among them there was one who rejoiced greatly [in the work]. One Saracen defender saw that the woman intended to discharge the burden. As she went to move forward he drew upon her and shot and the woman fell to the ground, mortally wounded. At once all the people came rushing up around the woman who was writhing in the agony of death. Her husband came up but she beseeched the people there, the good men and women, that for the sake of God and of their souls they should take her body to the ditch where she had taken [stones] for she did not wish that her physical body should be put to any other use. Her body was being borne there when God bore her soul away. The story tells us that such a woman should be remembered by all.

[3656–94]   Time passed and many an incident happened. Another thing happened in the army, indeed more than twenty more, but I cannot recall them all, nor keep a count of them. One day the Turks made a sortie out of Acre when they saw that our people had gone foraging, as is customary for men in times of war. Among them came an emir, a great man of high degree, by the name of Bellegemin; he was valiant, bold and of great renown. The barons who were protecting the army went against the Saracens. That day the army was very disturbed for so many had gone out to forage that they had difficulty in protecting the army itself. The army was in great trouble, both in front and behind, for the assault was very fierce. But our people managed to repulse them [. . .][262] except only for the emir, who remained purposefully, because he wished to burn our engines; this is what he had undertaken to do if he could get to them. He had in his hand a phial full of Greek fire, for he yearned to burn our engines. A knight went to strike him, wishing to pay him according to his deserts. He stretched him on the ground, emptying the contents of the phial on his private parts, so that his genitals were burned by the Greek fire which his men wished to put out but could not.

[3695–764]   Time passed and many an incident happened. It happened several times that the disloyal and false people who were holding Acre against God climbed onto the walls bringing the crosses which had been left in the churches. There they beat them, defiling them, spitting on them, doing all out of spite of

---

261 Stone adds '[to fill the trenches]', i.e. the ditches around Acre. That this is the purpose of the stone gathering, rather than as ammunition for the stone-throwing machines, is evident by the request the woman makes.

262 Lacuna, probably of one line, after l.3678, leaving an incomplete rhyme.

the Christian faith, for they hated nothing in the world so much. One day a Turk was up on the walls, bearing a wooden cross which he had found – he had already beaten and dishonoured it and did not want to stop there – he wanted to pee on it.[263] Just then a courtly crossbowman drew his bow and placed a bolt in its position; he wished to pay back the Turk who was defiling the cross. He aimed and struck the Saracen in his guts, piercing his body and his bowels. He fell down dead, his legs in the air. This enraged the people. Thus did God will that the cross, which he had defiled, should be avenged.

Time passed and many an incident happened. One day something happened that Ambroise relates in his writings. A Turk came out to shoot upon us and did not want to turn his back and a Welshman under provocation went out to fire in return. The Welshman was called Marcaduc and was not the son of a king nor of a duke. The Turk was called Grair; he was bold, strong, and seemed powerful. They immediately shot upon one another, the Welshman aiming at the Turk, the Turk at the Welshman. The Turk began to ask the Welshman where he came from, which country. The Welshman replied, "I am from Wales. It is mad of you to come down [here]." The Turk said, "You know how to shoot well. Would you like to play a game? I will shoot and you will stand still, not turning in any direction, and if I miss, I will stand still for you, not turning in any direction."[264] He said this so insistently and beseeched him so that the Welshman agreed. He drew against the Welshman and missed, for he misfired. The Welshman said, "Now I will shoot. Stand still for me." [But] he said, "No, let me draw again and I will let you draw twice." "Certainly", said the Welshman. But while he (the Turk) was searching for a bolt in his quiver the Welshman, who was near to him and who did not like these terms, fired, and shot him in the heart. Then he said, "You did not keep your agreement with me, nor shall I with you, in the name of Saint Denis."[265]

[3765–812]   The Pisans who were with the army and those who knew the sea well made a tower on galleys with two ladders that were large and wide. They covered all their vessels with leather and did the same with the tower. They attacked the Tower of Flies, bombarding it and shooting at it heavily.[266] Those in

263 Cf. Albert of Aachen, describing the Frankish siege of Sidon in 1108, where he refers to spitting and urinating on the Cross as characteristics of apostates and Saracens, *Historia Ierosolimitana*, ed. and trans. S.B. Edgington (Oxford, 2007), pp. 762–3. This cliché retained sufficient resonance to be used as one of the central accusations against the Templars in 1307, when they were accused of apostasy by the government of Philip the Fair of France, *Le Dossier de l'Affaire des Templiers*, ed. and trans. G. Lizerand, Les Classiques de l'Histoire de France au Moyen Age (2nd ed., Paris 1964), pp.18–19, and H. Finke, *Papsttum und Untergang des Templeordens*, vol.2 (Münster, 1907), pp.144–5. Cf *Itinerarium* 1.9, pp.22–3, on Muslim treatment of the Cross after the fall of Jerusalem on 2 October 1187.

264 1.3746. The text is corrupt here, but the parallel structure allows reconstruction.

265 The names look fictitious, but J.G. Edwards suggests that Marcaduc 'represents the ordinary Welsh name Maredudd and is therefore probably genuine'. See J.G. Edwards, 'The *Itinerarium Regis Ricardi* and the *Estoire de la Guerre Sainte*', in *Historical Essays in Honour of James Tait*, ed. J.G. Edwards, V. H. Galbraith and E.F. Jacob (Manchester, 1933), p.67. The reference to Saint Denis, unlikely from the mouth of a Welshman, is probably for the sake of the rhyme.

266 The Tower of Flies stood at the end of the east wall or breakwater of Acre's outer harbour,

the tower defended themselves well, selling themselves dearly. From the town, in galleys, came more than two thousand Saracens, armed, ready for battle, to support the rest of their pack. They shot and bombarded [the army], casting huge and heavy stones against them and sharp darts, breaking lances and shields. When those in the tower attacked the defenders did not fail. There you might have seen our people shoot well, shooting on the walls with many good shots; you might have seen there bolts raining down and the Turks having to take cover. There you might have seen daring, valiant men attack in relays. The ladders were set against the tower, put there by force and at great cost, for they hurled down great beams of wood on the heads of the Christians erecting them. They were not cowards. They kept coming back until they set fire to the tower, and those in it had to come out as they hurled flaming Greek fire and there was a great battle. But [meanwhile] out at sea there was a great massacre of the Saracens. The tower was speedily burnt down, as were the ladders and the vessels that carried them. Then the Turks were encouraged; when they saw our setback they yelled out loud, the hated race hurling insults against the army who served God.

[3813–90]   But the army of the Lord was discouraged by this, though encouraged by the great baronage that had arrived in Syria. First the Archbishop of Besançon[267] had built before Acre a battering ram to break down and destroy the walls. Built at great cost, it was strengthened with iron and well-protected above and below, before and behind, that no-one need fear the catapults for the archbishop wished that the best materials that should be used were used. Count Henry made another, well-covered and of great price, and the lords and counts made many other machines that I cannot number. But of the first, the one the archbishop made, the one we told you of, we will tell you what happened when it came before the walls.[268] The barons of the army planned the assault, conferring about the machines they had had made. Everyone brought to the walls his own engine. The archbishop had brought forward the ram of which I have told you. It was of such rich workmanship that it should not justly nor reasonably fear any creature. It was made as if [under] a house. A great ship's mast, straight and without knots, was in the middle, tipped with iron at both ends. Underneath the ram were those who would strike against the walls, having nothing to fear there. The Turks who loved them not at all, brought many dry bushes and threw Greek fire on it, and with their catapults, hurled down whole columns of heavy limestone and of marble, and threw down beams and trees, throwing over in vats and buckets, in jars and pitchers, sulphur and tar, tallow and pitch, then straight afterwards larger beams and on the top the people of Mohammed threw Greek fire, until the sappers fled from the ram, abandoning it. The Turks, still throwing

oriented south-west north-east. The attack on it took place on 25 September, Baha' al-Din, pp.127–8. See D. Jacoby, 'Crusader Acre in the Thirteenth Century: Urban Layout and Topography', *Studia Medievali*, 3rd series, 10 (1979), 9–10, and fig.4. For present remains and bibliography, see Pringle, *Secular Buildings*, pp.16–17.

267   Thierry of Montfaucon, Archbishop of Besançon, 1180–91.

268   The attack with the ram probably took place on 15 October. Baha' al-Din, pp.130–1, describes Muslim success at its destruction as 'one of Islam's best days'.

things down on the ram, came out of their cover on the walls. There you would have seen the archers drawing and fine shooting from the crossbows. There you would have seen great attacks and men injured on both sides. There you would have seen good vassals running up to defend and recover the ram and to remove what was thrown. [There you would have seen] Turks hurled down and Turks brought low, brought down from the defences, with their beautiful painted armour. They hurled and threw so much that they broke the ram, shattering the iron-work and other fittings and at once they threw down fire in order to burn all of our men. But the ram was bought at a price, for eighty of their best fighters and an emir died there, but they did much damage to us. Then the assault stopped, when they could not extinguish the ram and no-one could move. Then the Saracens mocked [us].

[3891–902]   Just after the end of August the Queen of Jerusalem died among the army; this was sad for a woman of her age, as she was considered to be a worthy lady. May God have mercy on her soul. There also died there two young girls, King Guy's daughters; fair were they.[269] Because of the death of his children who were the rightful heirs of the land, the king later lost his kingdom, that kingdom for which he had received many blows on his helmet.

[3903–54]   In October, after September, near the Kalends of November,[270] there came from Alexandria another fleet in full pride and glory, a fleet of fifteen vessels, according to the estimate of those of the army who afterwards counted them. The vessels had come to help the Turks who were in Acre, who had endured much hardship and little sleep. At the back of the fleet there came three great dromonds. The galleys and the galleymen who manned them watched this approach. When the Turks on the vessels saw them they were afraid and worried for there was not one so expert nor so valiant that he did not wish he was elsewhere. The evening was so dark and the wind so stormy that the Christian fleet did not dare [go out to] meet the pagan fleet. The storm did so much damage that everyone had enough to do with himself. So, as the Saracens sailed at full sail – having difficulties as they approached the chain – to rescue the pagan people, something shameful happened to them, for they could not prevent the vessels coming onto the rocks for God brought their ships onto the rocks in the port of Acre and the whole army hurled rocks on them; the ships were broken up and most of the people drowned. Then the Christians came down to the shore, yelling and killing the curs and took a large galley that had been forced aground, where they took a lot of food and killed the whole pack of curs. But the other vessels crossed the chain[271] [into the harbour] where the Turks were waiting faithfully for them. They reached out lances and spears towards them and lit so many lanterns that the Saracens were able to come to shore.

---

269 Sibylla died before 21 October 1190. Her daughters were Alice and Maria. As Guy was king by virtue of his marriage to Sibylla, her death undermined his credibility.
270 29 September 1190, *Itinerarium*, 1.60, p.114.
271 The chain could be drawn across the entrance to the inner or western harbour to keep out intruders. It also gave its name to the port area and to the various institutions associated with it, such as the court which decided maritime cases. See Jacoby, 'Crusader Acre', 13–17 and fig.4.

Using the Saracens who arrived they could re-arrange [their forces], ejecting those who were weak and keeping those who could be of use.

[3955–4032] At the great Feast of Saint Martin,[272] with already a shortage of food, the army was instructed to assemble the next day in the name of Mary's Son, to go into the mountains and fight the Turks. There a blessing and general absolution were given. The Archbishop of Canterbury,[273] with other bishops absolved them. Then they made plans and set apart the barons and the men who would protect the army. There in the morning, the army rose up; one could count many divisions of the finest Christian people ever seen by any people on earth; they were close together in ranks as if they were chained together. The front of the army was wide and broad and could well endure a severe attack; the rearguard had so many good knights in it that you would have difficulty seeing to the end of it unless from a great height; you could not throw a plum on it without hitting someone clad in burnished armour. So they headed straight for the Doc.[274] You could not have cooked a cock before Saladin would have known that he would have a battle if he chose to wait for the Christians. However, that night he made his army strike camp and leave the mountain where he was with his company. There came a spy to our army who told them that the hated race had left the mountain and were fleeing with abandon. It would have taken little for our people to follow, but it would have been madness for they could not have caught up. When they did not get a battle they turned towards Caiphas where there was said to be food, of which there was a shortage among the besiegers. So there they were at Recordane[275] when the Turks fell upon them, faster than a goshawk after a duck. They saw the Turks turn round and ride against the army, drawing against them, yelling and shouting and beating drums. That night the pilgrims pitched camp and waited for dawn the next morning. They were still [set] to turn and go straight to Caiphas but the food that they had been expecting was not there. The Turks had carried it off in the morning when they arose. When they looked around them they saw all the Turks in the world, or so it seemed to them, surrounding them, besieging their army. The land was so

272 This is probably the Feast of St Martin of Tours, 11 November. Baha' al-Din, p.135, gives Monday 12 November.
273 Baldwin was Archbishop of Canterbury from December 1184 until his death on 19 or 20 November 1190. He had taken the Cross on 11 February 1188, followed by a preaching tour of Wales, accompanied by Gerald of Wales, who wrote an account of these events. He left for the East in March 1190, in the company of Hubert Walter, Bishop of Salisbury (see below, p.92), and Ranulf Glanville, former justiciar of England under Henry II. They sailed to Marseilles and then directly to the Holy Land, arriving on 29 September. For his role in the crusade and its preparation, see Tyerman, pp.60, 61, 63–4, 66–9, 77, 84, 153–4, 156–8, and *DNB*, vol.3, pp.442–5. In letters of 25 January 1191, King Richard made it clear that he wished to see William, Archbishop of Monreale, elected in Baldwin's place, *Epistolae Cantuarienses*, pp.329–30.
274 There was a bridge over the River Belus at Doc (Tell Da'uk), Pringle, *Secular Buildings*, no.85, p.47.
275 Recordane (Tell Kurdana) was at the head of the River Belus, where the Hospitallers had operated a mill, *RRH*, no.1062, p.277; Pringle, *Secular Buildings*, no.133, pp.62–4 (map 3). The clash there took place on 13 November.

covered with them, beyond and behind, to the right and the left, that the army wished itself elsewhere. Never were such people seen. So, there was our army, immediately armed and ready for battle. But the Saracen curs did not dare fight against them and engage with such good men. The pilgrims turned to return to the place whence they had come, but they would have many attacks before they got back to their tents.

[4033–60]   At the head of the river that runs towards Acre, at its source, there was a great massacre of knights on both sides, before the armies separated. During that day's march the king of England's people and the Templars made up the rearguard and had to be on their guard, for God never created storm of snow or hail, nor shower in the dews of May, which fell more heavily than the storm of bolts that fell on the army before our men left there. They left in good order and returned towards Acre. Our army turned to the left of the river, theirs to the right; they went down either side of the river, harrying each other all the time. There came some who gave help to our men, for the foot-soldiers who came at the back of our rearguard, to protect it, advanced with their faces turned towards the Turks. They would endure much before the army would be safely in camp.

[4061–84]   In the morning, at dawn, our people set out to return to the siege of Acre. But the Turks were lying in wait for them at the bridge of Doc,[276] where they had to pass. They intended to destroy the bridge when the army came up and attacked them, but they were so thick on the bridge that the pilgrims did not know how to cross, they saw them so piled up there. Then Geoffrey of Lusignan rode up on a fresh horse with five good knights. They rode up with him, striking the Turks with such force that more than thirty fell and drowned in the river, in the sight of [the rest of] the enemy. They struck them and fought them until they crossed by force of arms and they returned to the siege, to the great joy of the army.

[4085–4138]   Towards the end of the sailing season few, whether wise or foolish, could make the journey; the time to voyage passed, yet still a few came.[277] As the people came and the numbers increased, the amount of food decreased. As time went by, so did the food go. Not a penny's worth arrived, except when a ship came. The rich were provided for, but the poor went without, complaining each day of the shortage from which they suffered. Some, suffering from such misery, wished to depart. The food when it did arrive, was detained at Tyre, kept there by the marquis and prevented from reaching the army.[278] Listen to this, about the disloyal marquis. He tried and endeavoured, by men of influence and by goods, to gain the kingdom. He so contrived, with great endeavour

---

[276] The battle at this bridge was on 15 November 1190.

[277] As Ambroise implies, it was possible (although risky) to sail across the Mediterranean out of season, but generally long-distance shipping was suspended between the beginning of November and the beginning of March, a situation which did not change until the late thirteenth century. See Pryor, *Geography, Technology, and War*, pp.87–8.

[278] Shipping usually approached Acre from the north, following the coast past Tyre, as can be seen by the route taken by Richard's fleet, see above, p.65. Conrad was therefore in a position to intercept it and would thus bring pressure to bear upon leading members of the Jerusalem nobility at the siege of Acre to agree to his proposed marriage to Isabella. See P.W. Edbury, *John of Ibelin and the Kingdom of Jerusalem* (Woodbridge, 1997), p.21.

and much machination, that a sister of the queen, who was dead by this time, wife of Humphrey of Toron, left this Humphrey and the marquis took her for his own, under an agreement that his forces would without fail join the army. He married her, in his house, against God and against all that is right. The archbishop of Canterbury railed against it, but the bishop of Beauvais married her to him.[279] It was very wrong of him to think of it for the marquis had married two lovely ladies, both young: one was in Constantinople, a beautiful woman, noble and fine, the other was in her own land, and now he had a third! For this reason the good archbishop and others, clerics and bishops, spoke against this marriage, excommunicating and daring to say that he had committed a triple adultery and that God was not present in such a marriage and at such a union.[280]

[4139–72] When the marquis had married the woman whom he had desired for a long time, he celebrated his wedding and held a feast; then he had three wives living, one in her land, one with the army, and a third in reserve. Evil and harm should come from such a marriage, and did, that very day. For when those who had come to the wedding had drunk a lot, they went to the field for recreation, as to a tourney. Saracens who were on the lookout for them, came against them and chased them. The men of the army leapt up at the shouts but the Saracens did not fail in what they attempted; they took away with them the butler of Senlis[281] and no-one knew what they did with him, whether he died or what became of him. Twenty were either taken or killed. They were well-paid for the marriage. Those in the army were dismayed. The wise feared more. Others still believed that the marquis told them the truth and that, as he had promised, he would send the food to the army. But he left at once, with his people and his bride and, though he had plenty, sent no provisions to the host, where it was in such short supply, except to those who had disgracefully made the marriage.

[4173–96] My lords, I can tell you nothing, of lies or truth, about the death of Alexander, whose death aroused such strong feelings, nor of the messenger of Balan, nor of the adventures of Tristan, nor of Paris and Helen who suffered so much for love, nor of the deeds of Arthur of Britain and his bold company, nor of Charlemagne and of Pepin, of Agoland and of Guiteclin, of the old epic tales of which the jongleurs make so much.[282] I can say nothing to support or

---

279 Conrad married Isabella on 24 November 1190, her half-sister, Sibylla, having died some time before 21 October, leaving Isabella as heiress to the Kingdom of Jerusalem. However, she had been betrothed to Humphrey IV of Toron since 1180 and married to him since 1183, WT, 22.5, p.1012; 22.29(28), pp.1053–4. Therefore, as Riley-Smith, *Feudal Monarchy*, p.116, points out, in canon law the marriage was both bigamous (since both parties were already married) and incestuous (since Sibylla had been married to William Longsword, Conrad's brother).

280 One of Conrad's wives was certainly still alive. He had been briefly married to Theodora Angela in 1187, and she was alive in 1195–8. See C.M. Brand, *Byzantium Confronts the West, 1180–1204* (Cambridge, Mass., 1968), pp.80, 84, 119.

281 Guy III of Senlis, butler of France. The family traditionally held the butlership in the French royal household and Guy had succeeded his brother in 1186, Baldwin, *Government of Philip Augustus*, p.32. He was captured on 24 November.

282 These are all well known in vernacular tales. A number of versions of the romance of Tristan and Yseut circulated, as did several different accounts of the Alexander story, both in the vernacular and in Latin. Classical tales were well known through the *romans d'antiquité*.

contradict them, nor can I find anyone to tell me if they are true or false – but of these which so many saw, and those who suffered themselves at Acre, of the sufferings they endured, the great heat and the dreadful cold, the injuries and the illnesses – I can tell you of this as truth, and it should be listened to.

[4197–222]   It was in winter, during Advent, when the wind and rain come, that the army there at Acre was filled with much complaining and suffering and moaning, among the lesser and middle-ranking people, because of the shortages which increased from day to day.[283] They complained unceasingly. They were fine, it is true, until the Feast of Nativity when there began the distress, famine and misery. As Christmas passed the shortages increased daily. A measure of corn of a weight that a man could carry under his arm would cost one hundred besants in the army.[284] This was cold comfort. Corn and flour were expensive. A hen was worth twelve sous and an egg could be sold for six deniers. Times were so dreadfully hard. Those who lacked would wage a war over bread. They cursed the marquis, who brought them to this sorry pass.

[4223–36]   My lords, I am not joking, in order that meat should not be totally lacking in the army of God, they skinned the fine horses and eagerly ate them. There was a huge crowd at the skinning [of the beasts] and it was still a costly meat. The misery lasted the whole winter and the flesh was sold for ten sous the piece. A dead horse was easily sold for more than a live one would have been. The flesh tasted good to them and they ate even the guts. Then they cursed the marquis who had brought them to this sorry pass.

[4237–46]   Times were bad and the need was great among the great folk and the lowly. Nevertheless, there were those who had the means who could get meat, but even if they wished to share it they did not dare hand it over as so many people came for it. For this reason everyone held on to what he had and cursed the marquis who had brought them to this sorry pass.

[4247–58]   Had it not been for the herbs they planted and the seed they sowed, from which everyone made his mess of pottage, the loss would never have been made up. There you would have seen fine men-at-arms, worthy and valiant men, brought up in riches, reduced by famine and distress that when they saw the grass growing they went to eat and graze it. Then they cursed the marquis who had brought them to this sorry pass.

[4259–308]   Then a disease ran through the army – wait while I tell you about it – it was the result of rains that poured down such as have never been before, so that the whole army was half-drowned. Everyone coughed and sounded hoarse; their legs and faces swelled up. On one day there were a thousand [men on] biers; they had such swelling in their faces that the teeth fell from their mouths.

Charlemagne, Pepin, Agoland, Balan and Guiteclin figured in *chansons de geste*, which were often taken to be true and even integrated into chronicle accounts, although only the first two mentioned were historical. On truth asssertions in vernacular historiography, see Damian-Grint, pp.157–60.

283   1.4202, *chierté*, translated here as 'shortages', also means 'expense, price', and *cher* translated in this paragraph as 'expensive' can also mean 'scarce'. The meanings are clearly linked and we have translated according to the context.

284   The measure is a *muis*, glossed in the *A-ND* as a 'bushel'.

There were those who would not be cured because they had no food.[285] Then they cursed the marquis who had brought them to this sorry pass.

My lords, necessity leads to many actions that are to be blamed and criticised. In the army were many men from many lands ashamed to beg for bread; they would steal bread from the bakers, coming right up and grabbing it.[286] One day a prisoner was taken for such a misdeed. He who had captured him took him away to his lodging place and tied him as best he could, with his hands behind his back, there being no support [to which he could be tied]. Those who were there, busy loading the oven, went up and down, paying no attention to the prisoner. God, who looks after his own, broke the bonds tying his hands. He was sitting on a heap of bread, so while the men-at-arms were idly looking elsewhere, he ate the bread and, hidden in the shadow of a seat, put one under his arm. Now he was not in such misery and when he saw the chance and opportunity he fled at speed, back to the army, where he related what had happened to his companion men-at-arms, who were dying from lack of bread. They ate and shared the bread that he brought them, which strengthened them for a while but not for long. So the hunger spread and the misery increased and they cursed the marquis who had brought them to this sorry pass.

[4309–26]   Those who remained with the army endured much hardship. No-one can tell you how their sufferings grew, how they endured and suffered during the siege from the time of their arrival. Hear how great is the loss and waste, how great the harm and shame, when a man, whom God made in his own image,[287] denies God because of his misery. In the army the shortage of all kinds of food was so great that many of our people went to the Turks and turned renegade. They denied that God did or could deign to be born of woman; they denied the Cross and baptism – everything.

[4327–54]   There were in the army two companions, poor men-at-arms who had nothing, except for one angevin coin. They were indeed in a bad way, for they had no more food nor belongings except for their armour and their clothes. They debated over the coin, how and in what way they could buy food for that day. They consulted their furs to know what they should do.[288] After much consideration they bought thirteen beans, among them one that had burst; to exchange it one of them had to travel across more than seven arpents of land.[289] The man who had to do this had great difficulty in exchanging it. He came back and they ate, nearly maddened with hunger. When the beans were consumed

---

285   This was probably scurvy and/or trench mouth (gingivitis).
286   1.4278 is obscure. Paris declines to translate it, giving the footnote 'le vers 4284 m'est obscur'. Stone has 'until they were well-nigh stuffed therewith' with a note that 'this clause is obscure in the original'. The verse reads *Si que tot pres les enpreinouent*, and we have assumed some confusion between the verbs *em/enprendre*, to proceed, begin or undertake, and *emprisoner*.
287   Genesis 1:26.
288   This probably refers to an attempt to trust to luck, similar to tossing a coin or drawing straws. Paris translates as 'ils consultaient le sort par les poils de leur fourrure'. Stone has 'they drew lots with hairs of their pelisses to determine what they should do', and HL have, 'They sought for omens that might guide/ Their conduct in their cloaks of hide'.
289   1.4346. An arpent is about one acre.

then was their misery doubled. Then they cursed the marquis who had brought them to this sorry pass.

[4355–74]   There was one thing for sale among the army, called 'carob-beans',[290] which were sweet to eat and could easily be acquired for one penny. The way was well trodden. Many people were sustained by those carobs and by little nuts. However, these who lay ill and who drank strong wine which was easily available, were so filled with wine and ate nothing, except what was least good to them, that they died in threes and fours; those who exercised got better and lived, but they had nothing to eat. They cursed the marquis who had brought them to this sorry pass.

[4375–90]   There was much suffering in the army before food was supplied to it; there is no rage like that born of starvation, of lack of bread, for hunger constantly presses on those who have the most need to eat – for they eagerly ate meat during Lent, and so sinned. This was at the beginning of Lent when everyone should fast – but they did penance when God had caused the time to pass. When they ate meat thus and thought of the sin they were committing, then they cursed the marquis who had brought them to this sorry pass.

[4391–4406]   The people of the army who sought God and waited upon His will for them suffered great shortages which lasted all winter, from Christmas until the end of Lent; I know this for a fact. I am not guessing, so that where God called the army to the siege people would scarcely look on one another. Charity became so cold that avarice increased and as avarice grew those with most became most avaricious, and avarice, without generosity, led to people dying in misery, cursing the marquis who had brought them to this sorry pass.

[4407–56]   This affliction lasted for so long that there was much talk about it. But God wished his people to learn that they should love and fear Him. The bishop of Salisbury[291] called his brothers and sons in God to him and preached to them and set them a good example. The bishop of Verona, who was worthy of his mitre, was not lazy in preaching, but spoke words that reached the heart. The bishop of Fano in Lombardy,[292] a bishop of holy life also preached in a touching way. It was not long before a collection was made throughout the army for those who were in distress, a collection that amounted to a great sum. Each did his utmost to satisfy the needy. Then you would have seen poor people thanking God as they ate what the rich had given. There was Walchelin of Ferrières, an open-handed man, not at all mean, and with him Robert Trussebot,[293] who put

---

290   According to the Russian abbot, Daniel, a pilgrim between 1106 and 1108, Mount Tabor 'is covered all over with trees of every kind, figs and carobs and olives in great abundance', *Jerusalem Pilgrimage 1099–1185*, ed. J. Wilkinson with J. Hill and W.F. Ryan, Hakluyt Society 167 (London, 1988), p.161. Carob trees, which are found throughout the Mediterranean, were valued in a period of dearth as they are evergreen and have edible pods, sometimes called 'St John's bread'. Usually, though, they were fed to animals.

291   Hubert Walter, Bishop of Salisbury, 1189–93, Archbishop of Canterbury, 1193–1205, Justiciar of England, 1193–8, Apostolic Legate, 1195–1200. On his role in the crusade, see C.R. Cheney, *Hubert Walter* (London, 1967), pp.33–7, and C.R. Young, *Hubert Walter, Lord of Canterbury and Lord of England* (Durham, NC, 1968), pp.33–42.

292   Monaldus, Bishop of Fano, 1178–1214.

293   Walchelin of Ferrières-St Hilaire (d.1201) and Robert Trussebot were Norman knights from

all he had into the common pot, and the count of Champagne who gave so freely, Sir Jocelyn of Montoire[294] who should be mentioned in this story, the Count of Clermont who was very generous and the bishop of Salisbury, who was not at all tight-fisted, and others who knew God and helped many people. The collection was distributed, generously and carefully, to the lesser men and the great, to knights and men-at-arms, to the poor, where the greatest need was seen, to each according to what he was and how he suffered. God saw that His people ardently desired the good and that there was charity among them and because of this He looked on them with the eyes of mercy.

[4457–76] You may have heard of the miracle the King of Heaven accomplished. Those who have heard of it should rejoice. There came to the port of Acre a small boat that was neither long nor wide. There was corn in this boat. Now you may hear how God saved Christianity and brought plenty out of a lean time – not that the lean times were so bad for there were provisions in the army, but the merchants held them back, in order to sell them at a higher price. But God who is Love and the Fountain of Humility, saw this evil in His people and commanded that the famine and misery should end and the price of corn fell.

[4477–506] It was on a Saturday, before nones,[295] that the small boat arrived with its provisions. Not much was said about the arrival of this boat, except by those who sold the corn, who were concerned about making a profit. The vessel came one Saturday, to the best of my knowledge, after midday. God himself brought it and took the grain that was lying in the barns and that the merchants were selling for one hundred besants and, by the next day, brought the price from one hundred besants to four. What a Merchant to bring down the price by so much, so quickly.

Listen how the Lord God brought down a man whose outrageous behaviour made this no bad thing. In the army before Acre was a man from Pisa who kept his grain at such a high price that he would not sell a single measure except at an outrageous price. God who knows every man, brought him to grief because he so determined. For a fire burnt his house so that all that was in it that he had wrongly accumulated was all lost and burnt to a cinder, and no-one could save it.

---

the Eure who arrived at Tyre mid-September 1190, with Archbishop Baldwin's party. Walchelin continued to act on Richard's behalf after the crusade, as he was among those gathered at Speyer in January 1194, shortly before the king's release, and was one of the guarantors of the treaty with Baldwin of Flanders in June or July 1197. Robert Trussebot also held a fee of ten knights at Warter in the East Riding (Yorkshire): Powicke, p.338; B. Siedschlag, *English Participation in the Crusades 1150–1220* (Randolph, Wis., 1939), no.130, p.124; Landon, pp.2, 5, 31, 37, 41, 54, 81–2, 100, 118, 126.

294 Not identified, but possibly from Montoire-sur-le-Loir (Loir-et-Cher) in northern Anjou, between Vendôme and La Chartre.

295 The actual time of nones varied as the hours of daylight were divided by twelve. In north-west Europe the canonical hours were matins (3.30 a.m. or 4.00 a.m. in the summer and 6.00 a.m. in the winter), prime (6.00 a.m. and 6.45 a.m.), terce (8.00 a.m. all year round), sext (11.30 a.m. and 12 p.m.), none (2.30 p.m. and 1.30 p.m.), vespers (6.00 p.m. and 4.15 p.m.), and compline (8.00 p.m. and 6.15 p.m.). See C.R. Cheney, ed., *Handbook of Dates for Students of English History* (London, 1948), p.9, and D. Knowles, *The Monastic Order in England 943–1216* (Cambridge, 1963), pp.448–53, 714–15.

[4507–44]   When God was seen to act in this way charity began to increase. Each good man became generous towards his fellow in every way. There you would have seen the poor satisfied and God thanked. All those who had eaten meat during Lent confessed and did penance for it, for they had done so, because of their misery. Each of them had three blows of a stick on his back, but not heavy blows, administered by the bishop of Salisbury, who chastised like a good father. On the Sunday after Easter,[296] after God had done this, there came to the army, truly and without doubt, King Philip of France. And with him came the count of Flanders, whose death was to be so much talked about, and with him came also the noble count of St Pol,[297] whose shield became him so well, and with him came also William of Garlande, with a great company of men, and with him came also William des Barres,[298] a good knight, worthy and alert, and with him came also my lord Dreux of Amiens, a man of nobility and means, and with him came also William of Mello,[299] a knight to be praised, and with him came the count of Perche,[300] who gave all he had, without restriction to this [cause]; then with the French, as I have been told, came the marquis. What else can I say? There did not remain in France any great men who did not come to the army at Acre at that time, either sooner or later.

[4545–62]   The king of France was there with the army of Christians from Easter to Pentecost,[301] that great and costly feast.[302] Then the king of England came to that land, having taken Cyprus. But I must follow the story and rejoin the material to tell of the siege of Acre; so Ambroise wishes to complete his tale here, carry on to his goal, tie the knot and join the tale of the two kings who came to the siege of Acre and what they did there and recall what he can remember of the story of how Acre was taken, as he saw it with his own eyes.[303]

---

296   The first Sunday after Easter is Quasimodo. Stone translates as 'Low Sunday'.

297   Hugh IV, Count of St Pol, 1174–1205.

298   The families of Garlande and Barres, along with that of the Cléments (see below, p.100) were key members of Philip II's military entourage, taking part not only in the crusade, but also in many other engagements, most importantly the battle of Bouvines, 27 July 1214. William of Garlande died in 1214 and William des Barres died in 1233, Baldwin, *Government of Philip Augustus*, pp.113–14.

299   Both these men acted as envoys for Philip II to Richard I in July 1191. Roger of Howden, *Chronica*, vol.3, p.123.

300   Routrou III, Count of Perche, 1144–91, died during the siege of Acre. He had been Philip's envoy to England in November 1189, during preparations for the crusade, Roger of Howden, *Gesta*, vol.2, pp.92–3.

301   Easter 1191 was 14 April.

302   Cf. *Itinerarium*, 3.4. Pentecost is Whitsun, 2 June 1191. We have retained the ecclesiastical reference to keep an element of the annominatio with 'cost'. The same terms are used in annominatio by Chrétien de Troyes in *Yvain*, ed. D.F. Hult (Paris, 1994), ll.5–16.

303   Ambroise makes it quite clear where he was an eyewitness and where he knows only from hearsay. See introduction p.1 above.

The Kings at Acre

[4563–4686]   As I have told you when King Richard of England came to the Holy Land he showed courtesy and nobility and generosity which should be recounted. The king of France had given freely to his people, so that each would have from his treasury three gold besants per month. This was much spoken of. King Richard, when he arrived and heard of this important business, had it announced throughout the army that any knight, of any land who wished to take his pay would receive four gold besants and that he would pay them this – and this was the right amount that should have been paid. The whole army rejoiced when they heard this. Then the lesser people, who had been there for some time, the lower and middle ranking men, said, "Lord God, when do we attack? Now the most valiant of kings has arrived, the best warrior in all of Christendom. Now let God's will be done." Their trust was in King Richard. Then the king of France,[304] who had arrived just after Easter, and had conducted himself well, sent to him a message that it would be good to attack and they should have the attack announced. However, King Richard was ill, his mouth and lips pale, because of an illness – may God curse it – called arnaldia.[305] He informed the king of his illness and told him that his fleet had not arrived, having been detained at Tyre by weather conditions, a wind called the 'Arsur'[306] and that his catapults were coming and would in time arrive, and that when his entourage arrived he would be willing to do all in his power to take Acre.[307] However, the king of France did not want to wait for this; may God protect me, he had the assault sounded. In the morning[308] they armed on all sides, for they very much wanted to attack. Then you would have seen so many armed men that they could scarcely be counted, so many fine hauberks, such a variety of burnished helmets, so many well-appointed horses, white saddle-cloths, elite knights. Never were seen so many good knights, noble and daring, proud, bold and renowned, so many pennons and banners worked in so many designs. Then they set apart and organised those who would guard the trench so that Saladin could not attack the army from behind with his fierce people. The people of God advanced towards the walls, firing and attacking strongly.

When the Turks in Acre saw that the Christians were attacking them then you would have heard a noise, as if God had caused it to thunder, the noise of basins and bells and drums. Those whose job it was to do this did nothing else but

---

304   The king of France is clearly supposed to be the subject here, but is in the wrong case, the object case.

305   1.4602, *leonardie, arnaldia*. Various theories have been put forward about it, including Vincent's disease (trench-mouth) and scurvy, although, given that Richard had only just arrived from Cyprus, where he had presumably eaten well, neither seems likely. See HL, p.196, n.4, and Gillingham, *Richard I*, p.160. It may, however, have been a recurrence of an illness from which he had suffered in the past which, according to William of Newburgh, p.306, manifested itself in pallor and swellings.

306   The wind was blowing from the south, thus preventing the fleet from sailing down to Acre.

307   Cf. *Itinerarium*, 3.5.

308   1 July 1191.

survey the army from the palace and make a lot of noise and smoke. This was to tell the Saracens that they should come to their rescue. You would have seen them rushing up to fill the ditch with faggots but they could not complete the task for Geoffrey of Lusignan, still fresh in prowess, came to the barrier where they were and which they had already taken from our men and repulsed them with force, sending more than ten of them to their graves using an axe that he carried. Everywhere resounded so to the sound of his blows that not since Roland and Oliver had there been such a praiseworthy knight.[309] The barrier that the Saracens had taken was reconquered. There was, however, a great free-for-all, tremendous fighting and such a racket that those who were attacking Acre, filling the ditches through force, had to withdraw to consider other options; this was to withdraw towards the archers[310] and no longer draw against them or hurl their projectiles. So the assault stopped; the people complained and cried out, lamenting the arrival of the long-awaited kings. Each one, in front of his own tent said, "Good Lord, what a feeble effort!" Our people went to disarm. There the Saracens mocked. Moreover, even as our men were disarming, the Saracens set fire to the machines and cercleiae of the king of France. This brought such anger to his heart, so I heard say, and it is known, that he fell ill and could not ride.

[4687–802][311]   So the armies were in this state, sad and melancholy, sorrowful and cast down, because the two kings who should have taken the city were ill. On top of this, the count of Flanders had died,[312] to the great sorrow of the army. What more can I say? The illness of the kings, the death of the count, put the armies into such distress that there was no joy or happiness, but for the arrival into this situation of the fleet of snacks.[313] There came then the bishop of Evreux with good men who were his vassals; there came also Roger of Tosny[314] with a very great company of knights and the brothers of Tournebu,[315] good

---

309 Roland and Oliver were legendary heroes of the time of Charlemagne whose exploits are celebrated in a number of *chansons de geste*, most famously in the *Chanson de Roland* (c.1100).

310 1.4669, *vers quarels se trestrent*. Paris assumes there to be an error in the manuscript and translates as 'retirer vers leur camp' (retire towards their camp).

311 Cf. *Itinerarium*, 3.6.

312 Philip of Flanders had died on 1 June 1191, Landon, p.50.

313 This group of crusaders arrived at Acre on 8 June, Landon, p.50. They were all vassals or household knights of Richard I from England and Normandy. On the importance of groupings based on lordship and family for crusade armies, see J. Riley-Smith, *The First Crusaders, 1095–1131* (Cambridge, 1997), pp.81–105.

314 Roger of Tosny (Eure, arr. Louviers) held lands on both sides of the Seine near Les Andelys. The family had been established in England since the eleventh century: Powicke, pp.355–6; Siedschlag, no.139, p.125. On this family, see L. Musset, 'Aux origines d'une classe dirigeante: Les Tosny, Grands Barons Normands du Xe au XIIIe siècle', *Francia. Forschungen zur westeuropäischen Geschichte* 5 (1977), 45–80. He took part in the important engagements of the crusade, including the battle of Arsuf (7 September 1191), and the attack on a Muslim caravan at the Round Cistern (Bir Khuwailifa) (23–24 June 1192). He remained in the royal service throughout the 1190s. See Landon, pp.17, 20, 54, 60, 65, 82–3, 118, 145.

315 Tournebu is near Louviers (Eure). It is not clear which members of the family are meant here, although Thomas, Richard, and John of Tournebu are all recorded in documents of the late twelfth and early thirteenth centuries, Powicke, p.355. William of Tournebu was present at Jaffa on 29 September 1191 in an incident in which Richard was nearly captured, Roger of

sons all from one father; there came also Robert of Neuborg[316] – no bolder men have I met; there came also Jordan du Hommet,[317] Constable of Séez; There came also at that time the chamberlain of Tancarville;[318] Count Robert of Leicester,[319] who wished to be there, came at that time; there came also Gilbert Talbot,[320] one of our noble vassals; my lord Ralph Teisson[321] came too – it would not be right to omit him; the viscount of Châteaudun[322] also came, and Bertrand of Verdun;[323] there came also the brothers of Tozel,[324] bold and courtly knights; there came also Roger of Harcourt, a companion of the king and one of his court; there came also those of Préaux[325] who were royal companions; there came also Garin FitzGerald,[326] with his company; there came also

Howden, *Chronica*, vol.3, p.133. They were related to Roger of Tosny, *Itinerarium*, 3.6, p.217.

[316] Robert of Neuborg (Eure), a member of the Beaumont family, Round, 478.

[317] Jordan du Hommet was the brother of William du Hommet, Constable of Normandy. He had fees in Cléville (Calvados).

[318] William III, hereditary Chamberlain of Tancarville, to which he succeeded on his father's death in 1173.

[319] Robert IV, Earl of Leicester (d. October 1204), succeeded his father on 1 September 1190 when he died at sea en route to the Holy Land. In 1172 there were 121 knights in the honour of Leicester. As major landholders at Breteuil, to the south-west of Evreux, as well, the earls were clearly key members of Richard's army, since their participation ensured the adherence of large numbers of their followers and fief-holders in the Eure region: Roger of Howden, *Chronica*, vol.3, p.88; Powicke, pp.343–4; Siedschlag, no.124, p.123. For the genealogy of this family, see F.M. Powicke, 'Loretta, Countess of Leicester', in *Historical Essays in Honour of James Tait*, ed. J.G. Edwards, V.H. Galbraith and E.F. Jacob (Manchester, 1933), p.272.

[320] Gilbert Talbot may have been lord of Linton in Herefordshire, Siedschlag, no.41, p.116. The *Itinerarium*, 3.6, p.217, gives Gerard Talbot, who was a different person, although also on crusade and probably related, Landon, pp.43, 50.

[321] Ralph Teisson, lord of St-Saveur-le-Vicomte, in Normandy, was with Richard at Barfleur in August 1189. He headed one of the parties of pilgrims allowed by Saladin to visit Jerusalem in September 1192, see below, p.187. He witnessed charters on Richard's behalf for the rest of the reign. Under John he served as seneschal of Normandy, although he joined Philip II after the conquest of the duchy in 1204: Landon, pp.2, 50, 69, 118, 130, 145; Powicke, *Loss of Normandy*, pp.352–3.

[322] The viscount of Châteaudun (Eure-et-Loir) is not identified, although Paris, p.535, gives his name as Ralph.

[323] Bertrand or Bertram of Verdun was an important Anglo-Norman with lands in Staffordshire, Ireland and the Avranchin. He had held the offices of seneschal of Ireland (1185) and sheriff of Warwick and Leicester (1168–84). He travelled with Richard to Marseilles, Messina and Acre. He and Stephen of Longchamp were appointed governors of Acre on 21 August 1191, when Richard took the main army south. He returned to the West in the autumn of 1192: R. Dace, 'Bertran de Verdun: Royal Service, Land and Family in the Late Twelfth Century', *Medieval Prosopography* 20 (1999), 75–93; Siedschlag, no.20, pp.113–14; Landon, pp.38, 43, 46, 50, 53, 71, 127.

[324] *Itinerarium*, 3.6, p.217, 'knights with the surname Torolens' (Nicholson, p.207).

[325] Préaux (Seine-Inférieur) is near Rouen. The brothers were household knights of Richard I. Three of them – John, William and Peter – accompanied Richard on crusade, while a fourth, Roger, one of the royal stewards, was with the king at Messina in 1191. William was captured at Jaffa in September 1191, but was ransomed by Richard a year later. Peter and John continued in Richard's service throughout the rest of the reign: Powicke, *Loss of Normandy*, p.350; Landon, pp.12, 18, 20, 46–8, 54–5, 59–60, 69, 129, 145.

[326] Garin or Warin FitzGerald travelled with Richard from Westminster in November 1189 to

the lord de la Mare,[327] in fine and rich accoutrements; there were many others whom I have not named, who came to serve God.

The two kings lay ill at the siege of Acre. It was not God's will that they should die, but that they should rescue the city. The king of France recovered some time before the other [king].[328] The catapults hurled stones at the walls without ceasing night and day. The king had one called Bad Neighbour, but in Acre there was one called Evil Cousin, which broke it constantly and he constantly had it set up again, so often that it broke the main wall, also causing considerable damage to the Cursed Tower.[329] The catapult of the duke of Burgundy also did its work well and that of the noble Templars struck many a Turk below the temple. The Hospitallers' catapult struck a blow that pleased all. They had constructed a catapult that was called the Catapult of God;[330] a good priest preached for it, inspiring the whole host and gathering enough money [for it] so that it had brought down the walls near the Cursed Tower for more than two perches.[331] The count of Flanders, when he was alive, [also] had a catapult, the best that could be found, which the king of England later acquired. The king also had another, a small one, considered to be very good. These two hurled missiles at a tower over a gate much used by the Turks, battering and beating so much against it that they brought half of it down. The king had built two new ones, so richly built that wherever they were placed they could fire under cover. He also had a tower built, which worried the Turks; it was so well covered and clothed in leather, cords and wood that it feared no stone hurled at it, nor Greek fire, not anything else yet created. He also had two mangonels made, one of which was so fast that when it hurled a stone into Acre it went as far as the Butchers' Row.[332] His catapults hurled stones day and night, without respite. As true as we are here one of them killed twelve men with one stone that was taken

---

Messina, arriving at Acre on 8 June 1191 with the other Norman crusaders. He was one of the guarantors of Richard's agreement with Tancred on 6 October 1190. He continued to witness Richard's charters after the crusade in Normandy and Anjou, as well as at Worms and Speyer in August 1193, while Richard was in captivity. Although never one of the leading figures of the reign, he was a member of the close circle of *familiares* around the king on the crusade and after, when he served as a chamberlain in the Norman Exchequer. Between 1192 and 1199 he was always in the top ten attestors of Richard's charters when the king was on the continent. See R. Heiser, 'The Royal *Familiares* of King Richard I', *Medieval Prosopography* 10 (1989), 35, 43, 45; Landon, pp.15, 20, 22, 43, 50, 59, 60, 79, 80, 82, 99, 120, 131–4, 137, 140–4.

327 Robert de la Mare held lands in East Anglia, Siedschlag, no.125, pp.123–4.

328 Cf. *Itinerarium*, 3.7.

329 The Accursed Tower was situated on the north-eastern corner of the city. At that time Acre had only a single line of walls; this became the inner wall when a new line was built sometime between 1198 and 1212, Jacoby, 'Montmusard, Suburb of Crusader Acre', pp.211–13.

330 Possible play on the similarity between *periere* (catapult, petrary) and *priere* (prayer).

331 1.4760. A 'perch' was a measure of length corresponding to approximately 5½ yards. A little more detail about the role of this priest is given in the *Itinerarium*, 3.7, p.219: 'A priest, a man of great probity, always stood next to it preaching and collecting money for its continual repair and for hiring people to gather the stones for its ammunition' (Nicholson, p.209).

332 According to Philip of Novara, when the Emperor Frederick II left Acre on 1 May 1229, he boarded a galley *devant la boucherie*, *Mémoires 1218–1243*, ed. C. Kohler, Les Classiques Français du Moyen Age (Paris, 1913), p.25. This suggests that Philip's catapult was so powerful that it had hurled a stone right onto the harbour front.

to Saladin to show him, for such stones[333] had been brought to the land by the king of England. They were stones from the sea that he had brought from Messina in order to kill Saracen people with them. However, the king was lying abed, very ill and taking pleasure in nothing. He came to see the fighting against the Saracens, those curs, so near the army and the ditches that the fact that he could not fight with them saddened him more than the illness that made him tremble.

[4803–60][334]   Acre was very hard to take, and before it was a great deal was spent on many machines that they made there and that were scarcely sufficient. When [no] attention was being paid to them the Saracens burnt them. The king of France had a cat made at great cost and expense and a richly covered cercleia from which resulted great loss. The king himself would sit under the cercleia and often fired his crossbow at the Turks who came to defend the walls. One day when the people were guarding the cat and those who worked it, there came a Saracen who brought and threw down many dry bushes on the cat and the cercleia – Ambroise saw this – then hurled Greek fire on it and set up a catapult to fire directly on the cat so that it was inevitable that the cat was destroyed and the rich cercleia burnt and broken. Then the king had such anger in his heart that he began to curse all who ate his bread because they did not wreak vengeance on the Saracens. That night he announced the assault. The next day was of a heat to be marvelled at.[335]

There they were in the morning; there they mounted, the proud and worthy people.[336] That day those who had no cowardice in them were set to guard the ditches. All around there were the best men in the world. There was great need of them that day for Saladin had said that he would be the first to enter and that he would show himself there. He did not come but his people came and dismounted by the ditch to take their stand there. There you would have seen such a defence made, with blows of mace and of sword; there the battle came to a standstill for the Turks outside Acre were enraged because of those in Acre who signalled to them using Saladin's banner. It was the Emir Saphadin and his men who put such pressure on the trench that by means of force they filled it, but our men repulsed them and those who were against the walls attacked Acre with might; may God give them their just reward.

[4861–4902]   The sappers who had given their allegiance to the king of France, dug under the ground to find the foundations of the walls, which they propped up, then set fire to the props so that a section of the wall collapsed.[337] However, it nearly brought harm to themselves, for as it fell the wall leaned over so that each man feared for his safety. A number of people came over to where they saw the wall brought down. There you would have seen many banners, cognisances of all sorts. There you would have seen in the press many evil pagans. There you

---

333 Mangonels and trebuchets were ineffective unless there were stones of the right size which would not shatter on impact. It was evidently thought worth transporting these from Sicily. See Contamine, p.104.

334 Cf. *Itinerarium*, 3.8.

335 2 or 3 July 1191, Landon, p.50.

336 Cf. *Itinerarium*, 3.9.

337 On mining, see France, pp.116–17.

would have seen them bringing up Greek fire to throw on us. There you would have seen both sides struggle to drag the ladders to the walls. There was a bold deed committed by Aubery Clément;[338] he had said that he would either die that day or enter Acre; he did not lie, but became a martyr there; he went to fight on the walls, against the Turks, who came upon him to knock him down, in such numbers that he died while defending himself. Those who were following him were already on the ladder, putting such a weight on it that it bent and then broke into pieces, throwing them into the ditch. The Turks mocked and jeered; some of our men died and others were dragged out. The whole army was distressed over the death of Aubery Clément and in order to mourn and lament him the assault was suspended.

[4903–20][339] It was not long after the death of Aubery Clément that the Cursed Tower, as I have called it, was undermined, with props put in place, then damaged and weakened. The Turks within were digging a countermine as straight as they could. Eventually they met and agreed a mutual truce. There were there Christians held in chains and bonds; they spoke together and arranged it that they managed to escape. The Turks inside, knowing of this, felt, you must know, great anger because of it. They repaired and mended the gap through which they had passed.

[4921–81][340] King Richard still lay ill, as I have told you; but he wished that the city of Acre should be attacked under his command. So he had a cercleia dragged to the ditches, a richly wrought construction. His crossbowmen, who carried out their work well, were in it. He himself, as God bears witness, had himself carried to the cercleia in a great silken quilt to [personally] work against the Saracens. With his ever-ready hand, he shot many bolts against the Tower, which his catapults were attacking and where the Turks shot back. His sappers continued to dig and prop up the mines; they mined it so much and weakened it with the catapults, that it fell down to earth. Then the king of England had his crier announce throughout the army, from a wall next to the tower, that he would give two gold besants to whoever removed from it a block of stone.[341] Then he promised three, then four, besants. Then you would have seen the men-at-arms struggle; then you would have seen much injury [. . .];[342] then you would have seen many knocked down, so that they did not dare hang about, nor did they dare remain under their shields. The wall was both high and wide; nevertheless they succeeded in dragging stones from the wall. Then you would have seen Turks storming in when they saw where the stones were being removed, coming out of cover in order to attack those who were destroying [the wall]. One Turk had

---

338 Cf. *Itinerarium*, 3.10. Aubery or Alberic Clément was the son of Robert Clément (d.1181), who had been tutor and guardian to Philip Augustus. This family, which originated in Mez-le-Maréchal in the Gâtinais in the eleventh century, provided several marshals of France, key figures in actually leading royal troops. Alberic, his brother Henry, and their father Robert, were all marshals, Baldwin, *Government of Philip Augustus*, pp.33–4, 113. Alberic died on 3 July 1191, Landon, p.50.

339 Cf. *Itinerarium*, 3.11.

340 Cf. *Itinerarium*, 3.12.

341 Cf. *Itinerarium*, 3.13.

342 After l.4949 there is a lacuna, probably of one line.

arrayed himself richly in the arms of Aubery Clément and that day he took too great a risk. King Richard struck him with a bolt square on the chest, which killed him instantly. There you would have seen Turks coming out of cover to assuage their sorrow for him; they laid themselves open to bolts and fired and struck great blows. Never was there such a defence. Everyone who considers it marvels at it. Armour, however good, strong or sure was of no use there – double pourpoints and double hauberks – they were of no more use than blue cloth against the framed crossbows, for the bolts were of such heavy calibre. Moreover, the Turks within countermined until our miners had to flee and withdraw. How the Saracens mocked.

[4982–5032][343]   When this tower, which had been attacked so much, was finally brought down, and the dust settled, so that many could enter, then the esquires[344] who were valiant and nimble, armed themselves. There was the banner of the earl of Leicester, and that of my lord Andrew of Chauvigny[345] in that place; similarly that of lord Hugh le Brun was there in glorious array, and of the bishop of Salisbury and of others of different status. It was at meal time that they gathered before the tower. The valiant esquires attacked [. . .][346] The watchmen on the walls cried out when they saw them climb up. How the city was stirred up when this was known; then you would have seen a storm of Turks and the esquires moving forward rapidly; they wanted to enter Acre. There you would have seen them meet together in battle, striking, hitting and knocking each other down. There were but few esquires and the number of Saracens continually increased, burning them with flaming fire. The esquires, alert to this, did not dare approach the fire and had to go back down. I do not know how many died in the attempt. Then the Pisans, who were men of great boldness, armed and went up [on the walls]; but the Saracens fought back, so well that the battle between the Pisans and the pack of curs was waged with such fury and

---

343 Cf. *Itinerarium*, 3.14.

344 Esquires should not be seen exclusively as a type of apprentice knight; more frequently, they were servants of a knight, looking after his horses and supplies, and carrying arms and equipment, as well as taking part in the fighting. On the role and status of the esquire as depicted in some chronicles, see M. Bennett, 'The Status of the Esquire: The Northern Evidence', and L. Paterson, 'The Occitan Esquire in the Twelfth and Thirteenth Centuries', in *The Ideals and Practice of Medieval Knighthood*, vol.1, ed. C. Harper-Bill and R. Harvey (Woodbridge, 1986), pp.1–11 and 133–51 respectively.

345 Andrew of Chauvigny (Chaveney) arrived at Acre on 8 June 1191 with the main group of Anglo-Norman crusaders, see above, p.96; *Itinerarium*, 3.6, p.218. He was an important member of Richard's *familia*, the recipient of an heiress from the king in August 1189. Throughout the crusade he appears among those who act as guarantors and witnesses of the royal enactments, including surety for the agreement with Tancred (6 October 1190), overseer of the regulations for the crusade (8 October), and witness of the dower granted to Berengaria (12 May 1191). During the crusade he was sent to Rome to gather information about the situation in Richard's lands in England (January to May 1192), and he was one of the leaders of the pilgrim parties allowed to visit Jerusalem by Saladin (September 1192). At the same time he was prominent in the fighting, at one point helping to rescue Robert of Leicester from a critical situation (20 December 1191), see below, pp.133–4. He continued to act on Richard's behalf during the 1190s, Landon, pp.3, 37, 43–4, 49–50, 57–60, 63, 67–9, 107, 127. He later attained the status of a legendary hero in the works known as 'the second cycle of the crusade'.

346 After l.4998, there is a lacuna assumed to be of one line.

fervour that never was such good defence nor attack seen. The Pisans had to leap down. Had the business been better known, then Acre would have been taken that day but, as most of the army was seated at their meal, the attack being made very suddenly, the assault came to nothing.

[5033–59][347]   There was a meeting in the army at which a much sought for and desired agreement was reached between King Guy and the marquis. The king of France was for the marquis and supported him and Richard, King of England, was for the king of that land, made king of Jerusalem. They distrusted one another and had no friendship for one another, for they disputed the kingdom; the agreement was that Guy would remain king but they would share what belonged to the kingdom, such as its income. In the meantime the marquis would have Tyre, Beirut and Sidon in order to establish a firm peace. If King Guy were to die first the marquis would have the crown and Geoffrey of Lusignan would have Jaffa and Ascalon[348] [and if Guy should die then Richard could][349] do as he willed with the land as if it were his own. But the marquis was envious of the two brothers all his life.

[5060–5097]   The people in the city were an incredibly proud and arrogant people. Had they not been infidels no better people could ever have been seen.[350] Nonetheless, they were afraid of the miracle that they now beheld, how the whole world was coming against them to destroy them; they saw their walls broken down, pierced and destroyed; they saw their people injured, killed and cut into pieces; yet there remained within the town more than six thousand, among them both Mestoc and Karakush.[351] But they were not sufficient nor had they any hope of help, and they knew well that the army was in deep sadness because of the death of Aubrey Clément, and because of their sons and their brothers, their uncles and their fathers, their nephews and their first cousins, whom they had killed with their own hands and because of whom they were

---

347 Cf. *Itinerarium*, 3.20.

348 On the circumstances, see above, pp.86, 88–9, and below, pp.147–8, 154.

349 ll.5055–6 in the manuscript are corrupt, resulting in a gap which Paris fills in his translation from the *Itinerarium* with 'Et s'il arrivait que le roi Guy, le marquis et sa femme mourusses, alors le roi Richard . . .', which I have translated here in order to make sense of the passage. The *Itinerarium*, 3.20, p.236, has: 'However, if King Guy, the marquis and his wife should all be taken from human affairs together while King Richard was in that region, then it would be left to King Richard's judgement to dispose of the kingdom as he wished' (Nicholson, p.222). The agreement was made on 27 July 1191 after the fall of Acre on 12 July. However, the conflict had existed since Conrad had refused Geoffrey of Lusignan entry to Tyre in the summer of 1188, which might explain why Ambroise places his account at this point, Landon, p.51. See above, p.70.

350 Cf. *La Chanson de Roland*, text F. Whitehead, revised T.D. Hemming (London, 1993), ll.899, 3164, and the *Gesta Francorum*, ed. and trans. R. Hill (London, 1962), p.21. See M. Ailes, 'Chivalry and Conversion: The Chivalrous Saracen in the Old French Epics *Fierabras* and *Otinel*', *Al-Masaq: Studia Arabo-Islamica Mediterranea* 9 (1996–7), 1–21, and *The Song of Roland – On Absolutes and Relative Values* (Lampeter, 2002), pp.71–4.

351 Saif al-Din 'Ali al-Mashtub, later governor of Nablus. He died on 1 November 1192. Baha' al-Din Qara-Qush had been made governor of Acre by Saladin in March 1189. He was a eunuch who had helped Saladin to power in Egypt in 1169 after the death of Shirkuh (Asad al-Din), Saladin's uncle. Both men are described by Baha' al-Din as 'the great military commanders and heroes of Islam', pp.237, 90, 157.

indeed hated. They knew for certain that our people would take them by force or die in the attempt. There was no other way. They had a wall constructed and built around and across the city that they thought to defend well – I tell you truly – but God caused them to make a decision that brought honour to us and death and harm to them, so that because of it Acre was taken without a bolt being fired or a stone hurled.

[5098–129] The Saracens who were in Acre held counsel and resolved to ask for a safe conduct from our people to send to Saladin, who had pledged faithfully that if he saw them in great distress that he would conclude a peace, according to their wishes; this was his pledge. They asked for a safe conduct from our people and sent to Saladin, that he should retain among them his position of respect and renown, his valour and the ancient law that Mohammed had established with their ancestors; that this law should not be damaged or brought low because of the Christians; that he should take counsel at once and listen to no other advice than this – to deliver the valiant men who had gone to Acre, guarded it for so long for him at the risk of being taken and put to the sword – that he would think of their poor households, left rudderless, whom they had not seen for three years, since the mustering of the army – that he should look to both themselves and their families; that they should not die through neglect, and that he should fulfil his pledge. Otherwise he should know for certain that they would make the best terms they could with the Christians.

[5130–59] Saladin heard the complaint of his people who were so hard-pressed; [he heard] of their misfortune and their distress, their despair and their weakness, and he replied as best he knew how, that he had received a message from Babylon and that in due course he would receive a noble company in ships and galleys that he had requested a long time ago, to save his valiant people of Acre, whom he had no desire to abandon, and that the Caliph had told him that they would arrive within the week.[352] However, if help did not come to him, by the faith that he followed,[353] he would make peace with Christendom for their salvation. The messengers went and returned to those suffering under misfortune. The catapults broke the walls, firing night and day without ceasing, and the Turks were so afraid that at night they would come to the walls and let themselves fall from them, for fear of worse to come.[354] The messengers went and came back and made it clear to Saladin that they were dead, unless peace was made or help came.

[5160–91][355] Saladin saw, with certainty, the great harm and loss and the great suffering of his people. He took counsel with his nobles and asked them what he should do about their request. The rich men and the emirs who were the friends and family of those who were defending Acre were vociferous in their reply that

---

[352] Paris, p.555, defines *mulaine* as 'nom donné avant Salahadin au calife fatimite de l'Egypte . . . mais il est vrai qu'en français ce nom . . . devint plus tard *amulaine* et désigna vaguement un prince sarrasin . . .' There was no caliph in Cairo after September 1171, when the last of the Fatimids had died, and Saladin had ensured that he was not replaced, thus ending the long-standing schism between Baghdad and Cairo. See Lyons and Jackson, pp.44–6.

[353] Literally, 'by the law which he upheld' (l.5145).

[354] Cf. *Itinerarium*, 3.16.

[355] Cf. *Itinerarium*, 3.17.

they wanted to get them out and that there was no alternative to seeking peace on the best terms they could get, before worse happened. When the Sultan heard the way his barons were thinking and knowing the suffering in Acre, which he could not bring to an end whether he wanted to or not, he said to the messengers, whom he knew to be valiant and wise, that he agreed to the surrender of the town when it could no longer be defended. Then before the messengers went they decided on the terms they would offer the Christians when they got back. The messengers returned looking not unhappy about it all. So there was a meeting between us and those in the city, who came to make the offer. The people were made to keep quiet about it.

[5192–213]   The Turks made their offer through an interpreter. The offer was as follows: that they would surrender the Cross in which Christians believe, that they would surrender the town to them, and with it two thousand of their important prisoners and five hundred lesser people, whom they had held for a long time, that Saladin would have their arms and other equipment searched for and gathered from the whole of his land and that when the Turks left Acre no creature would bear with him anything bar his tunic. Another condition was added that they would give two hundred thousand besants to the two kings who were there and that for this they would have as hostages the most important and most wise of the Turks to be found among those in Acre, the best chosen by appearance and reputation.

[5214–17]   Our people took counsel and examined the terms; the council agreed to them and granted peace.[356]

[5218–37][357]   The day that Acre was surrendered, as I have understood the matter, was four years after the Saracens conquered it; this was an established fact. As I remember it and can be sure of it the town was surrendered the day after the Feast of St Benedict,[358] despite the accursed race, whom God curses with his [own] mouth – I cannot refrain from saying this – you should have seen the churches as they left them in Acre, with their statues broken and defaced, the altars destroyed, crosses and crucifixes knocked down, to spite our faith and satisfy their wrong beliefs, and carry out their idolatries![359] But they later paid for this.

[5238–65][360] At that time, as I understand it, when the Turks were to surrender the Cross to us, after the surrender of Acre, the word spread through the army that the king of France, in whom the people had put such trust, wished to return to France and was preparing for his journey. God's mercy! what a turnabout!

356 Baha' al-Din's version was that the Franks should receive 'the city and all the engines, equipment and ships it contained', 200,000 gold dinars, 1,500 prisoners 'of common, unremarkable background', '100 prisoners to be specified by the Franks', and 'the Holy Cross'. Ten thousand dinars were to be paid to Conrad of Montferrat 'because he was the intermediary' and 4,000 dinars to his men. In return, the Muslims should leave safely, 'taking with them their personal wealth and goods and their children and womenfolk', p.161.

357 Cf. *Itinerarium*, 2.19; 3.18 contains material not in Ambroise.

358 The Feast of the Translation of St Benedict was on 11 July; the city therefore surrendered on 12 July 1191.

359 While this is clearly an epic topos it can nevertheless be found in sober chronicles as well, see for example, WT, 6.23, p.339.

360 Cf. *Itinerarium*, 3.21.

This was an unfortunate turn of mind, when he, who should support so many men, wished to go home. He was going back because of his illness, so the king said, whatever is said about him, but there is no witness that illness gives a dispensation from going with the army of the Almighty King, who directs the paths of all kings. I do not say that he was never there, nor that he had not spent iron and wood, lead and pewter, gold and silver, and helped many people, as the greatest of earthly kings known among Christians, but for this very reason he should have remained to do what he could, without failing, in the poor, lost land that has cost us so dear.

[5266–81]   The news was spread openly and certainly throughout the army, that the king was going back and that he was each day making his preparations. How the barons of France were filled with anger and rage, seeing the head of whom they were the members[361] in such a state of decision, not wishing to remain for their sakes, despite tears and complaints. When they could not change this, despite all that they would do, I tell you that they blamed him, coming little short of denying his kingship and lordship over them, they hated his power over them so much.

[5282–97]   The king of France was ready to leave, not wishing to allow any man to persuade him to delay his return to France. Following his example there returned with him a whole pack of barons and others. He left behind at that time, to stand in for him, with the men of his land, the duke of Burgundy, and he asked King Richard to lend him two galleys. So they set off for the port where they gave him two fine boats, well equipped and swift, given freely and poorly rewarded.[362]

[5298–321][363] King Richard, who remained in Syria in the service of our Lord God, made a request of the king of France, whom he distrusted, for their fathers had distrusted one another and often harmed one another.[364] Richard wished that Philip would reassure him and swear on the relics of saints that he would do no harm to his land, nor harm him at all while he was on God's journey and on his pilgrimage, and that when he had returned to his land, that he would cause no disturbance or war nor do him any harm, without warning him by his French [messengers] forty days before. The king made this oath, giving as pledges great men, of whom we still remember the duke of Burgundy and Count Henry, and other pledges, five or more in number, but I cannot name the others.

[5322–50]   The king of France took his leave but I tell you one thing, on leaving he received more curses than blessings. The marquis and he went by sea to Tyre,[365] taking with them Karakush and their share of the Saracens, who had been shared out, for whom the kings thought to receive one hundred thousand

---

361 This metaphor is used in the New Testament for the relationship between Christ and the Church and the relationship between man and woman, see Ephesians 5:23, 30; Colossians 1:18; 1 Corinthians 11:3.

362 According to the French chronicler, Rigord, however, Philip acquired three galleys prepared for him by the Genoese, Rufus of Volta, pp.306–7.

363 Cf. *Itinerarium*, 3.22.

364 See above, p.30.

365 Cf. *Itinerarium*, 3.23. 31 July 1191, Landon, p.52. Philip sailed from Tyre on 2 August, Roger of Howden, *Chronica*, vol.3, p.126.

besants of their treasury, with which they hoped to support and retain their people until Easter. However, all the hostages were abandoned [by their own side], many of them dying in sorrow, so that not a farthing was received for them,[366] nor anything of any worth at that time, nor any beast, except for half the equipment that the French found at Acre. They often reproved him for having no other payment and it was a subject of much dispute. In the end the king of England, from whom the duke of Burgundy asked for help, lent five thousand silver marks of his own to the duke, against the surety of the hostages, with which they could pay their men greatly to their advantage. But this was much later.

[5351–61][367]   The king of England saw that the whole enterprise and the cost of it now depended on him, because of the king who did not wish to stay, so he obtained from his treasury large amounts of gold and silver, which he gave most freely to the French, to encourage them where there had been only discouragement. He gave also to people of different tongues, that they could redeem their pledges.

[5362–85]   The king of France went home and King Richard, who did not wish to be neglectful of God, made his preparations.[368] Then he had summoned and called together the army, which remained for another two weeks, beyond the term set, then another week, for Saladin did not wish to fulfil his obligations to our people – or God did not wish it – whichever. So the armies waited and the king immediately had his mangonels and catapults loaded, so that he was prepared [to depart].[369] Now the summer passed and he got everything prepared. He had the walls of Acre rebuilt as high, indeed higher, than when they had been destroyed. He himself liked to go and see the workers working, for he was very keen to return God's heritage to him. The waiting wearied him. He would have recovered God's heritage had it not been for the workings of envy.

[5386–413]   The term came for their fulfilment of the agreement, the oath and the undertakings that the Saracens had made to the French. However, the Christians did not know that they were being toyed with by the Saracens; they asked for more time and respite, in order to look for the True Cross. Then you could have heard our people ask for news about when the Cross would come.

---

366 The sum actually referred to here as an expression of little value is the *maille* which was worth half a *denier*.

367 Cf. *Itinerarium*, 4.1.

368 Ambroise finds this dig at Philip II irresistible, but it may well be that, as the author of the Lyon *Eracles* claims, the king had just recovered from a serious fever. The *Eracles* adds that 'it was said' the reason for his anxiety to return was to make good his claim to Flanders following the death of the count, an idea which is not, of course, incompatible with the story of Philip's illness, *La Continuation de Guillaume de Tyr (1184–1197)*, ed. M.R. Morgan, pp.130–1. The rather surprising failure of Baldwin V, Count of Hainaut, to take the Cross in February 1188 at the meeting with the papal legate, Henry of Albano, may be explained by anticipation of these circumstances, for Baldwin V was designated regent by the count of Flanders before he left for the East, van Werweke, 60. Philip's departure did not enhance his reputation. See J. Richard, 'Philippe Auguste, la croisade et le royaume', pp.420–2.

369 Cf. *Itinerarium*, 4.2.

But it was not God's will to defend and protect those for whom it should have been exchanged. One would say 'it has come'; another would say 'so-and so, who was with the Saracens, saw it'. At the end of the day it was all lies. Saladin abandoned the hostages to perish, without rescue, for he hoped to bring about a more significant peace through the Cross.

During these delays the Christians sent messages to the marquis at Tyre,[370] asking and requesting that he surrender the captives to take and receive the proportion due to the king of France, half the agreed sum.

[5414–79] The bishop of Salisbury, Count Robert and one of the brothers of Préaux, the good knight, Peter, a valiant and loyal man, these three, took the message.[371] The marquis, who was enraged, replied to them, that he did not dare go to the army because of King Richard of England, whom he feared more than any man on earth. Moreover, if it happened that he gave up the Turks he held, he wanted the Cross to be shared, so that he would have his share. Then he would give them up without delay. They listened to these outrageous words coming from the dreadful marquis. You should know that they thought the less of him for this; they reasoned with him as best they could and said that one of them would remain behind as a hostage and that he could go before the king in safety. He swore an oath that he would not take his feet there. They returned to Acre, to the king, without taking their leave, and told him everything, omitting nothing. The king felt mocked and insulted and sent for the duke of Burgundy and lord Dreux of Amiens, who was so valiant and worthy, and Robert of Quency.[372] When the king saw them there he showed them the lack of moderation, the excesses and the pretext which the marquis gave for not coming and for keeping his hostages, how he wished to share the realm without bearing shield or helmet, how he had interfered with the provisions, so that not a pennyworth arrived at Tyre without being held and taken. The king said, "This is madness, my lord duke, you must go, for if we have madness in our minds we will do no good." Then the duke of Burgundy set off, with lord Dreux of Amiens and Robert of Quency, the valiant and alert. They went to the marquis at Tyre, admonishing him, in the name of God and in the name of the king of England, that he should come to reconquer and regain Syria, as he claimed a part of it. They spoke to him rashly but he replied foolishly, that he would not set foot in the army and that he would stay in his own city, where he feared no man alive. They debated hard until finally the three messengers, three noble men, took the hostages back to join the others with the army at Acre.

[5480–505][373] The hostages who had been held at Tyre arrived. The time set for the fulfilment of the terms passed; two more weeks passed, indeed more than that, from the time when they said they would keep their word to the Christians. In this way the sultan defaulted and in so doing he acted in a false and treacherous manner when he did not redeem or deliver those who were

---

370 Cf. *Itinerarium*, 4.3.
371 The emissaries were sent by Richard on 5 August, Landon, p.52.
372 Robert of Quency was the son of Saher of Quency, Earl of Winchester, Siedschlag, no.127, p.124.
373 This passage is not in the *Itinerarium*.

condemned to death. Because of this he lost his renown, which was great, for his name was celebrated in every court in the world. But God, having tolerated him for a time, brings down His enemy and upholds and supports His friend, glorifying and controlling His work. But He would not support and exalt Saladin any more, for whatever he did, resisting and working against the Christians, he accomplished only because it was God's will to work through these means to bring back His people who had gone astray and whom He wished to bring back to His way.

[5506–59][374] When King Richard knew for sure and realised without doubt that in truth Saladin was only putting him off, he was then very annoyed and displeased that he had not already moved the army on. And when he knew that Saladin would do nothing more for him and that he had no care for those who had defended Acre for him, then was the matter examined at a council where the great men gathered and decided that they would kill most of the Saracens and keep the others, those of high birth, in order to redeem some of their own hostages. Richard, King of England, who killed so many Turks in that land, did not wish to worry his head about it any more, but [in order to] bring down the pride of the Turks, disgrace their religion and avenge Christianity, he brought out of the town, in bonds, two thousand and seven hundred people who were all slaughtered. Thus was vengeance taken for the blows and the crossbow bolts.[375] Thanks be to God the Creator.

So the army was summoned and called together, at the setting of the sun [. . .][376] and that they would soon ride out and cross the river of Acre, in the name of God, the giver of all good things,[377] to go straight to Ascalon, to conquer the shoreline. Biscuits and flour, wine and meat, provisions were loaded. An order was given that they should carry provisions for ten days and that the seamen would ensure that they would come with their smaller boats, keeping close to the shore, near the army, with their loads, and that the snacks would similarly come closely after, loaded with provisions and people, armed and prepared. So it was said that they would journey in two armies, one travelling by land, one by sea, for no-one could conquer Syria any other way as long as the Turks controlled it.

---

374 Cf. *Itinerarium*, 4.4.

375 Landon, p.53, gives 20 August as the date for the killing of the prisoners, based on Roger of Howden, but see also *Itinerarium*, 4.4, giving 16 August. Baha' al-Din, pp.164–5, discusses these events in detail. He regards the massacre as justification for Saladin's negotiating tactics, since it was proof that Richard had always intended to act treacherously: 'Various reasons were given for this massacre. It was said they had killed them in revenge for their men who had been killed or that the king of England had decided to march to Ascalon to take control of it and did not think it wise to leave that number in his rear. God knows best.' See below, p.189.

376 Cf. *Itinerarium*, 4.5. Lacuna supplied in Paris's translation from the *Itinerarium*: 'Il fut crié partout qu'ils se mettraient en marche' (It was announced everywhere that they were setting out). This is included in Stone's translation without comment.

377 Matthew 7:11.

The Army on the March

[5560–605][378]   The army had been at Acre for two winters and a summer at
great cost and loss, until the middle of August when the king carried out the killings of those who had merited death for what they did to God and His pilgrims,
because of whom there were left behind so many orphans, so many unprotected
girls, so many widowed wives, so many abandoned inheritances, so many families brought down, so many bishoprics and so many churches left alone, without
their pastors; there died so many princes and counts – a clerk wrote down the list
of all those who died in the army who were of any renown, not counting the
middle-ranking and lesser men – for if he had wanted to write of all of them he
would never have completed the task because it would cost too much in writing
and expense. It is found and written in the account, written in his hand, that
there died in the army six archbishops, the patriarch and twelve bishops, apart
from priests and clerics about whose numbers no-one could be certain; there
died also forty counts, of whom the clerk kept the record, and five hundred great
landowners, who went to seek God; may God absolve them and welcome them
into His kingdom.[379] For all who died there, and for all who went there, for the
great and the lesser, who supported the army of God, for all together, we should
pray to God from our hearts that God in Heavenly glory, where it shall be
glorious to be, will welcome them among His friends, as He has promised to
them. For their benefit and for our own let everyone say "Our Father . . ."[380]
[5606–61][381]   When the pack of curs who had been holed up in Acre, where
they had released so many attacks on us, were killed, then King Richard had his
tents moved and set up beyond the ditches in readiness for the moving on of the
army. He had foot-soldiers stationed and lodged around him because of the false
Saracens who came baying with violence against us at any time, when our
people were least expecting it. The king, accustomed to these alarms, was the
first to leap to his arms and head straight for that hated race, performing great
deeds of knighthood.
    One day it happened that they harried us, beginning the skirmishing.[382] So
our men armed, the king and those who were with him, among them a count of
Hungary and a great company of Hungarians.[383] They sallied out against the

---

378 Cf. *Itinerarium*, 4.6.
379 Roger of Howden, *Gesta*, vol.2, pp.147–50, lists some of these by name. The patriarch was
     Heraclius of Caesarea, Patriarch of Jerusalem since 1180, Hamilton, *Latin Church*, pp.83–4.
380 Paris has the sentence break, a semi-colon, after 'for their good and for our own'. HL have a
     colon. Stone breaks the sentence as we do.
381 Cf. *Itinerarium*, 4.7.
382 Cf. *Itinerarium*, 4.8.
383 Geza, younger brother of King Bela III, together with 2,000 men, joined Frederick
     Barbarossa's army when it passed through Hungary in June 1189. See Z.J. Kosztolnyik, *From
     Coloman the Learned to Béla III (1095–1196): Hungarian Domestic Policies and their Impact
     upon Foreign Affairs*, East European Monographs, Boulder, 120 (New York, 1987),
     pp.214–15. It seems probable that the Hungarians mentioned here derived from this contigent,
     but 'the count of Hungary' is difficult to identify. The first part of the *Itinerarium*, 1.31,

Turks and there were those who did well, but they pursued them too long and misfortune followed. The count of Hungary who was of great renown in the army, was taken, as was Huguelot,[384] a knight from Poitou and marshal to the king. The king spurred on in great haste, thinking to rescue Huguelot, but he had been taken too far. The Turks had one advantage that brought much harm to us. The Christians are heavily armed and the Saracens unarmed, but for a bow, a club and a sword or metalled spear or knife of little weight. When they are chased after, they have such horses – there are no better anywhere in the world – they seem to fly like swallows. When the Turk is followed he cannot be reached. Then he is like an annoying venomous fly; when chased he flees; turn back and he follows. So did the cruel race harass the king; he rode and they fled; he turned back and they followed. At one point they suffered; at another they had the upper hand.

[5662–79][385]   King Richard was in his tent, awaiting the coming of the army. They were reluctant to come out across the ditches and the numbers increased but little. Yet the city of Acre was so full of people that it could hardly hold them all. There were at least three hundred thousand men within and around the town. The people were too reluctant because the town was delightful with good wines and girls, some very beautiful. They frequented the women and enjoyed the wine, taking their foolish pleasure, so that there was in the town such unseemliness, such sin and such lust that worthy men were ashamed by what the others were doing.

[5680–713]   The host was summoned and sallied out; as a protected candle is put out by the wind when exposed, so the wantonness that had taken hold in the army, had to be extinguished by force; for all the women would remain in the city of Acre except for virtuous elderly women pilgrims, the laundresses who were on the pilgrimage, who washed the clothes and heads, and were as good as monkeys at getting rid of fleas. So the army armed in the morning and set out in good order. The king was in the rearguard so that they would not suffer losses by being caught unprepared. That day the distance covered was small. As soon as the accursed tribe had seen the army on the move, then you would have seen them coming, like rain from the mountains, twenty here, thirty there. For their minds were full of sorrow because of the killings which they saw, the killing of their family members who lay dead; because of this they harried the army, following it and attacking it, but thanks to God, they did no harm. When our people left there and crossed the river of Acre they set up camp and put up their tents and waited for those of God's people whom it was difficult to draw out of

---

includes a Count Nicholas of Hungary in the list of arrivals at Acre in autumn 1189, and it is likely that this is the same person. See J.R. Sweeney, 'Hungary in the Crusades, 1169–1218', *The International History Review* 3 (1981), 471–2. Sweeney thinks that he was the Nicholas who was successively Count of Szatmár in 1181, Count of Zala in 1199, *Ban* of Slavonia in 1200 and Count Palatine of Hungary in 1205–6.

384 Huguelot has not been identified.
385 Cf. *Itinerarium*, 4.9.

Acre, for it was so difficult to get them out that they could not all be got out at once.[386]

[5714–815] The Christian army of which I tell you crossed the river on a Friday. The next day was a feast day, when no one did any manual labour; it was the Feast of the apostle St Bartholomew, one of the disciples of our Lord.[387] The Monday after it was in truth two years after the beginning of the siege of Acre, now taken by the Christians. On the Sunday the army moved on, in the name of God who directs and leads everything. Early in the morning the army mounted and drew up in their units.[388] There you would have seen chivalry, the finest of young men, the most worthy and most elite that were ever seen, before then or since. There you would have seen so many confident men, with such fine armour, such valiant and daring men-at-arms, renowned for their prowess. There you would have seen so many pennoncels on shining, fine lances; there you would have seen so many banners, worked in many designs, fine hauberks and good helmets; there are not so many of such quality in five kingdoms; there you would have seen a people on the march who were much to be feared. King Richard was in the vanguard, with such men as were not cowards. The Normans were around the standard; they often had the guard of it. The duke and the French, a proud people, formed the rearguard, but they took so long on the way that things inevitably went wrong.

The army went along the edge of the sea and the cruel race of Saracens were on the left, in the dunes, and could see our people well; a fog had risen that would bring trouble to the army. The column thinned out, attenuating where the carters who were transporting the food went. The Saracens rushed down, singling out the carters, killed men and horses, took a lot of baggage and defeated and put to rout those who led [the convoy], chasing them into the foaming sea. There they fought so much that they cut off the hand of a man-at-arms, called Evrart, so they told me, one of the bishop of Salisbury's men; he paid no attention to this and made no fuss when his right hand was chopped off, but taking his sword in his left hand, stood firm, waiting for them, so that he defended himself against them all. So the whole army was in chaos, but King Richard knew nothing about it. The rearguard was brought to a standstill, afraid and in disarray.

Then came riding up John FitzLucas,[389] and told the king at once. The king returned straight away, and with him his trusty companions, coming back from the vanguard and galloping against the Turks, as far as the rise. He went into their midst, quicker than a flash of lightning, and I do not know how many he killed, before they recognised him – they would have had a bad neighbour in him had he known of these events earlier. A Frenchman did well that day, the worthy William des Barres, who stretched many a Turk on the ground, and that day gave so much of himself that the king forgave him an offence that he held

386 The departure from Acre was on 22 August and the crossing of the River Belus the next day, Landon, p.53.
387 24 August.
388 Cf. *Itinerarium*, 4.6.
389 See the speculations of Round, 477, on this knight.

against him, so that he had no more bad feelings towards him.[390] They pushed
the Turks back to the mountains and killed I do not know how many Saracens.
Saladin was there in person with his pagan forces but after he saw his people
being repulsed they stopped and considered [matters]. The army, which they
had disordered, went on in good order, until they came to a river. Then they
tested the cisterns, set up camp and put up their tents in a large open area that
they could see and where Saladin had lain; it was clear that he had been there
with an immeasurably great army of the hostile people.

[5816–39]   This was how things went for the army on that first day, when the
Turk made war on them. This is what happens to a conquering army. God did
this for their salvation, so that the army would go on without misdeeds, closer
together and in better order than it had been when it was attacked. They made
great efforts and conducted themselves more wisely. But their task became
harder, for the filth, Saladin and his pack, had gone behind the mountain in the
narrow passes which our people had to cross.[391] They had set things up so that
the army would be dead or taken, or at least that they might be so exposed that
they would be utterly defeated. Our people left the river, making only a small
advance that day; they encamped below Caïphas, to wait for the lesser men.[392]

[5840–53][393]   Below Caïphas on the coast the worthy and proud people had
encamped all around in two groups, between the tower and the sea. They stayed
there for two days, preparing their equipment. They threw away what was of no
use and kept what seemed good to them. For the footsoldiers, the lesser men,
had come with such difficulty, so burdened with food and arms for the battle
that a number had to be left behind to die of heat and thirst.

[5854–85]   When the army of God had rested below Caïphas and had made
ready, they departed, on a Tuesday, drawn up in their divisions. The Templars
had the vanguard and the Hospitallers the rearguard. To any who saw the divisions made, the army seemed of great moment and it set out in better order than
it had been the other time. Because of the delay they had to make considerable
progress in one day. However, along the shore grew tall grasses and great thorny
bushes which troubled the footsoldiers and struck them in the face. The whole
land was a wilderness; there you would have seen much hunting of the plenteous
wildlife that was found along the shore, which would rise up at their feet, so
could be taken in plenty.

---

390 On the Barre family, see above, p.94. William des Barres had quarrelled with Richard during a
     mock tournament in Messina, 2–5 February 1191: Roger of Howden, *Gesta*, vol.2, pp.155–7;
     Roger of Howden, *Chronica*, vol.3, pp.93–4. However, the source of this hostility may well be
     found in an incident in 1188 when William was captured by Richard near Mantes. Placed on
     his honour not to escape, he nevertheless broke his pledge when the opportunity arose, thus
     depriving his captor of the ransom money. For his part William seems to have believed that he
     had been unfairly captured in the first place. See M. Strickland, *War and Chivalry: The
     Conduct and Perception of War in England and Normandy, 1066–1217* (Cambridge, 1996),
     p.52.
391 Cf. *Itinerarium*, 4.11.
392 26 August 1191, Landon, p.53.
393 Cf. *Itinerarium*, 4.12.

The king came to the castle of Capharnaum,[394] torn down by those whom we hate; he dismounted, ate, and waited for the army. Those who wished to, ate, and afterwards went as far as the castle of Destroit, which was not wide but narrow. They arrived there and dismounted, set up camp and pitched their tents. [5886–923] Every day when the army was encamped, in the evening, before they lay down, there was one man who would shout and the whole army shouted back, for his voice could be heard all around; he cried, "Holy Sepulchre, Help", and everyone would cry out after him and raise their hands towards Heaven, and weep and he would at once cry out again until he had shouted three times and they were invigorated by this.

During the day the army was quite safe but in the darkness of the night they were under considerable attack from stinging worms and tarantulas who harassed them greatly, stinging the pilgrims who would at once swell up.[395] However, the great men gave them some theriac which they had and which immediately cured them.[396] The tarantulas attacked but wise men were on the alert and when the vermin came and were seen then you would have heard such a racket – Ambroise testifies to this – such tumult and such banging, such noise and such a beating, beating of helmets and headgear, of casks and saddles and heavy cloths, shields, long shields and round bucklers, basins and pots and pans and the vermin would flee because of the dreadful racket, and as they got accustomed to doing this, they repulsed the vermin.

[5924–85] At the Casel where the army stopped,[397] there it made provisions and prepared itself against the cruel, hated people who would attack them frequently. The place and area was extensive.[398] The king and the army needed two days of respite and rest to wait for the food there. Then the vessels came, small boats and galleys, following the army along the coast, bringing food. They returned to the Casel. The king, who had lain at Merle, had prepared and made provision.[399] He decided that he would take the vanguard that day, that they would be protected from the front, and that the Templars would take the rear-guard and they would do this because the Saracens were close to the army and continually harried them.

That day the king of England, who should be much praised for this, spurred on and would have done great deeds of valour had it not been for the laziness [of

---

[394] Richard left Haifa on 28 August, passing through Capharnaum that day, and reached the Templar castle of Destroit, which he left the following day. See HL, p.456, for the dating. As the name implies, the passage between Mount Carmel and the sea was very narrow here, and the Templars had improved the fortification of Destroit (Khirbat Dustray) in order to defend the route between Haifa and Caesarea: Kennedy, pp.56–7; Pringle, *Secular Buildings*, no.90, pp.47–8 (map 5).

[395] Cf. *Itinerarium*, 4.13.

[396] Nicholson, p.241, n.32, notes that theriac was 'a classical Latin cure-all and antidote against poisonous snake-bites'. By *poignanz* Ambroise possibly means scorpions.

[397] l.5924. There is a textual problem here. The manuscript has, *se reusa*, 'recoiled', which is corrected in the text (following Paris) to *s'aresta*.

[398] l.5928. Paris and Stone point out that this is inconsistent with the description of the casel above, and that it doubtless refers to a wide place beyond the casel.

[399] Tantura. Cf. *Itinerarium*, 4.14.

others]. For the king and his men pursued [the enemy], but there were others whose lethargy brought them much blame at evening, and rightly so, for he who would have followed the king would have had a fine passage of arms. However, he repulsed the Turks and the army advanced along the sand, in order and at a slow pace, for it was excessively hot and the day's journey was long and arduous, not a short one. The heat was so intolerable that some died of it; these were buried at once. Those who could not go on, the worn-out and exhausted, of whom there were often many, the sick and infirm, the king, acting wisely, had carried in the galleys and the small boats to the next stage. That journey was made with difficulty and the harbingers went as far as the city of Caesarea. The enemy had been there and had destroyed the town, wreaking great damage and destruction. However, when Richard came, they fled and our people dismounted there, set up camp and pitched tents beyond a river that they found there. This river is still known as Crocodile River, for two pilgrims bathed in it and were eaten by crocodiles.[400]

[5986–6031] There is a great defensive wall around the city of Caesarea, a city where God did many works, for He and His dear companions spent much time along this coast.[401] There the king gave orders for the snacks that were coming after him; he had it announced in Acre, to bring out the lethargic, that they should board the ships and join the army, for the Lord's sake. A large number came before the army left. There could be seen, one evening, at Caesarea, the rich fleet, with its accompanying flotilla of small boats, following the army along the coast each day, supplying the army's needs for food, despite that pack of curs. At the hour of terce was the army ready to move – Ambroise knows this for certain – armed and well-equipped, in good order. It was decided that a short stage would be travelled because of the Saracens, who rained down on them each day as soon as they moved. That day they rode after the army but they lost there an emir, a man of renown and great boldness and such strength that no-one could knock him down, nor even dare attack him. He had a heavy lance of such weight that no two greater could be found in France. He was Ayas Estoï – I heard him called by this name.[402] The Turks lamented him so much that they cut off their horses' tails; they would have willingly carried off his body if the Christians had left it to them. The Christians left there and went on till they came to the Dead River, which the wicked, underhand Saracens had covered over, but it was uncovered and they drank of it and lay there for two nights.

[6032–113] When the bold people had rested there for two days they moved away from the river;[403] they travelled slowly, not in haste, through a poor, wasted

---

400 30 August. Crocodile River (Nahr al-Zarqa). The *Itinerarium*, 4.14, p.256, says that it had this name because 'crocodiles had once eaten two knights who were bathing there' (Nicholson, p.242).

401 31 August, Landon, p.54. Ambroise may be confusing here the town of Caesarea Maritima, the home of Philip the Evangelist (Acts 21:8), visited by Paul (Acts 9, 18, 21, 23) and Peter (Acts 10, 11) and the residence of Pilate, and Caesarea Philippi, at the foot of Mount Hermon, visited by Christ (Matthew 16; Mark 8).

402 Baha' al-Din, p.171: 'This day one of the brave knights of Islam was killed, Ayaz the Tall, a mamluke of the sultan.' On mamluks, see below, p.121.

403 They left the Dead River (Nahr al-Mafjr) on 3 September, Landon, p.54.

land.[404] That day they went by the mountain, for the shore was so wild and full of obstructions that they could not pass. That day the army moved in closer order than it would ever again. The rearguard was taken by the Templars, who furrowed their temples in the evening because they had lost so many horses during the day that they nearly despaired. The count of St Pol also lost many horses there, for he had with courage faced suffering from the Turks and their daring and all day had been so exposed that the whole army praised him for it. That day the king of England, who went after the Turks closely, was injured in the side by a dart from a Turk whom he had attacked.[405] However, he was not seriously hurt and quickly turned on them. There you would have seen bolts flying, horses dying and injured, such a storm of bolts that you would not have found four feet of empty land around where the army of God was. The hardship that the army suffered lasted all day until evening when the Turks withdrew to their camp and settled there and our men made camp. They settled by a salt water river.[406] There you would have seen a huge crowd around the fattest of the dead horses that had been killed that day. The soldiers bought the meat, though at a high price, and there was considerable brawling over them. When the king heard of this he had an announcement made that whoever had lost his horse to death and gave some of it to the worthy men-at-arms the king would exchange it for a live horse. So they had the dead horses without any problems. They took them, skinned them and ate the best cuts of meat with bacon.

They stayed there for two days.[407] On the third day at the hour of terce they moved on, in battle order, for it was said that the black and evil hordes of unbelievers had moved into the forest of Arsuf[408] and that during that day they would set light to it, and that they would cause such a great fire that the army would be roasted, but the whole army passed on its way through the forest of Arsuf in good order. Indeed, I do not think that any man saw nor would ever see in any place a finer march than they made there. They had no delays but marched on without hindrance. That day they crossed Mont Arsuf and passed through the forest and came out to open country. There they camped on the plain, by the River Rochetaille,[409] despite the people of circumcision who rained on them from every side. One who saw them, surveyed them and looked them over, estimated them at three hundred thousand, unless he was somewhat mistaken, while there were no more than an estimated one hundred thousand of our Christians.

[6114–295] The army of God and His household lay by the River Rochetaille. There they camped on a Thursday and stayed for the Friday.[410] At daybreak on

---

[404] Cf. *Itinerarium*, 4.15.

[405] l.6054. A *pilet* can be either a bolt from a crossbow or a throwing spear. Illustrations in Nicolle, *Arms and Armour*, pp.322, 804; 343, 815.

[406] They rested at the Salt River (Nahr al-Qasab) on 3 and 4 September, Landon, p.54.

[407] Cf. *Itinerarium*, 4.16.

[408] According to Baha' al-Din, pp.172–3, Saladin stationed his army on a *tell* in the wood of Arsuf near a village called Dair ar-Raheb (possibly Dair Asfin). This area extended for about 12 miles (19 kilometres) south of the Salt River. On this phase of the march, see Norgate, *Richard the Lion Heart*, pp.180–5.

[409] They camped by the River Rochetaille (Nahr al-Falek) on 5 September, Landon, p.54.

[410] 5 and 6 September, Landon, p.54.

the Saturday then you would have seen the men prepare, each to defend his own head, preparing in their units for they had heard that they could not go forward without a battle towards the hordes, who were coming upon them from all sides. So the Christian army got ready to go against the pagans in such order, so that in battle order they needed no re-organising or reproof. Richard, the worthy king of England, who knew so much about war and the army, set out in his own way who should go in front and who behind. They organised twelve battalions and split them into divisions made up of such men that, as the sky covers the earth, no better could be found. They were firm in their hearts, determined to serve God. The Templars that day had the vanguard and the Hospitallers the rearguard. Bretons and Angevins together went next, I think; the Poitevins and King Guy came after, so I believe; the Normans and the English rode behind, bearing the dragon[411] and the Hospitallers were at the back, for that day they formed the rearguard. The rearguard that day was furnished with great men and in such order, side by side and so close that an apple [thrown in their midst] could not have failed to strike man or beast; they extended from the Saracen army right down to the shore. There you would have seen so many banners and people of bold appearance. There was the earl of Leicester, who would not have wished to be elsewhere, and Hugh of Gournay[412] with his renowned men, and there was also William of Borris,[413] a man raised in that land, and there was Walchelin of Ferrières and all sorts of people; there was Roger of Tosny with a great host of knights and the worthy James of Avesnes, whom God took that day into his kingdom; there was Count Robert of Dreux and a number of his men, and the bishop of Beauvais, who had come to his brother. The lord of Barres and the lord of Garlande were also there with a great company; William and Dreux of Mello had not a few men with them. The men of different lineage marched together and came back together so that the army was so bound together that it could only with difficulty be split asunder. Count Henry of Champagne had charge of the army on the flank nearest the mountain. That day he was responsible for protecting the flanks and continually rode up and down the ranks; the foot-soldiers were behind the army, bringing up the rear. The equipment and

---

411 Richard's standard, see G.S.P. Tatlock, 'The Dragon of Wessex and Wales', *Speculum* 8 (1933), 226.

412 Hugh of Gournay-en-Bray was an Anglo-Norman vassal of Richard, who held lands along the rivers Epte and Bresle on the crucial frontier between Normandy and France, which were the subject of agreements between Richard and Philip in 1194–6. He also held other lands in Buckinghamshire, Norfolk and Suffolk. He arrived at Tyre on 16 September 1190, in Archbishop Baldwin's advance party, and he was named joint governor of Acre on 13 July 1191 after the city's fall. He continued to witness Richard's charters throughout the 1190s: Landon, pp.40–1, 51, 54, 78, 97, 107, 118, 127–8, 132–3, 137, 140; Powicke, *Loss of Normandy*, pp.108–9, 285–6, 340–1; Siedschlag, no.56, p.117.

413 Paris, p.533, suggests that William of Borris was a Norman knight from Boury-en-Vexin (Oise), south of Gisors, and that *terre* should read *guerre*, since no-one of this name can be identified in the East at this time. He may be the same person listed among the French at the great tournament held at Lagny-sur-Marne (about 10 miles, 17 kilometres, east of Paris) in 1180, *History of William Marshal*, vol. 1, l. 4521, pp. 230–1. However, the text makes sense as it stands, so he might have been brought up in the East, as Ambroise says.

provisions, carts, pack-horses, baggage, were down on the shore, so that they would be less vulnerable to loss.

Thus the army advanced with confidence, gently and slowly; the divisions advanced in this way. The duke of Burgundy with the king, with bold and fierce men of valour, went in front of the army and behind, to the right and to the left, to keep an eye on the Turks and their doings in order to guide and lead the army; it was necessary to make this effort for about one hour before the hour of terce the Turks came upon them, more than two thousand drawing their bows, surrounding the army.[414] After them came a black people; they were called 'blacks' – this is the truth – and the Saracens from the wild land, hideous and blacker than soot, with bows and crossbows, a people who were very quick and agile. They pressed upon the army without end or respite. Then you would have seen across the countryside such a rich company of Turks, so many pennoncels, so many ensigns, so many banners bearing devices, such fine, well ordered units. It was estimated that more than thirty thousand Turks came up, in fine array, coming with fury straight down on the army, on horses which were faster than lightning! Such dust was thrown up before them by their hooves! In front of the emirs came those who carried the trumpets, the drums and other timbrels; they had no other task than the beating of drums and making of noise, howling, shouting, baying. There one could not have heard God thundering, such a racket was made by the drums. The hordes fell upon the army, attacking and assailing them. For two leagues around you could not have found an empty plot of earth nor space the size of my lap, not any place free of those of an evil race. Land-ward and seaward they attacked so closely, with such strength and such excesses that they did them much harm by killing their horses, many of whom fell down dead. That day the good crossbowmen and the good men-at-arms, shooting from the rear did fine service to the army. They thought their lines would be broken for they were attacked so intensely that they did not expect to survive one hour or come out of it whole; know in truth that the cowards could not help throwing down their bows and arrows and taking refuge in the army, while the bold who remained, who supported the army from the rear, were so pressed back on their heels that day they advanced backwards more than in any other direction. In the whole army there was no man who was so confident that he did not wish in his heart that he had finished his pilgrimage. However, this should not be wondered at for the army was so harried on the right and on the left that never did any man born of the will of God see a people so up against it nor an army in such trouble; there you might have seen knights, when they lost their horses, go on shooting bows on foot with the men-at-arms; I can tell you and recount that never did rain or snow or hail falling in the heart of winter fall so densely as did the bolts which flew there and killed our horses – many would know if I were lying; there you could have gathered the bolts in armfuls like the gleaners gathering the corn in the cut fields, so did the violent horde shoot, so much did they press upon our units that they very nearly destroyed them. Then the Hospitallers sent a message

---

414 Cf. *Itinerarium*, 4.18. 7 September, 1191, Landon, p.54. Baha' al-Din, pp.174–6, for a Muslim account of the battle. For a plan of the battle, see N. Hooper and M. Bennett, *Cambridge Illustrated Atlas of Warfare: The Middle Ages 768–1487* (Cambridge, 1996), p.101.

to the king that they were doing so much damage to their unit that they could not endure it any longer unless they attacked. The king replied that they should hold firm and put up with the damage; they endured, perforce and with suffering, and held to their way.

[6296–350]   God had ordained that it should be very hot that day; the heat was great and the people fierce, harrying our people from behind. I tell you this that there is no people on earth, however brave, that would not fear if they saw the crowd and hordes of those hostile pagans, their fury and temerity, impelled by the devil, if they saw our suffering, if they did not know their ways; for as the smith strikes while the iron is hot on his anvil[415] so did their people strike eagerly on the rearguard, that day made up of many worthy men [. . .][416] They had no concern for themselves, as they ought to have had, and they did them much harm,[417] seeing them off with maces. There you would have seen empty places around men who might have been elsewhere, who would not acknowledge that they should give up their position on account of the Turks, nor withdraw by one foot for them. They did otherwise, fighting fiercely; they struck directly against the gathered hordes, in suffering and fear.[418] It is not to be wondered at, if anyone should wonder at it, for in all the forces of pagandom, from Damascus to Persia, from the sea to the Eastern limits, there was no bold race, no men of confidence and renown, none who was victorious, valiant or daring, whom Saladin had not sought out, hired, beseeched or requested, searched out and retained, because of the people of God who had come and whom he then thought to defeat. However, they could not have sufficed, for this was the flower of chivalry, the elite of the young knights, the experts in war; this was the gathering of the best of all Christendom, come to fight against the pagan, a people who were worthy and set apart; whoever could defeat them could say with confidence that nothing could prevail against him.

[6351–530][419]   The dust and the heat were great and the people of God were full of valour; the people of the devil were filled with pride and the people of God were valiant and defended themselves well. There the Turks were piled up, like a thick hedge. The Christians went on their way, the pagans pursuing them from behind, but they could do little damage to them. There you would have seen the Turks go mad with rage, the people of the devil of hell, who called us iron men because we were clad in armour, our men so protected that they felt less afraid of the pagans' attacks. They put their bows into their quivers and came upon us with clubs. There were in a short space of time more than twenty thousand of them who were hammering against the Hospitallers. Then one of the Hospitallers shouted out, "St George, will you let us be defeated like this? Now, Christianity should collapse since no-one offers battle to this pack of

---

415 The image here is quite clear but the actual construction in French of l.6310 is rather obscure.
416 After l.6313 there is a lacuna of at least one line.
417 It is difficult to know who is harming whom, which is the usual problem with the use of pronouns in Old French, exacerbated by the lacuna, which may have indicated a change of subject.
418 Paris suggests a change of subject.
419 Cf. *Itinerarium*, 4.19.

curs." This was Brother Garnier of Nablus, Master of the Hospitallers.[420] He came up to the king, spurred on in haste and said, "Sir, we are harried shamefully and wrongfully; everyone is losing his mount." And the king said, "Put up with it, Master, one cannot be everywhere at once." He went back to his unit. The Turks harried them from behind, so that there was neither prince nor count who was not ashamed in himself. They said, "My lords, let us charge them! We are being taken for cowards! Such shame has never been seen, nor was our army ever put under such reproach by the infidel and, if to await anyone,[421] we delay in defending ourselves, we may delay too long." God ! What loss, what misfortune, what sorrow and what suffering came to the army at this time, when so many Saracens would have died had sin not interfered with the attack that had been planned. If only they had carried out the plan of attack, which everyone agreed upon and which had already been decided: before the divisions spurred forward six trumpets would be placed in three different places in the army, which would sound when they were to turn against the Turks, two in front, two behind and two in the middle. Had they kept to this the Turks would all have been taken.

All was lost because of two men who could not hold back from charging; they rushed forward first and left two Turks dead. One of these two was a knight, the Marshal of the Hospitallers,[422] the other was Baldwin of Carew,[423] who was as bold as a lion, a companion of the king of England who had brought him from his land. These two began the foolish attack in the name of the Almighty King. They loudly invoked St George and the people of the Lord turned their horses round against the arrogant cruel people. Then the long-suffering Hospitallers advanced in order. There advanced the lord of Champagne, with his dear companions, James of Avesnes with those of his lineage, the Count Robert, the Lord of Dreux, I am sure of it, with him the bishop of Beauvais; the two advanced together, the earl of Leicester spurred towards the sea, on his left, and all those of the rearguard; there were no cowards there. After came the Angevins, the Bretons, the men of Maine and the men of Poitou and all the other units together. I tell you how it seems to me: that the valiant men who advanced there met the Turks with such [force] that each reached his [opponent]; he struck the iron of his lance into his body, so that he had to quit the saddle. It took the Turks by surprise, for our men came down on them like lightning. There you would have seen such dust fly; all those who had dismounted to fire their bows, which had hit our people hard, they all had their heads cut off – as they were knocked down

---

420 Garnier of Nablus, a former Prior of England and Grand Commander of France, was elected Master in late 1189 or 1190, and accompanied Richard on the journey to the East. He died in late 1192. Riley-Smith, *Knights of St John*, pp.107–8, 112, 117.

421 There is a textual problem in l.6392; the word *recoillier* does not appear to be attested elsewhere. Paris has in his glossary 'mot altéré non restitué' (corrupt term left uncorrected) and he omits this phrase in his translation; Stone has 'for any scruple'.

422 Riley-Smith, *Knights of St John*, pp.113, 318–19, refers to this incident, but does not name the individual. It is perhaps either Lambert (marshal in 1188) or William Borrel (marshal in 1193).

423 Baldwin of Carew was in fact from Hainaut, the son of Roger of Rumes (near Tournai). He had been a vassal of both Philip of Alsace and Baldwin V of Hainaut, but had joined Richard's army for the expedition to the East. He died sometime after 17 June 1192, van Werweke, 86.

the men-at-arms killed them. As soon as the troubled king saw that the army was disordered and had broken rank, he spurred his horse to the gallop without waiting any longer and let it run at speed, to help the first of the divisions. Faster then the bolt from a crossbow with his valiant and well-tried[424] entourage he came to a division of pagans on the right, a group of them, striking them indiscriminately so hard that they were stunned, because of the valiant men they encountered there, who made them quit their saddles. Then you would have seen them lying on the ground, as thick as sheaves of corn. The valiant king of England came after them and came down upon them. He did such deeds at that time that all around him, above and below, behind and beside were the bodies[425] of Saracens, who fell dead, so that the others fled. The line of the dead lasted for half a league. There you would have seen Turks stumble and Saracens unhorsed; there you would have seen the dust fly, which nearly undid our people, for when they came out of the press they could not recognise each other, because of the dust; this doubled their trouble. Then they struck blows to the right and to the left; there the Turks had trouble; there you would have seen blows given, bloodied men leaving the field of battle; there you would have seen banners and all sorts of pennoncels fall, such good sharp swords and steel-tipped spears; you could have picked up so many Turkish crossbows and many clubs, darts, bolts and arrows; you could have filled more than twenty carts with them; there you would have seen many bearded Turks lying as thick as sheaves of corn; you would have seen those who held firm fighting well, and those who had been defeated, who had lost their horses skulking in the bushes or climbing up trees, from where they were dragged out. You would have heard their howls as they were killed. Those who had fled towards the sea left their horses and leapt over the cliffs, to drop more than sixty feet. Their people were thoroughly repulsed, so that for two full leagues around you could see only fugitives of those who before were so cocksure. For all our men turned against them. Those who were guarding the standard (Normans – the most reliable race) took a long time to turn at their slow pace, I suspect, so that the business would have had to go very badly for harm to come to them.

[6531–622]   The warriors who were on God's side stopped their gallop and as soon as they stopped the Saracens recovered. More than twenty thousand came, holding clubs in their hands, to rescue the fallen. There you would have seen our men beaten. Those who were returning to the host the Saracens were shooting on continually, striking them with their clubs, breaking heads and arms, so that they leaned against their pommels. The valiant men recovered as soon as they recovered their breath, then they spurred on with great effort, striking the divisions [of the enemy] breaking them like fine threads; there you would have seen saddles turning and Turks fleeing and flying. There our men were under such pressure that they could not have advanced an arrow's flight; had the divisions not stopped they would have paid dearly for it. There was the Emir Dequedin, a

---

424   1.6468, *teste*. Paris's glossary has 'mot inconnu' and it is not in any of the dictionaries. It may
      be derived from *taster*, 'to put to the test'.

425   1.6479, *charriere*, cart-road/route. It could possibly be corrected to *charniere*, charnel house,
      but this would be rather obscure. Stone has 'a great open highway, filled with . . .'

relative of Saladin, who bore on his banner a strange device; his banner bore breeches, this was his true device.[426] This was the Turk who was most eager in his hatred of Christianity. He had with him more than seven hundred elite Turks, Saladin's own men, who could be conquered only at great cost. Each unit had a yellow banner with a pennoncel of a different colour[427] and came with such speed, such force and such impetus, to strike even those of experience who had turned to the standard, with the arms they bore, that there was none so valiant nor so clever who at that time would not have something to consider. There you would have seen our people wait; there you would have seen many attacks; there you would have seen many strong blows. For they returned to the main body of the army; for the Saracens pressed upon them so that the body of each man reeled so that few men turned back, and they paid the price with blows on their helmets.[428] Then the valiant William des Barres made an attack that everyone praised. He and his men threw themselves between our men and the press of the hostile race, striking them with such force that I do not know how many Turks fell, never to see battle again. The noble king of England charged on again, near the mountain, with his bold company. He was mounted on Fauvel of Cyprus, the best horse from here to Ypres, and did such acts of knightly prowess against the ugly race, the enemy, that they marvelled at him, how he and his people came together. They repulsed the enemy so well and held the ground until our men came back to the standard and immediately fell into line again. Then they rode and journeyed on as far as Sur[429] where they dismounted. There they pitched camp and erected their tents, for it was time to settle [for the night]. Any who wanted to collect some booty went to the scene of the battle; there they gathered some without difficulty. Those who went there said that they counted thirty-two lords of property, emirs, who died on the field of battle that day, whose bodies would later be sought, and seven hundred Turks left there, who lay dead in the fields, as well as the injured. There were not a tenth of that number dead among us, no not even a tenth of a tenth.

[6623–50][430] Oh God! What an affliction, what a dreadful loss we suffered there, where our men were, when the Saracens rallied, the loss of a valiant man whom they cut off and surrounded! This was the worthy James of Avesnes, may God make him [a saint] in His kingdom, for much misfortune came to us because of his horse, which fell under him. However, he defended himself so well, so we are told and understand, that after the end of the a battle, when his

---

426 Mayer, *Saracenic Heraldry*, pp.21, 243. For heraldry and the crusades, see A. Ailes, *Origins of the Royal Arms of England*, pp.35–7. The emir has not been identified.

427 These were Saladin's mamluks. See the description by WT, 21.22(23), p.991.

428 ll.6582–5. Paris bases his interpretation of this difficult passage partly on the Latin text: 'Les sarrasins les serraient de si près qu'il y eut peu qui osèrent retourner sur eux et que tous sentaient leurs corps trembler des coups qu'ils recevaient sur les heaumes.' Stone follows him quite closely. HL, p.263, have, 'we staggered 'neath the blows/ Dealt on our helmets by our foes,/ Who checked our progress with their might.'

429 Sur is normally interpreted as Tyre but it is clear from what follows that they are encamped outside Arsuf (medieval Arsur). The shortened name is perhaps simply because of syllable count.

430 Cf. *Itinerarium*, 4.20.

body was searched for, where he lay among the hordes of curs, that for some distance around his body the worthy men who went there, found a good fifteen Turks, all hacked down, the valiant man having taken his vengeance on them. He was the fourth of this family to die there[431] and there were some who did not come to his rescue, which gave rise to much talk; this was one of the barons of France, they said, the count of Dreux, he and his men. I have heard so many speak ill of this that the history cannot deny it.

[6651–74]   Before Arsuf that army was encamped, having checked the pagan army, and they would have checkmated them completely if they had been in better order. The news spread of our people who were lost, or not lost but found, tested for God, James of Avesnes and his household who were dead and slaughtered. So the army of God was in melancholy, troubled and shocked; not since Adam bit into the apple was such mourning, such regret and such complaining heard. And he was worthy of being mourned, for he served God well, without fail. He had already chosen his place in Heaven, his place was reserved, at the side of St James the apostle, whom he held as his patron and ours, James of Avesnes the martyr, who would not deign to flee before the Turks.

[6675–726]   The army was encamped before Arsuf, spread out along the river. They rested all night, wearied from the giving and receiving of blows and they did not want to move on until the third day when the army was again prepared. The battle took place on a Saturday. The next day was the Feast of the Glorious and precious Mother of God, the feast day celebrated in September, and recalled here in the history.[432] Then the Hospitallers and the knights of the Temple armed themselves, taking with them valiant Turcopoles and many others who went too. They went to the field where there lay those who had been killed in battle. They searched and looked over the whole field, neither eating nor drinking, until they had found the body of that sorely tried vassal, James of Avesnes, which they did find. First they washed his face, or he could not have been recognised, so many mortal blows had he received from the Saracens, whom he had stood firm against. They covered the body and lifted it up and returned to Arsuf.[433] There you would have seen a great company of men and of knights who came out to meet the body, all expressing such grief that there is no-one under the heavens who, if he saw them, would not have had great pity on them. One would regret the loss of his valour, another tell of his generosity. That day the king of England and King Guy were at the internment, in the Minster of Our Holy Lady,[434] may she pray to her Son for the soul which had lodged in that body! After the mass the clergy carried out the rest of the service, diligently, according to their

---

[431] The *Itinerarium*, 4.20, p.276, says that three of his kinsmen were found dead with him.
[432] 8 September 1191, Landon, p.54.
[433] Both orders considered this task an important part of their charitable role. See M. Barber, 'The Charitable and Medical Activities of the Hospitallers and Templars', in *A History of Pastoral Care*, ed. G. Evans (London, 2000), p.159.
[434] On this church, see D. Pringle, *The Churches of the Crusader Kingdom of Jerusalem*, vol.1 (Cambridge, 1993), no.11, pp.59–60.

practice. They put him in the ground.[435] The great men took the body in their
arms and buried it. There is no need to ask if they cried.

[6727–34][436]   Now let us leave this business, speak and tell no more of it at this
point and at this time. Not that it will divert us from our matter, for it is all to do
with our concern so we will return and talk of the hated race who had made the
attack on us.

[6735–59]   The race that had no good in them had been repulsed, as I have
already recounted, [They had not accomplished what][437] they had boasted to the
sultan in their arrogance, for they had said that without fail, no empty boasting,
and beyond any doubt Christianity would be overcome this time, killed and
conquered. However, things went otherwise. For who might have seen the mountain where the Turks fled! Those who saw it said to us that when their people
attacked ours they were repulsed with such force that they fled with all their
baggage and many camels fell dead there, and so many horses, both brown and
piebald, mules, both male and female, in their hundreds and thousands. They
lost so many at that time when our men attacked them that if they had been
better followed, better chased after and hunted down, the whole land would
have been ours and been inhabited by Christians.

[6760–89][438]   When the Turkish army had retreated and the whole battle was
over and Saladin, who was by the mountain, knew of it, when he saw his men,
the best, the elite, defeated, then, filled with rage and anger he began to say to
his emirs: "So, where is my beautiful, furious entourage? Now Christianity rides
through Syria as it wills and finds no-one who will turn it back. I do not know
which way to turn. Now, where are the great threats, the blows of the sword and
the club which they boasted they would make when they went to the battle?
Where are the beginnings of rich conquests from mighty armies and battles?
Where are the great defeats which we find in the writings were inflicted by our
ancestors, which are recounted to us daily, defeats which they used to inflict
upon the Christians? This business goes badly for now we are the butt of the
world in matters of war and battle, for besides those who once were, we are
worthless and they are worthy."[439]

[6790–825]   The Saracen emirs heard that Saladin had blamed them in such a

---

[435] l.6723 is added above by a different hand. The paratactic structure of this kind of writing
permits this abrupt juxtaposition. Paris changes the line order but then has to make further
alterations to keep the rhyme.

[436] Cf. *Itinerarium*, 4.21.

[437] After l.6737 there is a lacuna assumed to be of one line, filled by Paris in his translation from
the *Itinerarium*, 'et ils n'avaient pas accompli' (and they had not accomplished), translated
silently by Stone.

[438] Cf. *Itinerarium*, 4.22.

[439] The story of rage and recrimination is again typical of the genre and can be compared to the
words put into the mouth of al-Afdal, vizier of Egypt, after his defeat outside Jerusalem by the
First Crusade in August 1099: 'I led two hundred thousand soldiers hither to battle, and now I
see them all fleeing with slack reins down the road to Cairo, and they have not the courage to
rally against the Franks', *Gesta Francorum*, pp.96–7. Baha' al-Din, p.176, says only, 'On
account of the battle his heart was full of feelings that God alone could know. The troops, too,
were either wounded in body or in the heart.'

way that none of them could raise his head, except one, Sanguin of Aleppo,[440] who sat firmly on his Arab steed and said: "True Sultan, now listen to me. You have berated us insultingly and blamed us greatly. Why do you despise us if you do not know the reason? You are not being reasonable. It is not that we did not fight, nor strike boldly, nor shoot, nor strike with iron and steel against the Franks, nor endure their terrible blows, but nothing can prevail against them, for they wear such armour, strong, resistant and sound, with which they are covered so that we can do nothing more against them than against grey rock. He who has to deal with such a people, how is he to deal with them? What is to be even more wondered at is a Frank who is one of them, who kills and maims our men. You never saw anyone like him; he will always be at the front; he will always be found at the place of need, as a good and tested knight. It is he who cuts so many of us down. They call him Melec Richard, and such a melec should hold land, conquer and dispense wealth."

[6826–901][441]   Saladin, being, as I have told you, in this rage, called Saphadin, his brother, and said: "Now it is my will that the trust I have in my people should be obvious. Mount and go, without fear. Knock down Ascalon for me – we have no need to fight [in its defence]. Destroy the city of Gaza. Let it be broken like madder, but maintain Darum that my people may come that way. Destroy Galatia for me that the Franks do not make use of it. Destroy also the Castle of the Figs, that they may not rally there. Destroy for me the Blanchegarde, that we have nothing to fear from there. Destroy, and do it properly, Jaffa, Casel of the Plains, Casel Moien. Destroy for me Saint George and Ramla, the great city that we found. Belmont, high in the mountain, Toron, Chastel Arnould, Belveer and Mirabel;[442] destroy them for this seems good to me, with the castles of the

---

440 Sanguin of Aleppo is difficult to identify. HL are confident that it is az-Zahir, Saladin's fourth son, the ruler of Aleppo (d.1216), p.270, n.37. However, had this man been Saladin's son, it seems likely that Ambroise would have said so, for it would have heightened the drama of the scene. A further candidate is the emir referred to in the *Itinerarium* as Sanscous Alabiensis, tentatively identified by Mayer as Sunqur al-Halabi, *Das Itinerarium*, pp.256, 378.

441 Cf. *Itinerarium*, 4.23.

442 The Franks had created clusters of fortified places in the south around Gaza and Ascalon, as well as around Jerusalem and the routes to Lydda (St George), Ramla and Jaffa, still the main port for the Holy City. Blanchegarde (Tell as-Safi), 19 miles (30 kilometres) to the north-east of Ascalon, was built in 1142, as part of the strategic plan to bring pressure to bear upon the port which, in fact, remained in the hands of the Egyptians until 1153. Galatia (Qaratiya) was about 12 miles (20 kilometres) to the east of Ascalon. The southern approaches were further strengthened before 1170 with the addition of Darum (Dair al-Balah). The Castle of the Figs (Khirbat al-Burj) lay further inland, to the south-west of Hebron, about 28 miles (45 kilometres) to the west of the Dead Sea. Except for Mirabel (Majdal Yaba), built between 1134 and 1143, and part of the lordship of Ibelin further to the north, the castles referred to around Jerusalem all belonged to the military orders. Toron des Chevaliers (Latrun) and Chastel Arnould (*Castrum Arnaldi*, Yalu) were Templar and, before 1187, had guarded the routes from Jaffa to Jerusalem. The latter had originally been built on the initiative of William of Messines, Patriarch of Jerusalem, and various citizens, in 1132–3. Belmont (Suba) was constructed by the Hospitallers from c.1150 on a hill about 6 miles (10 kilometres) to the west

mountain, that not one will remain whole, neither castle nor casal nor city, that nothing will be left standing except for Kerak[443] and Jerusalem. As I wish it, so let it be." Saladin commanded him and he took his leave, knowing his commission well. Then a Turk, by name of Caïsac, spoke aloud, a noble Saracen of great renown.[444] He said to Saladin, "My lord, no-one should [trust in] his anger and rage as you do. Rather, now send out your watchmen and your spies and guards, to the heights, to the plains of Ramla, so that whichever way the French go your spies will go also and that they will know when they turn back which way their army will go. Then they could go on a way where harm could be done to them. By Mohammed, who is worshipped, one should look at the time and the hour and the reason before blaming people. You should not despise us for such are the vicissitudes of war that great defeats take place. I do not hesitate to tell you that if I have a good company of men I plan to keep such a hold on these French, that they would regret ever coming here." Then they elected thirty emirs, great men of high parentage, each having in his company, I believe, one hundred Turks, bold men; Saladin had them go to the River Arsuf and descend there. They were all there, on the look out for when the people of God would set out again.

The army of God, by defeating [them], had a little lessened the arrogance of the Saracens. On the third day, without fear, they left Arsuf, in order, [going] through the ravaged land, where they rode to avenge the shame of God.

[6902–31]   The Templars protected the rearguard that day,[445] where they were positioned, for it is a common saying that he who is prepared cannot be mocked. But in vain were they prepared, for they did not see a Turk that day, nor did the Turks appear to the army before [they reached] the river where our men lay down. There the Turks thought to harass them. However, they met with no

---

of Jerusalem and formed the centre of a collection of the Order's estates in the area. At the other end of the route, at 4 miles (7 kilometres) and 7 miles (12 kilometres) to the south-east of Jaffa respectively, stood Casel of the Plains (Yazur) and Casel Moien/Maen (Bait Dajan). Finally, Belveer (Qastal) was acquired by the Hospital in c.1168. Kennedy, pp.31–2, 38, 58–9; Pringle, 'Templar Castles between Jaffa and Jerusalem', *The Military Orders*, vol.2, *Welfare and Warfare*, ed. H. Nicholson (Aldershot, 1998), pp.89–109; Pringle, *Secular Buildings*, Blanchegarde, no.194, p.93 (map 7), Galatia, no.169, p.84 (map 7), Darum, no.80, p.46 (map 10), Castle of the Figs, no.59, p.37 (map 10), Mirabel, no.144, p.67 (map 8), Toron des Chevaliers, no.136, pp.64–5 (map 8), Chastel Arnould, no.231, pp.106–7 (map 8), Belmont, no.207, p.96 (map 8), Casel of the Plains, no.233, p.108 (map 7), Casel Moien, no.29, p.26 (map 7) and Belveer, no.R15, p.118.

443   Kerak was built about 9 miles (15 kilometres) to the east of the Dead Sea by Pagan the Butler, lord of Oultrejourdain, from 1142 onwards. It made use of a natural defensive position upon a spur of land where the ground falls away steeply on three sides. It was captured by Saladin in the autumn of 1188, but well before Hattin it had been a prime target for the Muslims, as it had been used as a base to attack caravans travelling between Egypt and Damascus: Kennedy, pp.45–52; Pringle, *Secular Buildings*, no.124, p.59 (map 10). On the ambiguity of this reference, see also below, p.132.

444   Alam al-Din Qaisar, a mamluk who was governor of Ascalon and later commander of Darum. Cf. *Itinerarium*, 4.24.

445   They encamped on the bank of 'the river of Arsuf', Nahr al-'Auja, in the evening of 9 September, Landon, p.54.

success; they harassed them and shot at them, but all had to retire. And our people set up camp and settled on the banks of the River Arsuf. In the morning those of lesser rank, held back with difficulty, moved on, with the foragers, soon arriving at Jaffa. Jaffa sits on the sea, but the cruel Saracen people had already so damaged and destroyed it that the army could not lodge within but set up camp to the left of it, in a fine olive grove. Why should I make a long tale of this? Three full weeks passed before the army marched there from Acre: it happened as I say.

[6932–77][446]   Before Jaffa, in the olive grove, in the fine garden, the army of God planted its banners [. . .][447] There was the cultivated land; there were grapes and figs, pomegranates and almonds, all around in great plenty, covering the trees so that they took enough, freely, that the army was well nourished. Then the fleet came to the port; ships came and went from Jaffa to Acre and back again, bringing them provisions, much to the annoyance of that pack of curs. Saladin, who did not dare fight, had the walls and towers of Ascalon destroyed.[448] One day around the hour of nones, the news came to the army by means of those of lesser rank, who had fled in the night [that Ascalon was . . .][449] mined and sapped from below and then shored up. Some, when this news came, held it to be the truth. Some thought it true, some lies, others thought it imaginings and a joke, that Saladin would ever show such weakness, whatever straits he was in and for whatever gain. [The doubts were such] that, to find out [the truth], King Richard and the barons sent the lord Geoffrey of Lusignan, who suffered so much for God, and William of L'Estang,[450] a worthy and noble knight, with others, in a strong galley. They stopped outside the city until they knew for sure that it was in truth being destroyed. They returned and told of this. The barons took council to decide what they would do and to decide whether they would rescue the town.

[6978–7019]   Before Jaffa, the council assembled, outside the town. Words were exchanged and different advice given, for each man had his own intentions and they are not all of the same age. So one would wish to do one thing where the other would wish to run counter. But there was no need for disagreement but rather that we should all agree. Some proposed that they should head towards Jerusalem, while others proposed that they should save Ascalon from the Turks if they could, for it would be a good place of refuge. Then you could hear each criticising others' plans, as men of great undertakings.[451] Then the king of

---

446   Cf. *Itinerarium*, 4.25.

447   After l.6934 there is a lacuna, probably of one line.

448   Cf. *Itinerarium*, 4.26.

449   After l.6953 there is a lacuna, probably of one line.

450   William of L'Etang helped thwart a mamluk attempt on Richard's life on 5 August 1192, and was one of the king's companions on his return from Acre between 9 October and his capture on 20 December. He was present at Richard's crown-wearing at Winchester on 17 April 1194, following the king's release. Thereafter he was a very frequent witness to Richard's charters in England, Normandy and Anjou during the rest of the reign, Landon, pp.68, 70–1, 80, 88, 90–2, 99–100, 102, 106, 110–11, 113, 117–20, 123–4, 127, 130, 132–4.

451   l.6995. We have translated this as it stands in the text, as does Paris, with 'et tous étaient'. We assume Ambroise has some ironic intention here. Stone rationalises with 'Yet were they . . .'

England, brought up to war, spoke to the duke and the French together and said, "My lords, it seems to me that we are of different minds. This can harm us greatly. The Turks are destroying Ascalon. They will not dare to fight us. Let us go to the rescue of Ascalon. All should hurry there. I believe it is a good thing to do!" What else shall I tell you of this but that the French replied in a way that many later repented, that it would be good to stay at Jaffa, to repair it and that this would be a quicker way to complete their pilgrimage.[452] However, they gave very bad advice when they did not go to Ascalon for had they helped it then the whole land would have been rescued, but they discussed it until they undertook to repair the defences at Jaffa.

[7020–39] When this task was agreed upon, there was the army stopped before Jaffa. A great sum was gathered to rebuild the castle. They redug the ditches and rebuilt the walls. There did the army settle. From day to day there was an increase in the army of sin and filth, ugly deeds and lust, for the women had come back among the army and behaved in a lewd way. They came in ships and small boats. Alas! for the mercy of God! What bad shields and defences with which to reconquer the land and heritage of God. How badly they prepared themselves who turned back to sin and because of their excesses failed to complete their pilgrimage.[453]

[7040–67] It was towards the end of September when, so I believe and so it seems, Jaffa was already partly rebuilt, when the army withdrew from the gardens. The princes and dukes put up their tents around St Habakkuk's[454] but the army was much smaller than at the beginning for some had returned to Acre and stayed there in the taverns. When the king knew of the indolence and lethargy of the pilgrims he sent to Acre by King Guy – this was observed – that the pilgrims should come to the army and keep their covenant with God. However, they responded with indifference to King Guy and held out until King Richard himself, who at first, and thereafter, took great pains over this, came back to Acre and preached until many came back with him.[455] He had the queens brought back and installed in Jaffa with their ladies. The army had to wait there

452 Jerusalem could never be held without a viable port. The Latins had captured Jaffa even before the fall of Jerusalem in July 1099, but their defence of the kingdom had been greatly hampered by their failure to take Ascalon until 1153, which meant that the Egyptians had been able to use it as a base.

453 The crusaders were undertaking the expedition as a form of penitential pilgrimage and therefore, in theory, should have abstained from sex completely. Ambroise interprets violation of this prohibition as invalidating the indulgence promised for participation in the crusade although, in practice, this would seem to be a highly questionable assumption. The author of the *Itinerarium*, 4.26, p.284, says that the women contaminated the people, diverting them from the proper goal of the their pilgrimage, but he does not go as far as Ambroise. See J. Brundage, 'Prostitution, Miscegenation and Sexual Purity in the First Crusade', in *Crusade and Settlement*, ed. P.W. Edbury (Cardiff, 1985), pp.57–65. Cf. *Itinerarium*, 1.23, p.52, where the author attributes Frederick Barbarossa's victory over the Turks of Iconium (May 1190) to the fact that 'there was chastity in the camp' (Nicholson, p.63).

454 This was a Premonstratensian house established c.1150. It was situated at Kafr Jinnis, outside Jaffa, just under 3 miles (4.5 kilometres) north of Lydda, Pringle, *Churches*, vol.1, no.127, pp.283–4.

455 Between about 10 September and 30 October.

for six weeks or nearly two months to let the people arrive.[456] This was to cause us many problems later.

[7068–134]   When the king had brought the people out of Acre and brought them to the army, it increased greatly, by more than had been the decrease. But, listen to the trials of the army at this time, trials that he who is writing this account saw. It nearly was brought low, for when an army loses its commander in a distant and foreign land, such as that land of Syria, it loses its way and breaks up. I say this because of [what happened to] the king of England, who had gone to seek out Saladin and spy the Saracens out in order to take them by surprise, but this spying went badly. The king had with him that time too small a company. It happened that he fell asleep and the enemies of nature, the Saracens, who were on the alert, were nearby and got so close that he was awakened only just in time. My lords, do not wonder at it that the king arose in haste, for a man alone hunted by so many people, is not at all safe. But God gave him such fortune that he mounted, as did his men, such as were with him, but they were too few in number. When the Turks saw them on their horses, the king gave chase and they fled as far as their ambush. Those [waiting] in ambush rushed out quickly, wishing to take the king, as he sat on Fauvel, but he put his hand to his sword. Already the Turks came upon him, each wishing to raise his hand against him, but no-one dared come within reach of his weapon. Perhaps they would have taken him had they recognised him at that time, but a worthy and loyal knight of his [company], William of Préaux, spoke and said, "Saracens, I am Melec." Melec, means king. The Turks seized him at once and had him led back to their army. There died Renier of Maron, who had the heart of a noble baron, and his nephew who was called Walter,[457] who was also of a noble and loyal heart. Alan and Lucas of L'Etable died there,[458] I tell you truly. When this was known [. . .][459] with joy and happiness, so the book says. There was no point in following the Turks for they went at speed, leading William prisoner. The hated race thought they led the king, but it did not please the Lord God who protected him. The Turks were already on the heights, believing they led the king, and our men returned to the army. However, the king and all the people of the army feared for William.

[7135–64]   When God in His Grace had, in this way, spared the king who was to lead the army, several, who knew him to be a man of courage and who feared

---

456   The chronology is as follows: 4 October, Guy returned from Acre; c.7 October, Richard went himself; 11 October, Richard wrote to the Genoese asking for help; 13 October, Richard granted a charter of privileges to the Pisans; 13 October, Richard returned to Jaffa: Landon, p.56.

457   The date of this foray (and thus the deaths of Renier and Walter of Maron, and Alan and Lucas of L'Etable) was 29 September 1191, Landon, p.55. Renier of Maron is listed among the barons of the kingdom in two charters granted by Conrad of Montferrat at Tyre in October 1187: RRH, nos.665, 666, pp.177–8.

458   Alain and Lucas of l'Etable have not been identified.

459   After l.7122 there is a lacuna of several lines. The Itinerarium at this point recounts the concern of the crusaders, then the reception of Richard with joy. l.7123, translated here as 'with joy and happiness, so the book says', is written after l.7132, and expunctuated. Paris puts it here because of the Latin and because it rhymes with l.7124; I have followed Paris.

for him, decided to say, "Lord, for the sake of God, do not do this! It is not for you to go on such spying expeditions. Protect yourself and Christianity. You have many good people. Never again go alone on such business. When you want to damage the Turks, take a large company, for in your hands is our support, or our death, should harm come to you – for when the head of the body falls, the limbs cannot survive alone, but will soon fail and fall and misadventure then comes." In this way many worthy men took great pains and put much effort into rebuking him but always, this is the sum of it, when he saw any skirmishes, very few of which were hidden from him, he would go against the Turks and bring things to a conclusion and he would always finish the business so that some were taken or killed and so that the greatest honour was his. God always brought him out of the greatest dangers of that hostile race.

[7165–94][460] When the army was equipped with great efforts and great difficulty, then was it summoned and gathered together by proclamation, in the name of the Son of Holy Mary, that they would go to the Casel of the Plains and that they would rebuild its walls, in order to protect the head of the army. Then it pleased the king to command that such men should remain at Jaffa as would protect the town and protect the port well, so that no-one could leave there except merchants for provisions. The bishop of Evreux, for certain, and the count of Châlons with him, and lord Hugh of Ribole[461] remained there for this purpose and had the work done. Then did the army mount and move on. Never was a finer host seen, nor a more richly equipped one, but the journey for the day was short. Between the two Casels they dismounted and pitched their tents. I know for sure, from several indications, that it was on the eve of All Saints' Day that we encamped there.[462] The army of the Turks was at Ramla. From there the hated race made great attacks and assaults against us.

[7195–220][463] For a full two weeks at least our army lay between the Casel of the Plains and Casel Moien, which the pagans had destroyed. The king had Casel Moien rebuilt stronger than before its destruction and the Templars rebuilt the other. But the Turks made strong attacks against us. One day, there came against the army a good thousand mounted men together, so it seemed to me. Then was our army in uproar, like an ants' nest that has been stirred up. The king and others mounted and made as much haste as they could and the Turks turned in flight. May the living devil take them! For their horses went so quickly, in every direction they turned, that the king could not reach them. However, he pursued and chased them. When he had followed them long enough and had not caught them up and he could see Ramla and the army of false and base people, he turned back to the army and with him his bold and valiant men.

[7221–415][464] On the sixth day after the great Feast of All Saints' that everyone celebrates,[465] the esquires went out from the army foraging for fodder. The noble

---

460 Cf. *Itinerarium*, 4.29.
461 Hugh of Ribole has not been identified.
462 31 October, Landon, p.57.
463 This paragraph is not in the *Itinerarium*.
464 Cf. *Itinerarium*, 4.30.
465 6 November, Landon, pp.57–8. ll.7221–2, annominatio similar to that used earlier about *Pentecoste/cost*, here *fest* (n.) and *feste* (vb).

lords of the Temple were guarding them at that time. The foragers, who left the army, spread out across the land looking for good grass, which was often sold to them, for often they paid for it [. . .][466] The Templars watched over the foragers,[467] but just when they were paying least attention to them there came four companies of Saracens, in great eagerness; they were by estimation at least four hundred [men], all mounted, well-equipped.[468] From near Bombrac[469] they came straight to the Templars and attacked them, surrounding them, for there is no more agile race in the world. They came upon them from several sides and closed in on them tightly. When the Templars saw them so close they dismounted. Then they did a most knightly deed, turning their faces to the wild barbarians, each one with his back against a brother, as if they were all sons of one father. The Saracens pressed in on them so tightly that they left three of our men dead. There you would have seen mighty blows given; there you would have heard helmets resounding and sparks flying from steel, and seen fine attacking and fierce defending. The Turks thought to take them by surprise and they wanted to capture them, they were holding them so close about, when, spurring on at great speed, there came those who had come out of the camp. It was said with perfect truth that Andrew of Chauvigny was the first of some fifteen knights to rescue the Templars at that time. At great speed he came down on the Turks and fought most valiantly, as did his companions. There was a very fierce fight, but it was not kept from the king. That day, amongst other things, he was having Casel Moien rebuilt and had sent for two counts who should be mentioned in all good accounts, the count of St Pol and the earl of Leicester. The king commanded that William of Caieux,[470] who held his place well that day, should be with them, and also Otto of Trazegnies.[471] They were men of high descent. Then came the noise and tumult that the foragers were making, and the king sent to the counts, said and commanded them to go to the rescue of the Templars and he would hasten to his arms. Then he hurried to arm himself as quickly as he could. They rode off at once. As they got close there surged out of

---

[466] Paris adds 'sold to them dearly'. Stone follows him. After l.7231 there is a lacuna, assumed to be of one line. Paris fills 'with their blood', from the *Itinerarium*.

[467] l.7232. The manuscript has the foragers watching over the Templars, but this makes no sense.

[468] l.7235. There is a textual error here. Manuscript *Od quatre desreiz* is nonsensical and is corrected by Paris to *od granz desreiz*, a correction we have kept in the text. The manuscript reading is probably caused by eye-skip, as the previous line has *quatre conreiz* and the following line *quatre cent*.

[469] Bombrac is about 4½ miles (7 kilometres) east of Jaffa.

[470] William of Caïeux was an important landholder in north-eastern Normandy, who was closely associated with Richard throughout the crusade. On 16 April 1192, with Henry of Champagne and Otto of Trazegnies, he was sent to announce to Conrad of Montferrat his election as king. However, he held most of his lands from the count of Flanders and, while Richard was in captivity, he defected to Philip II. He was reconciled with Richard in 1196 and remained on the Angevin side during John's reign. He was captured at the battle of Bouvines in 1214: Landon, pp.61, 96, 118, 121, 124; Powicke, *Loss of Normandy*, pp.108–9.

[471] Otto of Trazegnies (near Charleroi) was a vassal of Baldwin V, Count of Hainaut. He was one of the nobles of the region who took the Cross about 21 February 1188, in response to the preaching of the papal legate, Henry of Albano, at Mons. He had already been to the East between 1185 and 1187. He died after April 1192, van Werweke, 60, 71, 88.

a riverbed a good four thousand of the enemy, who divided into two groups. One group turned towards the Templars and the other towards the barons. The barons got into battle order and maintained it. The Turks approached and came closer. Then the count of St Pol suggested to the noble earl of Leicester a bold and foolish dare: that either Leicester would attack the Turks on the right while he would protect him, or he himself would attack while Leicester protected him wherever he went or whatever he did. The earl [of Leicester] took up the challenge. He advanced with his household and struck with speed against the columns of the dark race; he attacked with such violence that his prowess was praised and that he rescued two knights [albeit] at great cost. The struggle was in full force when the warrior King Richard arrived and saw our people in the middle of the hostile pagans. He had few men with him but his company was in fine order. Then some of them began to say to him, "In faith, sir, it could do much harm for you to go on, nor will you be able to rescue our men. It is better that they should suffer alone without you than that you should suffer there. For this reason it is good that you should turn back, for if harm comes to you Christianity will be killed." The king's colour changed. Then he said, "When I sent them here and asked them to go, if they die there without me then would I never again bear the title of king." He kicked the flanks of his horse and gave him free rein and went off, faster than a sparrowhawk. Then he galloped in among the knights, right into the Saracen people, breaking through them with such impetus that if a thunderbolt had fallen there there would have been no greater destruction of their people. He pierced the ranks and pursued them; he turned and trapped them, hewing off hands and arms and heads. They fled like beasts. Many of them were exhausted, many killed or taken. He chased them so far, following and pursuing them, until it was time to return. This is how that day went.

Whilst they were refortifying the two Casels that they were rebuilding the king saw how the army was emboldened against the Saracens – may they be cursed by God.[472] Then he called his messengers, noble men and wise, and sent them to Saladin and to his brother Saphadin,[473] making great demands, which were rich, noble and important – namely the realm of Syria, all of it from one end to the other, and everything that had belonged to it when the Leper King held it.[474] [With this he demanded] the tribute of Babylon, as the Leper King had received it, for he claimed this by right of inheritance and by the acquisition of his lineage.[475] The messengers sought out the sultan and delivered the message very clearly and he said that he would not do it and that the king was asking too much. He sent word by his brother, Saphadin, a wise Saracen, that he should

---

[472] Cf. *Itinerarium*, 4.31.

[473] Saphadin came to see Richard on 7 November and was received the next day, Landon, p.58.

[474] See above, p.66.

[475] Richard is referring here to the fact that Fulk V, Count of Anjou, 1109–29, and King of Jerusalem, 1131–43, was his great-grandfather. Fulk had married Melisende of Jerusalem, the eldest daughter of King Baldwin II, 1118–31, in 1129. See H.E. Mayer, 'The Succession to Baldwin II of Jerusalem: English Impact on the East', *Dumbarton Oaks Papers* 39 (1985), 139–47. Since that time their descendants had either succeeded to the throne or been the means of transmitting the crown.

leave all the land of Syria to Richard, in peace and without war, from the river to the sea, and that he could make no claim on it – but that on the condition that Ascalon would not be rebuilt by Christian nor Saracen. This message he sent by Saphadin. But the king did not distrust these false enemies; [he did not realise] that they tricked and delayed him while they destroyed the castles and deceived him. Let such a liaison come to a bad end. For Saphadin so deceived the king that he accepted his gifts. Messengers came and went, bringing these gifts to the king, for which he was much blamed and much criticised. However, Saphadin gave him to understand that he truly wanted peace and the king would at once have accepted any peace that was honourable to increase our faith and because of the departure of the king of France whom he feared and who, he knew, had no loyalty towards him. Messengers came and went, talking with the king, until he realised that the false Saracens, who were exceedingly false and disloyal, were creating delays. It was on account of the Kerak de Montreal[476] that the peace collapsed since the king wanted it destroyed as part of the peace agreement and they did not want to do this.[477]

[7416–33]   When the peace plans could not be concluded then the Turks made great attacks on our army, from the right and from the left, for they wished to do us much harm. The king fought against them and by [his] example showed those who had blamed him on account of the gifts with which the Turks deceived him that his intentions towards God and Christianity were entirely loyal. On a number of occasions he came against the Turks, on many occasions showing the army that he had cut many down. The army was no longer worried because of the gifts that he received and he would have rescued the land but for those who obstructed him by robbing from his treasury.

[7434–557][478]   When the Casels were armed and rebuilt and once more enclosed and the king had set his guard on them to look out over the heights, then was the army summoned and gathered at the setting of the sun. The next day[479] when they mounted, their men set on their way in good order, riding straight towards Ramla. As soon as we went, and Saladin knew for truth that he would have to leave Ramla because he did not dare fight, Saladin had the whole

---

476 Montréal (Shaubak) was established south of the Dead Sea by King Baldwin I in 1115. However, in 1142, Pagan the Butler, lord of Oultrejourdain, had moved his main base further north to his new castle at Kerak. Both castles threatened the routes between Egypt and Damascus, and it is not entirely clear that Ambroise means Montréal when he refers to 'Le Crac' in the imaginary rant he attributes to Saladin after the battle of Arsuf, see above, p.125, Kennedy, pp.23–5; Pringle, *Secular Buildings*, no.157, pp.75–6 (map 10).

477 Ambroise here compresses a complicated series of negotiations which had begun on 17 October and lasted until 14 November. They are described in detail by Baha' al-Din, pp.185–8, 193–6. The essence of Richard's proposal seems to have been that Saphadin (al-'Adil) should marry Richard's sister, Joanna. Saladin and Richard would then cede their respective holdings between the Jordan and the sea to them. Saladin's apparent acceptance was not serious, according to Baha' al-Din, since he did not believe that Richard had any intention of implementing the proposals. During this time, on 9 November, Saladin also considered an offer from Conrad of Montferrat for an alliance against Richard.

478 Cf. *Itinerarium*, 4.32.

479 Between c.15 and 22 November 1191, *Itinerarium*, 4.32, p.298, n.1, where Stubbs calculates the earlier date, but Imad al-Din, p.354, gives the latter.

town destroyed and was the first to turn in flight, straight to Toron des Chevaliers. He put his trust in the mountain while our army moved across the plain.
On good horses, fed on barley, the army arrived in two days between St George
and Ramla. There they set up camp to await more men and food. There once
again we suffered grievous attacks from the loathsome and hated enemy and we
suffered from heavy rains that fell and delayed us greatly, setting us back. These
rains forced our people to shelter in St George and Ramla, where we set up
camp and settled. We were there for a good six weeks[480] in great discomfort and
to our great distress.

While we were there and stayed there, a violent battle took place that should
not be forgotten.[481] It was near St George, on the left, between the valiant count
of Leicester and the Turks who were there, who often came near the army and
made many attacks. The count, with a small company, set out from the army to
chase them off, his steel helmet on his head. Three knights went ahead, foolishly
breaking rank, and galloped towards the Turks. All three would have remained
there, but the count, who did not wish to leave them to suffer, gave his horse its
head, coming against more than a hundred Turks, charging so hard that he
forced them across a river. However, he had charged too hard and too far for a
good four hundred Turks came with light spears and Turkish bows and put themselves between him and the army, and set about taking him. They had already
knocked to the ground, beaten and ill-treated Garin FitzGerald. There, where
the lord Garin fell, you would have seen fierce blows of war. Worse came to the
count, whom they knocked down after Garin, ill-treating him and beating him.
They also, in a short space of time, unhorsed Dreux of Fontenil[482] and after
Dreux, Robert Néel.[483] There were so many of them, Turks, Persians and renegades, who came upon the count, that he was submerged in the midst of them
and they could hardly [even] strike him down. There you would have seen men
fighting well. There was Henry FitzNicholas, with the count, in severe trial, and
also Robert of Neuborg.[484] No finer free man had ever lain in a cot than he. He
was well-built and of such valour and such a nature that he came down into the
great press of the hostile pagan race and gave his horse to the count and saved
both himself and the count from shame. Ralph of St Marie[485] was in the

---

[480] According to the mid-thirteenth-century compilation of Abu Shama, *Le Livre des Deux Jardins*,
       in *RHCr, Orientaux*, vol.5 (Paris, 1898), pp.44–9, they came on 22 November and left on
       10 January.
[481] Cf. *Itinerarium*, 4.33. 20 December 1191, Landon, pp.58–9.
[482] Dreux of Fontenil seems likely to have been a member of the family of the same name, which
       belonged to the lordship of Laigle, near Evreux. See Edwards, 'The *Itinerarium Regis Ricardi*
       and the *Estoire de la Guerre Sainte*', p.65, n.1. He was therefore probably one of the large
       number of followers of Robert of Leicester, as Mayer, *Das Itinerarium*, p.377, suggests.
[483] Robert Néel was probably related to the lords of St-Saveur (Manche), vicomtes of the
       Cotentin.
[484] Henry in the manuscript. Henry FitzNicholas arrived at Acre with the main party of Anglo-
       Norman knights on 8 June 1191, Landon, p.50. This suggests that he is the same person identi-
       fied by Siedschlag as holding a fee of 1½ knights in Dorset and Somerset, 1171–2, Siedschlag,
       no.46, p.116.
[485] Ralph of St Marie has not been identified.

company of the count and had it not been for Arnold of Bois[486] things would have been worse. Henry of Mailloc and William[487] took blows on their helmets with him; with him too was Saut du Breuil.[488] There never was and never was seen such great suffering, it seems to me, as these knights who held together against the number of Turks who were there, for not one could say how they would escape to freedom. This was the truth according to the book, that the count had fought so long and was so beaten and his companions similarly defenceless that the Turks had nearly killed them. The Turks were leading them, lying on the necks of their horses, straight to Toron, when there came from the army, as they passed close to it, a division of the true people, spurring [towards them] at speed. There were Andrew of Chauvigny and Henry of Graye[489] and Peter of Préaux, a good knight and a good warrior, and many other men of renown whose names I was not given. Each one on his arrival knocked his Turk to the ground. But the Turk struck by Peter, who perished there, body and soul, was so excessively strong that it caused Peter great effort and trouble. None could have made enough effort to bring him back alive, neither he, nor all of those who were with him, for he was killed with such great force.

[7558–90]   Listen my lords [to the account of] a strange joust. How valiant he is who jousts as my lord Andrew jousted. In their encounter he struck the emir with his lance so that the point went right through him. The emir came against him holding his spear so straight that the point entered Andrew's arm and broke it. It happened in this way. The emir fell. There you would have seen a fine rescue, with much brandishing of spears and bold brandishing of swords. Things would have gone badly for the first group if the others had not come up. There you would have seen the count of Leicester holding firm, striking to the left and to the right, until two horses had been killed under him. There were there men who will repeat that they have never seen greater valour in a man of his age, nor better men bar none than those who came to his rescue that day. So many came out from the army that none of our men perished. They were rescued and recovered [. . .][490] Our men defeated them and pierced their ranks, chasing them until through fatigue they gave up and returned to their tents.

[7591–604][491]   Saladin knew in truth and could readily see that our people made ready, each one preparing himself to go to the Holy City. As soon as he was told and knew our army to be two leagues away, knowing there was neither peace nor truce, he destroyed four or five towers and turrets of Toron to spite us

---

486   Arnold of Bois was a vassal of Robert of Leicester, Siedschlag, no.23, p.114.
487   William and Henry of Mailloc have not been identified, but probably came from one of the places of this name between Lisieux and Orbec in Calvados.
488   Saut of Breuil was sent by Richard to Palestine to inform Henry of Champagne that the king intended to return there at the time arranged. This appears to be part of the arrangements made by Richard at Mainz, 5 February 1194, when the final settlement of the terms of his ransom was agreed, Roger of Howden, *Chronica*, vol.3, p.233.
489   Henry of Graye, *bailli* of Verneuil (1193–5). This is probably Graye-sur-Mer (Calvados), about 14 miles north-east of Bayeux.
490   There is a lacuna after 1.7586, probably of one line.
491   Cf. *Itinerarium*, 4.34.

and left, so it was said, fleeing straight to Jerusalem.[492] The Turks left the plains to us and they took the mountain.

[7605–58]   When the Turkish army retreated and ours advanced then was the announcement given out and the arrangements made that they would go to the foot of the mountain, there to rest and bring up the provisions. So was it done. Then they mounted and rode off in their divisions. Then they were before Bettenuble.[493] There it was cold and overcast, with heavy rain and great storms that took many of our animals, for it rained there so excessively that it could not be measured in any way. Rain and hail battered us, bringing down our pavilions. We lost so many horses at Christmas and both before and after, so many biscuits were wasted, soggy with water, so much salt pork went bad in the storms; hauberks rusted so that they could hardly be cleaned; clothes rotted; people suffered from malnourishment so that they were in great distress. But their hearts were comforted by the hope that was in them that they would go to the [Holy] Sepulchre. They desired Jerusalem so much that all brought their food to keep the siege. Then you would have seen all the people coming to the army full of joy, full of the desire for worthy deeds. Those who were lying ill at Jaffa, or wherever they were, had themselves laid in litters, to be carried in great numbers to the army. Then came that hostile race, along the way where the [sick] were being carried and were being much comforted by those carrying them.[494] And their enemies waited for them and attacked them and killed and slaughtered them. These were true martyrs who thus left this world in good faith and with firm hope, as they all did, both wise and foolish, who made their pilgrimage there.

[7659–702][495]   In the army now was their joy complete, both deeply felt and fully expressed. There you would have seen hauberks being burnished, men nodding and saying, "God, we call on Your help! Virgin Lady, Holy Mary! God we worship You and praise and thank You. Now we will see Your Sepulchre!" There was there no-one who was angry nor sad, no one in anger or sadness. Everywhere was joy and happiness and [everyone], everywhere, rejoiced. Everywhere they said together, "God, now we are going on the right way, guided by Your Grace!" But there were those who paid little heed and delayed the journey. These were the wise Templars and the noble Hospitallers and the Poulains, those of that land.[496] They said to the king of England that in their opinion, in truth, whoever at that time were to lay siege to the city of Jerusalem would be attacked by Saladin, that while our men were at the siege the Turks would take the route that lay between the sea and the mountain and everything would go badly if that pack of curs took their provisions from the army. If it

---

492 Saladin moved to Latrun on 17 November and to Jerusalem on 12 December, leaving a protective force near Bait Nuba, Lyons and Jackson, pp.344–5.

493 22 or 23 December 1191, at Bait Nuba.

494 l.7650, manuscript *descomfortouent*, 'discouraged'.

495 Cf. *Itinerarium*, 4.35.

496 Ambroise here seems to be referring to Syrian-born Franks, although the term was sometimes applied specifically to the descendants of unions between Franks and Syrians. On its implications, see J. Riley-Smith, 'Peace never Established: The Case of the Kingdom of Jerusalem', *Transactions of the Royal Historical Society*, 5th series, 28 (1978), 96–9.

should happen, however, that they could not take it and that they could do no harm, and that the city was taken, it would still be a perilous undertaking, if it were not quickly peopled with such men as would stay, for all the travellers, the wise and the foolish, would have made their pilgrimage and would return to their own land from which they had come and the land would be lost again when the people scattered.

[7703–45][497]   On the third day of the New Year,[498] in the morning, fate had something in store [for us]. Some Saracens, that ugly brown race, had laid an ambush the evening before, among the dunes above the Casel of the Plains, and all night watched from there, until the morning when they sallied out, on the route of the army, where they saw two men-at-arms who passed there [attacking them][499] until they were cut down. But it was God's will that they should be avenged, for the king of England, aware of the ambush laid by the Turks, had lain that night at the Casel of the Plains. There was there [also] Geoffrey of Lusignan. It was on the third day of the New Year[500] when they let their horses run, thinking to rescue the men-at-arms, but they were [already] dead and slaughtered. The Turks, knowing Richard and his banner well and knowing his speed and his methods, turned away from there on the by-ways. At least eighty of them went towards Mirabel and the others then rode away. Seven were taken or dead. The king spurred on his worthy horse, after the eighty Turks who were going towards Mirabel in flight. He was mounted that day on Fauvel, who carried him with such great speed that he caught up the Saracens. Before the men came up and joined him he had already unhorsed two, knocking them down dead from their horses. Had the chase been better conducted they would have taken more. However, they took, either dead or prisoner, twenty of them. Then they returned.

Turning Back

[7746–65][501]   After Epiphany[502] the great men and captains held a council. They asked those of his men who were natives of that land, what course they would advise, to go back or to go on. They responded – first came the Hospitallers and the Templars – that in their opinion and at that time, they should not go on to Jerusalem but should return and fortify Ascalon, if they would take their word for it, to watch over the passage and the route which the Saracens took, bringing provisions from Babylon to Jerusalem. It was therefore decided to return and rebuild the walls of Ascalon.

---

[497] Cf. *Itinerarium*, 4.36.

[498] 1192.

[499] After l.7711 there is a lacuna, probably of one line. Paris adds in a footnote to his translation, 'ils les attaquèrent et les frappèrent', which Stone translates silently.

[500] 3 January 1192, Landon, p.60.

[501] Cf. *Itinerarium*, 5.1.

[502] Twelfth Night, 6 January.

[7766–95]   When this news was known, revealed and it was realised that the army was to turn back (let it not be called retreat), then was the army, which had been so eager in its advance, so discouraged, that not since God created time was there ever seen an army so dejected and so depressed, so disturbed and so astounded, nor so overcome with great sadness. Nothing remained of the joy that they had had before, when they were to go to the [Holy] Sepulchre, faced with the sorrow that they now had. There were those who would not be silent about this and cursed the delay and the fact that they had ever seen a tent pitched [there]. But had they known of the distress, the suffering and the weakness throughout Jerusalem, of the Turks who were suffering from the snow in the mountains, which was killing great numbers of their horses and other beasts – this is as true as you are here – had any known of their distress of body and lack of sustenance [. . .]⁵⁰³ then the Turks would have died in this undertaking and the city been taken.

[7796–827]⁵⁰⁴   It was at the Feast of St Hilary that the army suffered the reversal and distress because of the return.⁵⁰⁵ Everyone cursed the day he was born and each day of his life, since they were to turn back. Then were the people depressed and wearied and tired; they would not be comforted, nor could they carry back the food, for their pack-horses were weakened by the severe cold and the rain and reduced by fever. When they loaded the food and the pack-horses walked [. . .] they fell on their knees to the ground, and the men cursed and commended themselves to the devil. My lords, do not treat this as fiction, that such a good and chosen people were ever seen in such distress. Among the lesser people there were many who were ill, held in the grip of infirmity, in much distress. Had it not been for the king of England who had them looked for and searched everywhere so that he brought them all back, many would have been left there that day. All turned from there in their divisions. On the day we turned back the journey took us to Ramla.

[7828–53]⁵⁰⁶   The army was discouraged at Ramla, as I have said, and because of this discouragement, which could not be greater, at that time the army dispersed. Many French left, leaving out of bad feeling. Some went to Jaffa and stayed there for a while; others went back to Acre, where food was not scarce; others went to the marquis at Tyre, having been much implored by him; others, full of anger and shame, turned to the Casel of the Plains, with the duke of Burgundy and stayed there for eight full days. The king and his much depleted and angry army, with Count Henry of Champagne, his nephew, and those of his company, went straight to Ibelin. But they found the route so bad that when it came to settling for the night they could only complain.

[7854–81] The army lay at Ibelin, melancholy and more depressed than any living creature. In the morning, before the sun rose, the [scouts] went in front to find places [to rest]. They had their tents struck and the whole army rode off,

---

503   After l.7793 there is a lacuna apparently of several lines. As it stands the passage is rather odd with interrupted syntax and a change from a singular to a plural pronoun.

504   Cf. *Itinerarium*, 5.2.

505   The Feast of St Hilary, 13 January, Landon, p.60.

506   Cf. *Itinerarium*, 5.3.

fully armed. But never will a day of greater discomfort be recounted by any man alive. The day before was nothing compared to that day's travel. They passed such bad passes that they lost their provisions, because of the pack-horses that fell. This was the will of God, who tested them and who forcefully showed that he who is not willing to suffer discomfort for Him has no place of comfort by Him. So they came to Ascalon between midday and nones;[507] they found it so broken, fallen and destroyed that, when they climbed over the rubble, entering with such suffering after the hard day that they had endured, there was not one who did not want and desire rest. They were to have it in plenty.

Ascalon

[7882–917][508]   Ascalon sits on the Greek Sea – I heard it called this.[509] I believe that I never saw a city in a better situation, if it had only had a port or entrance, for it was in good countryside. However, the sea there is so tempestuous and dangerous that no vessel can survive. Because of this our people had to suffer much discomfort for no vessel could come by sea for eight days, I believe, with provisions to sustain the army, so because of the tempest, because of the storm, they tasted nothing but what they had brought with them.[510] Nor could man nor beast dare to move by land because of the cruel Saracen race. Eventually, in good weather, the fleet brought food from Jaffa. Then did battle recommence – a sea-tempest so great that meat became scarce, for the barges and galleys that had gone for food were at that time broken to pieces and most of the people were drowned and all our fine snacks were broken with them. The king then had them broken up to make long ships in which he hoped to embark, but this did not happen,
[7918–51][511]   Saladin, through his spies, knew that our people had gone down to the sea. Then he said to his Saracen people that they were to go to their homeland and stay there until May when it would again be the season for war. They did not have to be asked twice, but went willingly, having endured much for four full years in Syria, having endured fierce heat in summer and bitter cold in winter, which did not suit their constitution at all and because of which many had remained there [dead]. There you would have heard the lamentations of many Turks, many emirs, many powerful Turks, many Kurds and many Persians and many people from distant lands, who had been so often in so many wars without taking anything; at this leaving you would have seen them outraged over

507   At Ibelin, 19 January, and Ascalon, 20 January, Landon, p.60.
508   Cf. *Itinerarium*, 5.5.
509   This appears to be how the Mediterranean was described from the perspective of north-west Europe. According to Richard of Devizes, p.14, the Mediterranean Sea was entered through the 'Straits of Africa' and 'farther on is called the Greek Sea'.
510   Ascalon had no harbour, so it was not safe to try to land supplies during the winter months. See D. Pringle, 'King Richard I and the Walls of Ascalon', *Palestine Exploration Quarterly* 116 (1984), 139 (map), 144.
511   Cf. *Itinerarium*, 5.5.

their great losses and suffering; each was mourning those of his family whom he had lost in Syria! Nor was anyone ever so hated as Saladin was, nor so blamed by the Saracens, because of the Turks whom he left to suffer, without help or deliverance, before Acre, where so many perished. So the armies dispersed, except for the Sultan's own men, those from his own land.

[7952–79][512]   This happened near Candlemas[513] when several groups had left both our army and theirs, going in various directions. Then the king sent to the French who had left previously that they should come to Ascalon and that they should take council and consider and consult to know which way to turn and how to go on. For it would be better to go together than to sin by falling out. They sent back word that they would come and remain only until Easter, on the understanding that, if they wanted to go and should so decide in council, he would give them his safe-conduct and have them conducted safely over land to Acre or to Tyre. The king granted them this as each one asked him. So was the army again in one place and their joy made manifest.

[7980–8007]   When the army was thus brought together, gathered in agreement at Ascalon, though later they would split up again, they all stayed there together. Then they made ready and prepared to rebuild the walls of the city again. However, the barons who had stayed there since the return were so poor that the poverty of some was well known and apparent and no-one living who knew of it would not have great pity for them. Nonetheless, all set to work. They laid[514] the foundation of a gate where everyone worked so that they marvelled at the great work they were doing. The good knights, the men-at-arms and the esquires passed the stones from hand to hand. Everyone worked at it without respite; clerics and laymen came; so in a short space of time they accomplished much. Then afterwards they sent for masons to do the work that was completed at great cost.[515]

[8008–43]   In Ascalon there had been, in addition to the small turrets, fifty-three fine strong towers, now all destroyed. Five of them had been named according to their founders. So listen [while I tell you] about those who founded

---

512 Cf. *Itinerarium*, 5.6.

513 2 February.

514 1.7995, *delurerent* from *delurer*. *T-L*, vol 2, p.1349, cites only this instance *bloß legen*. Paris in his translation has 'déblayèrent' (tidy up, clear away), and in the glossary gives the *Itinerarium*: *portae majoris altuis fundamenta confodiendo perquirentes, usque ad ipsius maceriei solidatem dejecerunt directam lapidum congeriem*, with the comment that 'il doir manquer quelque chose dans le français'. This seems to be an unnecessary complication. The *A-ND* gives one instance of *delivrer* meaning to 'clear' or 'prepare (room)', vol.2, p.153.

515 Ascalon was a key city for both sides since, if held by the crusaders, it would threaten Saladin's communications with Egypt and serve as a base for attacks on his caravans. It had been the subject of a long conflict between the Latins and the Egyptians and, in contrast to most of the coastal cities, it had resisted the Christians until 1153. Saladin had therefore dismantled the gates, the towers, and some of the walls in the last two weeks of September 1191. Richard's rebuilding took place between late January and Easter 1192, under the supervision of Philip of Poitiers, his 'Clerk of the Chamber' (later Bishop of Durham, 1197–1208). Given the city's strategic importance and the cost and effort involved in the rebuilding, it was always likely that the fortifications would be a sticking point in the various attempts at a negotiated settlement, Pringle, 'King Richard I and the Walls of Ascalon', 133–47.

them, as we are told by those who know the truth. In the olden days there reigned a man named Ham who was noble and powerful and of great renown. He was the son of Noah who built the ark by which every creature was saved. The said Ham begat, according to him who remembers this, thirty-two sons who later reigned and founded Ascalon.[516] These sons sent throughout the lands they ruled, throughout the cities and the burhs, to find help to make the towers. They say that the girls founded the Tower of Maidens and that the Tower of Shields was founded by the knights of the time; the Tower of Blood was founded with fines and punishment money and the emirs made and built the Emirs' Tower; the Bedouin made the Tower [of the Bedouins], rich, strong and of great worth. These five towers bore these names and those who spoke of this knew it. The other people carried out the other works according to what they were.

[8044–72]   When the masons arrived they were retained for the work. The king came first with wholehearted efforts and then the great men. Everyone undertook what was appropriate. Where there was no-one else or where the barons did nothing, there the king caused the work to be done, to be begun and to be completed. And whenever the barons tired of the work and did not suffice the king had some of his goods carried there and encouraged them. He put so much into this and spent so much on it that for three parts of the city the cost was met by him. The city was built through the king and later destroyed through him, because of the French who failed when he and his noble men leapt from his galley into the sea at Jaffa.[517] There was his prowess proved as we will show at the right time and place, and we will prove it so that never according to our memory will the tale tell one word of a lie.[518] May God give me His glory.

[8073–120][519]   Listen to the account of a strange incident that should be written about, a true miracle, I do not doubt. Saladin was sending one thousand of our Christian prisoners in a convoy along the route to Babylon, escorted by his own men. There were among them French and Syrians. They had reached Darum. But God, who brought Lazarus from death to life, there brought them help and aid.[520] Listen to how He did this. One day King Richard left Ascalon with his proud men, between midday and nones, going to look at Darum, which

---

516   The story of Noah is found in Genesis, chapters 6–9. Noah had three sons, Shem, Ham and Japheth. Genesis 10:6–20 gives the names of four sons of Ham and their descendants. According to this account, from Ham were descended the people of Egypt, Ethiopia, Libya and Canaan.

517   This refers to Richard's rescue of the garrison at Jaffa, besieged in the citadel by Saladin's forces on 1 August 1192. However, within a month, Saladin and Richard had arranged a truce, a provision of which was the destruction of Ascalon's fortifications. See below, pp.175–80.

518   Paris assumed a lacuna here because the rhyming couplet is incomplete. What we actually have are three lines with the same rhyme. The last line, the benediction, may never have had a pair. This would be unusual but as neither the syntax nor the sense require another line I assume no lacuna here.

519   Cf. *Itinerarium*, 5.7.

520   The story of Jesus raising Lazarus from the dead is found in John 11. This sentence is reminiscent of the *prières du plus grand péril*, uttered by heroes of *chansons de geste*, wherein they ask for the help of God, who worked various miracles. See E.R. Labande, 'Le Crédo épique, à propos des prières dans les chansons de geste', in *Recueil de travaux offert à M. Clovis Brunel*, vol.2 (Paris, 1955), pp.62–80.

he later took by siege. The Saracens used to take refuge there in peace without disturbance or fighting when they brought provisions from Babylon to Jerusalem, before Darum was taken. There were those [Christians] who were being taken to die in shame. What more shall I tell you? As the king came that way with his bold men and the Turks saw his banner, they were afraid and took fright. Some of them went into the castle, leaving the prisoners outside, not daring to keep them when they saw the king's approach. The prisoners took refuge in a church; the poor wretches were left there. The king arrived and set them free. He put to death those Turks whom he could cut off and acquired many fine horse. That day he took twenty Turks alive, as well as those who were killed. If God had not guided him with His hand and the king and his men had not been there, the next day the prisoners would have been conducted to Babylon and would have died in captivity.

[8121–218]   When God had delivered his people who had been given over to death (giving to King Richard the role of St Leonard,[521] who freed prisoners), for which thanks were given to God, then did the king send to the marquis to come to Ascalon and take his place in the army, as he had requested several times, that he might merit the part of the kingdom that had been allotted to him before the king of France, by oath and faith.[522] This is the word that he sent to him. The marquis sent back the message that he would not set foot in the camp before he spoke with the king. Later, so it seems, they spoke together as Casel Imbert.

There where our men stayed at Ascalon, while they were re-fortifying it, there where they were in groups, there arose words between the king and the duke of Burgundy, which brought much harm to the work.[523] The French demanded their wages from the duke, pressing him for them, and he did not have the means to pay them. For this reason he went to try [his chance with] the king of England, to know whether he would lend him more wealth than he had already lent the French in the summer, against their share of Acre. However, the king did not wish to make any further loan. Because of this and other business many words were exchanged that are not written here; in the end the duke left there in anger with some of the French, and came rapidly to Acre. There they found the Genoese and Pisans fighting each other.[524] The Pisans nobly held to

---

521 St Leonard of Noblac perhaps lived in the sixth century, although there was no cult until a Latin *Life* was written before 1028. He was invoked by both women in labour and prisoners of war, in the former case because he was supposed to have prayed for the safe delivery of a child of the Merovingian king, Clovis, and in the latter because Bohemond of Taranto, one of the leaders of the First Crusade, had visited the shrine after his release from captivity by the Danishmend Turks in 1103. The saint's day is 6 November, *Butler's Lives of the Saints*, new full ed., revised by S.F. Thomas (Tunbridge Wells, 1995–7), November, pp.45–6. On the development of the cult, see M. Bull, *Knightly Piety and the Lay Response to the First Crusade* (Oxford, 1993), pp.235–49.

522 Cf. *Itinerarium*, 5.9.

523 Cf. *Itinerarium*, 5.9.

524 Cf. *Itinerarium*, 5.10. The Italian maritime cities often transferred their rivalries in the West to the crusader states, sometimes attaching themselves to contending parties there. See M.-L. Favreau-Lilie, *Die Italiener in Heiligen Land vom ersten Kreuzzug bis zum Tode Heinrichs von Champagne (1098–1197)* (Amsterdam, 1989), pp.257–97, and Mayer, 'On the Beginnings

King Guy and the Genoese attached themselves to the marquis because of the oath he had sworn to the king of France.[525] Then was there great confusion at Acre, with the town in a bad state, people killing and slaughtering, great disturbance and noise, so that the French and the duke and those who were there armed themselves. When the Pisans saw this they defended themselves boldly and brought shame and dishonour on the duke of Burgundy, for they killed his horse from under him and forced him to go on foot. Then they ran to close the city gates, for they did not want to shut into the city any who could harm it for the Genoese had sent a messenger to the marquis saying that they would give up the city to him. He came with his galleys and with his fully armed men, expecting to take the city by surprise. Then you would have seen the Pisans at the mangonels and the catapults, as men who were both bold and fierce. For three days they fought each other, while the Pisans sent hurriedly for the king of England. He had already come by land to Caesarea, as I ascertained, to go to speak with the marquis. The messengers met him. Then he rode on and journeyed to Acre, during the dark of night. When the marquis knew the fact that the king had come he could not be kept there, but went at once to Tyre, which was five leagues from Arsur.[526] The duke of Burgundy had gone there already with his Frenchmen. When the king learnt of this at Acre where he had lain, he mounted the next morning, and took the matter in hand, settling the quarrel, bringing peace to the parties involved. He made peace between the Genoese and the Pisans, considering that if he did not bring about peace things could go very badly indeed.

[8219–52][527]   When the Genoese and the Pisans had made peace in this way, having had war between them for such a long time, then the king of England sent to the marquis saying that they should meet at Casel Imbert and talk to see if they could arrive at an agreement. They came there and met together, the king and the marquis, talking together for a long time. But, so it seems to me, it came to nothing, for the marquis immediately broke his agreement with the king, partly because of the duke of the Burgundians and partly because of his other

of the Communal Movement', 456. Conrad of Montferrat had confirmed the privileges of both the Genoese and the Pisans in Tyre, but had quarrelled with the latter in the spring of 1189, when, reinforced by Archbishop Ubaldo, the papal legate, who arrived on 6 April with fifty-two ships, they had taken the side of King Guy in the dispute over the kingship. Richard arrived in Acre on 20 February 1192, and made peace between the parties on the following day, Landon, p.61.

525   The Genoese had a commercial link with Philip II since he had engaged their services for his transportation and supply, Richard, 'Philippe Auguste, la croisade et le royaume', p.414. See above, p.36.

526   I.8206. Paris considers this line corrupt and corrects in his translation on the basis of other references to Arsur to 'alors soufflait le vent d'Arsur', glossing this in his table of names as 'le vent du sud par rapport à Acre'. This seems an unnecessary alteration. Arsur is probably mentioned here to provide a rhyme for Sur (Tyre) and refers to Arsuf. The exact distance is probably not important as Ambroise is not at this point concerned with distance travelled in a day. HL, p.316, n.39, note that 'this verse makes no sense'. Paris translates it, 'Car alors souffleait le vent d'Arsur' (For now the Arsur wind blew). This makes little better sense and we have adhered to the literal translation of the text.

527   Cf. *Itinerarium*, 5.11.

companions, who turned him away from peace so that it all broke up. When the king knew of this [. . .][528] so the judgement was made, justly, that because he did not care about deserving his part of the kingdom, nor about serving God, that they should take his income from the kingdom and deprive him of it. From this came the discord between the barons of France and the marquis, who drew the French to him, both then and before, and brought such trouble to the land that the king of England, so I think and believe, for nearly three-quarters of Lent [. . .][529] did not dare leave Acre.

[8253–68][530]   On the third day before Palm Sunday[531] the young men [of the army] set out from Jaffa to Mirabel; this was a fine thing for many people because of a great booty that they found and brought back, killing thirty Saracens and taking fifty alive, coming quickly back to Jaffa. They kept half of their booty, scarcely knowing its total value, and half went to the count. The share of the men-at-arms was sold, so I have heard, for more than fourteen hundred good Saracen besants, of full weight.

[8269–308]   The Saturday afterwards for sure, once again all those who had horses set out in good order from Ascalon, after a booty of which they had knowledge, for it had been spied out. They did well on that occasion; those who were there tell that they went as far as Egypt, four leagues beyond Darum, and took horses and mares and also took seven hundred sheep and horned beasts, twenty asses and thirty camels. They also took, as I understand, more than one hundred and eighty of the infidels, men, women and children. They returned to Ascalon, with joyful countenances.

You have heard of the discord that I have already related between the barons who fell out.[532] The duke and the marquis sent a message from Tyre to the army at Ascalon, to all the French, that they should come soon to the marquis at Tyre and that they should support him and he them in faith, because of his homage to the king of France. Then was the matter made open, well known and clearly seen, the treachery and the cruel and mortal hatred on which the false marquis had acted because of the oath which they pledged together when the king of France left; because of this the French now left the king of England, who was concerned for the good of the land – as you will hear me tell, if it pleases you to pay a little attention.

[8309–62][533]   On Tuesday of Holy Week, when men are in a state of penitence,[534] the king returned to the army, angry and looking melancholy. On the Wednesday, the barons of France asked for him and said that he should provide them with escort as he had said to them and according to the agreement. He granted this at once and gave some of his men of Poitou, of Maine and of Anjou

---

528   After l.8237 there is a lacuna indicated by the incomplete rhyme. Paris suggests a lacuna of several lines, on the basis of the Latin, which recounts the marquis's removal to Tyre, giving up the war. See *Itinerarium*, 5.1.
529   After l.8251 there is a lacuna of at least one line.
530   Cf. *Itinerarium*, 5.12.
531   27 March 1192, Landon, p.61.
532   Cf. *Itinerarium*, 5.13.
533   Cf. *Itinerarium*, 5.14.
534   31 March, Landon, p.61.

and barons of Normandy; he himself escorted them in tears, pleading with them all the while to stay at his expense and that they should all keep together. But they did not wish to remain. When he could gain nothing and they would not hear his prayer he came back to Ascalon and sent at once to Acre, immediately and without delay, to his officers, that they should prevent the French from lodging there.

It was then on Maundy Thursday that sin took the barons of France from the army.[535] So there was the army, melancholy and sad and discouraged, considerably depleted by the loss of more than seven hundred knights, skilled in arms, valiant and agile, who did not dare remain any longer. There you might have seen many people crying because of the discords that there were. When the Saracens heard of it you may be sure that they rejoiced. Those who heard it say that Saladin ordered letters to be written and sent for the emirs of all the lands of which he was lord through conquest that they should come back to Syria for the Franks would not have any victories because there was such discord among them as had been told to him. So by his wealth and his ability he thought to take Tyre and Acre. They obeyed his command but came reluctantly. Nonetheless he gathered enough to be too many, it seemed to me.

Miracle in Jerusalem

[8363–408][536]   During the festival of Easter, on the Saturday,[537] according to those on whom I base my tale, the Sultan Saladin was [. . .][538] in Jerusalem, at the Sepulchre. There were there many Christians in dire straits,[539] prisoners in chains and bonds, both Latins and Syrians, who wept bitterly and, weeping before God, they asked for mercy for Christianity, reduced to the state of an orphan. As they wept thus, worshipping God, with tender tears, there came the fire of the Spirit, just as it was wont, to appear in the lamp.[540] As rapidly as the eyes of men rise, all saw it, young and old, Saracen and Christian; they saw the lamp lit as it had been in the past. So were the people moved when they saw this miracle. The Saracens wondered [at it] and said and asked whether it was by magic that it was lit in this way. Saladin wished to test this happening and commanded that the lamp be extinguished and his people at once put it out; but

---

535 2 April 1192. Maundy Thursday is Thursday of Holy Week, when the Last Supper which Christ took with his disciples is remembered. Cf. *Itinerarium*, 5.15.
536 Cf. *Itinerarium*, 5.16.
537 4 April.
538 After l.8365 there is a lacuna probably of one line.
539 l. 8367 translates *mucre*, which literally means damp, mouldy, musty, Godefroy, vol.5, p.434, figuratively, sad or discouraged, *T-L*, vol.6, p.397.
540 This is reminiscent of the appearance of the Holy Spirit as flames of fire to the first disciples at Pentecost in Acts 2. The Holy Spirit is also linked with fire in e.g. Luke 3:16, Matthew 3:11. For the Russian abbot, Daniel, this was the culmination of his visit, and he gives a vivid description of the event, Wilkinson, pp.166–71.

their intention achieved nothing [and they could not prevent][541] the lamp from re-igniting. He said it should be put out again but the Lord God willed that the truth should be made manifest in His name and in His City and He re-lit it for a third time. When Saladin saw the faith and belief of the Christians then he said to the Turks in truth and without doubt that he would die soon and the City would not long be his. According to my knowledge and as I understand it, he did not live after that day beyond the following Lent.[542]

Troubles for the Crusaders

[8409–58][543] At Easter, that great festival, the king held a full and great court for the encouragement of the men of his army, and had his pavilions carried and pitched outside Ascalon [and everyone might][544] take the food that he wished. The court lasted for only one day. The next day, with no delay, the king had the work on the walls begin again and continued the work that the French had abandoned when their people left. He had everything that needed to be completed done out of his own resources. Whoever among you pleased to listen has already heard me tell of the escort of his barons from Poitou and Normandy, Anjou and Maine, who had escorted the French as far as Acre and then had returned. Now listen to how the French behaved at Tyre, where they were, during the time they were there, and what good came out of their business and what service they did, what raids they made, what trials and tribulations they suffered there, for the love of God. Those who saw it tell how they danced the night away,[545] wearing garlands and crowns of flowers on their heads and how they would sit before the barrels and drink until matins, then returning with wanton young girls,[546] breaking the locks, saying very foolish things and swearing great oaths. This was their homecoming. I do not say that all said and did such base deeds, for the worthy men who were there and who remained there against their will were worried by the discord, which God did not wish to resolve; these men were very angry but the evil men rejoiced at the discord between the barons and the king of France.[547]

[8459–98][548] When the valiant King Charlemagne, who conquered so many lands and countries, went to campaign in Spain, taking with him the noble band

---

[541] After l.8393 there is a lacuna, probably of about of four lines. Paris fills from the context 'et ne purent empêcher' (and could not prevent), which seems to make sense.

[542] Saladin died on 4 March 1193.

[543] Cf. *Itinerarium*, 5.17.

[544] After l.8413 there is a lacuna assumed to be of four lines. Paris fills in his translation as 'et chacun put y pénétrer et' (and any could enter and), which Stone renders as 'and everyman might enter therein'. Nicholson, p.298, translates the Latin as 'providing plenty of food and drink for all who wanted it'.

[545] l. 8439. According to the *A-ND*, *tresches* refers to a specific form of dance, in a ring.

[546] l. 8444, *foles meschines*, lit. 'foolish girls', appears to be a euphemism for prostitutes.

[547] The *Itinerarium* has 'king of England', which seems more likely.

[548] Cf. *Itinerarium*, 5.21.

who were sold to Marsile by Ganelon to the dishonour of France,[549] and when he, Charlemagne, had returned to Saxony, where he did many great deeds and defeated Guiteclin, bringing about the fall of the Saxons by the strength of many valiant men and when he led his army to Rome, when Agoland, through a great undertaking had arrived at Reggio in the rich land of Calabria, when, in another war, Syria was lost and reconquered and Antioch besieged, in the great armies and the battles against the Turks and the pagan hordes, when many were killed and conquered, there was no bickering and quarrelling, at that time and before; then there was neither Norman nor French, Poitevin nor Breton, Mansel nor Burgundian, Flemish nor English; there was no malicious gossip nor insulting of one another; everyone came back with all honour and all were called Franks, whether brown or red, swarthy or white,[550] and when through sin they disagreed the princes brought them back into agreement with each other, and all were of one mind so that disagreement lasted little time. This is how things should be done and the affairs of today dealt with, that men may follow this example and not attack each other.

[8499–539][551]   After Easter, at the season for sea travel, a messenger came to King Richard, causing great trouble to the army. It was the prior of Hereford, a priory in England, who came to find him in Syria and brought him news that was neither good nor welcome, in written letters, sealed, written in great need, which told that his governors whom he had established in England had been removed from his castles and in the struggles people had been killed in the country. The prior himself had seen this. The letter also told that his brother had caused his chancellor[552] to leave England and that nothing remained in upper

---

549   The allusions are to various tales celebrated in the *chansons de geste*. The first is to the *Chanson de Roland*, in which Roland and the entire rearguard are betrayed by Ganelon. Jean Bodel's *Chanson des Saisnes*, ed. A. Brasseur, 2 vols (Geneva, 1989), tells of Charlemagne's campaigns against the Saxons under their king, Guiteclin. Agoland is in the *Chanson d'Aspremont*. The *Chanson d'Antioche*, ed. S.H. Duparc-Quioc (Paris, 1976), is an early thirteenth-century *chanson de geste* recounting the events of the First Crusade. This is an idealised presentation of these tales, here being used as exempla with little concern for an accurate presentation of the texts.

550   1.8490. The colours I have translated as 'red' and 'swarthy' are more frequently applied to horses and translated 'bay' and 'sorrel'.

551   Cf. *Itinerarium*, 5.22.

552   William of Longchamp had been Richard's chancellor in Aquitaine. In 1189 he became Bishop of Ely and Chancellor of England and, when Richard left for the crusade, he was appointed co-justiciar with Hugh, Bishop of Durham. In February 1190, Longchamp became chief justiciar, and in June he was made papal legate in England by Pope Clement III. While exercising these powers he came into conflict with, among others, Richard's brother, John. The situation led the king to send Walter of Coutances back to England in April, 1191, with delegated powers over all parties. See above, p.45, n.89. However, on 29 October 1191 Longchamp had been forced into exile to Flanders and had since conducted a vigorous campaign against John, which included complaint to Pope Clement III. According to the *Itinerarium*, 5.22, pp.333–4, Robert, Prior of Hereford, who arrived at Ascalon on 15 April 1192, was acting directly on Longchamp's behalf. Despite these problems, Longchamp remained an important member of Richard's inner circle after the king's release from captivity in 1194. He died end of January, 1197. *DNB*, vol.34, pp.381–3, and J. Appleby, pp.56–106, for Longchamp's exile and John's efforts to seize power. Robert, Prior of Hereford, was, according to Richard of Devizes, p.40, 'a monk who held himself in no small esteem and

room or cellar nor in any treasury (except in the churches) that he had not caused to be seized and taken, and that he dared go so far in his misdeeds that he had treated the chancellor, who was priest and bishop, lord and master, with such baseness and done him such harm that he had fled to Normandy. There was more. He wished so much harm to the king while he was on pilgrimage that he wished to receive the oaths of his barons [and the revenues][553] which came to the Exchequer. "Good lord, I therefore entreat you," said the prior, "that you return to your land and take vengeance against those who do you so much harm or they will do you more harm and you will not enter your land, which they pillage, without a battle."

[8540–579] My lords, do not wonder at the king, who had laboured for God in that distant land, where he had much pain and trouble; he was disturbed in his heart for such news brings despair and discouragement to any valiant man if he believes he will lose his dignities. So was the news made known. I do not think that there was ever seen in any place a people who were more angered or depressed over one man who had to leave the army. For the army would have split – if the king had left the dilemma would have been dreadful, for they were in disarray. There would never have been harmony between those of Tyre and those of Ascalon. The next day, between the hours of terce and nones the king assembled his barons and relayed aloud the whole message that had come to him from England,[554] that they wanted to take his land from him and that his chancellor, appointed by him to protect and maintain his interests, had been deposed, that he [Richard] would have to go, but, that if this happened, he would leave, at his own expense, three hundred chosen knights and two thousand men-at-arms, noble and valiant. He said that he wanted to know and have a response [concerning] who would want to come with him and he left the decision to them, whether to remain or to go, for he did not wish to force anyone.

The Marquis of Montferrat

[8580–625] The great men who were there spoke of this matter as the king asked. Each one gave much consideration to what they should say and do. They found themselves in this situation, that they had no overall leader in the kingdom but were divided into two; King Guy could not lead his own party and the marquis did not want to come back to the army whatever reassurance was

---

gladly meddled in matters in which he had no business so that he might promote his own affairs'. Richard agrees that he was sent by Longchamp, but remarks that 'to the disgust of many', he managed to obtain the abbacy of Muchelney from the king, apparently as a result of carrying the message.

553 After 1.8531 there is a lacuna of several lines. Paris, in his translation, supplies from the *Itinerarium*, 5.22, pp.333–4, 'et il avait tenté de s'emparer des rentes du roi', which Stone translates 'he had striven to lay hands on the king's revenues'. Nicholson, p.301, has, 'He had also reached out his hand to usurp the annual payments into the royal treasury, which are called "Exchequer payments".'

554 Cf. *Itinerarium*, 5.23.

offered him but stayed with the French. So there was much discord. When they had taken note of this they came back to the king and said, not secretly, that if he did not create in the land a lord who understood war and whom everyone could support, wherever they came from, that they would all follow him and abandon the land. The king, wanting to go on his way, responded at once, asking which of the kings they wanted and which they did not want, between King Guy and the marquis. All those who were asked and who kneeled before him, pleading and beseeching, the great and the lesser men and those of middle rank, all said that he should make the marquis lord, for he was the most able to aid and succour the kingdom.[555] When the king saw that everyone wanted him and that there was no-one who did not want him, he criticised some who were present and who had spoken ill of the marquis to him; since each had pleaded to have him he agreed and granted that great men should go for him and bring him with great rejoicing and that he and the French should come and that all should hold to one [lord].

[8626–43][556]   This election that I have recounted was not a minor affair. Everyone, both wise and simple wished it. The messengers got ready – Count Henry of Champagne and with him, in his company, my lord Otto of Trazegnies. They were men of high lineage. There was also William of Caieux. They put their helmets on their heads; they went to bear the message and to encourage the marquis and to tell him the good news, which was welcome to him and to the French who were at Tyre. They rode on their journey and you will hear what happened when they arrived.

[8644–693]   It is true and without doubt that the nobles of France had gone off with the marquis, whom King Richard had asked many times – as we bore witness and have told you – to join with the others and help the army to conquer that land and that he had not wanted to come and that ill came to him because of this. Now you shall hear what he wanted to do and how he wished to harm God; against the honour of the Crown and against the army of Ascalon he had agreed peace with Saladin and sworn that he would come to him and he would hold half of Jerusalem from him. He had concluded this villainous business, so it transpired.[557] He would have Beirut and Sidon and the area around and he would also have half the land. Saladin desired this peace, but the Emir Saphadin did not wish to grant it. We heard it said afterwards that he said to his brother the sultan, "My lord, let it not please God the Father that the Christians have peace on account of any man who tempts you [to it], except the king of England – there is no better Christian. I do not wish it or approve it." So the matter went no farther and it was known all over, for Stephen of Turnham[558] had been sent to

---

555   16 April 1192, Landon, p.61.
556   Cf. *Itinerarium*, 5.24.
557   On the negotiations between Conrad of Montferrat and Saladin, see above, p.132, n.477.
558   Stephen of Turnham was a knight from Kent, who held lands in Sussex. His brother, Robert, was one of Richard's fleet commanders and a justiciar in Cyprus after its conquest. Stephen may be the same person who had been seneschal of Anjou before the crusade, but had been imprisoned by Richard for some unspecified offence. If so, he was back in favour by the time the king set out, accompanying him on the journey to Sicily. According to the *Itinerarium*, 2.30, p.185, he was the royal marshal and treasurer at this time. He appears to have been among those entrusted with the protection of the queens Berengaria and Joanna, since he was

Jerusalem, to the sultan, when they came. He remembered the names of some, Balian of Ibelin,[559] who was more false than a goblin, and also Reynald of Sidon,[560] who came to seek and pursue this filthy and unclean peace. They should be hunted with dogs.

[8694–24][561] The messengers, of whom we have spoken, whom we saw depart with their message, journeyed by each stage as they had planned, arriving quickly at Tyre. There they dismounted and went straight to the marquis. They said to him what they wanted, greeting him courteously. He and those who were with him, greeted them with laughter. The Count Henry spoke and said with great willingness, "My lord marquis, the king and Christendom and all those at Ascalon have granted you the crown and the kingdom of Syria. Come with your assembled armies and conquer the kingdom with boldness." The history tells us reliably that he had such joy in his heart, that, in the hearing of all the barons, he raised his hands towards Heaven, saying these words, which would later anger many, "Dear Lord God, who made me [. . .][562] You who are the true and benign King, You know, Lord, if I am worthy to govern Your kingdom, then permit me

---

with them when they arrived at Limassol in May 1191, and accompanied them to Rome on the return journey at the end of the crusade: Landon, pp.20, 23, 31–4, 36, 38, 63, 75, 112; Siedschlag, no.144, p.125; Roger of Howden, *Chronica*, vol.3, p.228; vol.4, p.142.

559   Balian was the third son of Barisan of Ibelin and Helvis of Ramla. Barisan's origins are unknown, but he may have come from a Ligurian or Tuscan family. By 1115 he was constable of Jaffa and, by the time of his death in 1150, lord of Ibelin and Ramla. In 1177, Balian married Maria Comnena, widow of King Amalric and great niece of Manuel I, the Byzantine emperor. His prominence was further enhanced by the death of his eldest brother, Hugh, in 1171, and by the voluntary exile of his other brother, Baldwin, in 1186, following the seizure of the throne by Guy of Lusignan and Sibylla in 1186, see above, p.66. Balian was a notable soldier, having taken part in most of the important engagements of the 1170s and 1180s. Along with Raymond of Tripoli, he escaped from Hattin and was the chief negotiator with Saladin when Jerusalem fell on 2 October 1187. When Sibylla and her daughters died in 1190, he was in a unique political position since the heiress, Isabella, was his step-daughter, and he and Maria Comnena played a major part in forcing her to separate from Humphrey of Toron and to marry Conrad of Montferrat, see above, pp.88–9. As one of Conrad's negotiators with Saladin, he inevitably incurred Ambroise's hostility. See Edbury, *John of Ibelin and the Kingdom of Jerusalem*, pp.2–28, and table one for the genealogy of the Ibelin family in the twelfth century.

560   Between c.1171 and c.1200 Reynald of Sidon held one of the four most important lordships in the Kingdom of Jerusalem (the others were Galilee, Jaffa and Oultrejourdain). He was the great-grandson of Eustace Grenier, who had received the fief from Baldwin I in the early twelfth century, and it had remained in the family since that time. Together with the Ibelins he had supported the regency of Raymond of Tripoli in 1174 and had similarly been alienated by the *coup* of 1186 of Guy and Sibylla. He was part of the group which escaped from Hattin and, in 1189–90, had delayed the fall of his castle of Beaufort for nearly a year by a policy of prevarication and trickery. See above, n.213. His first wife was Agnes of Courtenay and when this marriage was dissolved he married Helvis, daughter of Balian of Ibelin and Maria Comnena. He, Balian, and Pagan of Haifa threw their weight behind Conrad of Montferrat's candidacy for the kingship. He regained the lordship of Sidon in the autumn of 1192. See La Monte, 'The Lords of Sidon in the Twelfth and Thirteenth Centuries', *Byzantion* 17 (1944/5), 193–200.

561   Cf. *Itinerarium*, 5.25.

562   After l.8718 there is a lacuna assumed to be of one line, filled in Paris's translation from the *Itinerarium* as 'and put my soul in my body'.

to go to be crowned; my Lord, if You do not know me to be so, do not permit
this to happen."

[8725–96]   The news was heard and spread throughout the land that the
marquis would be king and that the whole army asked for him. The joy was
great, the people filled with happiness and eager to equip and make ready, to
acquire and borrow gold and silver for expenses, according to what each considered necessary. There you would have seen arms being reached for, helmets
and caps burnished once more. There you would have seen fine swords being
polished by the esquires and hauberks rolled, knights and men-at-arms prepare
to fight against the hated race. There were men of great worth, had it been the
will of God, who knows them better than we do, to be with them. There you
would have seen many people rejoicing. It is right that one should know and hear
and one can know in truth, that no-one should rejoice too much in joy, nor
should any mourn too much in mourning. Everyone was eager and enthusiastic
about this business and the Count Henry and the barons who had brought the
message, had gone to borrow [what was needed] at Acre, where they already
made preparations and made ready to return to the army.[563]

This is indeed what happened at Tyre. The marquis had eaten with the bishop
of Beauvais, with great pleasure and joy and the time came for him to take his
leave. He was in front of the Exchange.[564] You will hear how joy can be
exchanged and quickly turned into sadness. As he went on his way, happy, two
young men, without cloaks, carrying two knives, came running up to him,
striking him in his body as they ran up, so that he fell. Of those who had
betrayed him, who were men of the Assassins,[565] one was killed straight away,
the other took refuge in a church, but this was no use to him, for he was seized
and dragged until he was dead. Before he died those who were there asked him
why they had done this, what harm the marquis had done them and who had sent
them. According to what he, the disloyal, said, and as was later known for sure,

---

[563]   Cf. *Itinerarium*, 5.26.

[564]   The murder took place on 28 April 1192, Landon, p.62.

[565]   When the Prophet died in 632, he was succeeded by Abu Bakr, one of his closest companions,
but almost from the beginning Islam was threatened by schism since some thought that a more
fitting ruler would be 'Ali, Muhammad's son-in-law and cousin. Thereafter, the party of 'Ali,
or the Shi'ah, frequently served as a focus for dissidents within the Muslim world. The Assassins were a Shi'ah splinter group who believed that a late eighth-century descendant of 'Ali
called Isma'il was the one true imam (doctrinal and political leader), and that since his death
there had been a series of secret imams, one of whom would eventually appear and declare a
new regime of justice and order. In 969 'Alid supporters managed to create the Fatimid
Caliphate in Egypt, but in time some of the Isma'ilites came to regard this government as
corrupt and, led by a Persian called al-Hasan ibn-as-Sabbah (d.1124), they established their
own power base at Alamut in north-west Iran. Although relatively weak as a military force
they made their presence felt by a series of political murders which gave them influence far
beyond their numbers. By the early twelfth century they had also moved into northern Syria
and during the 1130s and 1140s had gained a series of castles in the Lebanese mountains to the
east of the County of Tripoli, the most important of which was Masyaf. The name assassin
derives from the drug hashish, but it seems unlikely that sect members took this extensively
given the necessity for long-term strategies if they were to get close enough to political
opponents to murder them. See B. Lewis, 'The Isma'ilites and the Assassins', in *HC*, vol.1,
pp.99–132.

they had stayed near to the marquis for a long time in order to do this, that they had for a long time sought successfully to kill him, until the day came when many tears were shed, and that they had been sent by the Old Man of the Mountain[566] who hated him and who causes all those whom he hates with a [bitter] hatred to be killed in such a way, as you will hear if it pleases you to listen.

[8797–855]   The Old Man of the Mountain has the custom, handed on from generation to generation, to raise in his house many children, brought up to an age of reason, understanding and education. They learn how to behave and frequent the great and the wise, until they know all the languages of the age, throughout the world; their faith is so dark and cruel and black, taught to them with great care, that when the Old Man of the Mountain sends for them to come before him and orders them, as the price of remission for their sins and of his friendship, to go and kill some great man, it is the summit of their ambition; they are given fine, polished knives and they go away and spy out the great man and watch over him[567] and become part of his household, being clever in their speech, until they manage to take his life. Then they believe that they deserve the great joy of Heaven, which certainly cannot be. Such, my lords, were these two whom we saw,[568] who killed the marquis in this way. His men took him gently in their arms and took him from the place where he was hurt and carried him to this lodging. There you would have seen great mourning, as all the people hurried there. He lived for a short time, then died. But first he made confession and said secretly[569] to the marchioness, his wife, in whose eyes he saw tears, that she must turn her mind to the protection of Tyre and that she should surrender the city to the king of England himself or to the rightful lord of the land. Then he died and was buried. Both clerics and lay people mourned him. He was buried at the Hospital. There was much mourning; there has never been greater mourning. But this was God's will. So the news spread and the great joy, which had lasted such a short time, dissipated, throughout the land that was sworn to him who left it so soon. Now was the land distraught, and so filled with sorrow and grief that no-one could tell of it.

---

566   The name of 'the Old Man of the Mountain' had originally been applied to Hasan Sabbah, but the Franks used it for any current Assassin leader in northern Syria. At this time it was Rashid al-Din Sinan, who was born near Basra, but as a young man had left to live with the Assassins at Alamut. In c.1162 he was sent by Hasan II to the sect in Syria, where he seems to have created a power base independent of Alamut. He was well known both to the Franks – with whom he attempted to negotiate an alliance in 1173 – and to Saladin – whom he tried to murder in 1174 and 1176. After the second attack Saladin besieged Masyaf, a move which led to an agreement of mutual toleration. He died between 1192 and 1194. See B. Lewis, *The Assassins: A Radical Sect in Islam* (New York, 1967), pp.110–18. For the abortive negotiations with the Franks, WT, 20.29–30, pp.953–5.

567   Dittography in the manuscript. Paris supplies in his translation 'se familiarisent'.

568   Paris rejects the manuscript reading of l.8826 and corrects it to 'que nos deimes' (of whom we speak).

569   The word translated here as 'secretly', *saucession* (l.8836), is not attested elsewhere. Paris notes in his glossary 'mot altéré non restitué', giving in translation the guess 'en secret', which makes sense in the context. There is no reason to assume this is a corrupt reading.

[8857–86][570]   Listen to how the devil works, and how his works are revealed in evil and how they increase and spread out and how they spread as he unfolds them, from one word that was said by an envious and cursed people who hated the noble Richard and considered his deeds as naught – such men should be hunted down. They said that King Richard had pursued and sought the death of Conrad through payment. They sent to the king of France, saying that he should fear and protect himself from the Assassins, because they had killed the marquis and that the king of England had sent four of them to sweet France to kill him. God! What a foul thing to say; they did a vile deed when they sent the message.[571] As a result of it many people were later troubled, angered and grieved. For because of this evil deed the king was later imprisoned, through treachery and envy of the good works he performed in Syria.[572]

[8887–928][573]   When the marquis had been buried and mourning observed, they had done all that ought to be done, the barons of France were in their tents, outside the town; there were more than ten thousand of them, of high and low estate. The great men spoke together and sent a message to the marchioness that she should give up the city to them, peacefully and freely, to be held for the king of France. She replied without hesitation that when the king returned she would willingly surrender it to him if there were no other lord [chosen] before then. They were most indignant about this. Whilst they were struggling and striving to obtain Tyre, there came Count Henry into the town where he dismounted. He from whom I received this tells that as soon as the people saw him they waited no longer, but elected him king, as God willed it. They came to him and took him and beseeched him and said that he should receive the kingdom and lordship of Syria and that he should marry the marchioness who was left both heir and widow. He replied at once, taking no time to decide, that as God had called him and they had confirmed[574] him as heir to govern the land, that he wished to have the consent of his uncle the king of England, and when he sent to know his will and his intention regarding this election by the barons [. . .][575]

---

[570]   Cf. *Itinerarium*, 5.27.

[571]   Baha' al-Din, pp.200–1, says that the two murderers declared that 'the King of England put us up to it'. However, the Assassins did not act as hired killers even in the East (let alone in France), so it is more likely that Rashid al-Din had motives of his own for the murder. The French continuation of William of Tyre known as the Lyon *Eracles* gives the most likely explanation; it says that Conrad had seized a merchant ship belonging to the Assassins when it arrived in Tyre and refused to return it, despite Rashid al-Din's threats, *La Continuation de Guillaume de Tyr (1184–1197)*, ed. M.R. Morgan, p.141. Moreover, such a murder made no political sense for, by this time, Richard had already accepted that Conrad was the only practical choice for king once the crusade had finished. See above, p.148.

[572]   Richard was captured by Leopold of Austria at Vienna on 20 December 1192, while returning from the crusade, Landon, p.71. For the circumstances, see below, p.193.

[573]   Cf. *Itinerarium*, 5.28.

[574]   *ancelé* (1.8922) has not been attested elsewhere with similar meaning. The word *ancele* means 'handmaiden'; a more probable link is from *enseeler*, to seal, but this would give a hypermetric reading, or *enseller*, to saddle, so possibly by extension to burden.

[575]   Henry was elected on about 2 May, Landon, p.62. The syntax clearly makes no sense unless we posit a lacuna after 1.8928.

[8929–63]⁵⁷⁶   It was in May, when flowers and leaves are renewed, that the news came to the king that it had happened to the marquis as we recounted. The king was in the plains of Ramla where he was riding throughout the barren land, hunting a flight of Saracens who were fleeing from him as from one they greatly feared, for since God created the earth never did one man make such war on the Turks, nor through one did so many die. Many times he went after them, bringing back to the army the heads of Saracens, like those of wild beasts, ten or twelve, or twenty or thirty, to the great sorrow of pagandom. Sometimes the noble Richard would bring them back alive when he wanted to. In summary, never did any man cause so many to die at one time.

Then came the messengers, spurring on, seeking the king; they came to him and greeted him from the count and told him what happened to the marquis and how the people had chosen the count to be lord of the land [. . .]⁵⁷⁷ for the men of high and of low estate had elected him as lord and they wished him to take the marchioness [as wife], but he did not want to do this of his own will but for the good of Christianity.

[8964–9038]   For a long time was the king melancholy on account of the news of the marquis, who by such great misfortune had been killed so hideously, but he had great joy from knowing that the people were so anxious to give such honour to his nephew. He replied to this situation, "My lords, men-at-arms, I very much wish him to be king, if it pleases God, when the land is conquered, but he should not marry the marchioness, whom the marquis took; she hated her lord and lay with the marquis against God and against what is right, and he kept her so immorally that, if he believes me, the count should never in his lifetime take her in marriage, but let him receive the lordship [. . .]⁵⁷⁸ and I will give him Acre for his own and the income from the harbour dues⁵⁷⁹ and Tyre and Jaffa and jurisdiction over all of the conquered land, for I wish that he should hold it. Tell him to come to the army and bring with him the French, as soon as he can, because I wish to take Darum if the Turks dare to await me there." The messengers retained what they heard from the king and then left with his permission and without further ado, returning to the count at Tyre.⁵⁸⁰

They told the count and recounted to him all that they had from the king. What else should I say to you? There was great rejoicing on the count's behalf, at Tyre when the messengers returned. There you would have seen the great throng of high and proud men who were there, all urging him to take the marchioness as wife, but he did not dare do this for them against the wishes of the king of England. However, she was the heir and the count desired her greatly. It was so arranged that the marchioness herself, though she had been strongly

---

⁵⁷⁶ Cf. *Itinerarium*, 5.29. The *Itinerarium* lacks the *vers printanière*.

⁵⁷⁷ Cf. *Itinerarium*, 5.34. The *Itinerarium* has several episodes before this which are not in Ambroise. There is a lacuna after l.8957, assumed to be of one line.

⁵⁷⁸ After l.8982 there is a blank line in the manuscript. Paris adds in his translation [et le royaume de Syrie]. On the marriage of the marquis see above, p.89. l.8976 is clearly corrupt: the manuscript gives 'he who took away the marquis . . .', which has been corrected in the text.

⁵⁷⁹ The text has *chaaine* (l.8984), referring to the chain which closed the harbour, ensuring that no ships could enter without paying their dues.

⁵⁸⁰ Cf. *Itinerarium*, 5.35.

advised against it, carried the keys of the city to the count – I am telling the truth. The French acted at once and sent for the priest and they had the count marry the lady: and, by my soul, I would have done the same for she was very beautiful and noble and I believe that the count did not take much persuading to marry her, as God is my witness. So the marriage took place[581] there amid joy such as I believe I shall never see nor hear in my whole life; there was an event without envy, without contention, without trickery and so was the land in a good state and in high hopes because of the count, nephew of the king of France and nephew of the valiant king of England. The count sent throughout the land to Acre, Jaffa and elsewhere, to take possession of the castles and the towers and ensure that they would answer to him, and had the army called up and summoned the barons, being invited to come and take Darum.

[9039–78][582]   When the count had celebrated his marriage and called his people to him there on the advice of the barons and the Frenchmen of his own lineage, he wished to lead his men to Acre to prepare and equip, to buy barley and oats for the ride to Ascalon. Then he left good guards at Tyre who would look out over the heights, the city and the country [around] that no evil men could enter. The count took with him his wife, as fair as a gemstone. So did the army move out of Tyre. So came the news to Acre of the count's approach. Everyone was so overjoyed about the count that their joy could hardly be contained, night and day. There you could have seen a rich affair, processions formed, drapes hung in the streets, censers full of incense in front of the houses, in the windows! All the men of the town, about sixty thousand of them, went out from Acre, fully armed, to meet him until they saw him. This was to signify that they were coming to him to hold him as their rightful lord. The clergy led him to the great church and brought the relics to him. They made him kiss the Holy Cross and he and many others made offerings. They led him to the palace where they lodged him. There the count was richly housed – would that I could always be the same.

[9079–102][583]   When the count was in possession of Tyre, Acre, Jaffa and Arsuf then was King Guy without a kingdom, Guy who had received so many blows on his helmet who had paid so much and now found himself at a loss, [having endured] so many wrongs and such great misadventures, not only for his own sins, for no king had better qualities – he had one single lack, that of knowing no evil, which is counted as simplicity. This was the king who by his own valour had re-taken the city of Acre when the Saracens had taken it. Before all this the lords of the Temple had bought the land of Cyprus from the king who had conquered it but the purchase later collapsed and King Guy was later made emperor and lord of it, which was a great consolation to him.[584]

---

581 The marriage took place on 5 May, Landon, p.62.
582 Cf. *Itinerarium*, 5.37.
583 Cf. *Itinerarium*, 5.37.
584 Despite his success in conquering Cyprus, Richard must have realised that he had no realistic prospect of long-term direct government. He had therefore sold it to the Templars, whose Master, Robert of Sablé, had been one of his fleet commanders. See above, p.43. Although different accounts give different figures, the sum seems to have been 100,000 Saracen *besants*,

[9103–26]⁵⁸⁵   At the time when the marquis was stabbed to death at Tyre, then and before and after, as we saw, many times there came to the king of England messengers who brought him trouble, for some made him anxious and others reassured him; one would say that he should return, another that he should hold firm and remain in the service of God. Thus they spoke each in his own way: one would say that his land was in a state of peace, without war; another would say for certain that there was widespread disturbance; whatever some would say, others would contradict. So it is not to be wondered at that he did not know what to do nor that he was in great anxiety about the return of the king of France. For it is said that he who has a bad neighbour has a bad morning.⁵⁸⁶

Darum

[9127–69]⁵⁸⁷   While the French, the barons and Count Henry, of whom I have already spoken, were at Acre preparing for the campaign and equipping themselves for the siege of Darum, the king, not wanting to delay, went out from Ascalon in the name of God, the giver of all good things.⁵⁸⁸ He had his catapults embarked and taken to Darum by sea, and had his men armed, hiring men-at-arms, giving generous pay. He set guards and watchmen on all the castles, there and all around, and had them watch through the night so that no caravan could pass nor any Turks seek asylum at Darum as had been happening, causing us much harm. Then did the king mount, King Richard in whom much goodness is found. He came to Darum one Sunday,⁵⁸⁹ accompanied only by the men of his own dominions. There he was before Darum. The barons stood there, but there were so few men that neither they nor the king knew from which side they could besiege it, for if they spread themselves all around it and the Turks made a sally, or the army was attacked, they would not be able to withstand it, but would inevitably be defeated. Because of this they went to one side. [The

of which the Order initially paid 40,000. The Templars, however, failed to commit sufficient manpower to control the island, which, in any case, they seem to have regarded as a source of supply rather than a serious responsibility. Their actions provoked a rebellion in Nicosia on 5 April 1192, and they may well have been relieved to hand it over to Guy of Lusignan at some point after this. The transaction seems to have occurred at some point before the assassination of Conrad of Montferrat. See P.W. Edbury, 'The Templars in Cyprus', in *The Military Orders: Fighting for the Faith and Caring for the Sick*, ed. M. Barber (Aldershot, 1994), pp.189–91.

585 Cf. *Itinerarium*, 5.38.
586 This proverb is given in the *Dictionnaire des locutions en moyen français*, ed. G. di Stefano (Montreal, 1991), p.905, which quotes the prose *Tristan: De mal voisin vient mal matin* and *Pastoralet* where it takes the clearer form, *Qui a bon voisin a bon matin*. Philip II returned to Paris on 27 December 1191, but did not, in fact, make any serious incursions into Richard's lands until after the latter's capture in late December 1192. Philip's policy seems to have been to attempt to persuade John to betray his brother, a ploy which met with success in January 1194: Baldwin, *Government of Philip Augustus*, pp.87–9; Appleby, p.101.
587 Cf. *Itinerarium*, 5.39.
588 Matthew 7:11.
589 The siege of Darum began on 17 May 1192, Landon, p.63.

Turks sallied out].[590] They herded and harrassed [our men] until they re-entered the castle and prepared their defences, putting much care and thought into it, sealing their gate, which they considered very strong.

[9170–237] When the gate was closed behind the Turks, their men secure within, then did the catapults come up, disembarked from the vessels and brought to land in sections. The valiant Richard of England, he himself and his companions, carried on their shoulders the beams and wooded sections of the catapults, on foot, their faces sweating, along the sand, for nearly a league, burdened like a horse or beast of burden; this we saw with our own eyes. There were the catapults erected and handed over to the constables. The king had charge of one which attacked the Great Tower. The Normans, men of valour, had theirs, and the Poitevins, it seems, had one. All three hurled missiles at the castle. The Turks took fright though they would have had good protection in the strong castle and their resources. But the king had them attacked, night and day, without respite, wearing them down until they were confused. There were at Darum seventeen towers and turrets, strong and fine. One large tower dominated the others and was the strongest. Around it the ditch was deep, paved on one side and bare rock on the other. Fear made the people troubled because they could not escape. King Richard craftily dug underground until they came to the paving that they broke by force. Then they undermined [the wall] throwing the earth behind them. The catapults fired on the Turks, breaking a mangonel that they had erected on the main tower, which greatly dismayed them. Thus was the castle strongly attacked in different ways. There you might have seen the Turks defending on the battlements and at the loop-holes. Their darts raining down thickly struck our men in the faces. However, as soon as they moved out of cover our crossbowmen who were waiting for them in the open, shot arrows onto their shields as they drew,[591] injuring and striking so many that they were afraid to move and were indeed in some difficulty. Thus was the gate broken and set on fire and destroyed by the king's great catapult. There you would have seen a people in disarray, vigorously attacked, dismayed and in a bad way, for they were worn down night and day until everyone was disheartened.

[9238–309] King Richard and his barons laid siege around Darum; three days, day in, day out, they attacked, night and day, without respite. On the fourth day, a Friday,[592] the Turks I tell you of saw that they could not support it nor endure the great attacks that disheartened them and that many injured and hurt men lay around the castle; they were being attacked above and below ground. The king was about to take them with little difficulty. They did not delay but spoke of saving themselves and sent a message to King Richard, by three Saracens, that they would surrender on their terms, that they would go out, bodies and lives

---

590 There is a lacuna after l.9163, assumed by Paris to be of about five lines on the basis of the *Itinerarium*, 5.39, which recounts a sally made by the Turks.

591 ll.9225–6. Paris finds a difficulty with this: 'Ce passage . . . est altéré; on ne voit pas à qui se rapportent les mots: il getoient sur les targes; cela doit s'appliquer aux Turcs (car il s'agit sans doute des targes à l'abri desquelles les assiégeants attaquaient la muraille), mais ne va pas avec le contexte.' I do not share his concern. Ambroise has been describing the Turks' attempts at defence so it is no doubt the attackers firing on their shields.

592 22 May 1192, Landon, p.63.

saved, with their wives and their households. The king told them to hold their peace and defend themselves if they could. So they returned to the castle. Then did the largest catapult shoot, hitting a turret and greatly harming their cause, for the main tower fell,[593] having been undermined – as God willed it so it came to pass. Their people had [already fled]. All around our people rushed forward, [and] arming themselves, they attacked them, and, I believe, the Saracens all at once went into the main tower, but it was a premeditated act of evil-doing when they cut the hocks of their horses so that the Christians would not have them nor be able to ride them. The people of God climbed into the castle. Of the first to enter there, Seguin Baré was the very first, and an esquire, Espiard, was not far behind Seguin. Third was Peter the Gascon and there may have been others whose names I do not know.[594] Then the banners entered; there were several different ones. That of Stephen of Longchamp[595] was the first to enter, and it was not in one piece but had been greatly damaged. After that was raised the banner of the earl of Leicester. On the wall, to the right, was placed that of Andrew of Chauvigny, and with it the banner of my lord Raymond, the son of the prince, placed up on the wall.[596] The Genoese and the Pisans had many different banners. Our banners were raised on the walls and theirs thrown down from the walls. There you would have seen there Turks being cut down and thrown down from behind the parapets, attacked and held, killed, knocked and struck down, until there was found in the castle – this is the proven truth – sixty dead, those who had failed [to take refuge in] the great tower, who did not get away in time.

[9310–69]   The Saracens were in the great tower, keeping watch all around. They saw their castle taken and the Turks dead or in dire straits and they saw the shields being raised against the tower and directed so that the wall could be mined from below, while they were above,[597] and that the emir who was come to their rescue, was leaving them to suffer. He was called Caïsac, a Saracen of great renown. When they all saw that they would not be rescued they surrendered to

---

593 Paris suggests a textual correction to l.9266 which changes this to 'it [the turret] fell against the main tower'. It is not unusual in the paratactic style of medieval writers for the causal link to be left implicit.

594 These three are not recorded elsewhere.

595 Stephen of Longchamp was the brother of William of Longchamp, Richard's chancellor. He was a steward in the king's household. He crossed the Channel with the king in December 1189, and remained with him while he reached agreement with Philip II at Dreux in March 1190, and during the king's preparations for the crusade in the spring and summer of that year, see above, pp.33–7. He is one of those named as guarantors of the peace negotiated on Richard's behalf at Mantes on 9 July 1193. He was still alive in 1213: Landon, pp.8, 10, 11, 12, 14, 18–23, 25–7, 30, 33, 63, 65, 79, 107; Loyd, p.46. On his family connections, see Powicke, *Loss of Normandy*, pp.334–5.

596 Raymond (d.1197) was the son of Bohemond III, Prince of Antioch, and the godson of Raymond III, Count of Tripoli. Raymond III, who died in 1187, had no direct heirs and ceded his county to Raymond. On him, see H.E. Mayer, 'Raimund IV von Tripolis', in *Varia Antiochena: Studien zum Kreuzfahrerfürstentum Antiochia im 12. und frühen 13. Jahrhundert MGH, Studien und Texte* 6 (Hanover, 1993), pp.184–202.

597 l.9317 has *el desus e el desuz*, 'above and below', which makes no sense and seems to be an automatic and rather nonsensical use of formulae.

the warrior King Richard unconditionally, as prisoners and slaves, taken, captured, defeated and downcast, and a good forty Christians who were held in bonds had their lives saved, rescued and protected. The king had the Turks guarded in the tower and watched over throughout that Friday night. In the morning, the Saturday, on the Eve of Pentecost,[598] that great festival of great cost, he had them all brought out of the castle and straight away, without waiting he dealt with them so that he had their hands tied so tightly behind their backs that they howled loudly. Thus was Darum taken, giving great honour to those who took it, for it would have weighed on them and greatly distressed them, had they not taken it before the arrival of the French.

Then came the French, with Count Henry, spurring on, thinking to arrive in time,[599] but coming too late. The king and his people went out to meet his nephew the count. What more can I tell you than that they had great joy with one another, and the king, in the sight of many, gave Darum to the count, endowing him with his conquest. And there we stayed for the day of Pentecost and on the Monday we went towards Ascalon, passing through Gaza, straight to Furbia,[600] where the king and his entourage rested for the night; the rest of the men rode on until they came back to Ascalon where the French held a great celebration.

Dilemma for King Richard

[9370–407][601]   A little later there came to the king of England at Furbia, a spy, who came from around the Castle of the Figs where he spied on the Saracens. He said that there were at the Castle of the Figs a thousand or more, that he knew they were staying with Caïsac preparing the castle for defence against the Christians. The noble king mounted without delay and the whole army with him, and they lay that night I believe, by the reed-beds at Estornel.[602] The next day[603] it dawned fine and they moved on at sunrise and journeyed until they came before the Castle of the Figs which the Turks were to hold against them, but they made no defence. They found only two Turks there, whom they took with them. The rest of the Saracens had broken and destroyed the gates with Greek fire and abandoned the castle and fled incontinently when they knew that the army was coming for they recalled Darum, having heard the news that it was taken and the people lost. Because of this they abandoned the castle. Our people rode up till they saw that the castle was unguarded. Then they climbed the heights to see if they could find any Turk to fight. Finding none, they turned back and returned all the way to the reed-beds at Estornel.

---

[598] 23 May 1192. Darum had surrendered the day before, Landon, p.63.
[599] Cf. *Itinerarium*, 5.40.
[600] Furbia, or La Forbie (Harbiyah), was between Ascalon and Gaza.
[601] Cf. *Itinerarium*, 5.41.
[602] This seems to be near Tell al-Hasi, about 12½ miles (20 kilometres) south-east of Ascalon. Ambroise's description seems to confirm Pringle's belief that there was no crusader building there, *Secular Buildings*, no.R5, p.116.
[603] 27 May 1192, Landon, p.64.

[9408–35][604]   The army was encamped at the reed-beds, as I have heard, when they returned from the Castle of the Figs. He who tells the story says that there came to the king a messenger, a man from his own land, a cleric called John of Alençon.[605] He said to the king that disputes and quarrelling and war had sprung up throughout his land because of his barons and his brother who, because of the queen his mother, wanted only to do his own will and that the whole business had gone so far and seemed so bad because of the messengers that the king of France sent to England to his brother, turning him from the right path and wishing to make an ally of him, so much so that he dared to testify that if he did not soon return the land he held would soon be taken from those to whom he had entrusted it.[606] Indeed this is how it was when he returned. There is yet no evil [in the land] that has not come from this, as can be seen from Normandy, which was impoverished, wasted and beggared by this.

[9436–483]   When the king heard the news, which was neither good nor welcome, then was he melancholy, downcast and saddened and said to himself, "If you do not return now then indeed you will have lost your land." In this was his thinking confused, so he said resolutely that he would indeed go. When the good people heard it I can tell you they were not at all happy. Some knew this news in the army, others did not. One would say "He will go" and another would say "He will not." His enemies wanted him to go very much, but his friends did not, for his honour would have been decreased had he left the land before he ought to and before he had done more good.

So there where they were, all the barons gathered, French, Norman and English, men of Poitou, of Maine and of Anjou.[607] They held a council about what they would do and said that whatever King Richard did, wherever he went and whatever he said, they would go all together to Jerusalem. Then did someone – I know not who – slip away to the men of the army and tell them that the great men and the counts at their meeting had said that they would besiege Jerusalem. So there came among the army great joy among the men of great and of lesser estate, such hope and such joy, such splendour, lifting of gloom, such feelings of nobility, that in the whole army there was not a Christian soul, of high or low estate, young or old, who was not wildly joyful, except for the king himself, who was not at all happy but lay down, very upset about the news that he had heard. However, throughout the army the joy was such that they danced on, only going to bed after midnight.

[9484–527][608]   It was in June,[609] when the rising sun destroys the dew, when everything is full of the joys of life; then did the army move from the reed-beds

---

604 Cf. *Itinerarium*, 5.42.

605 John of Alençon, Archdeacon of Lisieux, was Vice Chancellor of England during Richard's preparation for the crusade in the winter of 1189 and the spring of 1190, during which time he sealed a number of royal charters. He was with the two kings at Vézelay on 3 July and remained with Richard until his departure from Lyons on 13 July, Landon, pp.5, 17, 18, 23–8, 30–7, 64, 93, 125, 174.

606 See above, pp.146–7, 155.

607 Cf. *Itinerarium*, 5.43.

608 Cf. *Itinerarium*, 5.44. Again the *Itinerarium* lacks the lyricism.

609 1 June 1192, Landon, p.64.

across the plains and down towards Ibelin of the Hospital, near Hebron,[610] which is close to the valley where St Anne was born, mother of the Holy Virgin mother and servant of God. There I saw the army full of joy because of the task they had pledged to undertake, to go to Jerusalem and besiege the city, but many people, rich and poor, desired this greatly, who would never enter there. Listen to what happened there – a strange penance and fierce persecution came among the army, a little fly, so small and as slight as a spark, which we called 'sparkles'. The army got such a reception from them as they crossed the land (St Celerin help me!)[611] they bit the pilgrims, their hands, neck, throat, forehead and face, so that there was no space between the bumps caused by the midge bites, so that everyone, old or young man, seemed like a leper; they had to make masks to cover their necks and faces. They suffered the pain there but always took comfort from the task ahead and the hope they had trusted. However, the king was melancholy and sad, because of the news that you have heard. He continually pondered it in his tent and gave himself up to this pondering.

[9528–655][612]   One day, when the king was sitting in his tent, silent and melancholy, he saw passing in front of the entrance a chaplain of his own country, William of Poitiers,[613] who would willingly have spoken to the king if he had dared address him. But he did not dare utter one word, for it was neither the time nor the place. The chaplain was shedding warm tears and was very distressed, but he did not dare say to the king what the men in the army said of him and how they criticised him because, on account of the news from England, he wanted to leave the Holy Land, poor, wasted and without a guide, where before he had himself guided it. The king called the priest and said to him, "Tell me the truth, by the faith you owe me, where does the trouble come from which has caused you to cry as I have seen? Tell me without delay." The priest, with little delay, still crying and in a low voice replied, "My lord I will not tell you until you assure me that you will not hold it against me." The king assured him, giving his word and swearing that he would not wish him ill, at any time or place, because of what he might say.

He said to him, "My lord, you are criticised and throughout the army the rumour of your return [to England] is spreading. May the day never come when you carry out such a plan. May you never suffer reproach, near or far, here or elsewhere!

---

610 Bait Jibrin or Bethgibelin, is about 8 miles (13 kilometres) to the north-west of Hebron, on the road to Ascalon. It was granted to the Hospitallers in 1136 (and was possibly the Order's first castle), having been built about two years before, Pringle, *Secular Buildings*, no.32, p.27 (map 8).

611 Paris, pp.xii–xiii, could find no other reference to this saint in medieval French literature. While accepting that it is intended as a rhyme for *pelerins*, he nevertheless argues that Ambroise still needed to know the name in the first place. Thus Paris believed that he was most likely to be identified with a seventh-century monk called *Cenericus*, to whom several churches in Normandy and Maine were dedicated.

612 Cf. *Itinerarium*, 5.45.

613 William of Poitiers has not been identified. It is possible that Ambroise invented the name in order to provide a vehicle for his own encounter with the king, or simply as a means of conveying his own thoughts on the situation.

"King, remember the great honour God has accorded you in many places, which will always be spoken of, for never has a king of your time suffered so little loss.

"King, remember what was said of you when I saw you as count of Poitiers, that there was no neighbour, however bold, however great, however renowned, that you would not defeat if he were to come in battle against you.

"Remember the great quarrels and bands of men of Brabant whom you defeated so often with few men and resources.[614]

"Remember the great defeat [you inflicted] and the adventure of Hautefort[615] which you set free when the count of St Gilles[616] had besieged it; you routed him and unceremoniously threw him out.

"Remember your kingdom, which you took over in peace and freely, as no-one had, without bearing shield and helmet.

"Remember your great undertakings, the people you have taken, Messina which you took, the deeds of valour that you committed when you defeated the Grifon, who thought to take you in battle, but God delivered you and gave them up to great shame.

"Remember your valour at the taking of Cyprus, when God showed great generosity to you, taking it in two weeks, when no-one had wanted to attempt this – apart from God the deed would have been impossible – and you took the emperor prisoner and put him in prison. King, take care you are not deceived.

"Remember the great noble ship, which was unable to enter Acre when God caused it to come your way; you took it with your galleys, with all eight hundred armed men, when the snakes were drowned.

"Remember how many times God had comforted you and comforts you still.

"Remember Acre and the siege in which you finally took [the town] where God caused you to expend your resources until the city surrendered. Good king,

---

614   As has often been pointed out, medieval rulers were usually reluctant to risk battle although, if successful, the rewards could be considerable. The defeat of the Brabançon mercenaries by Richard in May 1176 was in fact the only battle he fought before the Third Crusade, and thus it was considered especially memorable by Ambroise. This was part of a campaign by Richard to subdue his father's enemies in northern Aquitaine in the spring of 1176. The Brabançons had been hired by Vulgrin, son of William Taillefer, Count of Angoulême, Roger of Howden, *Gesta*, vol.1, pp.120–1. See Norgate, *Richard the Lion Heart*, pp.18–21, and J. Gillingham, 'Richard I and the Science of War in the Middle Ages', in *War and Government in the Middle Ages: Essays in Honour of J.O. Prestwich* (Woodbridge, 1984), pp.81, 83.

615   The castle of Hautefort, held jointly, if not harmoniously, by the brothers Constantine and Bertrand of Born, lay in the highly volatile borderlands of Limousin and Périgord. In the week 30 June to 6 July 1183, Richard had besieged and taken the castle, forcing Bertrand's submission. This was the final act in Richard's suppression of a widespread revolt among the baronage of the region, a revolt which Bertrand claimed to have initiated in 1183 and which, at one point, looked as if it would encompass Raymond of Toulouse and Hugh of Burgundy as well. The sudden death of Richard's elder brother, the young king, Henry, on 11 June 1183, however, deprived the opposition of a focus, and enabled Richard to re-establish his dominance. Moreover, Richard now became Henry II's direct heir. The fall of Hautefort, therefore, while a minor capture in the course of Richard's many wars, was a memorable event in the context of his overall career. See Norgate, *Richard the Lion Heart*, pp.40–56, and Gillingham, *Richard I*, pp.66–76.

616   Raymond V, Count of Toulouse, 1148–94.

did you not understand why you were spared the illness during the siege, the arnaldia that killed the other princes whom no doctor could help? King, remember and take good care of the land of which God has made you guardian, for he entrusted everything to you when the other king left.

"Remember the Christians whom you released from bondage at Darum, whom the Turks were leading away in captivity, when [God] caused you to come so quickly.

"King, you should well remember all God's goodness to you which has brought you to such renown that you fear no king nor baron.

"King remember Darum, which you took in four days – it took you no longer.

"Remember when you were in a great crowd of the infidel race, when you had through sin[617] fallen asleep, remember, gifted king, how God speedily delivered you. Now are we all given to death. Now everyone, great and small, everyone who wished to honour you, says that you are father and brother of Christianity and if you leave her without help now, then is she dead and betrayed."

[9656–695]   Now had the cleric[618] had his say, given the king his lesson and preached to him in this way.[619] The king uttered not one word in reply, nor did one word issue from the mouths of those who were sitting in the tent; but the king turned his thoughts to this sermon and all became clear in his thinking. The next day, at the hour of nones, came the army before the barons at Ascalon,[620] for everyone thought for sure, both barons and the army, that the king would prepare his army and would then return, but he had a change of heart, for he had received a message, first from God and [then] through the priest, showing him his true state. What else should I tell you, for he said to his nephew the count, to the barons, to the duke of Burgundy, that whatever the need of other affairs, whatever the messenger, whatever the message, whatever worldly quarrel, he would not go or quit the land before Easter. Then he called for his crier, Philip, his announcer, and had it announced throughout Ascalon, in the name of Him who gives all good things, that the king himself said with certainty that he would remain in the land until Easter without turning back and that everyone should be prepared, with all that they held from God, to go to Jerusalem, to lay siege there.[621]

[9696–808][622]   When the announcement was heard then were the people filled with joy, as is the bird at the [break of] day. Then they made ready without delay [. . .][623] Each one, for his part addressed God in His heaven and said, "May God be my help. God, we give You thanks and worship and adore You. Now we will see Your city. The Turks have lived there for too long. Bless our purpose, our stay here and the waiting that each of us has made and the suffering he has endured here." There you might have seen a people anxious and desirous of

---

617 l.9646, *pechié* can also mean 'misfortune'.
618 Manuscript 'king'.
619 Cf. *Itinerarium*, 5.46.
620 l.9667, obscure line. Paris in his translation corrects to 'before the gates of Ascalon', assuming the *barons* should be *bailles*, a word which is, however, not used anywhere else in the text.
621 4 June 1192, *Itinerarium*, 5.46, p.365. Easter 1193 fell on 28 March.
622 Cf. *Itinerarium*, 5.47.
623 After l.9699 there is a lacuna assumed to be of one line.

getting ready. The least of the people were so filled with joy that each one carried on his shoulder his provisions, saying in truth that they were carrying enough food for a month, they were so desirous of completing the task. What else should I tell you but that he who serves God does not count the cost.

It was in the octave of Pentecost, I believe, on the Saturday,[624] that the army was once again assembled, as I have said, and led out of Ascalon.[625] This was an easy thing to do for everyone wanted to do this and was pleased when he did. In the morning did the army move. I do not believe that ever was there seen a more valiant or better equipped army. That day they did not travel far, because of the heat. There you would have seen men of worth showing acts of honour, of humility, of courtesy, and charity, for those who had horses, or such beasts as would do, men of high status and young knights, placed on them the poor pilgrims and went after them on foot. There you would have seen fluttering on the wind, many fine banners and very fine pennoncels. There you would have seen so many mothers' sons, so many lineages, nephews and brothers, so many good hauberks and fine pourpoints, so many well-armed men, so many lances and spears, such as were never seen in the time of our ancestors, so many bright, expensive swords, so many fine men-at-arms, of cheerful countenance. There you would have seen so many men on the move, handsome horses and greys, mules and fine asses, knights, bold and confident who, I believe, could each have defeated forty such Turks. They rode on and journeyed until they passed a river of sweet water and came before Blanchegarde for the army to encamp that first night, under God's protection. One Sunday there died within two acres a knight and a valiant and agile man-at-arms, from two snake bites. May God see and hear their souls, for they died on His way.

We stayed there for two days, then on the third day we turned and the army, in serried ranks, filling the roads with iron-clad men, without any obstacles or disturbance, travelled directly to Toron des Chevaliers. There we lay for one night and the next day we did not move until we had eaten; then the king broke camp, with his own men and went ahead in person and had his tent pitched uphill and to the right a short distance from Chastel Arnould. The next day there came there the French and the others and they went towards Bettenuble.[626] The weather was fine, not cloudy. There the army stopped and stayed back, at the place where they had left in the winter, to await Henry the count. I shall tell you about this, for the king had sent him to Acre to those who had strayed from the way, who did not wish to join the army. Because of this we had to wait there for one month or more, just at the foot of the mountain, there where the palmers used to pass at will on their return from the Holy City, from which we had been disinherited. During that time when we were staying in the valley where we were, several things happened, disturbances and defeats that we saw but we were obliged to restrain ourselves.

---

624 7 June, Landon, p.64. Ambroise means the Octave of Holy Trinity.
625 Cf. *Itinerarium*, 5.48. The octave is the eighth day after any feast, counting the feast day. The Saturday after Whitsun in 1192 was 30 May. HL, p.364, n.1, note that Ambroise is giving the wrong date. According to the *Itinerarium*, 5.48, it was the Sunday after Trinity, 7 June 1192.
626 They reached Bettenuble (Bait Nuba) on 11 June, Landon, p.64.

[9809–919]   One day there came a spy, one sent out to spy and pry, who came from Mountjoy[627] to the king – I saw him coming back with joy – and he said, knowing this for the truth, that there were Saracens in the mountain guarding and keeping watch over the route, because of the army. The noble king mounted, before day, and taking with him the man who had told him, sought out the Turks, to their harm, as far as the spring at Emmaus.[628] At dawn he surprised them and succeeded in killing twenty and took Saladin's crier, his announcer, sparing him alone, and winning three camels and fine Turcomans. He also acquired there two fine mules, loaded with rich, exotic[629] robes, spices and aloes. These were all in bags. He pursued the Saracens into the mountains catching one up in a valley, knocking him from his horse, dead. When he had killed the villain he could see Jerusalem clearly. In Jerusalem,[630] so I have been told, they were so afraid that if the king had had the army with him, when it was seen, Jerusalem would have been set free and taken over by Christians, for all the Saracens came out of the city, fleeing, because they thought the army was coming, so there was no-one to hold the city, no-one daring to remain, whatever threats or constraint were made. Indeed Saladin had ordered his best horse to be got ready, not daring to stay, when he learnt the truth from a spy that the great army was not coming, for it did not at that time please God that the army should go so far.

On that very day, so it is remembered, when the king rode out creating disorder among that race, two hundred Turks came down from the mountain to the plain, to the tents of the French and attacked the army before it stirred, having already, to our shame, killed, close to the army, two men-at-arms who were out foraging.[631] On hearing their cries the French, the Templars and the Hospitallers rushed to the dying men-at-arms. The Turks took a stand against them at the foot of the mountain, not risking to venture onto the plain. There they rallied so well that they killed a knight, for which the French were much criticised. Valour is of more worth than gold or balm. A knight of the Hospital there did a deed of great valour and showed great skill, had he not gone beyond the bounds of his order, but valour carried him on. His name was Robert of Bruges.[632] He was already beyond the gonfanon[633] as he galloped out upon hearing the cries and getting further from his brothers [against the Master's rule][634] that they should not distance themselves from the army. He was so desirous of spurring on that he inevitably distanced himself from the others, spurring on the wonderful, strong horse which he was riding straight for a Turk

---

627   So-called because from here the pilgrims could see Jerusalem. It was also known as Shiloh and honoured as the burial place of Samuel.

628   12 June, Landon, p.65.

629   1.9830, *essaiees*. *T-L* gives *erprobt*, 'tested', but this makes little sense.

630   Cf. *Itinerarium*, 5.50.

631   Cf. *Itinerarium*, 5.51.

632   Robert of Bruges is not otherwise identified.

633   *A New Dictionary of Heraldry*, p.170, defines *gonfanon* as 'a personal flag, usually with tails'. See also Gayre, *Heraldic Standards*, pp.103–7. The text here suggests a larger, rallying flag.

634   After 1.9888 there is a lacuna of at least one line. Paris notes that 'la lacune contenait visiblement l'indication de la défense qui avait été faite aux Hospitaliers par le Maître de combattre isolément'.

he had spotted, elegant and well-turned out. He came at him at such speed that he pierced his yellow casignan[635] with his strong lance so that it came beyond the body an ell's length.[636] So did it happen to him. The Turk fell to the ground but his body was not left there. Then there came galloping up the Master of the Hospitallers, Garnier, that courtly knight, who said to the brother, "Dismount from your horse and learn how you should obey the rule." So the brother had to go on foot to their tent and wait there while great men pleaded with the Master, on their knees, asking that he should grant them a boon and pardon the brother the infringement of the rule because of the act of valour he had carried out, until he had mercy on him. "But," he said, "let him take care not to get carried away [again]."[637]

[9920–47][638]   One Tuesday,[639] I believe, our caravan came among the army all laden with provisions and equipment. That day it was to be conducted, or so we heard, by my lord Ferri of Vienne.[640] He was to protect the caravan for Count Henry, who was to have been in the rear-guard but had been sent to Acre. My lord Ferri had beseeched Baldwin of Carew and Clarembaud of Montchablon[641] to guard it for him that day, that the men would not behave foolishly, but foolishly they did behave and there were those who would pay for this. There was there Manessier of Lille,[642] who had a dappled grey horse, and Richard and

---

635   1.9898, *caïsan*, a form of *casignan*. Paris describes *casignan* as a 'cotte de mailles rembourée de coton'. There is a note on this term by A. Thomas, 'Ancien français *Casignan, -ingen, Gasigan, -ingan*', *Romania* 35 (1906), 598–601. Blair, *European Armour*, p.33, points out that it is difficult to be certain how the *pourpoint*, the *aketon* and the *gambeson* (possibly the same as the *casignan*) differ from each other, but that 'gambesons . . . are often described in the early inventories as being made of silk or some other rich material, decorated with embroidery and coats-of-arms, a fact suggesting that, sometimes at least, they were designed to be worn as independent defences or as surcoats'. Nicolle, *Arms and Armour*, p.591, glosses it as a 'fabric covered and padded mail hauberk'.

636   An ell was a varying measure of length, originally an arm's length.

637   The Templar Rule shows that the battle order of the military orders was strictly controlled by the Marshal and that no individual initiative of this kind was allowed, except to rescue any Christian who had unwisely strayed from the main body of the army. See Barber, *New Knighthood*, p.193, and M. Bennett, '*La Règle du Temple* as a Military Manual, or How to Deliver a Cavalry Charge', in *Studies in Medieval History presented to R. Allen Brown*, ed. C. Harper-Bill, C. Holdsworth and J.L. Nelson (Woodbridge, 1989), pp.17–18.

638   Cf. *Itinerarium*, 5.52. Paris posits a lacuna of several lines before 1.9921.

639   16 or 17 June, Landon, p.65. The *Itinerarium*, 5.52, p.373, gives 17 June, which was the Wednesday.

640   Ferri of Vienne was probably the third son of Matthew I, Duke of Lorraine (d.1207). See M. Parisse, *Noblesse et chevalerie en Lorraine médiévale: les familles nobles du XIe au XIIIe siècle* (Nancy, 1982), pp.400–1, for the geneaology. He witnessed several acts of Henry II and the Countess Marie in 1186–7, although he does not seem to have held a fief from the count. See H. d'Arbois de Jubainville, *Histoire des ducs et comtes de Champagne*, vol.4 (Paris, 1860), p.48.

641   Clarembaud was probably related to the castellans of Montchâlons (Aisne), 7 miles (about 11 kilometres) south-east of Laon. He is listed in the feudal register of Count Henry I in c.1178 as a knight in the castellany of Châtillon-sur-Marne/Fismes, *Documents relatifs au comté de Champagne et Brie (1172–1361)*, ed. A. Longnon, vol.1 (Paris, 1901), no.806, p.29.

642   Manessier was an important participant in the Fourth Crusade, for which he took the Cross in 1199. His involvement with this crusade continued until 1205. His name derives from

Thierry of Orques[643] – they were there in place of Ferri – [also] Philip and the companions of lord Baldwin of Carew. Otto[644] and a number of esquires were with them in this skirmish. They were their family and friends, and that day showed it in time of need.

[9948–10061]   The main company, fearing no-one, went on, as men who are unburdened, while the rearguard bore the burden. The company moved swiftly, while the others, as valiant and confident men, followed in fine order. Then from an ambush there burst out mounted Turks, spurring on outdoing each other in eagerness up to the vanguard then straight down upon the rearguard, right into the company. Those on swift horses went right into our company with such force that they penetrated it, so that Baldwin of Carew was unhorsed there; but he had the heart of a baron; he put his hand to his sword, which was much feared that day, for the Turks often felt it. During the rescue Richard of Orques and then Thierry were struck down. Baldwin fought until his men got him back on a horse that they had taken. There you would have seen a fierce fight, many fine blows and manoeuvres, many swords flaming, many intrepid attacks, many hard and fine combats, many riderless horses. There you would have seen many Turks in the attack and men fighting and defending well. When the Turks struck one down, the others would strike back, in the middle of the press, and re-mount him, helping each other as valiant men. However, it was an unequal struggle, for those of our party were swamped among them and it cannot be denied that many of the nobles fell and much harm came to them, for the bolts flew from the Turks, killing their horses. Then fell such a blow that Baldwin went down again; he had one of his own men dismount, [a man] who had defended himself well. Baldwin mounted his horse and he himself related that a little later he saw the man who had lent him the horse being decapitated. There were they taken. Baldwin's companion, Philip,[645] who acquired great praise from all those who were there, was taken. With Philip they led away a valiant man-at-arms, whom they took by force, and they killed Richard's brother.[646] There you would have seen a hard battle. Baldwin and his companions were caught in the mêlée while Clarembaud of Montchablon had left them and gone off, fleeing at speed as soon as he saw the Turks coming. There you would have seen Baldwin standing firm, struck again and beaten by so many maces that he nearly died. The blood was issuing from his nose and his mouth and his sword was blunted, notched and broken. Then he cried out loud to the valiant Manessier of Lille, who always defeated Turks, "Manessier, will you then abandon me?" My lord Manessier did not give up but came to his rescue. There you would have seen so many Turks

L'Isle-Adam (Seine-et-Oise), where his father, Anseau, had been lord. He is last mentioned in the period 1210–14. See L. Longnon, *Les Compagnons de Villehardouin: Recherches sur les croisés de la quatrième croisade* (Geneva, 1978), pp.42–5.

643   Richard and Thierry were two of four brothers from Orcq in the region of Tournai; the other two were Ivon and John. All died on the crusade, van Werweke, 87.

644   Otto is impossible to identify. Paris, p.556, suggests Otto of Trazegnies, see above, p.130, an idea rejected by HL, p.372, on the grounds that he was not an esquire. However, the sentence need not be read in that way.

645   Philip, companion of Baldwin, has not been identified.

646   Presumably meaning Thierry of Orques.

run up that they unhorsed Manessier, beating him, ill-treating and injuring him so badly that they cut into his leg, slicing the bone to the marrow. He and Baldwin were lost in the crowd when God sent to them the noble earl of Leicester, who had not known their situation. The earl, as he came spurring on, alert, struck a Turk so hard that he knocked him out of the saddle, sending him over the neck of the beast, and Ançon, companion of Stephen of Longchamp,[647] chopped off his head so that it fell into the field. My lord Stephen himself did very well both at first and later and our people increased in numbers when the news was known so that when the Turks saw them increase they fled towards the mountain, except for those who were caught. Our injured, who lay there, were gently put onto horses and carried back to the army. This is how it happened and it well deserves to be written down.

[10062–109][648]   On the third day before the Feast of St John,[649] there came some news to the army where they were. It brought great encouragement to the army for it was brought by a holy abbot who encouraged all the people. The holy abbot was from St Elias[650] and he lived on bread and rape. He had a long beard, allowed to grow naturally and he seemed a holy creature. He said to the king that he knew of a place that he had long protected where a cross was hidden that the Lord God had put in his care. It contained a piece of the True Cross, of which there are many pieces. The good Christian, who was not an aged man, had by himself concealed and hidden it, until the land should be conquered. It had cost him dearly, for Saladin had asked for it a number of times from the abbot but the abbot had deceived him, so he had been restrained and put into tight bonds, but whatever harm they did him they could not force him to say where it was nor to give it up, but he said that he had lost it when Jerusalem was conquered. When the king had inquired into the matter he had the holy abbot of whom I am speaking mounted, with the barons and a large number of young men. They set off in tight formation. They rode and travelled following the dawn[651] the whole way until they reached the place of which I have spoken, where the Cross was hidden. That day the Cross was glorified for so many people came to kiss it that they could not be calmed. They carried it straight back to the army that drew great encouragement from it. Many tears were shed in its adoration.

---

647 Ançon, companion of Stephen of Longchamp, has not been identified, but could be the same person as Ançon of Faï, see below, p.178.

648 Cf. *Itinerarium*, 5.54; 5.53 contains an incident not recounted in Ambroise.

649 21 June. HL, p.376, interpret this to mean Monday 22 June on the basis that Ambroise is counting the Feast of St John itself in the way contemporaries calculated dates based on kalends, nones and ides. However, Ambroise also says that Richard set out for Galatia (Qaratiya) on the Sunday evening, having heard that there was a rich Muslim caravan travelling from Cairo to Damascus, see below, p.170. The early hours of 21 June is then the only feasible time for his pursuit of the True Cross, giving him time to return by the evening to hear the news about the caravan. Galatia was about 15 miles (25 kilometres) east of Gaza on the road to Blanchegarde.

650 According to the Greek pilgrim, John Phocas, who visited the holy places in 1185, this monastery, situated about 3 miles (5 kilometres) south of Jerusalem on the road to Bethlehem, had been ruined by an earthquake, but was being rebuilt by its Syrian abbot: Wilkinson, p.332.

651 1.10100, *Apres l'aube*. Paris makes an unnecessary correction to *après l'abés*, which is followed by Stone and HL.

[10110–200]652   As the Cross was exalted, then did the army rejoice, and they had kept it a long time. Then did the poor people of the army begin to say, "Good and gentle Lord God, what are we doing? What will be done? Are we going to Jerusalem?" In brief they bemoaned [the situation] until the king and the great men heard of it and spoke of it, deliberating over several plans, over the plan to adopt and whether they should go to Jerusalem. The French appealed to the king several times, saying to him, some of them, that they would advise besieging Jerusalem. The king replied, "That cannot be. You will never see me lead a people [in an undertaking] for which I can be criticised and I do not care if I am disliked for it. Know for certain that wherever our army may go Saladin knows what we are about and what our strength is. We are a long way from the sea and if he and his Saracens were to come down on the plains of Ramla and intercept our provisions, so that we could not receive them, this would not be wise for the sake of those who would be besieging. Rather I believe it would cost them dear. Moreover, I have been told that the city's defences are so great at every point that it would need so many people [. . .]653 that we would not be able to save the army if it were attacked by the Turks, but it would be damaged and destroyed. And if I were to lead the army and besiege Jerusalem and such a thing were to happen to their loss, then I would be forever blamed, shamed and less loved. I know in truth and without doubt that there are those here and in France who have wanted and who want and greatly desire that I should do such a thing, which would everywhere be told to my shame. We, men of foreign lands, do not know their roads, nor the paths and the moors654 nor the dangerous passes and the narrow defiles by which we could conquer them. We must work through those who live in this land, who want to recover their fiefs, and through the advice of the Templars, with the agreement of the Hospitallers, and through those who used to live in this land and who knew it and still know it. I will pass it to them to resolve, after deliberation, if it would be good to undertake the siege, or to go to take Babylon or Beirut or Damascus, so we will not be in disagreement, for never was there such disagreement among men" [. . .]655 so that they made a decision.656 They took four or five Templars and as many Hospitallers and Syrian knights and as many barons of France, so that there were twenty of them in all, to resolve the disputes among them. They would put them on oath and put them on their loyalty in what they would decide. They looked into it and decided, saying that the greatest good of the land would be to conquer

---

652 Cf. *Itinerarium*, 6.1.

653 After l.10147 there is a lacuna, with a line left blank in the manuscript.

654 The word *larroiz* (l.10165), translated here as 'moors', is not attested elsewhere. Paris comments in his glossary 'mot sans doute altéré'. After l.1066 Paris assumes a lacuna of two lines which he fills with, 'Nous ne pouvons rien faire de sérieux sans cette connaissance', based on the *Itinerarium*, 6.1, pp.380–1; Nicholson, p.336, has 'we . . . know absolutely nothing about this region, its thoroughfares, or its passes. If we knew them we could advance more safely and carefully, and so we would be able to win our desired success.' This seems an unnecessary correction.

655 After l.10183 there appears to be a lacuna, possibly of four lines.

656 Cf. *Itinerarium*, 6.2.

Babylon. When the French heard it, it is true that they rebelled and said that they would go to the siege [of Jerusalem] and would not go anywhere else.

[10201–38]   When the king heard the disagreement, where God did not will there should be agreement, and that it was because of the French, then he said, in truth, that had the French trusted him they would have moved towards Babylon, "You can see my fleet lying at Acre, which I have made ready for them, to take their equipment, their armour and their baggage, their biscuits and their flour. The army would travel along the coast. Seven hundred knights and two thousand men-at-arms with them, paid for at my expense would have gone from here to there; and they would know in truth that no valiant man would go short of my money for any reason. Since they do not want to do this I am completely ready to go to the siege, by St Lambert of Liège,[657] but they should know that I would not lead them but be one of their company." Then he ordered without any delay that all his men should gather in the Hospitallers' tent and that there they should consider what support they could give to the siege when they went to Jerusalem. They came and sat there and made great promises; some made generous offers who had little in their coffers. But had they at that time laid siege it would have been a great folly since those who had made an oath in good faith advised against it.

[10239–284][658]   As they were making promises about what they could bring to the siege, there came Bernard the spy, a man born in Syria,[659] and with him two other barbarians, dressed as Saracens. They were coming back from Babylon, having no other task than that of spying on the Saracen army. I swear to you that I never saw anyone look so like Saracens nor speaking their language better with the people listening. All three of them had received a hundred marks of silver from King Richard before they left. They said to the king courteously, that he should mount at once, with his men and they would lead him to loaded caravans that were coming from Babylon, which they had spied upon. As soon as the king heard this he rejoiced in his heart and sent to the duke of Burgundy to join him in this business and to bring the French with him. He did so, first saying that they would want one third of the booty, which the king agreed to. Then they mounted and the king mounted. There were then counted five hundred well-armed knights and a thousand valiant and skilled men-at-arms whom the king maintained at his expense, and, at the front, the king himself. It was on a

---

657 St Landebert (later Lambert) was born between 633 and 638 into a noble family from Maastricht. He became bishop when his predecessor and mentor, St Theodard, was murdered, although political circumstances obliged him to retire to the monastery of Stavelot between 674 and 681. He was very active in converting pagans in the region. He himself was killed in c.705, perhaps as a result of a family feud, and the place where this occurred became a cult centre. His relics were kept there and miracles occurred. His successor, St Hubert, moved the see to this place which, in time, became the city of Liège. His saint's day is 17 September, *Butler's Lives of the Saints*, revised ed. H. Thurston and D. Attwater, vol.3 (New York, 1962), pp.579–80.

658 The manuscript has a blank here left for a large initial; no guide letter is visible. Cf. *Itinerarium*, 6.3.

659 Bernard the spy was presumably a local Christian, perhaps Armenian or Maronite.

Sunday evening.[660] They travelled by moonlight, all through the night, stopping but briefly, until they reached Galatia. There the bold men dismounted, all set for battle, and sent to Ascalon for provisions, remaining there until the esquires returned.

[10285–510]   As soon as our men, the king and those who were with him, moved on there was a spy who set off for Jerusalem, to tell Saladin that he had seen the king mount, to set out to take his caravans. Saladin, without delay, took five hundred chosen knights, among the best he had, and sent them straight to the caravans, armed with bows and javelins. When they joined up with those who were leading the caravans they numbered two thousand on horseback, apart from those who went on foot. There came to the king a spy, galloping straight to Galatia,[661] encouraging the king to come quickly, to keep the army quiet, for at the Round Cistern,[662] all around it, there was a caravan newly arrived, and that he who could take it would have great gain. The spy had been born in that land and the king did not trust him, but he sent at once a Bedouin and two men-at-arms, Turcopoles, who were valiant and skilled, to find out and spy out. He had the Turcopoles wrap their heads in cloth like the Bedouin and just like other Saracens, and it was by night that they travelled. They scaled the heights, climbing up and down, until they saw on a height I know not how many Saracens on the watch. The spy and the Bedouin approached them, step by step making his companions be silent that they would not be noticed, so deceiving the Turks. Those there asked our men whence and from what part they came. The Bedouin came out of cover and said that they came from Ascalon, where they had taken some booty. One of them replied in this way, "But you come to do us harm; you are with the king of England." The Bedouin said, "You lie." Then he wanted to move on and went towards the caravan, and the Turks followed them and came after them, with their bows and javelins, until they got fed up and let them go, thinking they were on their side. The Bedouin turned back when he knew that in truth the caravan had arrived; this was seen as a wise move. Then did he turn back to the king and said to him that for sure he could take the caravan. The king, in the name of St George, had the horses fed with barley, then they ate and then mounted, travelling all night until they came to the place where the caravan and the Turks lay. There he stopped. It was as fine as a summer's day. The king armed and they all armed and got into their divisions. The French formed the rear guard and the king was in the van. He had it announced throughout the army that those who did not wish to forget their honour would not think about the booty but only about defeating and breaking through the Turks and striking with their swords of steel.

While they were getting their divisions into order and rank there came another spy to the king, coming galloping in great haste, telling him that since daybreak the caravan had been prepared and that they had been seen. When the

---

660   21 June. See above, p.167.
661   Cf. *Itinerarium*, 6.4.
662   The Round Cistern was near Bir Khuwailifa, about 6 miles (10 kilometres) south-west of the Castle of the Figs (Khirbat al-Burj), see above, p.158. Pringle, *Secular Buildings*, no.52, p.34 (map 10).

king had learnt this he sent forward archers, Turcopoles and crossbowmen to harass the Turks and hold them back until he could get to the Turks. While they harassed the Turks and drew near to their divisions those of the army drew close. When the Turks saw them they drew back to the mountain slopes behind them; [the Turks were] all set out in battle order, but not fired up for the fight. The king divided his divisions into two groups. As they drew near the divisions [of the enemy] they attacked and shot at them, [the arrows] falling as numerous as the drops of dew. The caravan was stopped. The good king, in the van, paid the first instalment, striking with such force into their first division that I can tell you for sure that he and his other divisions struck them with such ferocity that any they encountered were struck down. No Turk escaped, unless he turned and fled, nor did they make a recovery, but as the greyhound hunts the hare in the countryside, so did our men in the mountains hunt their men, causing them so much harm that they fled, scattering, defeated and dispersed and the caravan was left behind. Our men, filled with enthusiasm, pursued them to the right and to the left. One who knew the situation said that the pursuit lasted so long into the desert that they dropped dead from thirst and those who were caught were struck down by the knights and killed by the [mounted] men-at-arms. There you would have seen saddles turned and men in a very bad way; there you would have seen the valiant king of England striking fierce blows. Do not think that I undertake to flatter him here for so many men saw his fine blows that they make me dwell on them. There you would have seen the king chasing the Turks, his sword of steel in his hand, that those whom he caught as he pursued them, no armour would protect from being split to the teeth, so that they fled him as sheep who see a wolf. While the front runners were chasing and pursuing the Saracens in the mountains in this way, some thirty Saracens turned down a path, in anger and hatred, coming upon Roger of Tosny; they killed his horse under him and very nearly took him. A companion, Juhel of Mayenne,[663] came then against the pagan race and was at once struck down and Roger, who had been fighting, came to his aid on foot. There you might have seen our men running up, striking to the right and to the left. There came the earl of Leicester and there came Gilbert Malmain[664] with two others, or at least one other. Alexander Arsie[665] came and fifteen or twenty knights; Stephen of Longchamp came, in the middle of the pagans, bringing such help to Roger that he once again got him mounted on his horse. There you might have seen such a defeat of that unnatural people.

---

663 Juhel of Mayenne, lord of Sainte Susanne, was an Angevin vassal of Henry II and Richard. He stood surety for Richard in the peace treaty made with Baldwin of Flanders at Les Andelys in June or July 1197: Loyd, pp.62–3; Landon, p.118. However, like most Angevin lords, he supported Arthur of Brittany in the succession dispute with Richard's brother, John, in 1199. In March 1203 he was among those who offered liege homage to Philip II, pending the release of Arthur, whom John had captured at Mirebeau on 1 August 1202. He remained a partisan of Philip II thereafter, Baldwin, *Government of Philip Augustus*, pp.192–3.

664 Gilbert Malmain had travelled to the East via Messina. He appears on a charter of Richard at Vaudreuil in June 1195. He was the fourth husband of Eleanor of Vitry, Countess of Salisbury, whom he married after 1196: Landon, pp.41, 60, 102; Powicke, *Loss of Normandy*, pp.354–5.

665 Alexander of Arsic, lord of Cogges (Oxfordshire) (d.1202): I.J. Saunders, *English Baronies: A Study of their Origin and Descent 1086–1327* (Oxford, 1960), p.36; Siedschlag, p.112.

There you might have seen great blows of the sword, feet and hands and heads lopped off, slashing of eyes and mouths, so many dead bodies, lying like so many logs, so that they hindered our men, causing them to stumble. They struck hard, the men of Poitou, the Normans, the English and the Angevins, and the good king, bold and valiant, did better than all the others. There you might have seen such a slaughter of Turks, such as was never seen in the days of our ancestors; they were killed and the [survivors so demoralised] that as it was well known and ascertained that a young lad of little renown could have killed seven or ten of them. There you might have seen the drivers of the caravan give themselves up to the men-at-arms and the knights and give to them, by the halter, the great laden camels, the mules and asses, which carried such great and precious goods and such riches, gold and silver, silk and samite, from the land of the lord of Damis,[666] brocaded silks, silks from Baghdad, Greek ciglaton and rich oriental cloth, casignans and quilted pourpoints and fine elegant clothes, fine pavilions and good tents, worked with great care, biscuit, wheat, barley, flour, electuaries and medicines, basins, skins and chess-boards, silver pots and candlesticks, pepper and cumin and sugar and wax, so much that I could not tell you it all. [Also] all sorts of spices, so many other precious things, such fine armour, strong, light and protective, such riches and such goods that they said there, truthfully, that never in time of war had there ever been such booty [taken] in that land.

[10511–64][667] When the curs were killed and the rich caravan taken,[668] they had a rich prize, but they had great trouble in gathering together the swift camels, who caused trouble to the whole army, for they fled with such speed when those on horseback chased them that God made nothing so swift, stag or doe, fallow dear or gazelle, which could have caught up with them if they had once got away. Those who gathered them together, counting them without help from the men-at-arms, said that there were three thousand eight hundred camels gained there and as many mules and asses and so many sturdy pack-donkeys that they could not count them. They were only an encumbrance. They said, moreover, that in that chase there were killed one thousand seven hundred mounted Turks, of high and low estate, in the mountains and in the valleys, not counting those on foot who were killed without ever getting away.

Then they moved on, by such stages as they had decided, until they came before Betaffa, four leagues from Jaffa.[669] There they divided up the booty. When they left there their next stage on their return took them to Ramla. There came the army from Acre, Count Henry with his men. They all came back with the army. There you might have seen the fullness of joy because of the marvel they saw, the animals which filled the camp. The king distributed the camels,

---

666 Stone, p.139, n.228, notes that 'it is possible that Ambroise here uses the form Damiz for Damas (Damascus) in order to furnish a rhyme for samiz (samite)'.

667 Cf. *Itinerarium*, 6.5.

668 The caravan was taken on 23 June 1192: Roger of Howden, *Chronica*, vol.3, p.182; Baha' al-Din, pp.206–8. The latter says, 'It was a disastrous incident, the like of which had not befallen Islam for a very long time', p.207.

669 Cf. *Itinerarium*, 6.6. Betaffa is about 14 miles (22 kilometres) east of Ascalon.

which were as fine as were ever seen, both among the knights protecting the army and those who had gone out. Similarly, he distributed the mules and asses among them generously. He had the donkeys given to the men-at-arms, both great and small. Then was the army so burdened with animals that they could scarcely keep them all together. However, they killed the young camels and eagerly ate the meat, for it was white and full of flavour when roasted with fat.

[10565–610]   When the animals had been given out and distributed among the army,[670] some people began to complain about the lack of barley [to feed the animals]. Then did those who were full of anger begin to moan again about the siege of Jerusalem, which they greatly desired, and they would not be appeased.[671] But those who had sworn [the oath] and considered that they would not go re-stated their reasons, that if they besieged the city they would find around it so little water that neither horse nor beast nor any man would be able to drink without great harm and trouble, whatever the Turks could do. For it was around St John's Day[672] when the heat dries up everything in the land, such is its nature, and indeed the Saracens had knocked down and destroyed all the cisterns around the city. Thus, where we had neither peace nor truce, no water could be found without difficulty for a good two leagues around, apart from a tiny stream, Siloam, which runs from the Mount of Olives into the Valley of Jehosaphat – this was known to be true.[673] So it was not advised by them to surround the city and lay siege to it in summer.

When this was known, revealed and spread about, that they would not go to Jerusalem but would turn back, then you might have seen such a sorrowful people that they cursed the delay which had passed and the tents they had erected, as Jerusalem would not be besieged and could not be conquered for they would not ask to live beyond the day when Jerusalem would be set free.

[10611–54][674]   My lords, you should not wonder at it that God had allowed the pilgrims to labour in vain, as we have said, for it is true that we often saw when we were encamped, in the evening, when they were [tired from][675] travel, that the French went apart from the other men and pitched camp by themselves, aside, so that the army was so split that some would not agree with others – [I say this in] in truth and without lies. So one would say "You are such and such" and the other reply "You are so and so." Moreover, Henry the duke of

---

670 Cf. *Itinerarium*, 6.7.

671 Whether it is those who are complaining, or those who had taken the oath, who would not be appeased, is unclear from the syntax and depends on how the sentence is split. I have translated according to sense.

672 24 June 1192, Landon, p.65.

673 The Mount of Olives overlooks Jerusalem on the eastern side. The Siloam channel, leading from the Gihon spring to the Pool of Siloam, was one of the principal sources of water for Jerusalem from biblical times. The channel goes through the Kidron valley which has been identified in Christian, Jewish and Muslim tradition as the 'valley of Jehosaphat', the name given in Joel 3:2 for the place of final judgement. Most twelfth-century pilgrims describe these sites, e.g. Theoderic, a German pilgrim, who visited the Holy Land in c.1170, Wilkinson, p.276.

674 Cf. *Itinerarium*, 6.8.

675 Something has been omitted in l.10616, presumably to the effect that they were tired.

Burgundy, made matters much worse when in arrogance and impertinence, he had a song made about the king, a base song, full of baseness, which spread throughout the army. What could the king do but reciprocate with a song about those who worked against him and mocked him through envy? Never will a good song be sung about such uncontrolled men, nor will God look upon their deeds as on those who went on a different pilgrimage,[676] when Antioch was besieged and taken by force by our men. The story is still told of those for whom God gave the victory, of Bohemond and Tancred, who were distinguished pilgrims, and of Godfrey of Bouillon and high princes of high renown and of the others who died in the service of God, so that He gave back to them according to their desires and plans. He raised their deeds to great heights and they and all their family are exalted and still honoured.[677]

[10655–690][678] The army remained as I have described for ten or twelve days after the taking of the caravan[679] – so I believe and as I can best tell the truth of it. When, whatever efforts they might put into it [they realised] all could come to nothing; they would not worship at the Holy Sepulchre which was four leagues away, their hearts were filled with sorrow and they turned back so disheartened and miserable that you never saw such a chosen people so depressed and dismayed. They set the rearguard and as soon as they left the Saracens came down from the mountain and pursued them until they killed one of our men-at-arms. However, those who were mounted on good horses repulsed them and chased them off. Then they rode and journeyed on until they reached between St George and Ramla. That very day, when we made that journey, it was exactly five years since the land had been lost through war.[680] The French were on the left and the king and his men on the right. They journeyed like this also on the following day. They came back to Casel Moien where they pitched camp and came to a halt. Some left the army and returned to Jaffa because of the suffering and privations they had endured in the army.

[10691–713][681] When Saladin knew for certain that our men could make no plans but to retreat then was he full of joy and cheerfulness. He quickly had letters written and took swift messengers to send to the Turks who owed him allegiance that the Christians were leaving and that they were in disagreement and had left without any agreement and that any who wished to have some of his wealth should come to Jerusalem under his pay. Then were there so many men gathered both within and without the city that they were numbered at some twenty thousand mounted, well-armed Turks, as well as those on foot, who could not easily be counted, all of whom knew our situation well and proved it to us [. . .][682] as soon as our men returned where they stayed.

---

676 There is, inappropriately, a marginal mark indicating a new paragraph at this point in the manuscript, l.10639.

677 The exploits of Bohemond, Tancred and Godfrey were celebrated in the *Chanson d'Antioche*.

678 Cf. *Itinerarium*, 6.9.

679 Somewhere between 30 June and 2 July 1192.

680 4 July 1192. For a discussion of the various versions given by the sources, see *Itinerarium*, trans. Nicholson, pp.344–5, n.20.

681 Cf. *Itinerarium*, 6.10.

682 After l.10711 there is a lacuna, probably of one line.

[10714–57][683]   Day after day, discouraged, men left and turned back to Jaffa, because of the privations of the life they led. When the king saw them turn back and realised that he could not succeed in leading the army on the right way – what more can I say? But that he sent to Saphadin, asking that he should speak to Saladin and find out if he could [still] have the truce which was offered in the plains of Ramla, as we have told you, until he [Richard] could come back again from his own land. He went to inquire from the sultan, but the sultan had known of our turning back from the first day and he did not wish to grant the truce unless Ascalon was destroyed.[684] Then did the news reach the king who was with the army but the king did not show any awareness of it nor did he wish to listen to it. Rather he commanded at once that the Templars and Hospitallers with three hundred other knights should mount and he commanded that they should destroy Darum and protect Ascalon, that it might not be lost through being unguarded. They went and destroyed Darum and then returned to the army, and the army, melancholy and wrapt in thought, moved back to Jaffa, and from Jaffa immediately moved [to Acre]. Many men remained behind at Jaffa, men of good health and ill, who later knew great fear. Then, one Sunday,[685] the army was once again at Acre, [having returned] by the same route as when it had come, disappointed and confused. This is what happens to those who are led by sin.

[10758–904][686]   As soon as Saladin and his brother Saphadin knew that we left Jaffa, as we have said, and that we had gone away in such discouragement as we have described, then was the army of proud men of pagandom summoned and assembled. At that time and season the sultan had more than twenty thousand mounted Turks, among them the emir of Byla and the son of the Assassin[687] and at least one hundred and six emirs as well as foot-soldiers from the mountain. They covered the whole plain. Then did the army descend from Jerusalem and encamp below on the plains of Ramla. There you might have seen many a fine horse.

On the Sunday, the very day when we returned to Acre, the army of enraged pagans was encamped[688] at Jaffa. On the Monday they attacked [while our men went out towards them].[689] They met outside [the town] in the gardens where they struggled against each other for the whole day. During that day they could

---

683   Cf. *Itinerarium*, 6.7.
684   The negotiations took place between 4 and 20 July 1192. Baha' al-Din, p.216, confirms that they foundered over Richard's refusal to dismantle Ascalon.
685   26 July 1192, Landon, p.67.
686   Cf. *Itinerarium*, 6.12.
687   If Mayer, *Das Itinerarium*, pp.255, 364, is correct, then this is the lord of al-Bira, who was the Ortoqid Turk, Shihab al-Din Mahmud. Al-Bira is on the Euphrates about 75 miles (120 kilometres) north-east of Aleppo, Lyons and Jackson, pp.171, 174, 275. According to the *Itinerarium*, 1.5, p.12, he was in Saladin's army at Hattin, as well as 'the emir of Mossetar', or Masyaf, who may have been Rashid al-Din or another Assassin leader, perhaps his son. Both Ambroise and the author of the *Itinerarium* appear to be trying to convey the size and comprehensiveness of the Muslim army by showing that it included even these diverse elements.
688   Cf. *Itinerarium*, 6.13.
689   After l.10782 there is a lacuna. Paris supplies 'les notres sortirent de la ville' on the basis of the *Itinerarium*.

not approach the castle so thoroughly were they harrassed. Similarly the next day, which was Tuesday, and on the third day. But on the Thursday the town was besieged all round and the people inside were in anguish. Saladin had four strong and light catapults erected, and two mangonels for hurling [missiles].

There you might have heard the Christians in the town, more than five thousand of them, both those who were well and those who were lying ill, lamenting, as all went about full of lamentation, saying, "Ah, king of England, why did you go to Acre? Christianity, how you are fallen!"

There you might have seen men being attacked with great force and violence, so many men killed or injured, defending themselves so boldly, rising and falling so quickly, that under the heavens there is no-one who seeing this would not have [great] pity. The catapults continually hurled their missiles and the mangonels did not cease. Those within had catapults but did not know how to help themselves with them. The Turks fired against the gate on the Jerusalem side until, to the great distress of our people, the upper arches gave way and the wall to the right fell; that Friday there fell two perches of the wall.

There you would have seen a hard battle when the Turks entered the town. There they fought hand-to-hand.[690] But the Turks, who were constantly increasing by those units which came out of the army, increased in number until they broke through them and pursued them down as far as the hill of Toron,[691] in front of the tower.

There you would have seen an ugly sight as they killed the invalids as they lay in the houses. There was there many a good martyr.

There you would have seen men leave and flee towards the sea. The cruel Saracen race took the houses and pillaged them, carrying off all the cereals and pouring out all the wines. Some attacked the Toron where the people of God were defending themselves valiantly. Others ran to the sea, to the boats and barges which were there, in which our men sought to flee to safety and protection. Many of the last of our men were killed there. Aubri of Reims,[692] who was supposed to guard the castle, was seen to behave as a low coward; he was already in a barge to flee across the wide sea when the valiant men cried out so much to him that they forced him to return and enter the Toron so that he said, "As it cannot be otherwise, let us all die here, for God's sake!" All around them, to the right and to the left, so many Turks were attacking at the foot of the Toron that they did not know which part to defend.

There you might have seen bolts flying, falling as thickly as hailstones. They were side-by-side, higgledy-piggledy. The battle lasted all day. Our men would not have survived the great assault or great charge, had God not caused the

---

690 *achamaillé* (l.10822). *T-L* gives *ins Handegemenge bringen*, 'come into hand-to-hand fighting', 'scuffle', citing only Ambroise. Paris glosses 'engagés dans une mêlée, aux mains'.

691 The Toron was the citadel of Jaffa. Citadels were typical of Byzantine fortification and could be defended even when the town walls were breached. They were usually built on one side of the city in order to retain outside access.

692 Aubri of Reims is listed as a knight of the count in the feudal register of Henry I of Champagne in c.1178 for the castellany of Sézanne. His son, Simon, did homage for the fief in c.1190, which might indicate that his father died during the crusade, *Documents relatifs au comté de Champagne et de Brie*, vol.1, no.1748, p.62.

newly-appointed patriarch[693] to remain there; he would not have hesitated to die to save those who were there, fighting to the death. He sent to Saladin, the generous and valiant Saracen, and Saphadin, beseeching them to grant a truce to be granted just until the next day. He would undertake himself that if, before the hour of nones, there had not been seen the men of Acre or of Ascalon, or the men of King Richard of England, which he had sent for, then he would give himself over as hostage with other men of noble family, to be put in irons and bound and that each Christian who was fighting in the Toron would pay to Saladin in ransom ten gold besants, and similarly the women would give five besants and three for each child. Just as he asked, Saladin ordered that it should be agreed and pledged. Then did the messenger return; then was the truth agreed and the matters arranged thus: they gave up to the Turks two hostages who went with the patriarch. One was Aubri and the other Theobald of Troyes[694] who was valiant and handsome. He was a man-at-arms belonging to Count Henry who had brought up his father. There may have been others whose names I do not know.

[10905–11004][695]   You have heard me tell and relate, and the tale should be told again because of the great good which came from it, how the army returned to Acre, all discouraged and dispirited and crushed with shame, all expecting to leave and heading for their ships. King Richard himself, we saw with our own eyes, had at that time taken leave of the Templars and the Hospitallers and had seen that his galleys were well prepared. The next day, according to the written account, he and his household were to leave for Beirut. He had already sent ahead seven galleys which had fought with those of the castle, who fled and had not waited to see if they could see more galleys [on the way]. In the evening at vespers, as the king was in his tent making his preparations, there came a barge, with all haste arriving at Acre. Those who came out of the barge came to the king without delay and told him that Jaffa was taken and the people besieged in the Toron and that if he did not rescue them they would all be killed and perish, as I have told you. The noble king in his goodness abandoned his plans and said, "I will certainly go!" and at once summoned the army. But the French did not want to respond; rather these jealous men, looking at him with hatred, replied that they would not take any steps in that direction and would no longer follow him in the army – nor did they, neither with him nor any other man – but they died – that is the sum of it. Nonetheless those who feared God, of any land, Templar and Hospitaller and many other good knights, mounted and got ready, rode and travelled by land straight to Caesarea, while the worthy king of England went by sea with his galleys. Then did they arm themselves so richly that none could be better armed. There was the earl of Leicester and Andrew of

---

693   This seems to have been Ralph II, Bishop of Bethlehem, Hamilton, *Latin Church*, p.131. He was executed after the siege of Jaffa, having only just been appointed Patriarch of Jerusalem in succession to Heraclius, who had died in the summer of 1190.

694   Theobald of Troyes appears therefore to have been a member of the household of the counts of Champagne. The reference is to Henry I (1152–81). According to the *Itinerarium*, 6.13, p.403, Aubri and Thibaut, together with the patriarch and three other hostages, were all later taken to Damascus in captivity.

695   Cf. *Itinerarium*, 6.14.

Chauvigny and Roger of Sassy; there was seen Jordan des Homez, who died later that year; there was Ralph of Mauléon, who bore a lion banner and Ançon of Faï,[696] who fought many a Saracen; there were the men of Préaux, who were companions of the king and many another renowned man, not named to me. They went in the service of God, with the men of Genoa and of Pisa who played an important part in time of need.

Listen to what happened. Those who were going by land to Jaffa and thought to go [straight] there had stopped at Caesarea and had scarcely arrived there when it was said to them that Saladin was having the route watched, so that they were besieged therein. This was [done by] the son of the Assassin who was between Arsuf and Caesarea. The others, the king and his galleys, were held up by an unfavourable wind so that for three days they could not stir from off Caïphas, where they lay. The king said, "Mercy, my God, why do you keep me here when I go in Your service?" But God in His grace sent them a north wind which brought the whole fleet to Jaffa, late on the Friday night. The truce was to end at the hour of nones on the Saturday;[697] the men [would have been] killed and ill-treated, given up to death and sorrow, had God not delivered them through the king in this way, as we will briefly tell.

[11005–207]   The noble king and his renowned men had lain in their galleys through the night till Saturday [. . .][698] He and his men armed themselves. Now hear about the protection agreement, how the town was protected, and of the treachery and agreement which the Turks had planned against those who had bought their protection with the promised besants. They were made to pay in the morning. In the end they did pay. They made their payment and even as they paid, the Saracens came and cut off their heads. They thought this was a job well done, but such a cur's faith should be accursed. They had killed seven and disposed of them in a ditch when those in the Toron realised. Those who were there have said that there you might have seen a piteous sight before the tower in the Toron, for, condemned to death, they were afraid. There you might have seen men weep and go down on their knees to worship, to make their confession and say their *mea culpa*[699] and those who were without forced their way within, into the great press of people, that they might die later, for all beings, when pursued by death, seek a short space [of time]. They awaited their martyrdom. We can say in truth that tears were shed there which pleased God for they came from the distress of death and the depth of their hearts which yearned for Him. So they awaited death with no other expectation but to die.

---

696   All of these men, except for Ançon of Faï, are listed among the main body of Anglo-Norman knights who arrived in Acre on 8 June 1191, Landon, p.50. Roger of Sassy (Calvados), north-east of Falaise, appears to have returned to the West in Queen Berengaria's party, for he was with her in Rome in April 1193, Landon, p.75.

697   1 August 1192, Landon, p.67.

698   After l.11007 there is a lacuna indicated by an incomplete rhyme. Paris proposes that the copyist conflated two lines through eye-skip and the passage should read, 'All that Friday night. On the morning of the Saturday . . .'

699   Prayer asking for forgiveness. See J.C. Payen, *Le motif du repentir dans la littérature française médiévale (des origines à 1230)* (Geneva, 1968), pp.112, 147, 210 n.31, 214–15, 381, 549. On collective penance and absolution, see p.49.

Then did the Turks notice the galleys in the harbour.[700] They came on foot and on horseback down to the shore until the strand was so full that it could scarcely contain them. They had round shields and long shields and shot at the barges and the king's galleys. There you might have seen a fierce struggle as those who were on horseback fought in the sea, firing and fighting so that our men could not disembark. The noble Richard, I believe, drew all his vessels together, to speak to his company. Then he said to his knights, "Good knights, what shall we do? Shall we go or shall we disembark, or how can we manage this?" Such was the situation that there were those who replied that in their view there was no point in trying to disembark or take the port. They all thought unanimously that those in the castle had been killed. Even while they were considering whether they should disembark the king of England saw a chanting priest leap into the sea from the land; he swam straight to the king who brought him into his galley. The priest said to the king, "Good king, those who await you here are lost if you and God do not have mercy." "What!" said the king, "Do some still live, my friend? Where are they?" "Yes, my lord. Lined up before this tower they await their death." As soon as the king heard how it was he tarried no longer. Then he said, "God brought us here to endure and suffer death, and since we must die may he be shamed who does not come." Then he had his galleys advanced and, with his legs unprotected, he jumped into the sea, [only] waist-deep – fortunately for him – and came by force to dry land, first or second, as was his custom. Geoffrey du Bois[701] and the noble Peter of Préaux, a companion of the king, leapt in after him; they reached the Turks who filled the strand and the king himself attacked them with his crossbow and his valiant bold and ever-ready men, followed him along the shore. The Turks fled before the king, not daring to draw near to him. He took his sword in his hand and rushed upon them, harrying them, so that they had no opportunity to defend themselves. They did not dare await him and his experienced company, who hit the Turks like madmen who struck them and pressed them until they freed the strand of Turks, forcing them all back and after this took barrels and beams and wide planks, old galleys and old barges and made a barrier across the strand between them and the Saracens. The king placed there knights and men-at-arms and crossbowmen who fought the Saracens, who yelled and shouted and hastily withdrew. Then the king climbed a twisting stair which led to the Templars' lodging. There he was the first to enter, forcing his way into the town where he found more than three thousand Saracens pillaging the castle and carrying everything off. As soon as Richard, the boldest king in the world, was up on the wall he had his banners unfurled and shown on high to the Christians so that they would see them. As soon as they noticed them they cried "Holy Sepulchre", took their arms and armed themselves without delay. Then was there great alarm among the pagans when they saw our men descend on them.

---

700 Cf. *Itinerarium*, 6.15.

701 Geoffrey du Bois-Arnault (Eure) was a member of an Anglo-Norman family with extensive holdings in both the English Midlands and the honour of Breteuil in Normandy. They were vassals of the earls of Leicester. On the family, see D. Crouch, *The Beaumont Twins: The Roots and Branches of Power in the Twelfth Century* (Cambridge, 1986), pp.109–11.

There you might have seen many Turks stretched out, knocked to the ground by the king. None waited to receive his blow who did not lose his life. Then did our men descend among the streets.

There you might have seen men defeated, cut down and killed. There were the wounds of the invalids, found in the town and killed when they could not stir, there were those wounds avenged.[702]

There you might have seen men storming down, bringing shame to the Saracens. Why should I make a long tale of it? All those who were caught, who were in the town, who could not get out in time, they were killed at once. Then was the town set free and its [Saracen] people given over to shame.

The king came out after them, having carried out such deeds that day and having then only three horses.[703] Never, even at Roncevaux, did any men, young or old, Saracen or Christian, conduct himself so well.[704] For when the Turks saw his banner they trembled on the right and on the left. No coward would have wished to be there, for God made no rain nor snow, however destructive, which fell more heavily than the storm of bolts and arrows which rained down on them; there could not have been more [bolts and arrows] among them. Then was the news brought to Saladin and the account given of the assault on his people. He, the defeated man, more angry than a wolf, was feverish with fear. He did not dare wait there any longer but had his pavilions struck and his tents moved back into the plains. The king and his valiant and proud men followed and chased them, striking and pursuing them with their crossbowmen whose bolts struck them, killing their horses. They pursued them and fired on them until they retreated by two leagues. The king had his camp pitched where Saladin had not dared await him. In that very place did Richard the Great encamp.

[11208–35]   When the day was done and the Turkish army retreated, then was that army ashamed and embarrassed at having been repulsed by footsoldiers who had such a small force compared to the Turks, but God had set His hand to it for He did not wish His people to be harmed. Then did Saladin call upon his Saracens and his most nobly born Turks and asked them, "Who is chasing you? Has the army returned from Acre to attack my people? Were they on foot or on horseback, those who came against you?" Then a traitor who knew the matter and who had seen the king said: "My lord, they had no mounts with them, not even a mule or she-mule, except for three horses which the king, that valiant lord,[705] found in Jaffa. That is all they have or can have and they can get no more for any sum of money. If there were someone who wished to undertake it he himself could be taken without great effort, for he lies all alone in his tent."

[11236–71][706]   It was on a Saturday, according to the tale I tell, that the town was reconquered and delivered from the Saracens, for wonders were done there which will always be recounted, for they had taken Jaffa again and killed the

---

702 Baha' al-Din, who was a participant, describes the capture of Jaffa by Saladin and Richard's rescue of the garrison in the citadel, pp.217–23.
703 Cf. *Itinerarium*, 4.16.
704 l.11175. The heroic battle in the *Chanson de Roland*.
705 l.11228, *li bon vassals*, means that he is endowed with all the feudal virtues.
706 Cf. *Itinerarium*, 6.17.

Christians they found there, as they lay ill. It is a known truth that they found there in the town so many pigs, which they killed and slew, that there was an infinite number of them. It is known in truth that they do not eat pork and, therefore, wilfully killed them, for they hate nothing more on the earth than the Christian faith. So they had mixed in death the men and the pigs, lying side by side. But the Christians in the service of God took the bodies; they buried the Christians and threw out the Saracens killed that Saturday, with the pigs that stank so much that they could not endure it.[707]

Then did the king have work done on the walls of Jaffa on the Sunday, the Monday and the Tuesday, to repair them where they were broken, until they were rebuilt as best they could be without lime or mortar, for defence, if there was need of it.[708] However, the army was outside the city in tents, where there was greater need of alertness.

[11272–313][709]   The Mamluks of Saladin, those of Aleppo and the Kurds,[710] the light division of the hated pagan race, gathered together for a discussion. They said they were all shamed by having left Jaffa before such men as ours, with no mounts. This they said discussing the matter together, the men of high and low estate, until they swore together, boasting that they would take the king in his tent and bring him before Saladin. This was the deed that was sworn.

Then did the Count Henry of Champagne arrive in a galley from Caesarea, he and his company.[711] The army had come to Caesarea and, against its will been held there because of the Saracens who kept watch over the rivers and the crossings, with the result that the king had neither help nor aid from their whole company except from his nephew the count. Nor did he have much [protection] against that terrible day which had been planned for him, beyond fifty knights, sixty at the most, and men-at-arms and crossbowmen who were valiant and knew their work well, and men of Genoa and of Pisa, who had committed themselves in the service of God, and about two thousand other men. Nor, since the rescue of the town, did they have as many as fifteen horses, good or bad. This

---

[707] This was a calculated insult.

[708] Cf. *Itinerarium*, 6.18.

[709] Cf. *Itinerarium*, 6.19.

[710] The Kurds came from the mountainous region of southern and eastern Anatolia and northeastern Iraq. Although very conscious of their identity, they had had no independent political power since the Seljuk invasions of the eleventh century, when most of the minor ruling dynasties of the region had been eliminated. However, they were often to be found in the armies of various Turkish rulers and, not surprisingly, given Saladin's own origins, they were prominent in the Ayyubid forces as well, where they held both civil and military positions. See *The Encyclopedia of Islam*, ed. C.E. Bosworth, E. van Donzel, B. Lewis and Ch. Pellat, vol.5, new ed. (Leiden, 1986), pp.447–55, for a concise history of the Kurds in this period. The *Tractatus de locis et statu sancte terre Jerosolimitane*, an anonymous description of the Kingdom of Jerusalem in the 1170s and 1180s, which may have been written during the siege of Acre, presents the Kurds as the best soldiers in Saladin's army, comparing them to the Varangian guard at Constantinople. See B.Z. Kedar, 'A Western Survey of Saladin's Forces at the Siege of Acre', in *Montjoie: Studies in Crusade History in Honour of Hans Eberhard Mayer*, ed. B.Z. Kedar, J. Riley-Smith and R. Hiestand (Aldershot, 1997), pp.113–22.

[711] Cf. *Itinerarium*, 6.20.

shortage of horses would have brought much suffering and loss of life if God had not protected him from the Turks and their hatred.

[11314–77][712]   Now listen to the great miracle that all the world wonders at, for our men would have been taken on that Wednesday,[713] through the plan to take the king, had not God concerned himself in the matter. That night, at the hour of matins, the Saracen men mounted and ordered their divisions. The laced their ventails[714] and rode in the moonlight. Then did God in His glorious grace do a deed of goodness – and when He carries out great works the tale of it should be told. There they were on the plain, riding in tight formation when God caused a quarrel to arise between the Kurds and the Mamluks over which of them would dismount and await our people to prevent them returning to the castle for protection. Each said, "It's up to you to dismount", "No, you", "No you", "It's only right. We would be better on horseback." They came, arguing, down the valley and their quarrel lasted so long between them that, as God had planned, they saw the day dawn. The king was asleep in his tent.

Listen to the fine deeds and good fortune of a Genoese who had risen and gone out to the wasteland just at the break of day. As he made to come back he heard the Turks who were coming up and saw their helmets shining. So he lowered his head and raised his voice, calling out without ceasing that our men should arm and go to arms. The king, who had worked hard that day, woke at his cry and leapt out of bed and put on, I believe, a white hauberk, strong and tough. He immediately gave orders that his companions be warned. It is no wonder that,[715] so taken by surprise, they got into a muddle in dressing and arming themselves. For I can indeed confirm that they were in such haste there that the king and several others fought that day with their legs unprotected and covered only by fresh air; some were even naked, without breeches, attacked and injured that day, but their undress harmed them more than anything else.

[11378–620]   While our men were arming and the Saracens drawing nearer, then was the king mounted, and with him were no more than ten mounted men. The tale tells truly that Count Henry of Champagne was on horseback, with his company; so was Robert the earl of Leicester, who certainly ought to have been there, and, I believe, Bartholomew of Mortemer on his horse and Ralph of Mauléon, who never had enough of fighting. There was Andrew of Chauvigny, who was strong and valiant in his saddle. There was Gerard of Furnival, mounted with the king. There was Roger of Sassy, seated on a poor hack. There was William of L'Estang, on an exhausted horse.[716] There was Hugh of Nevill, a bold and noble man-at-arms. Henry le Tyois bore the king's banner in that

---

712   Cf. *Itinerarium*, 6.21.

713   5 August 1192, Landon, p.68.

714   Ventails are the part of the coif which covers the lower part of the face, Nicolle, *Medieval Warfare*, p.310. Illustrations in Nicolle, *Arms and Armour*, pp.291, 782; 300, 786; 354–5, 822.

715   Cf. *Itinerarium*, 6.22.

716   One should probably not take the descriptions of the horses too seriously. Ambroise is having fun with words and punning on the forms of the names; thus *estanc* meaning 'worn out, exhausted' of a horse is rhymed with the name of the knight, in Old French *Estanc*.

company.[717] There were our men ranged against the cruel and furious race, set out in their divisions, each under his own constable. The knights were on the left, towards St Nicholas, along the strand,[718] against the Saracen race. That was where they were to be for there that was where most of the Turks were shooting, beating their drums and yelling. People of many nations were positioned in front of the gardens. There were Pisans and Genoese. The tale is not easily told or recounted, the tale of the attacks that they encountered from that hated race. The Turks began to shoot on them with yells and cries and howls. You would have seen marvels and our good people under pressure. They went down on their knees, placing their round shields and long shields before them, lances in their hands.[719] The king, who was skilled in arms, had hidden behind the shields between two men, a crossbowman and another man to prepare his crossbow for him and hand it to him when it was ready. In this way was the army thoroughly protected. In this way were they ready for action. Now, there should be no doubt that those who were tried like this, seeing so many Turks against them, were afraid for their heads. It is as true as you are here that the king went about exhorting them and addressing them, with John of Préaux who went about preaching to them. They said, "Now it will be apparent who will take pains to do well while God will guard him, for here we have no business but to sell ourselves dearly and await our martyrdom when God sends it to us. We are on the right path when in his goodness God grants to us that which we are seeking. Here lies our real reward."

Then were the divisions established and then did the companies of Turks come and our men hold fast, their legs firm on the sand, their lances stretched out, ready to receive them. Then did the divisions of the false Saracen race advance with such violence and such force that had our men budged they would have broken through. There were, if I am to be believed, one thousand Turks in each division. When they came up to our men and saw that they did not budge they turned to ride across our front. The crossbowmen drew; the Turks did not dare wait. They struck their bodies and their horses, knocking them to the ground. They came back again and again, in their battalions and again they drew near to them striking and fighting. They did this a number of times. When the

---

[717] All these men were close associates of Richard. Gerard of Furnival appears on the king's charters in Normandy and Anjou throughout the 1190s and was present at the siege of Chalus where Richard died on 5 April 1199. He also served John, from whom he received the fief of Conteville in north-eastern Normandy (Seine-Inférieur). In c.1203 he returned to the East on pilgrimage, perhaps influenced by his experience in September 1192, when he had been among those who had visited the holy places under the protection of the treaty of Jaffa: Powicke, *Loss of Normandy*, pp.221–2, 245–6; Landon, pp.99, 118, 130, 132, 143, 145. Hugh of Nevill (Néville, Seine-Inférieur) was a member of a powerful Anglo-Norman family established in England since the time of William the Conqueror, Loyd pp.72–3. He was one of the sources of information about the Third Crusade used by the chronicler Ralph of Coggeshall, *Chronicon Anglicanum*, p.45.

[718] The parish church of St Nicholas was situated on the cliffs just to the north of the city walls of Jaffa. It belonged to the canons of the Holy Sepulchre and had existed since at least 1167, Pringle, *Churches*, vol.1, no.110, pp.268–9.

[719] l.11426. The word *glaive* translated here, and by Stone, as 'lance' can also mean sword.

king and his men saw how many mounted men there were and that they would keep this up, they lowered the points of their lances, each threw himself forward, striking into the middle of the great press of the devilish unbelieving race. They came together with such force that the whole company trembled back to the third row. Then did the king look round and saw to his right the noble earl of Leicester fall, his horse struck from under him. He fought well until the king came to his rescue. There you would have seen so many Turks rush towards the Lion Banner![720] There was Ralph of Mauléon taken prisoner by the Turks; the king spurred on his valuable horse until he had delivered him from their hands. The powerful king was in the press, against the Turks and the Persians. Never did one man, weak or strong, make in one day such efforts. He threw himself against the Turks, splitting them to the teeth.[721] He fought so often; he struck so many blows; he did himself such injury in striking that the skin of his hands cracked.

Then there came spurring up, apart from the other Turks, on a swift and speedy horse, a single Saracen. It was the noble Saphadin of Arcadia,[722] a man of valiant deeds, kindness and generosity. As I said, he came galloping up with two Arab horses which he sent to the king of England, beseeching him and begging him, because of his valiant deeds, which he, Saphadin, knew and because of his boldness, that he would mount one [of the horses] on condition that, if God brought him out of this safe and sound that if he lived then Richard would ensure that he received some reward. He later received a large recompense. The king took them willingly and said that he would take many such, if they came from his most mortal enemy, such was his need.

Then did the battle intensify. Never was another such battle seen. The ground was completely covered with bolts sent by the base race, gathered in armfuls. There you might have seen so many injured men that the sailors fled back to the galleys whence they had come. He who flees at such a time greatly dishonours himself! Then did the cry rise from the town that the Turks were arriving in force, wishing to take our people by surprise, from the front and the rear. The noble king with his banner, came there, with two other knights [. . .][723] As soon as he entered [the town] he met on the way three Turks, with rich accoutrements. He struck them down in kingly manner, striking with such force that he instantly gained two horses, killing the Turks. He forced the other [Turk] out [of the town] and had the gate by which they had entered blocked against the outside[724] and set guards to guard it. Then did he go straight to the galleys where his men had gone in great fear and distress.[725] Richard, the son of valour, encouraged them all and had them steer back to land, bringing them back together, so that in each galley there remained no more than five men. He came back with the others to the army, which had no respite. Then did he undertake a daring charge. Never

---

[720] On the Lion Banner, see Ailes, *Origins of the Royal Arms*, pp.71–2.

[721] It is difficult to know how far such epic style expressions can be taken literally.

[722] In the *Itinerarium*, 6.22, p.419, it is one who 'came on behalf of Saphadin' (Nicholson, p.364).

[723] After l.11548 there is a lacuna, probably of one line.

[724] *desqu'en l'or* (l.11558) is obscure.

[725] Cf. *Itinerarium*, 6.23.

was the like seen. He charged into the accursed people, so that he was swallowed up by them and none of his men could see him, so that they nearly followed him, breaking their ranks, and we would have lost all. But [the king] was not troubled. He struck before and behind, creating such a pathway through [the Turks] with the sword he was holding that wherever it had struck there lay either a horse or a corpse, for he cut all down. There, I believe, he struck a blow against the arm and head of an emir in steel armour whom he sent straight to hell. With such a blow, seen by the Turks, he created such a space around him that, thanks be to God, he returned without harm. However, his body, his horse and his trappings were so covered with arrows which that dark race had shot at him that he seemed like a hedgehog. In this way did he return from the battle which lasted all day from morning till night, a battle which was so cruel and fierce that if God had not supported our people evil would have come of it. Truly He was there, we say this, for that day we lost no more than one or two men and they lost more than fifteen hundred horses, which lay on the slopes and in the valleys, and more than seven hundred Turks who lay dead there. Nor, for all their impetus, did they take with them the king, who, in front of the hated race, had done deeds of knighthood so that all were amazed by the great deeds of valour committed by him and by those who, with him, were willing to give, even unto death.

[11621–58]726   When God in His grace spared in this way the king and the Christian race from the pagan race and men, and the army had retreated, then were there told the words of Saladin. He addressed his Saracens, to mock them over their defeat, "Where are those who have taken the king? Where is he who is bringing him?" A Turk from a distant land said to him, "My lord, I will tell and I will tell no lie. Never was such a man seen, so valiant and so skilled; no-one can bear arms better. He was to be found wherever there was need. We made great efforts and struck great blows, but we could not take him, for no-one dares to await his blow; he is so bold and skilled." My lords, do not hold it as a myth that the Turks did not know him well, nor that they would have taken him but for God and his great prowess, for he did great deeds of valour and endured much that day, as did the other valiant men, so that [while] near to the race that is accursed by God, they fell ill,727 both from the effort of their deeds in that undertaking and from the stink of the carnage that so polluted the town and disrupted their constitution, so that they all nearly died, both the king and those who were there.

[11659–91]728   There where the king was ill and in a poor way, there did Saladin send to him, saying that he and his Saracens would come there and take him, if he dared to wait for them. The king replied at once that, if he could believe and trust this, that he would wait there for him and that, as long as he could stand on his feet, or hold firm on his knees, that he would not flee from him the distance of one foot.729 This was the way of war. And God knew his condition when he spoke in these strong terms. Then he sent, by Count Henry

726 Cf. *Itinerarium*, 6.24.
727 Cf. *Itinerarium*, 6.25.
728 Cf. *Itinerarium*, 6.26.
729 This kind of boast is a commonplace of heroic literature, e.g. Vivien in *La Chanson de*

(so goes the story and the tale)[730] for the French at Caesarea, sending for those who had come before and for other men to come to defend the land. He appealed to their commitment and told them of his poor condition. But they did not want to rescue him, but left him to suffer, if he had not made a truce [. . .][731] but no-one should be upset by this for the Turks would have come to take him and ill-treat him and he would have lost Ascalon which would certainly have been taken, and perhaps Tyre and Acre.

[11692–717]   The king was at Jaffa, in fear and trouble and suffering, and he considered what he would do and that he would leave the town, which was weak and was neither strong nor firm [in its defence]. Then he sent to Count Henry,[732] whom his sister had raised, and he sent for the Templars and for the Hospitallers and reminded them of his sickness of mind and heart. He said to them that some should go and guard Ascalon and others remain at Jaffa and take care of it and he would go to Acre, there to receive medical care. He said he could not do otherwise. What else shall I say? All refused. All replied that they could not guard or protect a castle without him. They left without saying another word. Then was the king very angry.

[11718–67]   When the king saw that everyone, everyone had let him down, no-one was either loyal or blameless, then was he troubled and disturbed and very perplexed. My lords, do not wonder at it that he did the best he could in the time that he had. For he who shuns shame and seeks honour chooses the lesser of two evils. So he would rather seek a truce than leave the land in danger, for everyone else was leaving, openly making for their boats. Then he sent to Saphadin, who was brother to Saladin and who respected him because of his valour, asking that, sparing no effort, he would seek for him the best truce that he could and that he, Richard, would agree to it. Saphadin made great efforts and conducted talks until a truce was arranged and devised by Saladin in these terms: that Ascalon, which was a threat to his crown, would be knocked down and destroyed and that no-one would fortify it within three years, but then whoever was most capable of doing so could hold it and rebuild it. Jaffa would be strengthened and inhabited once again by Christians. The rest of the plain, between the mountain and the sea, where no-one lived, would be held in truce, in stability and safety. Anyone who wished to observe the truce and travel in safety there and back could seek out the Sepulchre. Merchandise could be transported throughout the land without the payment of tribute. These were the terms and in such terms was the truce written and conveyed to the king. He, being without support and so close to that hated race, with their army at a distance of

---

Guillaume, ed. and trans. P.E. Bennett (London, 2000), ll.291–2, p.48, declares 'I shall not turn back, for I have promised God that I shall never flee for fear of death', repeated by him, ll.586–7, p.62; ll.598–9, p.63; later, as he prays, he is more precise, 'defend me . . . that it may never enter my head to flee one pace' (ll.808–10, p.73; repeated ll.911–12, p.78).

730   Such tags do not necessarily mean that Ambroise does not know about this. He is punning on Conte meaning 'count' and conte meaning 'tale'.

731   After l.11685 there is a lacuna, probably of one line. Paris supplies 'cette trêve fut blâmée de plusieurs' (this truce was criticised by some).

732   Cf. Itinerarium, 6.27.

no more than two leagues, accepted in this way the truce.[733] Anyone who tells the tale differently is lying.

[11768–97][734] When the truce had been brought to the king and he had granted it, then he could no longer keep silent about what was in his heart. Then he sent a messenger to Saladin, in the hearing of many noble Saracens, saying, in these terms that he should know for sure that he had only agreed to the truce for three years, one to return to his land, one to seek and assemble his men, the third to return and take the land, if Saladin dared to wait for him. The sultan sent back to him, by those whom he had sent there, saying that by his faith and by the God whom he supported, that he so honoured his valour, his great-heartedness and his skill, that if his land were taken in any way during his lifetime, then from among all the princes he had seen, Richard would be the prince whom he would be most willing to have take it from him by force and conquer it. The king believed he would do this and reclaim the Sepulchre, but he neither saw nor heard what was in store for him.

[11798–66][735] When this truce was sworn on both sides, and confirmed, the agreements drawn up and the charters made, the good king was taken to Caiphas on the sea to be strengthened and healed and there he received medicine.[736] The French who were staying there wanted to go to France [. . .][737] that they would continue their pilgrimage. They had greatly criticised the truce, with scorn and mockery, and did not want to rescue Jaffa in its need nor support the king. When it was made known to the king that they wished for safe-conduct to make their pilgrimage, then the king sent his messenger to Saladin and to the Emir Saphadin, saying that if they wished that he would be in their debt they should not let any Christian, young or old, go to Jerusalem without his letters [of authorisation] or those of Count Henry. The French were very angry when they heard of this message so that many of them, as soon as they could, boarded a ship and made ready and returned to France.

When the large company of French had left, [that is] the greater part of those who had been speaking ill of the king and causing the greatest trouble, those whom he could never trust, then did the king announce that his men should go to the Sepulchre and carry their offerings to Jaffa, to help build the walls. What else shall I tell you of this business but that this is how they were organised? They went to the Sepulchre together in three troops under three constables.[738] One of the constables was I believe Andrew of Chauvigny – there are worse monks than he at Cluny. Another was Ralph Teisson, lover of notes and

---

733 The Treaty of Jaffa, 2 September 1192, Landon, p.68. The crucial element seems to have been Richard's agreement to demolish Ascalon. It is clear however, from Baha' al-Din's account, that Saladin believed his troops had reached the end of their endurance, Baha' al-Din, pp.230–2.

734 Cf. *Itinerarium*, 6.28.

735 Cf. *Itinerarium*, 6.29.

736 The king went to Haifa on 9 September 1192, Landon, p.69.

737 After l.11807 there is a lacuna of at least one line. Paris posits three and fills the gap from the *Itinerarium*, 6.30, p.431, 'toutefois ils déclaraient d'abord' (nonetheless they first declared).

738 Cf. *Itinerarium*, 6.31. The pilgrim groups visited Jerusalem during the month of September 1192, Landon, p.69.

sounds.[739] The bishop of Salisbury, since then made archbishop, led the last group. I know all this very well and for certain. When they were in possession of the charters then did the pilgrims set off in a tight press. Listen to how sin[740] can trouble many people of good intent in many places and over many matters. Along the route they took, in the plains of Ramla which they passed through, there did the barons talk together and decide to send word to Saladin that they were going to Jerusalem bearing the letters of the king of England and [that they] wished to see the Sepulchre.

Jerusalem

[11865–11978] Those who took the message were most valiant and wise men, but their sin, or their laziness, was detrimental to their valour. One of these [men] was William des Roches,[741] whose helmet became him well. Another was Gerard of Furnival and [another] Peter of Préaux. They rode across the plains of Ramla, journeying and travelling until they came to Toron des Chevaliers. There they stopped and waited for Saphadin, whom they sought, desiring his safe-conduct. It is true that they fell asleep and delayed there so long that the afternoon passed; the main body was travelling in orderly fashion and had crossed the plain and were near to the mountain. Then my lord Andrew and those who were with him saw those who came, who should have delivered their message. When they saw them and recognised them they stopped, shocked. There you might have heard the high men say, "Ah! Lord God, evil will befall us if the Saracens come near us. There are those who should have carried our message! Things will not go well for us! It is nearly nightfall and this savage people have not yet left their army. If we go this way without sending notice in advance they will come before us and we will lose our heads. We, and the men who have set out, are all unarmed." The messengers were criticised but nonetheless beseeched to go again with their message and they were strongly pressed to go. They came near to Jerusalem and found, outside the town, more than two thousand Turks. They sought the Emir Saphadin until they found him and said to him that our men were coming and asked for his safe-conduct. They were

739 l.11846. I have accepted Paris's correction of *noces*, 'weddings', to *note*, 'musical notes'.
740 l.11867, *pechié*, could also mean misfortune; see above, n.617. While it is the laziness of the messengers that almost causes a disaster, Ambroise is careful not to be too critical of them.
741 William des Roches (d.1222) was the seneschal of Anjou, Maine and Touraine, and the son-in-law of Robert of Sablé, whose lordship he inherited. He returned to the West with Berengaria and thereafter appears on Richard's charters. He was present at the king's funeral on Palm Sunday (11 April) 1199, Landon, pp.50, 60, 75, 123, 143, 145. In the disputed succession which followed Richard's death he was a pivotal figure, initially supporting Arthur's cause, but quickly changing to John's side when he thought that Philip II's influence was becoming too great. John's treatment of Arthur after his capture in August 1202 led him to change sides once more and thereafter he remained loyal to Philip II, playing a decisive part in the Capetian campaign in the Loire valley. In 1209 and 1219 he participated in the Albigensian Crusades against the Cathar heretics of Languedoc, Baldwin, *Government of Philip Augustus*, pp.94–5, 191–5, 234–7.

bearing the king's charters and asked that he would help them. But Saphadin reproached them greatly and said that he had been very foolish and had given foolish advice who led such people here and that they did not value their lives when they journeyed there without a safe conduct. They spoke there for so long that night was falling. Then did the main body arrive, lacking both arms and good advice. When the Saracens saw them they looked at them, eyeing them in such a way that I truly tell you there was not in that company one man so bold that he would not have happily been at Tyre or back at Acre. That night they lay in the lee of a wall. You may know that they were in great fear. The next day the Saracens came before Saladin and knelt at his feet,[742] begging and beseeching him, saying, "Oh, true sultan, now it is right and it is time for us to take vengeance for the massacre that they did to us before Acre. My lord, let us avenge our fathers, our kinsmen, our sons and our brothers, whom these men killed and slaughtered. Now each man can wreak his vengeance." He replied, as was right, that he would speak to his friends about it. They gathered together before the sultan and discussed it in detail. There were the great Saracen lords, Mestoc, with Saphadin, and Bedreddin Dorderdon.[743] They said, "My lord, we will say what is pertinent to your highness. It would be a dreadful deed and great blame would come to the pagan faith if these Christian people, who were here in our power and who are come in good faith, were killed in this way while there is a truce between you and the king. How can you ever hold land if you break faith in this way, for any reason? And who could ever trust us?" Saladin immediately took his men-at-arms and sent to Saphadin who commanded that the Christians should be guarded and should have his safe-conduct to make their pilgrimage to the Sepulchre and complete their expedition. He honoured them greatly until they returned to Acre.

[11979–12066][744] As they were returning, those of our band were journeying. It was at daybreak. The sultan had set his men to guard the route where the pilgrims were passing, so that we passed in safety and crossing the mountains we came to Mountjoy. There our hearts were filled with joy at the sight of Jerusalem. We went down our knees, as all should. We could see the Mount of Olives, the starting point for the procession when God submitted to His Passion. Then we came to the city where God conquered His inheritance. Those who had ridden could kiss the Holy Sepulchre. The horsemen of our company said that Saladin had shown them the True and Holy Cross that we had lost in battle, to kiss and to adore it. Those of us who were on foot saw what we could. We saw the monument where the very Body of God was placed when He had suffered death. There some gave offerings, but the Saracens took them as soon as our people left them, so few made offerings there. [Rather] we divided our offerings among the prisoners who were there as slaves, in bonds, Franks and Syrians; to them we took our offerings. They were in slavery and said, "May God render it back unto them!" Then we made a farther pilgrimage to Mount Calvary on the

---

742 Cf. *Itinerarium*, 6.32.
743 Badr al-Din Dildirim al Yarinqi ibn Baha al-Daula, Lord of Tell Bashir: Baha' al-Din, pp.59, 234.
744 Cf. *Itinerarium*, 6.33.

right, where He died who humbled Himself to be born [in human form], where the Cross was set up and the Holy Flesh pierced with nails, where the rock broke and split as far as Golgotha. We saw and kissed that place.[745] From there we went to Mount Sion, to the church, which lay in ruins. There we saw on our left the place where the mother of the King of Heaven went through the heavens to God her Father, who made of her His sweet mother. We kissed that place, weeping. Then we hurried on to see the Holy Table where God was willing to sit and eat. We eagerly kissed it.[746] We did not spend a long time there because the Saracens were taking some of our pilgrims and hiding them in caves, here three, here four. These were our fears and our dread. Then we all, both those on foot and those on horseback, went down the Valley of Jehosaphat to Siloam, as we were told and advised.[747] There we saw the Sepulchre of the body where God became flesh. That did we kiss eagerly, our hearts moved and full of pity. There in great fear we went into that same cave where God was when they took Him, those who killed His precious Body. We kissed this place, with no loss of time, full of pity and desire, weeping warm tears. It was the time and place for weeping for there were the stables for the horses of these men of the devil who polluted the Holy Places of God and ill-treated our pilgrims. We, the pilgrims, hurried on; we left Jerusalem and came again to Acre.

[12067–118][748]   The third company was led by the bishop, who later became archbishop of Canterbury. It is true that because of his valour, his reputation and

---

745   The crusaders had rebuilt and remodelled the Church of the Holy Sepulchre, which was conse-crated on 15 July 1149, fifty years after the fall of the city. The original Constantinian church had been substantially damaged both by the Persians in 614 and by the Caliph al-Hakim in 1009, so that the structures which the first crusaders encountered were those rebuilt by the Byzantines in the mid-eleventh century. The two-storeyed chapel encompassing Mount Calvary (upper) and Golgotha (lower), situated on the east side of the main south doorway of the Holy Sepulchre, had been covered with four vaults in 1119. This was naturally the focal point of any pilgrimage. For two pilgrim accounts among several, see Theoderic, c.1170, and John Phocas, 1185, Wilkinson, pp.285, 324. On the church, see J. Folda, *The Art of the Crusaders in the Holy Land, 1098–1187* (Cambridge, 1995), pp.175–245.

746   Although the Hospitallers disputed this, twelfth-century pilgrims were unanimous in their belief that the place where the Church of Mount Sion stood, just beyond the south-west corner of the city, was where Mary died and was assumed into Heaven. According to Theoderic, 'As soon as you enter this you find to the left of the main apse a venerable place decorated with marble outside and mosaic within, in which our Lord Jesus Christ transferred to heaven the soul of his beloved Mother, our Lady Saint Mary. The structure is square at the bottom and on top it bears a round ciborium.' Here too was the room of the Last Supper. 'On the right you go up about thirty steps to the Upper Room, which is located beyond the apse. A table is to be seen there on which our Lord supped together with his disciples, and after the traitor had gone out, he shared with his disciples the mystery of his body and blood', Wilkinson, p.297. This room is described by the Abbot Daniel, less than ten years after the capture of Jerusalem in 1099, as 'a chamber, beautifully made, standing on pillars and with a roof, decorated with mosaic and beautifully paved and with an altar as in a church at the end', Wilkinson, p.141. It was thought to be the earliest Christian church, although the twelfth-century visitors saw a rebuild of 965. Several mention seeing the actual Table of the Last Supper, Wilkinson, pp.217, 226, 235, 297, 323–4. Although Ambroise describes this church as in ruins, it seems curious that it was still possible to view the table if this were really the case. For this church, see Folda, pp.469–71.

747   The Pool of Siloam was the site of one of Christ's miracles, John 9:1–12, Luke 13:11–13.

748   Cf. *Itinerarium*, 6.34.

his high dignity, Saladin did him great honour, as I am about to tell you. For he sent to meet him some of his own men, to beg him to stay with him, at his expense. But the bishop made the excuse to the Saracens that as he was a pilgrim he could not accept his expenses for any reason nor in any place. As he could not accept his expenses Saladin gave his people to understand that the bishop and his people should be honoured; he gave them many fine gifts and had them conducted around the sites which our Lord God frequented. Then he requested a meeting that he might see what he was like. Saladin had him shown the Holy Cross, then had him sit in his presence and they remained together, talking for a long time. He began to ask about the king of England, about his qualities and what we Christians thought of those who were with him. The bishop replied, "My lord, I can tell you of my lord for he is the best knight in the world and the best warrior, and he is generous and talented. I say nothing of our sins[749] but if one were to take your qualities and his together then we will say that nowhere in all the world would ever two such princes be found, so valiant and so experienced." The sultan listened to the bishop and said, "I know indeed that the king has great valour and boldness, but he rushes into things so foolishly! However high a prince I should be I would prefer to exercise generosity and judgement with moderation, than boldness without moderation."

[12119–58]   When Saladin had talked like this for a long time with the bishop, through interpreters, and had willingly listened to him, then he said that he should ask for and request a gift, whatever he wanted, and he should know that, if it was in his power to grant it, he would have it. The bishop thanked him and said, "By my faith, there is here a great opportunity for him who understands it, but, if I may, I would like to wait and take counsel of God tonight and return tomorrow." The sultan granted this. The next day the bishop made his request and it was a great thing he achieved: that at the Sepulchre, where he had worshipped where there was no service of God, except for the Syrians who worshipped in their own way, that two of our Latin priests, with two deacons to support them, would every day, evening and morning, worship with the Syrians and that they would live off the offerings. The same was to be done in Bethlehem and in Nazareth as in Jerusalem. The sultan was willing that this should be done, for as long as he held the land. The good bishop sent for priests and had [the offices] sung. For this reason can the archbishop boast that he gave back to God the sung offices when He was given none [. . .][750] Having done what they wished they took their leave from Saladin and left Jerusalem to return to Acre.

---

749 Stone has 'your sins', following the *Itinerarium*.
750 After l.12154 there is a lacuna probably of two lines.

Departure

[12159–220]751   When all had returned, those of high and of low estate, when all had come back from the Sepulchre, the ships were made ready, the pilgrims boarded and, when they had a good wind, they set sail.752 The ships were separated, split into groups. Some came safely to port, where they were thrown up; others came into danger and were in peril in many places. Some died at sea, where they had a bitter shroud? – bitter? No sweet! – for they taste the sweetness of on high.753 Others became ill, of an illness that will never be cured. Others left behind their fathers, cousins, brothers, dead in battle or of sickness and because of them they are in deep mourning. Just as the martyrs who leave this world suffer different martyrdoms for God, so, if I dare say it, did those who undertook this pilgrimage suffer in different ways, endure different events. But many ignorant people say repeatedly, in their folly, that they achieved nothing in Syria since Jerusalem was not conquered. But they had not inquired properly into the business. They criticise what they do not know and where they did not set their feet. We saw it who were there; we saw this and knew it, who had to suffer, we must not lie about others who suffered for the love of God, as we saw with our own eyes. So I dare to say, in the hearing of those who were there, that some one hundred thousand men died there, because they did not lie with a woman, men who held to the love of God and would not have died without such abstinence. I also dare to say, to pledge, that more than three thousand died of illness and of famine at the siege of Acre and in the town. The valiant men who had their chaplains and listened to the offices [of God], such as a bishop or a holy archbishop, and who died in such a life, caught by illness which spread there, they will be at the right hand of God in the heavenly City of Jerusalem, and such people with the good that they acquired, conquered that other Jerusalem.

[12221–313]754   When Richard, King of England, had been in the Holy Land, when it was time to return, then he had his crossing prepared, his ship made ready, so that nothing was lacking, men, arms and equipment. Then he acted as a noble, loyal and valiant man, because he gave up ten valuable Saracens, who would have brought him great goods, for William of Préaux, who had been taken prisoner in his service; he gave them up to have William back. He had his pay proclaimed abroad that here would be neither complaints nor plundering and had much paid and handed over.755 Anyone who witnessed his leave-taking would have seen the people in tears, following him and praying for him, lamenting [the loss of] his prowess, his deeds of valour and his generosity, and

---

751 Cf. *Itinerarium*, 6.35.
752 Berengaria and Joanna sailed from Acre on 29 September 1192, Landon, p.69.
753 ll.12172–3, Ambroise plays on the homophony of *amer*, 'bitter', and *la mer*, 'the sea'. This is almost a cliché, the most famous example being in the version of the romance of Tristan and Yseut by Thomas of England, see *Tristan et Yseut: Les poèmes français, la saga norroise*, ed. D. Lacroix and P. Walter (Paris, 1989), Carlisle fragment ll.40–2.
754 Cf. *Itinerarium*, 6.36.
755 Cf. *Itinerarium*, 6.37.

saying, "Alas, Syria! Now you are without help. God!! If the truce were now broken, as it often has been, who is there to protect us now that the king is leaving?" Then you would have seen many men weep and the king, who was also distressed, without delay set to sea, having taken leave and raised the sails to the wind, sailing through the night, by the stars.[756]

In the morning, in the light of day, he turned his face towards Syria and said, that his men could hear and others could listen, "Ah! Syria! I commend you to God. May the Lord God, by His command, grant me the time, if it is His will, that I may come to your help! For I still expect to save you." Then did his ship begin to travel at speed. But he did not know the evil that lay before him nor the sufferings that awaited him, because of the premeditated treachery, sent from Syria to the king of France about the Assassins,[757] because of which he was thrown [into prison] and taken when on pilgrimage under the protection of God. Because of this was his inheritance taken, with his castles in Normandy, through envy and jealousy. Later he was ransomed by fine silver, for which he imposed a tax on all his people, through the taking of crosses and reliquaries, chalices and vessels of gold and silver from the great churches. He was in such great need that never was there a saint of God, man or woman – and there have been many saints – who suffered for God, short of death, more than did the king in his prison in Austria and in the rich realm of Germany. He knew nothing of this, but God, whom he served with his mind, his generosity, his prudence and his valour [. . .][758] and the barons who stood as surety for him, who sent their sons for him, until he was able to reclaim his land from the king of France, waging war against him. He put in such effort and did so much that he recovered all that had been taken from him and more.[759] This is how God works, justly, that he who labours in His service will receive again his portion.

---

[756] Richard departed on 9 October 1192, Landon, p.69.

[757] See above, p.152.

[758] After l.12292 there is a lacuna of at least two lines.

[759] It appears that Richard intended to return the way that he had come, that is via Marseilles, but that he was deterred by the enmity of Count Raymond of Toulouse and Philip II of France. He therefore turned back to Corfu, arriving on 11 November, from where he planned to sail to Venice and then to travel north-east towards Bohemia and Moravia, territories whose rulers were allied to his brother-in-law, Henry the Lion, the former Duke of Saxony and Bavaria. However, on 20 December 1192, while travelling in disguise through the lands of Leopold of Austria, whose hatred he incurred during the crusade (see Richard of Devizes, pp.46–7), he was captured at Vienna. He was eventually handed over to the Emperor Henry VI on 23 March 1193, and did not obtain his release until 4 February 1194, by which time two-thirds of a ransom of 150,000 marks had been paid and he had agreed to hold the Kingdom of England as a fief of the Empire. In the interim John had done homage to Philip II for the Angevin lands and had agreed to marry Philip's sister, Alice (January 1193), while, in April and May, Philip had invaded Normandy, taking the important Vexin castles of Gisors, Neaufles and Châteauneuf, and besieging Rouen. On his return to England, Richard at once set about restoring his position. His crown-wearing at Winchester on 17 April reaffirmed his lordship and soon afterwards he began a series of campaigns against Philip II. By the end of 1198 he had recovered most of his Norman losses and had isolated Gisors and Neaufles, as well as gaining new ground in Berry. See Gillingham, *Richard I*, pp.222–53; Norgate, pp.264–329; Baldwin, *Government of Philip Augustus*, pp.87–94. For the chronology, Landon, pp.71–88.

Epilogue

May all who are here and all who are to come, know that this is where our story ends and know in truth that the year when the Cross was lost [. . .][760] as confirmed by this writing was the year one thousand one hundred and eighty-eight[761] from the incarnation when the Son of God was born who lives and reigns with His Father – May He take us all to His kingdom.

Amen

Explicit

---

[760] After l.12307 there is a lacuna, probably of one line as the rhyme is incomplete. In his translation Paris conjectures 'et prise par les Sarrasins' (and taken by the Saracens).
[761] Ambroise means 1187.

References

Editions and Translations

L'Estoire de la Guerre Sainte par Ambroise, ed. and trans. G. Paris, Documents inédits sur l'Histoire de France (Paris, 1897)

The History of the Holy War, trans. E.N. Stone, in *Three Old French Chronicles of the Crusades*, University of Washington Publications in the Social Sciences (Seattle, 1939), pp.1–160

The Crusade of Richard Lion-Heart by Ambroise, trans. M.J. Hubert, notes J.L. La Monte, Columbia Records of Civilization 34 (New York, 1941, reprint 1976)

'L'Estoire de la Guerre Sainte: An Edition', ed. P.J. Amash (unpublished Ph.D. thesis, University of North Carolina, 1965)

Colker, M.L., 'A Newly-Discovered Manuscript Leaf of Ambroise's *L'Estoire de la Guerre Sainte*', *Revue d'Histoire des Textes* 22 (1992), 159–67

Sources

Abu Shama, *Le Livre des Deux Jardins*, in *RHCr, Historiens Orientaux*, vol.5 (Paris, 1898)

Albert of Aachen, *Historia Ierosolimitana*, ed. and trans. S.B. Edgington (Oxford, 2007)

Baha' al-Din Ibn Shaddad, *The Rare and Excellent History of Saladin*, trans. D.S. Richards, Crusade Texts in Translation 7 (Aldershot, 2001)

Benoît de Sainte-Maure, *Chronique des ducs de Normandie*, ed. C. Fahlin, Bibliotheca Ekmaniania 56 and 60 (Uppsala, 1951–4)

Beroul, *Le Roman de Tristan*, in *Tristan et Iseut: les poèmes français, la saga norroise*, ed. D. Lacroix and P. Walter (Paris, 1989)

Jehan Bodel, *La Chanson des Saisnes*, ed. A. Brasseur, 2 vols (Geneva, 1989)

Boethius, *Consolation of Philosophy*, trans. V.E. Watts (Harmondsworth, 1969)

La Chanson d'Antioche, ed. S.H. Duparc-Quioc (Paris, 1976)

La Chanson d'Aspremont, ed. L. Brandin, Classiques français du Moyen Age, 2 vols (Paris, 1923–4, reprint 1970), trans. M.A. Newth (New York, 1989)

La Chanson de Guillaume, ed. and trans. P.E. Bennett (London, 2000)

La Chanson de Roland, text of F. Whitehead, revised T.D. Henning (London, 1993) (trans. G. Burgess, Harmondsworth, 1990)

Chrétien de Troyes, *Le Chevalier au Lion ou Le Roman d'Yvain*, ed. D.F. Hult (Paris, 1994)

La Chronique d'Ernoul et de Bernard le Trésorier, ed. L. de Mas Latrie, Société de l'Histoire de France (Paris, 1871)

La Continuation de Guillaume de Tyr (1184–1197), ed. M.R. Morgan, Documents relatifs à l'histoire des Croisades publiés par l'Académie des Inscriptions et Belles-Lettres 14 (Paris, 1982)

Documents relatifs au comté de Champagne et de Brie (1172–1361), vol.1, ed. A. Longnon, Collection de documents inédits sur l'histoire de France (Paris, 1901)

Le Dossier de l'Affaire des Templiers, ed. and trans. G. Lizerand, Les Classiques de l'Histoire de France au Moyen Age (2nd ed., Paris, 1964)

Edbury, P.W., trans., *The Conquest of Jerusalem and the Third Crusade: Sources in Translation* (Aldershot, 1996)

Epistolae Cantuarienses, in *Chronicles and Memorials of the Reign of Richard I*, vol.2, ed. W.Stubbs, Rolls Series 38 (London, 1865)

Geffrai Gaimar, *Estoire des Engleis*, ed. A. Bell, Anglo-Norman Text Society, vols 14–16 (Oxford, 1960)

Gerald of Wales, *Topographia Hibernica*, vol.5, ed. J. Dimock, Rolls Series 21 (London, 1867)

Gesta Francorum, ed. and trans. R. Hill (London, 1962)

L'Histoire de Guillaume Le Maréchal, vol.1, ed. P. Meyer, Société de l'Histoire de France (Paris, 1891)

Historia de expeditione Friderici imperatoris, in *Quellen zur Geschichte des Kreuzzuges Kaiser Friedrichs I.*, ed. A. Chroust, *MGH SS*, n.s., vol. 5 (Berlin, 1928)

History of William Marshal ed. A.J. Holden, with English translation by S. Gregory and historical notes by D. Crouch, Anglo-Norman Text Society, 3 vols (2002–6)

Ibn al-Athir, *The Chronicle of Ibn al-Athīr for the Crusading Period from al-Kāmil fī'l-ta'rīkh*. Part 2, trans D.S. Richards. Crusade Texts in Translation 15 (Aldershot, 2007)

'Imad al-Din al-Isfahani, *Conquête de la Syrie et de la Palestine par Saladin*, trans. H. Massé (Paris, 1972)

Itinerarium Peregrinorum et Gesta Regis Ricardi, in *Chronicles and Memorials of the Reign of Richard I*, vol.1, ed. W. Stubbs, Rolls Series 38 (London, 1864). Trans. H.J. Nicholson, *Chronicle of the Third Crusade: A Translation of the Itinerarium Peregrinorum et Gesta Regis Ricardi*, Crusade Texts in Translation 3 (Aldershot, 1997)

Das Itinerarium: Eine zeitgenössische englische Chronik zum dritten Kreuzzug in ursprünglicher Gestalt, ed. H.E. Mayer (Stuttgart, 1962)

Jerusalem Pilgrimage 1099–1185, ed. J. Wilkinson, with J. Hill and W.F. Ryan, The Hakluyt Society 167 (London, 1988)

Jordan Fantosme's Chronicle, ed. R.C. Johnston (Oxford, 1987)

Die lateinische Forsetzung Wilhelms von Tyrus, ed. M. Salloch (Leipzig, 1934)

Libellus de Expugnatione Terrae Sanctae per Saladinum, in *Radulphi de Coggeshall Chronicon Anglicanum*, ed. J. Stevenson, Rolls Series 66 (London, 1875), pp.209–62

La Lumiere as Lais, by Pierre d'Abernon of Fetcham, ed. G. Hesketh, Anglo-Norman Text Society 53 (London, 2000)

Niketas Choniates, *O City of Byzantium: Annals of Niketas Choniates*, trans. H.J. Magoulias (Detroit, 1984)

Papsttum und Untergang des Templeordens, ed. H. Finke, vol. 2 (Münster, 1907)

Le Petit Plet, ed. B.S. Merrilees. Anglo-Norman Text Society 20 (Oxford, 1970)

Philippe de Novare, *Mémoires, 1218–1243*, ed. C. Kohler (Paris, 1913)

Les Poèmes de Gaucelm Faidit, ed. J. Mouzat (Paris, 1965)

Ralph of Coggeshall, *Chronicon Anglicanum*, ed. J. Stevenson, Rolls Series 66 (London, 1875)

Ralph of Diceto, *Ymagines Historiarum*, in *The Historical Works of Master Ralph of Diceto*, vol.2, ed. W. Stubbs, Rolls Series 68 (London, 1876)

La Règle du Temple, ed. H. de Curzon, Société de l'Histoire de France (Paris, 1886)

Richard of Devizes, *The Chronicle of Richard of Devizes of the Time of King Richard the First*, ed. and trans. J.T. Appleby (London, 1963)

Richard, J., *L'Esprit de la Croisade* (Paris, 1969)

Rigord, *Histoire de Philippe Auguste*, ed. and trans. E. Carpentier, G. Pon and Y. Chauvin. Sources d'Histoire Médiévale publiées par l'Institut de Recherche et d'Histoire des Textes 33 (Paris, 2006)

Riley-Smith, L.and J., trans., *The Crusades: Idea and Reality 1095–1274*, Documents of Medieval History 4 (London, 1981)

Robert de Clari, *La Conquête de Constantinople*, ed. P. Lauer (Paris, 1924). Trans. E.H. McNeal (New York, 1966)

Roger of Howden, *Gesta Regis Henrici II et Ricardi I*, 2 vols, ed. W. Stubbs, Rolls Series 49 (London, 1867)

Roger of Howden, *Chronica*, vols 3 and 4, ed. W. Stubbs, Rolls Series 51 (London, 1870)

Rotuli de Liberate ac de Misis et Praestitis, Regnante Johanne, ed. T.D. Hardy (London, 1844)

Rotuli Normanniae, ed. T.D. Hardy (London, 1835)

Villehardouin, *La Conquête de Constantinople*, ed. J. Dufournet (Paris, 1969). Trans. M.R.B. Shaw (Harmondsworth, 1963)

Wace, *Le Roman de Brut*, ed. I. Arnold, 2 vols, Société d'Anciens Textes Français (Paris, 1938–40)

Wace, *Le Roman de Rou*, ed. A.J. Holden, 3 vols, Société d'Anciens Textes Français (Paris, 1970–3)

William of Newburgh, *Historia Rerum Anglicarum*, in *Chronicles of the Reigns of Stephen, Henry II and Richard I*, vol.1, ed. R. Howlett, Rolls Series 82 (London, 1884)

William of Tyre. Guillaume de Tyr, *Chronique*, ed. R.B.C. Huygens, vol.2, Corpus Christianorum Continuatio Mediaevalis 63, 63A (Turnhout, 1986)

'Ein zeitgenössisches Gedicht auf die Belagerung Accons', ed. H. Prutz, *Forschungen zur deutschen Geschichte* 21 (1881), 449–94

Reference

Anglo-Norman Dictionary, ed. W. Rothwell, Publications of the Modern Humanities Research Association 8, 7 vols (London, 1977–92)

Atlas des formes et des constructions des chartes françaises du 13e siècle, ed. A. Dees, Beihäfte zur Zeitschrift für romanische Philologie 178 (Tübingen, 1980)

Atlas des formes linguistiques des textes littéraires de l'ancien français, ed. A. Dees, Beihäfte zur Zeitschrift für romanische Philologie 212 (Tübingen, 1987)

Butler's Lives of the Saints, rev. ed. H. Thurston and D. Attwater, vol.3 (New York, 1962)

Butler's Lives of the Saints, new full ed., revised by S.F. Thomas (Tunbridge Wells, 1995–7)

Cheney, C.R., *Handbook of Dates for Students of English History* (London, 1948)

The Dictionary of the Middle Ages, vol.1, ed. J.R. Strayer (New York, 1982)

Dictionary of National Biography, vols 2, 3, 5, 13, 18, 30, 34

Dictionnaire de l'ancien français, ed. A.J. Greimas (Paris, 1968)

Dictionnaire des locutions en moyen français, ed. G. di Stephano (Montreal, 1991)

The Encyclopedia of Islam, vol.5, new ed. C.E. Bosworth, E. van Donzel, B. Lewis and C. Pellat (Leiden, 1986)

Godefroy, F., *Dictionnaire de l'Ancienne Langue Française*, 10 vols (Paris, 1881–1902)

Landon, L., *The Itinerary of Richard I*, Pipe Roll Society n.s. 13 (London, 1935)

Moisan, A., *Repertoire des noms propres de personnes et des lieux cités dans les chansons de gestes*, vol.1 (Geneva, 1986)

A New Dictionary of Heraldry, ed. S. Friar (London, 1987)

Old French–English Dictionary, ed. A. Hindley, F.W. Langley and B.J. Levy (Cambridge, 2000)

Opll, F., *Das Itinerar Kaiser Friedrich Barbarossas (1152–1190)* (Vienna, Cologne and Graz, 1978)

The Oxford Dictionary of Byzantium, ed. A.P. Kazhdan (Oxford, 1991)

Tobler-Lommatzsch Altfranzösisches Wörterbuch, 11 vols (Stuttgart, 1989–)

Secondary Works

Ailes, A., *The Origins of the Royal Arms of England: Their Development to 1199* (Reading, 1982)

Ailes, M.J., 'Chivalry and Conversion: The Chivalrous Saracen in the Old French Epics *Fierabras* and *Otinel*', *Al-Masaq: Studia Arabo-Islamica Mediterranea* 9 (1996–97), 1–21

Ailes, M.J., 'The Medieval Male Couple and the Language of Homosociality', in *Masculinity in Medieval Europe*, ed. D.M. Hadley (London, 1999), pp.214–37

Ailes, M.J., *The Song of Roland – On Absolutes and Relative Values* (Lampeter, 2002)

Ailes, M.J., 'Heroes of War: Ambroise's Heroes of the Third Crusade', in *Writing War. Medieval Literary Responses to Warfare*, ed. C. Saunders, F. Le Saux and N. Thomas (Cambridge, 2004), pp. 29–48

Appleby, J.T., *England without Richard 1189–1199* (Ithaca, 1965)

Arbois de Jubainville, H. d', *Histoire des ducs et comtes de Champagne*, vol.4 (Paris, 1860)

Baldwin, J.W., *The Government of Philip Augustus: Foundations of French Royal Power in the Middle Ages* (Berkeley and London, 1986)

Baldwin, M.W., *Raymond III of Tripolis and the Fall of Jerusalem (1140–1187)* (Princeton 1936; reprint Amsterdam, 1969)

Barber, M., *The New Knighthood: A History of the Order of the Temple* (Cambridge, 1994)

Barber, M., 'The Charitable and Medical Activities of the Hospitallers and Templars', in *A History of Pastoral Care*, ed. G. Evans (London, 2000), pp.148–68

Beer, J., *Villehardouin, Epic Historian* (Geneva, 1968)

Beer, J., *Narrative Conventions of Truth in the Middle Ages* (Geneva, 1981)

Bennett, M., 'The Status of the Squire: The Northern Evidence', in *The Ideals and Practice of Medieval Knighthood*, vol.1, ed. C. Harper-Bill and R. Harvey (Woodbridge, 1986), pp.1–11

Bennett, M. '*La Règle du Temple* as a Military Manual, or How to Deliver a Cavalry Charge', in *Studies in Medieval History presented to R. Allen Brown*, ed. C. Harper-Bill, C. Holdsworth and J.L. Nelson (Woodbridge, 1989), pp.7–19

Bennett, P.E., 'La Chanson de Guillaume, poème anglo-normand?' in *Au carrefour des routes d'Europe: la chanson de geste. X congrès international de la Société Rencesvals pour l'étude des épopées romanes, Strasbourg, 1985*, Senefiance 21 (Aix-en-Provence, 1986), pp.259–81

Blair, C., *European Armour, circa 1066 to circa 1700* (London, 1958)

Bradbury, J., *The Medieval Archer* (Woodbridge, 1985)

Bradbury, J., *Philip Augustus, King of France 1180–1223* (London, 1998)

Brand, C.M., *Byzantium Confronts the West, 1180–1204* (Cambridge, Mass., 1968)

Broughton, B.B., *The Legends of King Richard I Coeur de Lion: A Study of Sources and Variations to the year 1600* (The Hague, 1966)

Brown, E.A.R., 'Eleanor of Aquitaine: Parent, Queen, and Duchess', in *Eleanor of Aquitaine, Patron and Politician*, ed. W.W. Kibler (Austin and London, 1976), pp.9–34

Brundage, J., 'Prostitution, Miscegenation and Sexual Purity in the First Crusade', in *Crusade and Settlement*, ed. P. Edbury (Cardiff, 1985), pp.57–65

Bull, M., *Knightly Piety and the Lay Response to the First Crusade* (Oxford, 1993)

Bulst-Thiele, M.-L., *Sacrae Domus Militiae Templi Hierosolymitani Magistri: Untersuchungen zur Geschichte des Templeordens 1118/9–1314* (Göttingen, 1974)

Cartellieri, A., *Philipp II. August, König von Frankreich*, vol.2 (Leipzig, 1906; reprint 1984)

Chalandon, F., *Histoire de la domination normande en Italie et en Sicile*, vol.2 (Paris, 1907)

Cheney, C.R., *Hubert Walter* (London, 1967)

Contamine, P., *War in the Middle Ages*, trans. M. Jones (Oxford, 1984)

Corley, C., 'Editing *Le Bel Inconnu* and Other Single Manuscript Texts', in *The Editor and the Text*, ed. P.E. Bennett and G.A. Runnals (Edinburgh, 1990), pp.11–19

Corner, D., 'The *Gesta Regis Henrici Secundi* and *Chronica* of Roger, Parson of Howden', *Bulletin of the Institute of Historical Research* 56 (1983), 126–44

Croizy-Naquet, C., 'Les figures du jongleur dans l'Estoire de la Guerre Sainte', *Le Moyen Age* 104 (1998), 229–56

Crouch, D., *The Beaumont Twins: The Roots and Branches of Power in the Twelfth Century* (Cambridge, 1986)

Dace, R. 'Bertran de Verdun: Royal Service, Land and Family in the Late Twelfth Century', *Medieval Prosopography* 20 (1999), 75–93

Damian-Grint, P., *The New Historians of the Twelfth-Century Renaissance: Authorising History in the Vernacular Revolution* (Woodbridge, 1999)

Daniel, N., *Heroes and Saracens: An Interpretation of the Chansons de Geste* (Edinburgh, 1983)

DeVries, K.R., *Medieval Military Technology* (Peterborough, Ontario, 1992)

Dunbabin, J., 'William of Tyre and Philip of Alsace, Count of Flanders', *Mededelingen var de Koninklijke Academie voor Wetenschappen, Letteren en Schone Kunsten van België. Klasse der Letteren* 48 (1986), 110–17

Edbury, P.W., *The Kingdom of Cyprus and the Crusades 1191–1374* (Cambridge, 1991)

Edbury, P.W., 'Propaganda and Faction in the Kingdom of Jerusalem: The Background to Hattin', in *Crusaders and Muslims in Twelfth-Century Syria*, ed. M. Shatzmiller (Leiden, 1993), pp.173–89

Edbury, P.W., 'The Templars in Cyprus', in *The Military Orders. Fighting for the Faith and Caring for the Sick*, ed. M. Barber (Aldershot, 1994), pp.189–91

Edbury, P.W., *John of Ibelin and the Kingdom of Jerusalem* (Woodbridge, 1997)

Edbury, P.W., 'The Lyon *Eracles* and the Old French Continuations of William of Tyre', in *Montjoie: Studies in Crusade History in Honour of Hans Eberhard Mayer*, ed. B.Z. Kedar, J. Riley-Smith and R. Hiestand (Aldershot, 1997), pp.139–53

Edbury, P.W., *The Continuators of William of Tyre* (Aldershot, 1998)

Edwards, J.G., 'The *Itinerarium Regis Ricardi* and the *Estoire de la Guerre Sainte*', in *Historical Essays in Honour of James Tait*, ed. J.G. Edwards, V.H. Galbraith and E.F. Jacob (Manchester, 1933), pp.59–77

Falmagne, J., *Baudouin V, Comte de Hainaut 1150–1195* (Montreal, 1966)

Faral, E., 'A propos de l'édition des textes anciens: Le cas du manuscrit unique', in *Recueil de Travaux offert à M. Clovis Brunel*, vol.1 (Paris, 1955), pp.409–21

Favreau-Lilie, M.-L., *Die Italiener im Heiligen Land vom ersten Kreuzzug bis zum Tode Heinrichs von Champagne (1098–1197)* (Amsterdam, 1989)

Flori, J., *Richard the Lionheart. King and Knight*, trans J. Birrell (Edinburgh, 2006)

Folda, J., *The Art of the Crusaders in the Holy Land, 1098–1187* (Cambridge, 1995)

Foulet, A. and M.B. Speer, *On Editing Old French Texts* (Lawrence, 1979)

France, J., *Western Warfare in the Age of Crusades 1000–1300* (London, 1999)

Garsoïan, N.G., 'Geography and History of Armenia', in *Dictionary of the Middle Ages*, vol.1, ed. J.R. Strayer (New York, 1982), pp.470–87

Gayre, R., *Heraldic Standards and Ensigns* (Edinburgh and London, 1959)

Gibb, H.A.R., 'The Arabic Sources of the Life of Saladin', *Speculum* 25 (1960), 58–72

Gibb, H.A.R., 'The Aiyubids', in *A History of the Crusades*, vol.2, ed. R.L. Wolff and H.W. Hazard (Madison, 1969), pp.693–714

Gibb, H.A.R., *The Life of Saladin from the Works of 'Imad ad-Din and Baha' ad-Din* (Oxford, 1973)

Gillingham, J., 'Richard I and Berengaria of Navarre', *Bulletin of the Institute of Historical Research* 53 (1980), 157–73

Gillingham, J., 'Richard I and the Science of War in the Middle Ages', in *War and Government in the Middle Ages: Essays in honour of J.O. Prestwich*, ed. J. Gillingham and J.C. Holt (Woodbridge, 1984), pp.78–91

Gillingham, J., 'Roger of Howden on Crusade', in *Richard Coeur de Lion: Kingship, Chivalry and War in the Twelfth Century* (London and Rio Grande, 1994), pp.141–53

Gillingham, J., *Richard I*, 2nd ed. (New Haven and London, 1999)

Gillingham, J., 'Royal Newsletters, Forgeries and English Historians: Some Links between Court and History in the Reign of Richard I', in *La cour Plantagenêt (1154–1204). Actes du Colloque tenu à Thouars du 30 avril and mai 1999*, ed. M. Aurell (Poitiers, 2000), pp.171–86.

Gillingham, J., *The Angevin Empire*, 2nd ed. (London, 2001)

Gransden, A., *Historical Writing in England c.550–c.1307* (London, 1974)

Hamilton, B., *The Latin Church in the Crusader States: The Secular Church* (London, 1980)

Hamilton, B., *The Leper King and his Heirs: Baldwin IV and the Crusader Kingdom of Jerusalem* (Cambridge, 2000)

Hanley, C., 'Reading the Past through the Present: Ambroise, the Minstrel of Reims and Jordan Fantosme', *Mediaevalia* 20 (2001), 263–81

Heiser, R., 'The Royal *Familiares* of King Richard I', *Medieval Prosopography* 10 (1989), 25–50

Hiestand, R., ' "precipua tocius christianismi columpna": Barbarossa und der Kreuzzug', in *Friedrich Barbarossa Handlungsspielraume und Wirkungsweisen des Staufischen Kaisers*, ed. A. Haverkamp, Vorträge und Forschungen 40 (Sigmaringen, 1992), pp.51–108

Holt, R., *The Mills of Medieval England* (Oxford, 1988)

Hooper, N. and M. Bennett, *Cambridge Illustrated Atlas of Warfare: The Middle Ages 768–1487* (Cambridge, 1996)

Jacoby, D., 'Crusader Acre in the Thirteenth Century: Urban Layout and Topography', *Studia Medievali*, 3rd series, 10 (1979), 1–45

Jacoby, D., 'Montmusard, Suburb of Crusader Acre: The First Stage of its Development', in *Outremer: Studies in the History of the Crusading Kingdom of Jerusalem presented to Joshua Prawer*, ed. B.Z. Kedar, H.E. Mayer and R.C. Smail (Jerusalem, 1982), pp.205–17

Jacoby, D., 'Conrad, Marquis of Montferrat, and the Kingdom of Jerusalem (1187–92)', in *Atti del Congresso internazionale 'Dai feudi monferrine e dal Piemonte ai nuovi mondi oltre gli Oceani', Alessandria 2–6 aprile 1990* (Alessandria, 1993), pp.187–238

Jamison, E., *The Norman Administration of Apulia and Capua*, ed. D. Clementi and T. Közler (Darmstadt, 1987)

Johnston, R.C., 'Jordan Fantosme's Experiments in Prosody and Design', in *Mélanges offerts à P. Jonin* (Aix-en-Provence, 1971), pp.355–67

Kay, S., 'The Nature of Rhetoric in the Chansons de Geste', *Zeitschrift für romanische Philologie* 94 (1978), 304–20

Kealey, E.J., *Harvesting the Air: Windmill Pioneers in Twelfth-Century England* (Berkeley and Los Angeles, 1987)

Kedar, B.Z., 'A Western Survey of Saladin's Forces at the Siege of Acre', in *Montjoie: Studies in Crusade History in Honour of Hans Eberhard Mayer*, ed. B.Z. Kedar, J. Riley-Smith and R. Hiestand (Aldershot, 1997), pp.113–22

Keen, M., 'Brotherhood in Arms', *History* 47 (1962), 1–17

Kennedy, H., *Crusader Castles* (Cambridge, 1994)

Knowles, D., *The Monastic Order in England 943–1216* (Cambridge, 1963)

Kosztolnyik, Z.J., *From Coloman the Learned to Béla III (1095–1196): Hungarian Domestic Politics and their Impact upon Foreign Affairs*, East European Monographs, Boulder, 120 (New York, 1987)

Labande, E.-R., 'Le Crédo épique, à propos des prières dans les chansons de geste', in *Recueil offerts à M. Clovis Brunel*, vol.2 (Paris, 1955), pp.62–80

La Monte, J.L., 'The Lords of Sidon in the Twelfth and Thirteenth Centuries', *Byzantion* 17 (1944–5), 193–211

Levy, B., 'Pèlerins rivaux de la 3e croisade: les personnages des rois d'Angleterre et de France d'après les chroniques d'Ambroise et d'Ernoul, et le récit Anglo-Normand de la *Croisade et Mort Richard Coeur de Lion*', in *La Croisade – réalités et fictions: Actes de colloque d'Amiens, 1987* (Göppingen, 1989), pp.143–55

Lewis, B., *The Assassins: A Radical Sect in Islam* (New York, 1967)

Lewis, B., 'The Isma'ilites and the Assassins', in *A History of the Crusades*, vol.1, ed. M.D. Baldwin (Madison, 1969), pp.99–132

Lindemann, R.H.F., 'The English *Esnecca* in Northern European Sources', *Mariner's Mirror* 74 (1988), 75–82

Longnon, L., *Les Compagnons de Villehardouin: Recherches sur les croisés de la quatrième croisade* (Geneva, 1978)

Loyd, L.C., *The Origins of Some Anglo-Norman Families*, Publications of the Harleian Society 103 (Leeds, 1951)

Lyons, M.C. and D.E.P. Jackson, *Saladin: The Politics of the Holy War* (Cambridge, 1982)

Maksoudian, K. H., 'The Armenian Church', in *Dictionary of the Middle Ages*, vol.1, ed. J.R. Strayer (New York, 1982), pp.498–505

Markowski, M., 'Richard Lionheart: Bad King, Bad Crusader?' *Journal of Medieval History* 23 (1997), 351–65

Marnette, S., *Narrateur et points de vue dans la littérature française médiévale: une approche linguistique* (Bern, 1998)

Marnette, S., 'Narrateur et point de vue dans les chroniques médiévales: une approche linguistique', in *The Medieval Chronicle: Proceedings of the First International Conference on the Medieval Chronicle, Utrecht, 13–16 July 1996*, ed. E. Kooper (Amsterdam, 1999), pp.176–90

Martindale, J., 'Eleanor of Aquitaine', in *Richard Coeur de Lion in History and Myth*, ed. J.L. Nelson (London, 1992), pp.17–50

Matthew, D.J.A., *The Norman Kingdom of Sicily* (Cambridge, 1992)

Mayer, H.E., 'On the Beginnings of the Communal Movement in the Holy Land: The Commune of Tyre', *Traditio* 24 (1968), 446–57

Mayer, H.E., 'The Succession to Baldwin II of Jerusalem: English Impact on the East', *Dumbarton Oaks Papers* 39 (1985), 139–47

Mayer, H.E., *The Crusades*, 2nd ed. (Oxford, 1988)

Mayer, H.E., 'Raimund IV von Tripolis', in *Varia Antiochena: Studien zum Kreuzfahrerfürstentum Antiochia im 12. und frühen 13. Jahrhundert, MGH, Studien und Texte* 6 (Hanover, 1993), pp.184–202

Mayer, L.A., *Saracenic Heraldry* (Oxford, 1933)

Möhring, H., 'Eine Chronik aus der Zeit des dritten Kreuzzugs: das sogennante *Itinerarium peregrinorum* 1', *Innsbrucker historische Studien* 5 (1982), 149–62

Morawski, J., *Proverbes français antérieurs au XVe siècle* (Paris, 1925)

Musset, L., 'Aux origines d'une classe dirigeante: Les Tosny, Grands Barons Normands du Xe au XIIIe siècle', *Francia: Forschungen zur westeuropäischen Geschichte* 5 (1977), 45–80

Nicolle, D., *Arms and Armour of the Crusading Era, 1050–1350*, 2 vols (New York, 1988)

Nicolle, D., *Medieval Warfare Source Book*, vol.1: *Warfare in Western Christendom* (London, 1995)

Norgate, K., *Richard the Lion Heart* (London, 1924)

Painter, S., 'The Houses of Lusignan and Chatellerault', *Speculum* 30 (1955), 374–84

Painter, S., 'The Lords of Lusignan in the Eleventh and Twelfth Centuries', *Speculum* 32 (1957), 27–47

Painter, S., 'The Third Crusade: Richard the Lionhearted and Philip Augustus', in *A History of the Crusades*, vol.2: *The Later Crusades, 1189–1311*, ed. R.L. Wolff and H.W. Hazard (Madison, 1969), 45–85

Parisse, M., *Noblesse et chevalerie en Lorraine médiévale: les familles nobles du XIe au XIIIe siècle* (Nancy, 1982)

Partington, J.R., *A History of Greek Fire and Gunpowder* (Cambridge, 1960)

Paterson, L., 'The Occitan Squire in the Twelfth and Thirteenth Centuries', in *The Ideals and Practice of Medieval Knighthood*, vol.1, ed. C. Harper-Bill and R. Harvey (Woodbridge, 1986), pp.133–51

Payen, J.C., *Le motif du repentir dans la littérature française médiévale (des origines à 1230)* (Geneva, 1968)

Phillips, J., *Defenders of the Holy Land: Relations between the Latin East and the West, 1119–1187* (Oxford, 1996)

Pope, M.K., *From Latin to Modern French* (Manchester, 1934, revised ed. 1952)

Power, D.J., 'Between the Angevin and the Capetian Courts: John of Rouvray and the Knights of the Pays de Bray, 1180–1225', in *Family Trees and the Roots of Politics: The Prosopography of Britain and France from the Tenth to the Twelfth Century*, ed. K.S.B. Keats-Rohan (Woodbridge, 1997), pp.361–84

Powicke, F.M., 'Loretta, Countess of Leicester', in *Historical Essays in Honour of James Tait*, ed. J.G. Edwards, V.H. Galbraith and E.F. Jacob (Manchester, 1933), pp.247–72

Powicke, F.M., *The Loss of Normandy 1189–1204*, revised ed. (Manchester, 1961)

Prawer, J., *Histoire du Royaume Latin de Jérusalem*, vol.2 (Paris, 1970)

Pringle, D., 'King Richard I and the Walls of Ascalon', *Palestine Exploration Quarterly* 116 (1984), 139 (map), 133–47

Pringle, D., *The Churches of the Crusader Kingdom of Jerusalem*, vol.1 (Cambridge, 1993)

Pringle, D., *Secular Buildings in the Crusader Kingdom of Jerusalem: An Archaeological Gazetteer* (Cambridge, 1997)

Pringle, D., 'Templar Castles between Jaffa and Jerusalem', *The Military Orders*, vol.2: *Welfare and Warfare*, ed. H. Nicholson (Aldershot, 1998), pp.89–109

Pryor, J.H., 'Transportation of Horses by Sea during the Era of the Crusades: Eighth Century to 1285 A.D., Part I: To c.1225', *The Mariner's Mirror* 68 (1982), 9–27, 103–25

Pryor, J.H., 'The Naval Architecture of Crusader Transport Ships', *The Mariner's Mirror* 70 (1984), 171–219, 275–92, 363–86

Pryor, J.H., *Geography, Technology and War: Studies in the Maritime History of the Mediterranean, 649–1571* (Cambridge, 1988)

Rausing, G., *The Bow: Some Notes on its Origin and Development*, Acta Archaeologica Lundensia 6 (Lund, 1967)

Riant, P., *Expéditions et pèlerinages des Scandinaves en Terre Sainte au temps des croisades* (Paris, 1865)

Richard, J., 'Philippe Auguste, la croisade et le royaume', in *La France de Philippe Auguste: Le Temps des Mutations*, ed. R.-H. Bautier (Paris, 1982), pp.411–24

Richard, J., 'Les Turcopoles au service des Royaumes de Jérusalem et de Chypre: Musulmans convertis ou Chrétiens orientaux?' *Revue des études islamiques* 54 (1986), 259–70

Richards, D.S., 'Imad al-Din al-Isfahani: Administrator, Littérateur and Historian', in *Crusaders and Muslims in Twelfth-Century Syria*, ed. M. Shatzmiller (Leiden, 1993), 133–46

Riley-Smith, J., *The Knights of St. John in Jerusalem and Cyprus c.1050–1310* (London, 1967)

Riley-Smith, J., *The Feudal Nobility and the Kingdom of Jerusalem, 1174–1277* (London, 1973)

Riley-Smith, J., 'Peace never Established: The Case of the Kingdom of Jerusalem', *Transactions of the Royal Historical Society*, 5th series, 28 (1978), 87–102

Riley-Smith, J., ed., *The Atlas of the Crusades* (London, 1991)

Riley-Smith, J., *The First Crusaders, 1095–1131* (Cambridge, 1997)

Riley-Smith, J., *The Crusades. A History*, 2nd ed. (London, 2005)

Rodger, N.A.M., *The Safeguard of the Sea: A Naval History of Great Britain*, vol. 1: *660–1649* (London, 1997)

Rogers, R., *Latin Siege Warfare in the Twelfth Century* (Oxford, 1992)

Round, J., 'Some English Crusaders of Richard I', *English Historical Review* 18 (1903), 475–81

Rudt de Collenberg, R.H., 'L'empereur Isaac de Chypre et sa fille (1155–1207)', *Byzantion* 38 (1968), 123–79

Runciman, S., *A History of the Crusades*, vol.2 (London, 1952)

Saunders, I.J., *English Baronies: A Study of their Origin and Descent 1086–1327* (Oxford, 1960)

Schulze-Busaker, E., *Proverbes et expressions proverbiales dans la littérature narrative du moyen âge français* (Geneva, 1985)

Siedschlag, B., *English Participation in the Crusades 1150–1220* (Randolph, Wis., 1939)

Smail, R.C., 'The Predicaments of Guy of Lusignan', in *Outremer: Studies in the History of the Crusading Kingdom of Jerusalem presented to Joshua Prawer*, ed. B.Z. Kedar, H.E. Mayer and R.C. Smail (Jerusalem, 1982), pp.159–76

Strickland, M., *War and Chivalry: The Conduct and Perception of War in England and Normandy, 1066–1217* (Cambridge, 1996)

Sweeney, J.R., 'Hungary and the Crusades, 1169–1218', *The International History Review* 3 (1981), 467–81

Tatlock, J.S.P., 'The Dragons of Wessex and Wales', *Speculum* 8 (1933), 223–35

Thomas, A., 'Ancien français Casignan, -ingen, Gasigan, -ingan', *Romania* 35 (1906), 598–601

Tibble, S., *Monarchy and Lordships in the Latin Kingdom of Jerusalem, 1099–1291* (Oxford, 1989)

Tyerman, C., *England and the Crusades, 1095–1588* (Chicago and London, 1988)

van Werweke, H., 'La contribution de la Flandre et de Hainaut à la troisième croisade', *Le Moyen Age* 78 (1972), 55–90

Vielliard, F., 'Richard Coeur de Lion et son entourage normand: le témoignage l'*Estoire de la guerre sainte*', *Bibliothèque de l'Ecole des Chartes* 160 (2002), 5–52

Vising, J., *Anglo-Norman Language and Literature* (London, 1925)

Warlop, E., *The Flemish Nobility before 1300*, trans. J.B. Ross and H. Vandermoere, vol. 1 (Kortrijk, 1975)

Warren, W.L., *Henry II* (London, 1973)

Young, C.R., *Hubert Walter, Lord of Canterbury and Lord of England* (Durham, NC, 1968)

Index

9 781843 836629